LIGHTER
T·H·A·N
AIR

LIGHTER · T·H·A·N · AIR

AN ILLUSTRATED HISTORY OF THE AIRSHIP

LEE PAYNE

ORION BOOKS · NEW YORK

TO MY WIFE, MARILYN,

WHO SPELLED ALL THE WORDS.

Published by Orion Books, a division of Crown Publishers, Inc., 201 East 50th Street, New York, New York 10022. Member of the Crown Publishing Group.

ORION and colophon are trademarks of Crown Publishers, Inc.

Manufactured in the United States of America

Library of Congress Cataloging-in-Publication Data

Payne, Lee.
     Lighter than air: an illustrated history of the airship/Lee
Payne.
          p.   cm.
     Includes index.
     1. Airships—History.   I. Title.
TL650.P39   1991
629.133'24'09—dc20   90–20156
                                                                    CIP

Book design by Deborah Kerner

Frontispiece courtesy of
Culver Pictures (see page
181 for description)

ISBN 0-517-574764

10 9 8 7 6 5 4 3 2 1

Revised Edition

· C O N T E N T S ·

· A C K N O W L E D G E M E N T S ·

If this book were only words, the list of acknowledgments would be much shorter, for writing is a relatively solitary business. But in the search for historic photographs, an author can use all the help he can get. Without the people listed below, this book would not have been possible.

Dr. Douglas Robinson—the leading authority on the German Naval Airship Service whose excellent books are listed in the bibliography—read the manuscript and also contributed rare photographs from his own collection.

Dr. A. D. Topping—editor of *Buoyant Flight*, who corrected the new chapters in the second edition.

Professor Henry Cord Meyer—an authority on Germany and the Zeppelin Company.

Patrick Koughan and Walter Boyne—without whose efforts there would never have been a second edition.

Rudi Niedzielski—who searched among the archives of Germany.

Lisa Drake—who searched in San Francisco.

Bishop John Myers—who prayed in Washington, D.C.

General Umberto Nobile—for his comments on his historic airship voyages to the North Pole and also for the use of his personal photographs.

Arch Whitehouse—a World War I pilot and author, for the use of photographs from his collection.

Hertha Mathy—for permission to publish, for the first time, her wedding portrait.

Jack R. Hunt—former president of Embry-Riddle Aeronautical University and the navy blimp pilot who broke the *Graf Zeppelin*'s nonstop endurance record.

Roy Belotti—who has flown navy balloons, navy blimps, Goodyear blimps, German blimps, and Japanese blimps.

Jim Winker of Raven Industries in Sioux Falls, South Dakota.

Hugh V. Morgan for his work at the Air Force Museum in Dayton, Ohio.

John R. Jenson, Assistant Curator, Special Library Collections, University of Minnesota.

Comprehensive collections of aviation history are rare—those with lighter-than-air material are rarer still—yet four of the most complete turned out to be near at hand and all offered exceptional cooperation. A glance at the photo credits in the following chapters will show how much is owed to them all.

The Aviation History Collection of Northrop University in Inglewood, California, and Research Professor of Aviation History, David D. Hatfield.

The Hallett Everett Cole Airship Collection at the University of Oregon in Eugene, Oregon, and Mr. Walter J. Wentz.

The James Carruthers Memorial Aviation Collection in the Sprague Library at the Claremont Colleges, Claremont, California, and librarians David Kuhner and Ruth Hauser.

The San Diego Aero-Space Museum in Balboa Park, San Diego, California, and archivist Brewster C. Reynolds.

Special thanks are due to Louise L. Lewis, the research librarian at the Costa Mesa Library, who located more than one hundred books for me, many of them long out of print. Without California's Interlibrary Loan Service, it would have been impossible to research this book.

To anyone dealing with the history of a technical subject, I should like to recommend the back issues of the *Scientific American* and the *Scientific American Supplement*. Between 1870 and 1920, this publication gave major coverage to the development of aviation. Old issues of the *Literary Digest* also proved invaluable for their reprints of eyewitness accounts of major contemporary news events as reported in the pages of newspapers, many of which no longer exist. The *National Geographic* has also published dozens of firsthand accounts by aeronauts from Walter Wellman to Joe Kittinger.

Acknowledgment is given to the following publishers for allowing material to be reprinted here:

Material from *Slide Rule*, by Nevil Shute reprinted by permission of William Morrow & Co., Inc., from *Slide Rule*, by Nevil Shute, copyright 1954 by Nevil Shute.

Material from *My Life as an Explorer*, by Roald Amundsen, copyright 1928 by Doubleday, Doran & Co. Reprinted by permission of Doubleday & Co., Inc.

Material from *Beyond Horizons*, by Lincoln Ellsworth, copyright 1937, 1938 by Doubleday & Co., Inc. Reprinted by permission of Doubleday & Co., Inc.

Excerpts from "The Last Trip of the Hindenburg," by Leonhard Adelt, *The Reader's Digest*, November 1937, copyright 1937 by The Reader's Digest Assn., Inc. Used with permission.

Putnam & Co. for the extracts from *My Zeppelins* by Hugo Eckener.

Material from "I Was on the Hindenburg," by Margaret Mather, copyright 1937 by *Harper's Magazine*. Reprinted from the November 1937 issue by special permission.

Material from *Andrée's Story*, by S. A. Andrée, translated by Edward Adams-Ray, copyright 1930, copyright renewed 1958 by The Viking Press, Inc. Reprinted by permission of The Viking Press, Inc.

Material from *My Polar Flights*, by Umberto Nobile, copyright 1961 by General Umberto Nobile. Reprinted by permission of G. P. Putnam's Sons.

Material from *Double Eagle*, by Charles McCarry, Ben Abruzzo, Maxie Anderson, and Larry Newman. Copyright 1979, by Charles McCarry and Double Eagle II. By permission of Little, Brown and Company.

Material from *Zeppelin*, by Ernst Lehmann and Leonhard Adelt, copyright 1937 by Longmans, Green & Co. Reprinted by permission of David McKay Co., Inc.

· I N T R O D U C T I O N ·

Since Etienne and Joseph Montgolfier made their historic flight on June 5, 1783, lighter-than-air has been part of the romance of aviation. Fixed-wing aircraft developed rapidly in the seventy years of this century and seemingly all but eclipsed LTA.

Energy shortages combined with the need to move heavy, outsized payloads have produced renewed interest in LTA. In the military, there is a perceived need for LTA regarding logistics, and perhaps antisubmarine warfare. On the civilian side, there is a growing awareness that our existing transportation network may not be able to accommodate cargoes of the future. For example, we currently have no way to economically move large components for nuclear factories.

While numerous articles and books have been devoted to particular aspects of LTA, Lee Payne has filled a void with his comprehensive work *Lighter Than Air: An Illustrated History of the Airship.* The general reader will find before him the history of man's ingenuity in trying to adapt or conquer the air above our earth. Those engaged in aviation research will find a truly valuable reference work. All will enjoy this picture record of success and failure that ends in a question mark.

BARRY GOLDWATER
Former member, Senate Committee
on Aeronautical and Space Sciences

· I N T R O D U C T I O N ·

Since Etienne and Joseph Montgolfier made their historic flight on June 5, 1783, lighter-than-air has been part of the romance of aviation. Fixed-wing aircraft developed rapidly in the seventy years of this century and seemingly all but eclipsed LTA.

Energy shortages combined with the need to move heavy, outsized payloads have produced renewed interest in LTA. In the military, there is a perceived need for LTA regarding logistics, and perhaps antisubmarine warfare. On the civilian side, there is a growing awareness that our existing transportation network may not be able to accommodate cargoes of the future. For example, we currently have no way to economically move large components for nuclear factories.

While numerous articles and books have been devoted to particular aspects of LTA, Lee Payne has filled a void with his comprehensive work *Lighter Than Air: An Illustrated History of the Airship.* The general reader will find before him the history of man's ingenuity in trying to adapt or conquer the air above our earth. Those engaged in aviation research will find a truly valuable reference work. All will enjoy this picture record of success and failure that ends in a question mark.

B A R R Y   G O L D W A T E R
**Former member, Senate Committee
on Aeronautical and Space Sciences**

1
· T H E ·
BALLOON

Will you walk with me a while in the paths of adventure? For that is what this book is to deal with—adventures in Polar Ice, far out upon the broad sea, and high up in the air which covers them both. By adventure I mean strange and thrilling experiences which come to one who sets out, not for adventure, not for hardships, not for narrow escapes from death, but with a desire to achieve something in the way of exploration and scientific progress for the good of mankind and the advancement of knowledge; and who, in this spirit endeavoring, experiences more of adventure, danger and hardship, and ill fortune followed by the fair that leaves life intact after hope had almost gone, than he had ever dreamed of—so much, perhaps that if he could have forseen it all he would never have had the courage to venture forth from the quiet of his home.[1]

Walter Wellman in the introduction to *The Aerial Age*, 1911

Joseph and Etienne Montgolfier were wealthy French paper manufacturers. Their family had been in the paper business for more than three hundred years, and the product of their prosperous mills at Annonay near Lyons found its way even to the desk of King Louis XVI at Versailles.

As educated men of the eighteenth century, Joseph and Etienne were interested in science. Joseph in particular was fascinated by the problems of flight.

Like others before them, the Montgolfiers watched steam rising into the air from a kettle and tried to use it to lift light paper bags, but the steam condensed into water as soon as it was enclosed in the bag. They tried to fill their bags with the gas that scientists called hydrogen. It had been known for many years that acid poured on metal released an inflammable gas. The British scientist Henry Cavendish had recently shown that this gas was different from all others in that it was lighter than air.

OPPOSITE: The Montgolfier brothers' first public demonstration. On June 5, 1783, after weeks of experimentation with small paper balloons, they were ready for a public demonstration in the town square at Annonay, thirty-eight miles south of Lyons. A large crowd watched in amazement as the 110-foot balloon soared skyward. The silk and paper panels of the balloon were fastened together with buttons and buttonholes. *Courtesy Northrop University.*

·

Joseph and Etienne Montgolfier. Joseph Michel Montgolfier (1740–1810) was the elder of the two brothers and led their research into aeronautics. He was forty-three when they invented the balloon in 1783. Jacques Etienne Montgolfier (1745–99) was five years younger than Joseph. Both men were trained in science and mathematics and had been experimenting with flight for some years before Joseph hit upon the idea of the hot-air balloon. *Courtesy Carruthers Collection, Claremont Colleges.*

Experimenters in several countries had tried without success to find a light container that would hold it. The Montgolfiers tried to use their paper bags but the gas passed right through the paper.

Joseph's mind was on other matters as he sat before a friend's fire on a winter afternoon in Avignon. He was idly watching the bits of ash from the fire swirl up the chimney when the idea struck him. He took a piece of paper from the table, folded it to enclose the smoke, and watched it rise up the chimney along with the ashes. Further experimentation resulted in a bag of tightly woven silk rising to the ceiling of the room, where it stayed for more than a minute. Joseph was delighted. He rushed a letter off to Etienne back home at Annonay. "Prepare a supply of taffeta and cordage and you shall see the most astonishing thing in the world!"[2]

He hurried home and the two brothers built a small bag and filled it with the smoke from an open fire. When they released it, the bag rose seventy feet into the air. After a number of tests they were ready for a public demonstration. On June 5, 1783, as hundreds of curious spectators crowded into the market square at Annonay, the brothers built a large fire with bundles of straw and wool that produced a great cloud of black smoke and a terrible smell.

Etienne Montgolfier

The aerostatic machine was constructed of cloth lined with paper, fastened together on a network of strings fixed to the cloth. It was spherical; its circumference was 110 feet, and a wooden frame 16 feet square held it fixed at the bottom. Its contents were about 22,000 cubic feet, and it accordingly displaced a volume of air weighing 1,980 pounds. The weight of gas was nearly half the weight of the air, for it weighed 990 pounds, and the machine itself, with the frame, weighed 500; it was therefore impelled upward with a force of 490 pounds. Two men sufficed to raise it and fill it with gas, but it took eight to hold it down till the signal was given. The different pieces of the covering were fastened together with buttons and buttonholes.[3]

When Joseph gave the signal for its release, the bag sailed into the air and rose to six thousand feet before drifting to earth a mile and a half away.

Fire, cloth, and paper, ingredients available to man since ancient Egypt, yet this simple combination had eluded him for five thousand years. And even the Montgolfiers did not really understand what they had done. The great quantity of smoke and smell that issued from their bundles of straw and wool convinced them that they were filling their *balon* with a previously undiscovered gas similar to Cavendish's hydrogen. The idea that hot air was less dense and thus lighter than cold air never occurred to them. The fact that the air eventually cooled and the balloon lost its lift only indicated to them that their mysterious gas had escaped through the bag's buttonholes, and these were eliminated on subsequent machines.

Word of the Montgolfiers' achievement spread across France. In Paris the French Academy of Sciences invited them to give a demonstration at the capital. While awaiting their arrival, the academy commissioned one of its members, a young physicist, Jacques Alexandre César Charles, to construct a similar machine for further experimentation. Charles had no idea what kind of gas they were using in far-off Annonay but he knew of Cavendish's hydrogen and he had recently met two brothers, Marie-Noel and Anne-Jean Robert, who claimed to have developed a method of sealing silk with a rubber solution that made it impervious to hydrogen.

Using this new material, the construction of the balloon proved to be the easiest part of the project. Though it was only twelve feet in diameter, they had great difficulty in generating enough hydrogen to fill it. For three days they struggled, consuming five hundred pounds of sulfuric acid and one thousand pounds of iron before the bag was filled.

Finally on August 27, 1783, in the Champ de Mars before a crowd of fifty thousand cheering Parisians that filled the streets and rooftops, Charles's balloon rose to a height of three thousand feet and drifted out of sight. It came to earth fifteen miles away near the village of Gonesse, where the peasants, recognizing a work of the devil, tore it to shreds with pitchforks.

To prevent further panic, the government took action. It issued a proclamation:

Public notice on the ascent of balloons or globes in the air. The one in question has been raised in Paris this said day, 27th August, 1783, at 5 p.m., in the Champ de Mars.

A discovery has been made, which the Government deems it right to make known, so that alarm be not occasioned to the people.

On calculating the different weights of inflammable and common air, it has been found that a balloon filled with inflammable air will rise towards heaven till it is in equilibrium with the surrounding air; which may not happen till it has attained a great height.

The first experiment was made at Annonay, in Vivaris, by MM Montgolfier, the inventors; a globe formed of canvas and paper, 105 feet in circumference, filled with inflammable air, reached an uncalculated height.

The same experiment has just been renewed at Paris (27th August, 5 p.m.) in presence of a great crowd. A globe of taffetas, covered by elastic gum, 36 feet in circumference, has risen from the Champ de Mars, and been lost to view in the clouds, being borne in a northeasterly direction; one cannot foresee where it will descend.

It is proposed to repeat these experiments on a larger scale. Any one who shall see in the sky such a globe (which resembles the darkened moon during an eclipse), should be aware that, far from being an alarming phenomenon, it is only a machine, made of

Professor Jacques Alexandre César Charles (1746–1823) built the first hydrogen balloon. He had been experimenting with hydrogen for some time but was successful only after the Robert brothers developed a method of impregnating silk with rubber to make it gastight. The balloon's construction was financed by a subscription raised by members of the French Academy of Sciences. *Courtesy San Diego Aero-Space Museum.*

•

The peasants at Gonesse destroy Charles's first balloon. "For on first sight it is supposed by many to have come from another world; many fly; others, more sensible, think it a monstrous bird. After it has alighted, there is yet motion in it from the gas it still contains. A small crowd gains courage from numbers, and for an hour approaches by gradual steps, hoping meanwhile the monster will take flight. At length one bolder than the rest takes his gun, stalks carefully to within shot, fires, witnesses the monster shrink, gives a shout of triumph, and the crowd rushes in with flails and pitchforks. One tears what he thinks to be the skin, and causes a poisonous stench; again all retire. Shame, no doubt, now urges them on, and they tie the cause of alarm to a horse's tail, who gallops across the country, tearing it to shreds." —Hatton Turnor, Astra Castra, Experiments and Adventures in the Atmosphere. London: 1865. *Photo Courtesy San Diego Aero-Space Museum.*

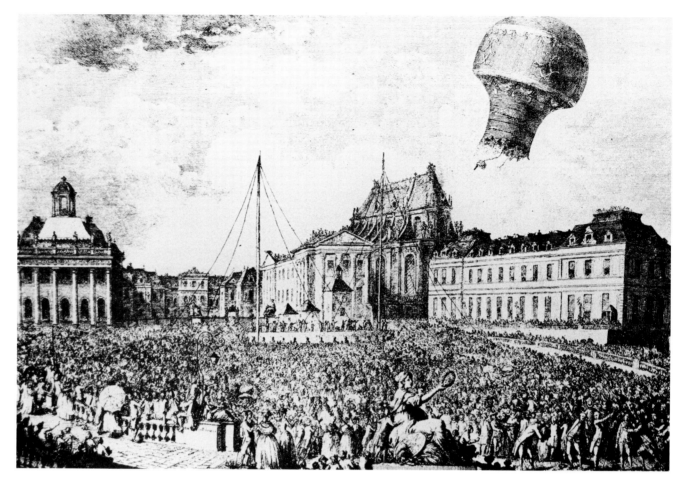

The first creatures aloft. Would the air above the earth support life? Some scientists claimed that the breathable air was only a few hundred feet deep and lay like a blanket clinging to the mountains and valleys of the earth. Above that, no one knew for certain if life could exist. The first aeronauts to explore this unknown region were a duck, a rooster, and a sheep launched from the grounds of the Palace of Versailles on September 19, 1783. The balloon was actually the second built by the Montgolfiers in Paris. Their first had been caught in a sudden shower and reduced to a soggy wreck. *Courtesy San Diego Aero-Space Museum.*

•

taffetas, or light canvas covered with paper, that cannot possibly cause any harm, and which will some day prove serviceable to the wants of society.

Read and approved, 3rd September, 1783.

De Sauvigny Lenoir[4]

Two weeks later the Montgolfiers arrived in Paris ready to launch their latest "aerostat." It was made of cotton lined with paper, fifty-seven feet high and forty-one feet in diameter. King Louis XVI commanded that the ascension take place in his presence at the Palace of Versailles. For this great occasion, Joseph Montgolfier decided to send living creatures aloft to see if it were possible for life to exist in the air above the earth. Some scientists had suggested that the breathable atmosphere might be only a few hundred feet deep.

On September 19, 1783, the gaily decorated balloon soared up from the palace grounds before the king, Marie Antoinette, and the entire court. In a wicker basket swinging below the balloon were the first aeronauts, a sheep, a duck, and a rooster.

The hot air carried them up to fifteen hundred feet, and, after eight minutes, as the air in the globe cooled, they descended slowly to earth in a forest two miles away. The aeronauts emerged unscathed except for a slight injury to the rooster when the sheep stepped on him. King Louis was so delighted that he gave the brothers the Legion of Honor, the Order of St. Michael, an annual pension and, for their father, a patent of nobility.

The Montgolfiers' next step was to build a machine large enough to carry a man aloft. A contemporary print shows it as a great lemon-shaped bag decorated with gold fleurs-de-lis, Louis XVI's royal monogram, and the signs of the zodiac on a bright blue background. It was seventy-five feet high and capable of holding eighty thousand cubic feet of hot air. Actually two passengers were required for balance, one on each side of a narrow wicker balcony around the mouth of the balloon. They were to be supplied with bundles of straw and wool that they would feed into a fire in a brazier in the neck of the balloon to maintain their lift.

On October 15, 1783, everything was ready and a young scientist, Jean-François Pilatre de Rozier, volunteered to make the first tethered test flight. The balloon was held by eighty-foot ropes firmly staked to the ground. With a 110-pound weight on one side of the balcony for balance, Rozier climbed aboard, was cast off, and rose to the end of the ropes. He stayed aloft for four and a half minutes and then, as the air cooled, slowly sank to the ground.

Four days later Rozier again made a tethered flight, this time on a two-hundred-foot rope. By the end of the day, the lines had been lengthened to over three hundred feet and two other aeronauts, Giraud de Villette and the Marquis d'Arlandes, had taken a turn flying with Rozier.

As the day of the first free ascent drew near, the king decided that, despite the success of the tethered flights, the safest plan would be to send up two condemned criminals. If the flight was a success, they would be allowed to live as a reward. If something went wrong, they would only lose their lives a little sooner than expected.

Rozier felt that the honor of man's first flight should go to someone more worthy and begged his friends the Duchess de Polignac and the Marquis d'Arlandes to plead his case before the king.

Pilatre de Rozier

Shall vile criminals, foul murderers, men rejected from the bosom of society, have the glory of being the first to navigate the field of air? Never, while Pilatre de Rozier draws breath![5]

ABOVE: The first aeronauts: Pilatre de Rozier and the Marquis d'Arlandes. Jean-François Pilatre de Rozier (1745–85) was twenty-nine years old when he made man's first flight. He taught chemistry and physics and was curator of the natural history and physics collections of the Count de Provence. His friend, the Marquis François-Laurent d'Arlandes, was an army officer and a favorite at court. *De Rozier, courtesy Carruthers Collection, Claremont Colleges. D'Arlandes, courtesy San Diego Aero-Space Museum.* LEFT: The first flights of the manned balloon were made at the end of long ropes. It was allowed to rise eighty feet into the air the first time, then two hundred feet, and finally three hundred feet. The two poles were used to raise the balloon up over the fire pit and hold it in place until it was fully inflated. Then the rope at the top was cast off and the balloon was allowed to rise. *Courtesy Carruthers Collection, Claremont Colleges.*

The Marquis d'Arlandes must have been a persuasive advocate, for the king finally relented and allowed Rozier to make the flight—with only one condition. Since the marquis had explained how safe it was, he would be allowed to accompany his friend into the air.

On November 21, 1783, half a million cheering Frenchmen watched Pilatre de Rozier and his slightly surprised friend, the Marquis François-Laurent d'Arlandes, become the first men to leave the earth in free flight.

The marquis has left us a description of the historic voyage in a letter to a friend:

I was surprised at the silence and the absence of movement which our departure caused among the spectators, and believed them to be astonished and perhaps awed at the strange spectacle; they might well have reassured themselves. I was still gazing, when M. Rozier cried to me:

"You are doing nothing, and the balloon is scarcely rising a fathom."

"Pardon me," I answered, as I placed a bundle of straw upon the fire and slightly stirred it. Then I turned quickly, but already we had passed out of sight of La Muette. Astonished, I cast a glance towards the river. I perceived the confluence of the Oise. And naming the principal bends of the river by the places nearest them, I cried, "Passy, Saint-Germain, Saint-Denis, Sevres."

"If you look at the river in that fashion you will be likely to bathe in it soon," cried Rozier. "Some fire, my dear friend, some fire."

They were up to three thousand feet drifting slowly over the city when the marquis discovered that sparks from the fire were burning holes in the side of the balloon.

The Marquis d'Arlandes

"Look!" I said. At the same time I took my sponge and quietly extinguished the little fire that was burning some of the holes within my reach. I then perceived that the bottom of the cloth was coming away from the circle which surrounded it.

"We must descend," I repeated to my companion.

He looked below. "We are upon Paris," he said.

"It does not matter," I replied. "Only look! Isn't there any danger? Are you holding on well?"

"Yes, I am," he answered.

I examined the situation from my side, and saw that we had nothing to fear. With my sponge I then tried the ropes which were within my reach. All of them held firm. Only two of the cords had broken.

I then said, "We can cross Paris."

During this operation we were rapidly getting down to the roofs. We made more fire, and rose again with the greatest ease. I looked down, and it seemed to me we were going towards the towers of Saint Sulpice; but, on rising, a new current made us quit this direction and bear more to the south. I looked to the left, and beheld a wood, which I believed to be that of Luxembourg. We were traversing the boulevard, and I cried out all at once:

"Get to the ground!"

But the intrepid Rozier, who never lost his head and who judged more surely than I, prevented me from attempting to descend. I then threw a bundle of straw on the fire. We rose again, and another current bore us to the left. We were now close to the ground, between two hills. As soon as we came near the earth I raised myself over the gallery,

Half a million Parisians watched in awe as man first rose from the surface of the earth in free flight. The large, elegantly decorated machine ascended from the garden of the Chateau de la Muette, rose to three thousand feet, and was carried five miles across Paris. The two aeronauts fed bales of hay and wool into a blazing fire on a metal plate in the open mouth of the balloon. After twenty-five minutes they ran out of fuel and the balloon floated gently to earth. It was seventy-five feet high, forty-eight feet in diameter, and held eighty thousand cubic feet of hot air. *Courtesy Carruthers Collection, Claremont Colleges.*

•

and leaning there with my two hands, I felt the balloon pressing softly against my head. I pushed it back, and leaped down to the ground. Looking round and expecting to see the balloon still distended, I was astonished to find it quite empty and flattened. On looking for Rozier I saw him in his shirt-sleeves creeping out from under the mass of canvas that had fallen over him. Before attempting to descend, he had taken off his coat and placed it in the basket. After encountering much trouble, we were again all right.

As Rozier was without a coat I urged him to go to the nearest house. On his way there, he encountered the Duke of Chartres, who had managed to follow our flight very closely, for I had had the honor of conversing with him just before we ascended.[6]

The flight lasted twenty-five minutes and carried the two intrepid aeronauts five miles across Paris. The only difficulty was experienced when the sparks from the brazier set the balloon on fire, but this the Marquis quickly extinguished with a wet sponge brought along for just such an emergency.

The first manned flight of a hydrogen balloon took place on December 1, 1783, just ten days after the Montgolfiers' first manned flight. Though Professor Charles's balloon was much smaller—it was only twenty-six feet in diameter—it had more lift and remained in the air for two hours, carrying Professor Charles and Marie-Noel Robert twenty-seven miles from Paris. Henceforth, all hydrogen balloons were popularly called *Charlières* and all hot-air balloons were known as *Montgolfières*. *Courtesy Northrop University.*

One of the most interested spectators at the ascension was the American ambassador to France, Benjamin Franklin. He had also been in the royal party at the animals' flight. After the manned flight, the marquis and Etienne Montgolfier visited Franklin at his home to discuss this new world that had suddenly been opened to mankind.

Benjamin Franklin

It appears, as you observe, to be a discovery of great importance, and what may possibly give a new turn to human affairs. Convincing sovereigns of the folly of wars may perhaps be one effect of it, since it will be impracticable for the most potent of them to guard his dominions. Five thousand balloons, capable of raising two men each, could not cost more than five ships of the line. And where is the prince who can afford to so cover his country with troops for its defense as that ten thousand men descending from the clouds might not in many places do an infinite deal of mischief before a force could be brought together to repel them?[7]

Now it was Professor Charles's turn. In just over a week he had a new hydrogen balloon ready for a manned flight. His efforts were financed by public subscription, with each contributor being allowed into a special enclosure to watch the ascension. But the tremendous success of the manned flight had caused a number of Charles's supporters to wonder if they were backing the right machine, for it was obvious to everyone that his balloon operated on a completely different principle than did the Montgolfiers'. And what was more, Charles's appeared to be the inferior of the two. It was considerably smaller with no colorful decoration, and while the manned balloon had been filled in a few minutes, Charles had struggled for three days to generate enough hydrogen to fill his first tiny test machine.

In order to silence these rumbles of discontent among his sponsors, the professor announced that he would make the first ascent in person.

The flight was scheduled for December 1, 1783, and four hundred thousand spectators, half the population of Paris, gathered at the Tuileries Gardens for the great event. Everyone was aware of the professor's problems and was eagerly choosing up sides between the Montgolfières and Charlières.

As the moment for the launch approached, the professor stepped over to Joseph Montgolfier standing nearby and offered him a small balloon with which to test the wind direction. "It is for you, monsieur," Charles said, "to show us the way to the skies." It was a gallant gesture and the crowd roared its approval as Montgolfier released the small balloon. Then Professor Charles and Marie-Noel Robert stepped into the basket suspended beneath the gasbag and prepared to cast off.

Prof. J. A. C. Charles

The balloon which escaped from the hands of M. Montgolfier rose into the air and seemed to carry with it the testimony of friendship and regard between that gentleman and myself, while acclamations followed it. Meanwhile, we hastily prepared for departure. . . . After the balloon and the car were in equilibrium, we threw over 19 pounds of ballast, and we rose in the midst of silence, a silence resulting from the emotion and surprise we all felt.

Nothing will ever equal that moment of joyous excitement which filled my whole being when I felt myself flying away from the earth. It was not mere pleasure, it was perfect bliss. Having escaped from the frightful torments of persecution and of calumny, I felt that I was answering all in rising above all.

To this sentiment succeeded one more lively still—the admiration of the majestic spectacle that spread itself out before us. On whatever side we looked, all was glorious; a cloudless sky above, a most delicious view around. "Oh, my friend," said I to M. Robert, "how great is our good fortune! I care not what may be the condition of the earth; it is the sky that is for me now. What serenity! What a ravishing scene! Would that I could bring here the last of our detractors, and say to the wretch, 'Behold what you would have lost had you arrested the progress of science.' "

While we were rising with a progressively increasing speed, we waved our bannerets in token of our cheerfulness, and in order to give confidence to those below who took an interest in our fate. M. Robert made an inventory of our stores; our friends had stocked our commissariat with enough provisions for a long voyage—champagne and other wines, garments of fur, and many other articles. . . .

At the end of 56 minutes, we heard the report of the cannon which informed us that we had, at that moment, disappeared from view at Paris. . . . We gave ourselves up to the contemplation of the views which the immense stretch of country beneath us presented. From that time, though we had no opportunity of conversing with the inhabitants, we saw them running after us from all parts; we heard their cries, their exclamations of solicitude, and knew their alarm and admiration.

We cried, "Long live the King!" and the people responded. We heard, very distinctly—"My good friends, have you no fear? Are you not sick? How beautiful it is! Heaven preserve you! Adieu, my friends."

I was touched to tears by this tender and true interest which our appearance had called forth.

We continued to wave our flags without cessation, and we perceived that these signals greatly increased the cheerfulness and calmed the solicitude of the people below. Often we descended sufficiently low to hear what they shouted to us. They asked us where we came from, and at what hour we had started.[8]

They landed near Nesle, twenty-seven miles from Paris, after two hours in the air. As soon as Marie-Noel Robert stepped out, the lightened balloon bounded into the air again, carrying the startled professor nearly two miles straight up. After landing safely for the second time, Professor Charles, one of flying's most distinguished pioneers and the first to use ballast, the net-enclosed balloon, the suspended car, and the gas valve, never set foot in a balloon again.

Others did not share the professor's sudden lack of enthusiasm. On January 19, 1784, at Lyons, the Montgolfiers prepared to launch their fourth creation, a half-million-cubic-foot hot-air balloon. Joseph Montgolfier and Pilatre de Rozier were to be the passengers.

Suddenly, four young noblemen leaped from the crowd into the car, drew their swords, and slashed the mooring lines. Montgolfier and Rozier scrambled aboard. So did a spectator named Fontaine. The people of Lyons were beside themselves with excitement as the two-man balloon sailed away carrying a crowd of seven.

That night at the opera, all the aeronauts were given a standing ovation. Like Professor Charles, Joseph Montgolfier decided that his first aerial voyage would also be his last.

Balloon ascensions became a national mania. By April 1784 the French government was forced to pass an ordinance prohibiting the launching of aerostatic machines unless the proper safety precautions were observed.

The first aerial crossing of the English Channel took place on January 7, 1785. Dr. John Jeffries, an American physician with Royalist sympathies who had moved to England after the American Revolution, had agreed to finance the construction of a hydrogen balloon designed especially for the crossing by Jean-Pierre François Blanchard, an experienced French aeronaut.

When the day for the historic event arrived, Dr. Jeffries was surprised to learn that Blanchard did not plan to take him along. The aeronaut had even hidden a few lead weights in his trousers in order to convince Jeffries that the balloon would lift only one man.

The balloon was being inflated inside the walls of Dover Castle and Dr. Jeffries, after explaining his problem to a group of sympathetic British sailors, led them in a march on the castle. The castle's alarmed governor slammed the gate on the approaching mob, but after hearing the doctor's grievances, the governor interceded on his behalf with Blanchard, who finally agreed to allow him to go, but only after Jeffries promised to jump overboard if the ship appeared to be in any danger.

A magazine correspondent with a literary turn of mind was on hand to report the thrilling takeoff:

TOP: Jean-Pierre François Blanchard (1753–1809) was the best and by far the most active of the early aeronauts. In addition to the first crossing of the English Channel, he made the first balloon flights in Germany, Belgium, the Netherlands, Poland, Bohemia, Switzerland, and the United States. A contemporary described him as a "petulant little fellow, not many inches over five feet, and physically well suited for vaporish regions." *Courtesy San Diego Aero-Space Museum.* ABOVE: Dr. John Jeffries (1744–1819) was born in Boston, graduated from Harvard in 1763, studied medicine in London and Scotland, worked in British military hospitals during the American Revolution, and was surgeon major for the British troops fighting around Savannah and Charleston. He went to England after the war and became interested in ballooning as a means of studying the upper atmosphere. He returned to Boston in 1790 and lived his last years there. *Courtesy Carruthers Collection, Claremont Colleges.*

The Gentleman's Magazine

Now the awful moment came, every remaining cord was loosened, and this large stupendous body seemed struggling to get loose to float in purer climes. The particular friends of our two aerial heroes on each side of the boat, kept it gently gliding on the ground till it came to the utmost edge of the cliff. Then was realized that famous description of Shakespeare, in his tragedy of King Lear, when Gloster is about to throw himself from the cliff on the other side of town:

> How fearful
> And dizzy 'tis to cast one's eye so low!
> I'll look no more,
> Lest my brain turn, and the deficient sight
> Turn me down headlong.

From a precipice like this let the admiring world be told that these two men were launched to swim in air—or meet inevitable death; and from this precipice, to the rapturous astonishment of thousands of spectators, these bold adventurers floated safe in the atmosphere, buoyed up by a power lighter than air itself. The sight was truly sublime, the spectators were all eyes, and their hearts all feeling. The serenity and composure visible on the countenances of these two extraordinary characters, the display of two beautiful flags, the Red Ensign of England and the Royal Standard of France, the elegance of the little wherry that sustained the passengers, the expansion of the silken oars, and the stupendous magnificence of the balloon itself, with the sunbeams full upon them, was a sight which leaves all description at a distance, and requires indeed a thousand witnesses to establish the truth of this most wonderful spectacle to the absent public.

The salutations from the Castle, the beach, the ports and the town were general, and gracefully returned by the two Aeronauts moving their hats and waving their flags; this was repeated again and again, while, by an almost imperceptible transition, they gradually lessened to the eye.[9]

The first crossing of the English Channel by air took place on January 7, 1785, only fourteen months after man learned to fly. Blanchard hoped to assist his crossing from Dover to Calais by the use of large oars, but they proved to be useless and were among the first articles thrown overboard when the balloon began to sink toward the sea. *Courtesy Carruthers Collection, Claremont Colleges.*

•

As the raw winter wind grew colder, the hydrogen contracted and the balloon began to fall. They had taken off with only thirty pounds of ballast, which was quickly thrown overboard. The ship continued to sink, so they threw out their lunch. Next came the "silken oars" that didn't work anyway, the ornaments on the gasbag, all their ropes and lines, and, finally, the anchors.

As they settled slowly toward the sea, Blanchard discarded his outer coat and Dr. Jeffries his only coat. Just as the doctor was about to suggest that they empty their bladders they encountered a warm breeze and the ship began to rise. At three in the afternoon they sailed over the French coast near Calais. The French were overjoyed. Louis XVI showered the aeronauts with medals. The English were slightly less enthusiastic about this first aerial breach of their kingdom's insularity.

The first man to fly in a balloon was also the first to die in one. In 1784, Pilatre de Rozier ascended to a record altitude of 11,732 feet in a hot-air balloon. After Blanchard crossed the Channel from England to France, the French government offered Rozier a large grant to build a balloon capable of making the crossing in the opposite direction. Five months after Blanchard's flight, Rozier was ready. In order to overcome Blanchard's ballast problems, he had built a combination ship. Beneath a forty-foot hydrogen balloon he suspended a ten-foot hot-air balloon that he hoped would supply the added lift that Blanchard had lacked.

At 7:00 A.M. on the morning of June 15, 1785, Rozier and Pierre Ange

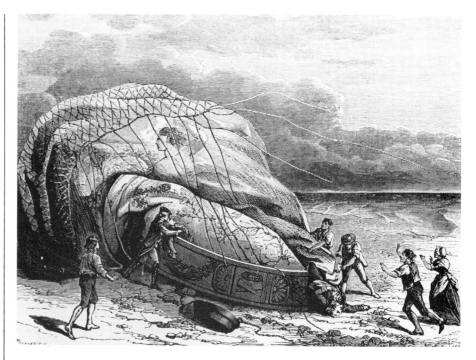

The first ballooning fatality. The attempt by Pilatre de Rozier to reverse Blanchard's flight and cross the Channel from France to England was financed by the French government. With the prevailing winds against him, Rozier built this combination hot-air and hydrogen balloon with the idea of changing his lift as the flight progressed in order to search for favorable winds at different altitudes. But by combining the open fire of a hot-air balloon with highly inflammable hydrogen, his friend Professor Charles warned him, "You are putting a chafing-dish under a barrel of gunpowder." Aware of the danger, Rozier took special precautions. To make the hydrogen bag as gastight as possible, he used three layers of goldbeater's skin, the gastight intestine of the ox, pressed onto taffeta with a solution of oil, honey, and sugar of lead. It was to no avail. Rozier's fiancée witnessed his fatal fall and is reported to have died eight days later of a broken heart. Rozier's death, the first ballooning fatality, occurred nineteen months after he ushered in the aerial age. *Courtesy Carruthers Collection, Claremont Colleges.*

•

Romain, a Boulogne physician, cast loose their moorings and rose into the air. At first the ship drifted slowly toward the sea, but at five thousand feet they met an adverse air current that blew them back over the land. Twenty-three minutes into the flight, the fabric caught fire at the top around the copper gas valve. As the fabric burned away, the balloon crashed to the ground. By the time friends reached them, both Pierre Romain and Pilatre de Rozier were dead.

In spite of these occasional setbacks, ballooning was being taken up by ever-increasing numbers of people all over Europe. Soon the public grew accustomed to ordinary ascensions and demanded more spectacular stunts. The aeronauts complied by taking horses aloft, shooting off fireworks, and dropping from their balloons by parachute.

Stuart Amos Arnold planned to make one of the first parachute jumps in England. Arnold, his son, and a sailor named Appleby, who claimed to be an expert parachutist, cast off on a bright August day in 1785. As the balloon rose from the ground, Appleby's parachute became entangled in a fence and he and his chute had to be cut away. Then they struck a cart, overturning the balloon basket and dumping Arnold out on the ground. The younger Arnold was left clinging to the broken cords as the balloon finally soared skyward where it burst. The boy fell into the Thames and was rescued unhurt. The excited spectators agreed that it was the most original ascension they had yet witnessed.

The first balloon flight in the United States took off from the yard of the Walnut Street Prison in Philadelphia, the nation's capital, on January 9, 1793. Among the spectators was President George Washington. The balloonist was Jean-Pierre Blanchard, the man who first flew the English Channel.

The Federal Gazette and Philadelphia Daily Advertiser

As soon as the clock had struck ten, everything being punctually ready, Mr. Blanchard took a respectful leave of all the spectators, and received from the hands of the President a paper, at the same time the President spoke a few words to this bold adventurer, who immediately leap'd into his boat which was painted blue and spangled; the balloon was of a yellowish color'd silk highly varnished, over which there was a strong net work—Mr. Blanchard was dressed in a plain blue suit, a cock'd hat and white feathers. As soon as he was in the boat, he threw out some ballast, and the balloon began to ascend slowly and perpendicularly, whilst Mr. Blanchard waved the colours of the United States and also those of the French Republic, and flourished his hat to the thousands of citizens from every part of the country who stood gratified and astonished at his entrepidity.[10]

Blanchard rose to twelve hundred feet, where a strong breeze drove him eastward across the Delaware River into New Jersey. After covering fifteen miles in forty-six minutes, he landed in a plowed field near Woodbury.

Now his only problem was to get back to Philadelphia. A farmer was staring at him in open-mouthed amazement from the edge of the field.

Jean-Pierre Blanchard
I spied him and enjoyed his whole surprise when he saw through a tuft of trees such a monstrous machine, balancing on itself, and sinking in proportion as the spirit wherewith it was animated, left it. He seemed to be frightened, and I was afraid he would go away again. I let him hear my voice, inviting him to draw near.[11]

The farmer did not appear to be reassured when Blanchard started shouting at him in French so the aeronaut tried another tack.

Jean-Pierre Blanchard
Recollecting that the exhilarating juice of the grape was always amongst mankind the happiest sign of friendship and conciliation, I showed a bottle of wine.

That did the trick, and after a couple of drinks, Blanchard showed the farmer the paper that Washington had given him back in Philadelphia. It introduced the balloonist and directed all citizens to aid and assist him. The farmer admired the document but was forced to admit that he had never learned to read, and Blanchard didn't speak any English. A crowd began to gather and finally someone arrived who was able to read Washington's passport.

Jean-Pierre Blanchard
I could not, nor did I know how to answer all the friendly questions which they asked me; my passport served me instead of an interpreter. In the midst of a profound silence was it read with a loud and audible voice. How dear the name of Washington is to this people! With what eagerness they gave me all possible assistance, in consequence of his recommendation.[12]

That evening Blanchard was returned in triumph to Philadelphia, where he presented President Washington with the American flag he had carried aloft. Unfortunately, in spite of the huge crowd that witnessed the ascension, Blanchard was able to collect less than a third of the two thousand dollars that the flight had cost him. When he could find no one willing to sponsor a second flight, he returned to Europe, where ballooning was a more profitable enterprise. He made a total of sixty ascents, including the first flights in the Netherlands, Belgium, Germany, Poland, Bohemia, and Switzerland before his death in 1809 at the age of fifty-six.

Ballooning soon became a worldwide mania, and a number of professional aeronauts began traveling around the countryside giving exhibitions and taking paying passengers for rides. Many spectacular long-distance flights were made, including John Wise's 809-mile voyage from St. Louis to Henderson, New York, in 1859, a record that stood until Count Henry de La Vaulx's 1,195-mile flight from Paris to Russia in 1900. As shown here, the landing was often the most exciting part of the voyage. *Courtesy Carruthers Collection, Claremont Colleges.*

•

Blanchard was only one of several professional balloonists, highly skilled aeronauts who made their living giving aerial exhibitions and selling rides. One of the best was England's Charles Green, who set a distance record in 1836 of 480 miles from London to Germany in his *Royal Nassau* balloon. He regularly made ascensions from London's Vauxhall Gardens, and the writer Henry Mayhew reported on one such flight in an 1852 issue of the *Illustrated London News.*

[W]e were raised some fifty feet in the air to try the ascensive power of the machine that was to bear us through the clouds. Then, having been duly dragged down, the signal was at length given to fire the cannons, and Mr. Green loosening the only rope that bound us to the Gardens, we shot into the air—or rather the earth seemed to sink suddenly down . . . instantaneously there appeared a multitude of upturned faces in the Gardens below, the greater part with their mouths wide open. . . . Then, as we swept rapidly above the trees, I could see the roadway immediately outside the Gardens, stuck all over with rows of tiny people, looking like so many black pins on a cushion, and the hubbub of the voices below was like the sound of a distant school let loose.

And here began that peculiar panoramic effect which is the distinguishing feature of a view from a balloon, and which arises from the utter absence of all sense of motion in the machine itself. The earth appeared literally to consist of a long series of scenes, which were being continually drawn along under you, as if it were a diorama beheld flat upon the ground, and gave one almost the notion that the world was an endless landscape stretched upon rollers, which some invisible sprites were revolving for your special enjoyment.

The strange absence of any sense of motion noted by nearly all balloon passengers is due to the complete silence of the machine together with the lack of even the slightest breeze. The wind may be blowing the balloon along at fifty miles per hour, but since both are moving at the same speed, the passenger feels no wind at all. After marveling at the scene below ("we could see the gas-lights along the different lines of road start into light one after another all over the earth"), Mayhew and his nine fellow aeronauts prepared to descend into what proved to be one of the *Royal Nassau*'s rougher landings.

Henry Mayhew

A bag of ballast was entrusted to one of the passengers to let fall at a given signal, while Green himself stood with the grapnel ready to loose immediately as he came to a fitting spot. Presently the signal for the descent of the ballast was given, and as it dropped it was curious to watch it fall; the earth had seemed almost at our feet as the car swept over the fields, but so long was the heavy bag in getting to the ground that, as the eye watched it fall and fall, the mind was filled with amazement at the height the balloon still was in the air. Suddenly the sound as of a gun announced that the bag had struck the soil, and then we were all told to sit low down in the car and hold fast. Scarcely had we obeyed the orders given than the car was suddenly and fiercely jerked half round, and all within it thrown one on top of another; immediately after this, bump went the bottom of the car on the ground, giving us so violent a shake that it seemed as if every limb in the body had been simultaneously dislocated. Now the balloon pitched over on its side, and lay on the ground struggling with the wind, and rolling about, heaving like a huge whale in the agonies of death.

"For Heaven's sake! hold fast," shouted Mr. Green, as we were dashed up and down in the car, all rolling one on the other, with each fresh lurch of the giant machine stretched on the ground before us, and from which we could hear the gas roaring from the valve, like the blast of a furnace.

"Sit still, all of you, I say!" roared our pilot, as he saw someone endeavouring to leave the car.

Again we were pitched right on end, and the bottom of the car shifted into a ditch, the water of which bubbled up through the wicker-work of the car; and I, unlucky wight, who was seated in that part of which the concussions were mostly confined, soon began to feel that I was quietly sitting in a pool of water.[13]

It was ten o'clock at night and they had landed in a swamp. But with the help of some nearby farmers, they soon had their balloon rolled up, stowed in the wicker car, and loaded aboard a farm wagon. Then, as they opened up the food and wine, everyone rode off toward town.

It wasn't long before the inventive mind of man found a way to use the balloon in warfare. The year was 1793. While Blanchard was sailing over far-off New Jersey, his king, Louis XVI, was losing his head to the French Revolution, and the armies of the new republic were beset on all sides by monarchs anxious to contain the spread of liberalism. That same year the new French government authorized the formation of a balloon corps. Eight months later on June 2, 1794, the first Compagnie D'Aerostiers went into action against the Austrian army at Maubeuge on the Belgian frontier. The Balloon Corps created a mild sensation on its first arrival in camp.

Capt. Jean Marie-Joseph Coutelle

The officer to whom I delivered my order could not understand my mission . . . and still less an aerostat in the middle of the camp. He threatened to have me shot, as a suspicious character, before listening to me; but ended by relenting and complimenting me on my devotion.[14]

After the initial confusion was cleared up, Captain Coutelle and his corps went on to give a good account of themselves in their first engagements.

The balloon at the battle of Fleurus. Capt. Jean Marie-Joseph Coutelle was Napoleon's captain of aerostiers and the world's first military balloon observer. He hung suspended over the battlefield at Fleurus in Belgium on June 26, 1794, for nine hours spotting for the French artillery. He used signal flags to relay his information to the ground. The French republican army's victory in this battle was due, at least in part, to the Austrians' confusion at having their movements observed from the air. *Courtesy San Diego Aero-Space Museum.*

•

Capt. Jean Marie-Joseph Coutelle

I will not claim, as do those who praise or blame with exaggeration everything that is new, that the balloon won the Battle of Fleurus. On this memorable day, every corps did its full duty. What I can say is, that well served by my glass, despite the oscillation and movement caused by the wind, I was able to distinguish clearly the corps of infantry and cavalry, the parks of artillery, their movements, and in general, the massed troops. . . .

Generally the soldiers of the enemy, all who saw the observer watching them and taking notes, decided that they could do nothing without being seen. Our soldiers were of the same opinion, and consequently they regarded us with great admiration and trust. On the heavy marches they brought us prepared food and wine, which my men were hardly able to get for themselves so closely did they require to attend to the ropes. We were encamped upon the banks of the Rhine at Mannheim when our general sent me to the opposite bank to confer. As soon as the Austrian officers were told that I commanded the balloon, I was overwhelmed with questions and compliments.[15]

The world's first aerial bombardment took place in 1849 when the Austrian army was attempting to recapture the city of Venice. A number of unmanned hot-air balloons, each carrying a thirty-pound bomb with a long fuse, were sent up to drift out over the city. The plan was imaginative but unsuccessful, though the Austrians took the city anyway. *Courtesy Carruthers Collection, Claremont Colleges.*

The Austrians paid careful attention to their inventive foe, and some years later they came up with an aerial first of their own. While besieging Venice in 1849, they won the dubious honor of dropping the first aerial bombs. They launched small unmanned hot-air balloons upwind of the city, each carrying a thirty-pound bomb with a slow-burning fuse. As the hot air in the bag cooled, the balloons dropped into the city, where the bombs would explode. It seemed like a good idea until the wind changed. The small amount of damage both to the Austrians and to Venice failed to justify the effort and expense, and the experiment was not repeated.

Observation balloons were used by both sides in the American Civil War, but the most systematic efforts were made for the Union army by Thaddeus Lowe, a professional aeronaut.

Lowe began his military career by accident. While preparing for a trans-Atlantic balloon crossing, he made a test flight from Cincinnati that carried him southeast across Kentucky, Tennessee, and North Carolina. After covering 350 miles in eight hours, he landed at Pea Ridge, South Carolina, where he was taken for a

The *Intrepid,* one of several Union army balloons, is being inflated at the battle of Fair Oaks. Lowe and his men also saw action at Richmond, Manassas, and Chickahominy. President Lincoln strongly supported Lowe's Balloon Corps and some battlefield commanders made good use of the aerial observers, but many were too busy to use the balloons properly. Part of the difficulty was in moving this bulky hydrogen-generating equipment fast enough to keep up with the army. *Official United States Air Force photo.*

•

visitor from the infernal regions. The natives were convinced of his terrestrial origin only when he pulled a Colt revolver and commandeered a wagon to carry him and his equipment to the nearest railroad station. He caught a train to Columbia, South Carolina, where he narrowly escaped being arrested as a Union spy, Fort Sumter having been fired upon only a few days earlier. He then proceeded by train to Nashville where, with his high silk hat and black frock coat, he was mistaken for a member of the Tennessee legislature, which was convening to withdraw formally from the Union. When he finally arrived back in Cincinnati, Lowe telegraphed President Lincoln the first news of Tennessee's decision to join the Confederacy.

Lincoln was impressed by the balloon's potential and ordered the formation of an aerial observer corps under the direction of Thaddeus Lowe. For two years he and his men made hundreds of ascents with various Union armies. In July 1861 Lowe himself directed the first artillery fire from the air in his balloon high over the besieged suburbs of Washington, D.C.

Lowe always wore a top hat and frock coat when he went into combat, much to the disgust of the regular army officers with whom he worked. They would have preferred a more conventional uniform, but Lowe may have been looking forward to the day when once again he would drift down into the middle of the Confederacy and have to take another train north.

The Confederates' balloon experience was much more limited.

Gen. James Longstreet

The Federals had been using balloons in examining our positions, and we watched with envious eyes their beautiful observations as they floated high up in the air, well out of range of our guns. While we were longing for the balloons that poverty denied us, a genius arose for the occasion and suggested that we send out and gather silk dresses in the Confederacy and make a balloon.

It was done, and soon we had a great patchwork ship of many and varied hues which was ready for use in the Seven Days' campaign.

We had no gas except in Richmond, and it was the custom to inflate the balloon there, tie it securely to an engine, and run it down the York River Railroad to any point at which we desired to send it up. One day it was on a steamer down the James River when the tide went out and left vessel and balloon high and dry on a bar. The Federals gathered it in, and with it the last silk dress in the Confederacy. This capture was the meanest trick of the war and one I have never yet forgiven.[16]

General Longstreet loved a good story even if it was not precisely true. The Confederacy employed several balloons during the war, none made of silk dresses.

After two years, Lowe's Balloon Corps was disbanded. Not only was his uniform nonregulation, his organization didn't fit into the chain of command. It was transferred from the Topographic Engineers to the Quartermasters and then to the Corps of Engineers where it finally expired in June 1863. While some commanders used aerial observers to advantage, others felt it was unsportsmanlike to spy on the enemy's movements from the air. In addition, the balloon and its hydrogen-generating equipment often proved to be too slow and cumbersome to keep up with an army on the move.

Napoleon had disbanded the French army's Balloon Corps in 1802. The United States Army made one last try during the attack on Santiago, Cuba, in the Spanish-American War of 1898.

Lt. C. de W. Willcox

[A]s the Spaniards saw it rise from the ground, they got its range at once and destroyed it before it could be of any material use. Indeed it is charged that it caused serious loss to the advancing infantry by revealing their position and attracting the enemy's fire.[17]

It was not until the static trench warfare of the western front in World War I that the tethered observation balloon again proved useful. The free balloon, on the other hand, proved its worth at the siege of Paris during the Franco-Prussian War of 1870. Prussian armies encircled the city in September and kept it completely cut off from the rest of France for four months. The only avenue of communication left open was the skies. A circus balloon that happened to be in the city was pressed into service along with a professional aeronaut, Jules Duruof, who volunteered to fly over the Prussian lines to French-held territory with news of the city's encirclement.

A French journalist, Wilfrid de Fonvielle, described the flight.

Wilfrid de Fonvielle

Duruof did not hesitate an instant to brave the fire of the Prussians with an old balloon leaking at every seam. An order arrived in the evening, and next morning at eight o'clock the Neptune soared above the buttes of Montmartre. Duruof perceived that his only chance of safety lay in the force of the impulse with which he started. He therefore launched his balloon like a projectile which issues from a monster mortar. The Neptune described a parabola like that of a bombshell whose descent had been miraculously prolonged. By sacrificing seven hundredweight of ballast, the descent took place about 19 miles from the Place St. Pierre, in the Department of Eure, not far from the Prussians, but still beyond their range. A true son of Paris, Duruof could not let the opportunity escape of enlivening a situation so terrible. He threw his calling cards down upon the heads of the enemy, who, furious at seeing the blockade thus forced, saluted the Neptune with a salvo of artillery, and a rolling fire of musketry.[18]

The success of the flight galvanized the city into action. The empty and useless railway stations were quickly converted into balloon factories. Every scrap of silk and linen was commandeered as Paris's seamstresses, used to sewing the latest in women's fashions, went to work on balloons.

The prevailing winds made it much easier to fly out of Paris than to fly back in again, so each balloon that left the city carried up to thirty homing pigeons. After the aeronaut had examined the Prussian defenses, he sent his information back into the city by pigeon. In spite of Prussian hawks sent up to intercept them, the pigeons returned with letters and dispatches that had been copied on microfilm. Using a special process developed by the Paris photographer Dagron, each pigeon could carry up to five thousand microfilmed messages that were then projected on a large screen and transcribed back into letter form before being delivered through the post office.

During the four-month siege, sixty-six balloons rose from the center of the city. They carried two and a half million letters, four hundred pigeons, and 102 passengers including Leon Gambetta, the head of the French provisional government, who flew out to direct the formation of a relief army in the provinces.

Only two balloons were lost when they were blown out to sea. Another sailed all the way to Norway, where its two occupants received a hearty welcome. A different kind of reception awaited the two balloons that came down in Germany. Three others were also captured by the enemy but all the rest landed safely.

The balloon was extremely useful at the siege of Paris but it was a losing cause. The city was forced to surrender on January 28, 1871, and France had to cede the provinces of Alsace and Lorraine to Germany. Still, in the ninety years since the Montgolfiers' first flight, the siege of Paris stands almost alone on the balloon's list of practical accomplishments. For though a balloon ascension is interesting, colorful, sometimes dangerous, always exciting, and a great crowd pleaser at circuses and fairs, even its most enthusiastic adherents seldom claim that it is practical.

In 1870 one disillusioned French aeronaut wrote:

Our age is the most renowned for its discoveries of any that the world has seen. Man is borne over the surface of the earth by steam; he is as familiar as the fish with the liquid element; he transmits his words instantaneously from London to New York; he draws pictures without pencil or brush, and has made the sun his slave. The air alone remains to

ABOVE LEFT: Microfilm messages being enlarged and copied. Sixty-six balloons were built and launched during the siege that lasted from September 1870 until the end of January 1871. The city's pigeon fanciers were enlisted in the cause, and four hundred of Paris's best birds were flown out by balloon. A special microfilming process was developed to reduce thousands of messages to a single tiny piece of film that was then carried back into the city by homing pigeon. Here the messages are being enlarged and copied for delivery through the Paris postal system. *Courtesy Carruthers Collection, Claremont Colleges.* ABOVE RIGHT: Balloons being built in a Paris railway station. Several leading aeronauts were in Paris when it was encircled, including Nadar, Gaston Tissandier, Jules Duruof, Eugene Goddard, and his brothers Jules and Louis. After Duruof, Louis Goddard, and Gaston Tissandier flew balloons out, the rest realized that the supply of pilots would soon be exhausted and a training school was started. They found that sailors, of whom there were a large number in the city, made the best aeronauts. It was the beginning of the navy's long association with lighter-than-air flight. Here the city's seamstresses work with sailors building balloons in one of Paris's empty railway stations. *Courtesy Carruthers Collection, Claremont Colleges.*

•

Salomon August Andrée (1845–97) is seated in the center with Knut Fraenkel, a twenty-seven-year-old civil engineer, at the left, and Nils Strindberg, a twenty-five-year-old physics teacher, at the right. Andrée was a graduate of the Swedish Royal Institute of Technology. His outstanding work on an international meteorological expedition to Spitzbergen in 1882 led to his appointment as head of the technical department of the Swedish Patent Office in 1885. *Courtesy Andrée Museum, Gränna, Sweden.*

•

him unsubdued. The proper management of balloons has not yet been discovered. More than that, it appears that balloons are unmanageable, and it is to air vessels, constructed more nearly upon the model of birds, that we must go to find out the secret of aerial navigation. At present, as in former times, we are the sport and the prey of tempests and currents, and aeronauts, instead of showing themselves now as the benefactors of mankind, exhibit themselves mainly to gratify a frivolous curiosity, or to crown with éclat a public fete. . . . The balloon is not the master of the atmosphere; on the contrary, it is its powerless slave.[19]

One who dreamed of more practical work for the balloon was Salomon August Andrée, the chief engineer of the Swedish Patent Office. He envisioned the trade winds that blow constantly over the oceans as that "magnificent, regular system of winds, which only waited for aerial vessels—giant balloons carrying cargo and passengers."[20]

Others were intrigued by the same possibility. Various proposals had been put forward for an Atlantic balloon crossing using the trade winds that blew from America to Europe. A few aeronauts actually got off the ground but, fortunately for them, they were invariably blown inland instead of out to sea. In 1859 Thaddeus Lowe was at Philadelphia preparing to try his luck over the Atlantic in a 725,000-cubic-foot balloon, the *Great Western*. It was 130 feet in diameter, the largest hydrogen balloon yet built. Thirty minutes before the scheduled takeoff, a sudden windstorm destroyed it completely.

Salomon Andrée remained fascinated by the idea of a dirigible balloon. He made an intensive study of aeronautics and finally, with the help of a Swedish foundation, purchased a balloon in France and brought it home to Sweden. He christened it *Svea (Sweden)* and made nine flights between 1893 and 1895. Altogether he spent forty hours in the air and covered nine hundred miles.

At the end of his experiments, Andrée announced a bold plan, a balloon voyage to the North Pole. At a meeting of the Swedish Academy of Sciences, he challenged the assembled explorers and scientists:

Has not the time come to see if we do not possibly possess any other means than the sledge for crossing these [polar] tracts? Yes, the time for doing so has certainly come, and we need not search very long before we find a means which is, as it were, created just for such a purpose. This means is the air balloon; not the dreamed-of, perfectly dirigible air balloon, so devotedly longed for, since we have not yet seen it, but the air balloon which we already possess and which is regarded so unfavourably merely because attention is focussed on its weak point. Such an air balloon is, however, capable of carrying the explorer to the Pole and home again in safety; with such a balloon the journey across the waste of ice *can* be carried out.

These words may seem bold, and even reckless, but I ask you to suspend your judgment on the matter until you have heard my arguments. For I am assured that then your judgment will be different. We have merely to rid ourselves of preconceived opinions and then allow facts to have all the weight they may possess.[21]

Andrée then listed the four requirements that he felt a North Pole balloon must fulfill. First it must be able to carry three men and enough provisions for four months, about sixty-six hundred pounds. Second, the envelope must be so gastight that it can remain in the air for thirty days. Third, it must be filled and launched as near the

Pole as possible, and fourth, "the balloon must, to some degree, be dirigible."

His first three requirements were, according to Andrée, well within the limits of current balloon science. Bigger balloons had already been built and flown successfully. The fourth requirement, dirigibility, Andrée felt he himself had solved in his nine test flights. He had worked out a system of drag ropes and sails with which he said he was able to alter the course of his balloon up to thirty degrees off the direction of the wind.

Salomon Andrée

How soon the Pole can be reached depends, of course, on the velocity and direction of the wind. Under favourable conditions it can be done in a very short time. With a wind-velocity like that which, on November 25, 1870, carried a French balloon from Paris to Livfjeld in Norway (600 miles in 13 hours), and that which on November 29, 1894, carried my balloon from Gothenburg to Gottland (240 miles in under four hours) there would be required about ten hours for the journey to the Pole. If, on the other hand, the balloon does not move at a greater speed than 16.5 miles per hour, which is the speed that can be obtained with the average wind-velocity at a height of 800 feet above the surface of the earth, then about 43 hours would be needed for a journey from Spitzbergen to the Pole. . . .

If the journey lasts thirty days, then, according to the above calculation of the probable average speed of the balloon, it will cover a distance of about 11,800 miles. The journey from Spitzbergen across the Pole direct to the Bering Straits—a distance of 2,200 miles—will not take more than six days, i.e., one-fifth of the time during which the balloon can remain in the air.[22]

Andrée estimated the cost of the expedition at $34,500. Four months after giving his speech, he had the entire sum in hand. Alfred Nobel contributed half, Sweden's King Oscar gave eight thousand dollars, and two other donors gave the rest.

In December of 1895 Andrée signed a contract with Henri Lachambre, a French balloon maker, and in June of the following year his expedition was on a steamer bound for Dane Island just off the coast of Spitzbergen. There they built a large hangar, inflated their balloon, the *Ornen (Eagle)*, and waited for the south wind that would blow them to the Pole.

For two weeks the wind blew the wrong way. By then it was the middle of August, the end of the Arctic summer, and too late to attempt the voyage, so they deflated the *Ornen*, packed up, and headed home. A year later they returned to Dane Island. The balloon house needed only minor repairs and by the first of July everything was ready. Andrée was then forty-three. He was to be accompanied by Nils Strindberg, a twenty-five-year-old physics teacher at the University of Stockholm, and Knut Fraenkel, twenty-seven, a civil engineer. Shortly before their departure, the three men issued a final press statement:

We have taken all into account. We are prepared to face whatever may happen. . . . Having during these last years thought, worked, and calculated in preparing for this expedition, we have, so to speak, mentally lived through all possibilities. Now we only desire to start, and have the thing finished some way or other. . . . one year, perhaps two years, may elapse before you hear from us, and you may one day be surprised by news of our arrival somewhere. And if not,—if you never hear from us,—others will follow in our wake until the unknown regions of the north have been surveyed.[23]

The *Ornen* starting on its way.

The balloon was visible over an hour and presented a beautiful sight as it sailed away toward a point a little north of Franz Josef Land.

The Scientific American, September 18, 1897.

This was the last sight of the explorers for thirty-three years. Most of their drag lines had already fallen off. By trailing these ropes behind him over the ice, Andrée planned to make the *Ornen* go slower than the wind. His sail could then catch the wind and alter the course of his balloon, he believed, by up to thirty degrees off the wind direction. But with the loss of the drag lines the *Ornen* would move at the same speed as the wind and the sail would be useless. *Alexis Machuron, courtesy Carruthers Collection, Claremont Colleges.*

•

ABOVE LEFT: The balloon down on the ice. With her heavy drag ropes lost in the first minutes of the flight, the *Ornen* rose too high, her hydrogen expanded and was blown off through the safety valve. Then, with part of her lift gone, the balloon dragged across the frozen ocean for three days before they were finally forced to land on July 14, 1897. They were four hundred miles north and east of Spitzbergen and five hundred miles short of the Pole. *Courtesy Northrop University.* ABOVE RIGHT: For almost three months the men struggled across the drifting ice, dragging their supplies behind them. On October 5, they reached White Island, a desolate, ice-covered island never before visited by man. They were found there thirty-three years later frozen and preserved in the bitter Arctic cold. Even the images on the film in their camera were preserved. When this photo was developed in 1930, both Andrée and his polar bear had been dead for a third of a century. *Courtesy Andrée Museum, Gränna, Sweden.*

•

On July 11, 1897, the south wind began to blow and the three men climbed aboard. The *Ornen* was cast off and rose slowly to six hundred feet as she drifted out over the harbor. Then she started to sink, and with a sharp jolt, the car dipped into the water for an instant before rising again and sailing off into the Arctic vastness. Most of the drag lines were left lying on the beach where they had unscrewed themselves and fallen off.

Four days later the captain of a Norwegian sealing vessel shot a strange-looking bird that landed on his ship's rigging. It was a carrier pigeon with a message from Andrée written on July 13, two days after they took off. It gave their position some miles north of Spitzbergen and said only "All well on board."

For nearly two years, nothing more was heard from the explorers. Not even their pigeons returned. Then a buoy was found washed up on the coast of Iceland. A message was inside.

> This buoy is thrown out from Andrée's balloon at 10.55 G.M.T. [Greenwich mean time] on July 11, 1897, in about 82° latitude and 25° long. E.fr.Gr. We are floating at a height of 600 meters (1950 feet).
>
> All well
>
> Andrée   Strindberg   Fraenkel[24]

This message that took so long to reach the outside world had been thrown from the balloon at 10:00 P.M. on the evening of the first day, only ten hours after they set out and two days earlier than the message already received by carrier pigeon.

Two other buoys were found later. One was empty; the second had another message from the first day. The lost aeronauts had written, "Weather magnificent. In best of humours."

A pigeon with a message from the third day, three buoys, two with messages from the first day. Nothing more. Three men sailed away into the wilderness of ice and snow and the Arctic night had closed around them.

Then thirty-three years later, the mystery of Andrée and his expedition was solved. In 1930 seal hunters found their frozen bodies on White Island where they had camped after trudging from their fallen balloon for months over the ice.

In trying to make the balloon envelope as gastight as possible, it had been made too heavy. The loss of the 1,160-pound drag lines at the very beginning of the flight allowed the balloon to rise too high. The precious hydrogen expanded and escaped through the gas valve. Then they had drifted into fog, which froze on the

envelope and rigging, weighing them down. As they descended the gas contracted and there wasn't enough left to keep the *Ornen* in the air.

After sixty-five hours of flight, much of it with the balloon basket being dragged across the ice, they were finally forced to land at 7:30 on the morning of July 14. They had covered nearly five hundred miles, but only half of it was toward the Pole.

For days they trudged across the shifting sea ice, dragging heavy sledges loaded with supplies. For food they shot seals, birds, and polar bears. All through July, August, and September they struggled onward over the ice until they reached White Island. There they died, possibly from carbon monoxide generated by the stove as they sat cooking dinner inside their tightly sealed tent.

Their bodies were found on the remote ice-bound island thirty-three years later and returned to Sweden, where the entire nation turned out to honor them.

Shortly before the balloon came down on the ice, Salomon Andrée sat alone on top of the car and thought of death. His words were found in a journal beside his frozen body a third of a century later.

It is not a little strange to be floating here in a balloon. How soon, I wonder, shall we have successors? Shall we be thought mad or will our example be followed? I cannot deny that all three of us are dominated by a feeling of pride. We think we can well face death, having done what we have done. Isn't it all, perhaps, the expression of an extremely strong sense of individuality which cannot bear the thought of living and dying like a man in the ranks, forgotten by coming generations? Is this ambition?

The rattling of the guide-lines in the snow and the flapping of the sails are the only sounds heard, except the whining [of the wind] in the basket.[25]

•

Dr. Solomon Andrews offered his airship to Congress in 1863 for use in the war against the Confederacy. When he claimed a secret power source that enabled him to fly for miles in any direction without the aid of an engine, he was dismissed as an eccentric and Congress turned to other matters. Dr. Andrews was, however, a respected citizen, a physician, an inventor, and the former mayor of Perth Amboy, New Jersey. He built his airship, the *Aereon,* without government assistance and it did fly. Several reputable witnesses claimed to have seen him fly against the wind over New York City in 1865. Dr. Andrews never revealed his secret power source but he apparently took the *Aereon* to an altitude of several thousand feet and released a large amount of gas. The ship would then descend in a long glide using the underside of the three connected balloons as a lifting surface or wing. At the bottom of his glide, if enough ballast was thrown off, he may have been able to turn around and, in a long ascending glide, return to his starting point. *Courtesy Library of Congress.*

•

2

· T H E ·
SEARCH
· F O R ·
DIRIGIBILITY

The fact that so many gifted scientists and engineers are engaged on the problem of artificial flight affords, in itself, a strong presumption that sooner or later a successful motor-driven flying machine will be an accomplished fact. It is only in recent years that the question of artificial flight has been recognized as deserving a high place among the many unsolved problems which are worthy of the serious efforts of the scientist and mechanic. It was not so long ago that the flying machine was classed as a kind of first cousin to the perpetual motion device, and the mere suggestion that anyone was attempting to fly caused a smile of pitying contempt.

Scientific American, January 8, 1898

The first balloon was hardly off the ground before the search began for a way to direct its flight. Though the spherical balloon was the most natural shape and the easiest to build, it was quickly recognized as the most difficult to drive through the air.

The first elongated or cigar-shaped balloon was designed by Professor Charles and built by the Robert brothers for the Duc de Chartres in 1784. But finding a suitable method of propulsion proved to be a much more difficult problem. The Roberts tried rapidly opening and closing umbrellas. Joseph Montgolfier suggested cutting holes on one side of a hot-air balloon bag to allow the escaping air to push it in the opposite direction. Jean-Pierre Blanchard was the first to try oars, but muscle power alone proved insufficient. Trained birds were widely recommended with vultures, eagles, and pigeons being favored. The Abbé Bertholon proposed using the recoil of cannons fired in rapid succession.

OPPOSITE: Alberto Santos-Dumont won the Deutsch Prize on September 19, 1901, with a seven-mile round-trip from St. Cloud to the Eiffel Tower in thirty minutes. It was a performance unequaled by any other airship of its day. In fact, there were no other airships of its day. Count Zeppelin's unwieldy *LZ-1* had been dismantled a year earlier and the Wright brothers would not fly for two more years. Alberto's *No. 6* was 110 feet long and 20 feet in diameter with a top speed of twenty-five miles per hour. *Courtesy Carruthers Collection, Claremont Colleges.*

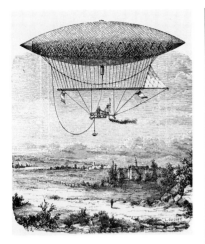

Henri Giffard (1825–82) built the first practical airship and flew it from the Paris Hippodrome on September 24, 1852. He had already, at the age of twenty-four, invented the injector used in all steam engines. His ship was powered by a specially designed three-horsepower steam engine that drove it at six miles per hour. The engine was suspended twenty feet below the 144-foot-long, eighty-eight-thousand-cubic-foot balloon. The total weight of the ship and pilot was three thousand pounds, which left a disposable lift of 250 pounds for coal and water. *Courtesy Carruthers Collection, Claremont Colleges.*

•

The fact remained that the only power available to man capable of withstanding the force of the wind was the steam engine, and those with enough horsepower to do the job were too heavy to lift off the ground. It wasn't until 1852 that Henri Giffard, a leading steam designer, developed a special three-horsepower engine that weighed only 350 pounds. He mounted it below a 144-foot-long elongated balloon and on September 24, 1852, rose from the Paris Hippodrome before a large crowd to demonstrate man's first powered flight. With a top speed of six miles per hour, he was unable to fly against the light breeze that was blowing but he was able to steer his ship in large circles. He made several more flights but no one followed up on his experiments. At six miles per hour his ship was capable of controlled flight only in a dead calm, and the sight of Giffard's highly inflammable hydrogen-filled airship trailing a shower of red-hot cinders behind it was enough to convince most people that this was not the solution to powered flight, even if a lighter, more powerful steam engine were available. Giffard built a second, larger gasbag that was wrecked on its first test flight. Thereafter, he turned his attention to building a series of large captive balloons culminating in an 883,000-cubic-foot giant, the largest hydrogen balloon ever built. It was a great success at the Paris World's Fair of 1878, carrying fifty-two passengers aloft at one time.

The first attempt to use the newly invented internal combustion engine in an airship was made by a German, Paul Haenlein, in 1872. His engine was a very early five-horsepower Lenoir that used gaseous rather than liquid fuel. The ship proved to be too heavy and made only a few tethered flights at Brunn in what is now Czechoslovakia. Haenlein ran his engine on coal gas pumped from the balloon bag, so that the longer it ran, the less gas was left to lift the ship.

The Paris Electrical Exhibition of 1881 featured a scale model electric-powered airship built by the well-known balloonists Gaston and Albert Tissandier. They were encouraged to construct a full-sized version that flew in a series of tests in 1883 and 1884, but the ship's 1½-horsepower Siemens motor was barely able to drive it at three miles per hour. Its twenty-four bichromate of potash batteries weighed over four hundred pounds and actually produced less power per pound than Giffard's steam engine. The only advantage of the electric engine was its flameless operation.

As the Tissandiers' ship was launched, a much more efficient airship was also being completed. Named *La France,* it was the creation of two French army engineers, Charles Renard and Arthur Krebs. An improved battery developed by Renard weighed more than fifteen hundred pounds, but it furnished eight horsepower to Krebs's specially designed motor. On August 9, 1884, after waiting several weeks for calm weather, the two men ascended from the aeronautical park at Chalais-Meudon. Finding the ship completely controllable, they set out on a circular, five-mile flight that brought them back over the park, where they landed after twenty-three minutes in the air. It was the first time that an aircraft had ever been able to return to its starting point. They made six more flights over the next several months, four times returning to their point of departure, but *La France*'s top speed of fourteen miles per hour was still too slow to permit completely controlled flight on any but the calmest days. They were also limited by the amount of electricity stored in their batteries.

The most advanced steam and electric engines of the day had been tried and had failed. They were simply too heavy for the amount of power they produced. Even the earliest internal combustion engines required more than one thousand

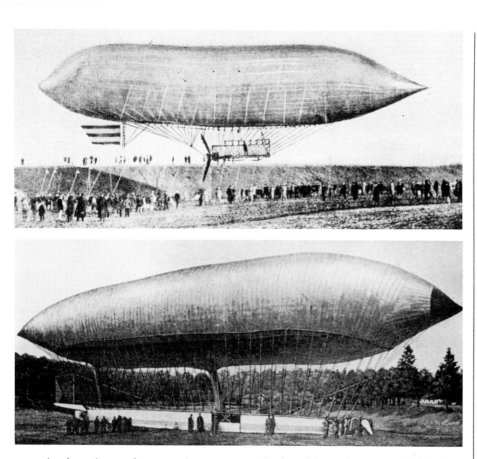

pounds of machinery for every horsepower. The breakthrough came in 1886 when Gottlieb Daimler was able to build a gasoline engine that weighed only eighty-eight pounds per horsepower.

The first to try Daimler's new engine in an airship was a German, Dr. Karl Woelfert, a Protestant minister who gave up his pulpit to become a professional balloonist. While pursuing his career as an aeronaut, Woelfert built two small, manually powered airships. Both were unsuccessful, but Gottlieb Daimler became interested and asked Woelfert to try one of his engines. A two-horsepower single-cylinder motor was installed in a new ship at the Daimler factory and several test flights were made in the summer of 1888. Though the power was inadequate, the ship handled well, and Woelfert was determined to build a larger one. Daimler's ignition system used an open flame and, though the engine was quite close to the hydrogen-filled gasbag, it luckily did not catch fire. Woelfert does not seem to have appreciated the danger.

Lack of money delayed him for nearly eight years, but in August 1896, his new ship, the *Deutschland,* was ready for display at the Berlin Trade Fair. It was powered by an eight-horsepower two-cylinder Daimler engine. The ignition system still required an open flame, and once more Woelfert had slung the car close up under the gasbag.

Kaiser Wilhelm took an interest in the project and ordered the Royal Prussian Aerial Navigation Department to assist in a test flight at Tempelhof Field in Berlin. It was scheduled for May 12, 1897, at seven in the evening when the wind usually died down. A large number of military and diplomatic observers were present as Woelfert and his mechanic, Robert Knabe, climbed aboard, were cast off, and climbed rapidly to three thousand feet.

ABOVE LEFT: Paul Haenlein (1835–1905) was the first to use the internal combustion engine in this 1872 airship. His engine burned 250 cubic feet of coal gas per hour, drawing it from the gasbag. Coal gas has about half the lift of hydrogen. Haenlein's ship proved to be too heavy and made its only flights led around on ropes held by soldiers. The gasbag was 164 feet long, thirty feet in diameter, and held eight-five thousand cubic feet of gas. *Courtesy Northrop University.* ABOVE RIGHT: The car of the Tissandier brothers' airship. Albert Tissandier (1839–1906) and his brother, Gaston (1843–99), were both experienced balloonists. Gaston flew out of Paris by balloon during the war of 1870. The gasbag of their airship was ninety-two feet long, thirty-two feet in diameter, and held 37,500 cubic feet of hydrogen. A series of test flights showed that their ship was seriously underpowered and they abandoned the project. *From* Histoire de Mes Ascensions, *by Gaston Tissandier, Paris, 1887.* LEFT: Renard and Krebs's *La France.* Capt. Charles Renard (1847–1905) was the commandant of the French army's balloon establishment at Chalais-Meudon. Capt. Arthur Krebs was his assistant. Their ship, *La France,* was financed by the government. The gasbag was 165 feet long and twenty-seven feet in diameter with sixty-six thousand cubic feet of hydrogen. The ship weighed two tons including Renard's fifteen-hundred-pound chromium-chloride batteries and Krebs's 210-pound electric motor that turned the twenty-three-foot-long propeller at the front of the car. With a top speed of fourteen miles per hour, *La France* was the first airship to return to her starting point against the wind. *Courtesy Carruthers Collection, Claremont Colleges.*

Dr. Karl Woelfert was the first to mount a gasoline engine in an airship. The *Deutschland* was his fourth ship and his second with a Daimler motor. With the car connected directly to the underside of the balloon bag, he was able to use his engine power more efficiently in driving the ship, but it was much more dangerous when compared with the respectful distance between car and gasbag on Giffard's airship, which also featured an open engine flame. *Courtesy Deutsches Museum, Munich.*

•

The Berlin Tageblatt

Scarcely had the attempts at propulsion been begun when a violent explosion shook the air. Basket and balloon were at once wrapped in flames, and the blazing mass was soon falling to earth with ever increasing speed. The rudder also was caught by the flames, got loose and reached the ground first. For some seconds there seemed to be danger that the aerial furnace should be precipitated on a goods train laden with hay. This additional catastrophe, however, did not take place.

The military aeronauts were the first to pick up the mutilated and charred remains of the unfortunate balloonists, who, but a few minutes ago, had left the solid earth healthy and strong. As the balloon was 2,500 feet above the earth when the explosion took place, and was still in full ascent, there can be no doubt that the gas, escaping from the valve with too great force, reached the furnace and caught fire. The doctor should have made his experiments with the machine only after reaching the zone of equilibrium.[1]

The *Tageblatt*'s analysis was probably correct. As the *Deutschland* rose rapidly into the air, her hydrogen expanded and blew off through the gas valve. It combined with the oxygen in the air to form a highly explosive mixture that was ignited by the engine flame. If Woelfert had waited until the ship had risen into equilibrium before lighting his engine, most of the free hydrogen would have been dissipated and there would have been little chance of an explosion.

Woelfert and Knabe were the first victims of powered flight, but the cause of their deaths was well known. The dangerous combination of hydrogen and fire was recognized from the beginning—yet more were to come.

By far the most unusual of the early airships was the all-aluminum balloon of David Schwarz. Except for the twelve-horsepower Daimler motor, the leather belts driving the three propellers, and some miscellaneous brass bearings, the entire 156-foot-long ship was made of aluminum. Even the outer cover was of .008-inch-thick sheets of aluminum supported by a framework of aluminum tubing. The whole thing weighed just under three tons.

Though the idea that a metal ship could float in the air was almost beyond comprehension, Schwarz, an Austrian timber merchant, had carefully calculated all the factors involved and had even solved the difficult problem of filling it with gas. A balloon is easy to fill. It is flattened out on the ground so that no air remains inside, then it is filled with hydrogen. But you can't flatten a metal balloon, and hydrogen pumped into it simply mixes with the air already inside, losing most of its lift. How did Schwarz do it? He made several fabric balloons that fit inside the metal hull, completely filling it. These were inflated with air. When the ship was ready to be filled, hydrogen was pumped in between the hull and the fabric balloons forcing the air out of the balloons until they were deflated and could be withdrawn leaving the airship filled with gas.

Schwarz's first ship was built in 1894 in Russia but never flew. His second was begun in 1896 in Berlin. Construction took a year but before it could be test-flown, Schwarz died. His widow, Melanie, arranged a test by the Prussian Balloon Corps at Tempelhof Field, where Woelfert had died six months earlier. It was an unfortunate choice, though probably the only one open to her, for the officers of the Balloon Corps did not believe that the ship could possibly fly. They began by removing everything they considered excess weight, and some of the parts they took off were necessary to fly the ship. The difficult job of filling the aluminum hull took two full days, but by November 3, 1897, everything was ready. Though the officers of the Balloon Corps were a little surprised to find the airship straining at the ropes that held it to the ground, they still doubted its lifting power and refused to allow any of their men to fly it. A pilot who had never flown before was finally hired.

As the ship rose into the air, the leather belt driving the two front propellers began to slip. The mechanism that held it in place had been removed. Rather than fly it as a free balloon using the rear propeller for partial control, the inexperienced pilot threw open the gas valve. The ship fell from eight hundred feet, landing heavily in an empty field. The four shock-absorbing landing legs had also been removed and, though the pilot escaped without injury, Schwarz's metal airship was smashed beyond repair.

The brief history of powered flight had so far been dominated by events in France and Germany. Now the scene changes to far-off Brazil where a young man,

David Schwarz was a timber merchant in Slavonia. He built his first metal airship at St. Petersburg in 1894 with financial backing from the Russian government and engineering help from Carl Berg, a German aluminum manufacturer. Two attempts were made to fill the ship with hydrogen but the bags inside the hull first leaked, then burst. When the hull was finally filled and sealed, a sudden drop in air temperature began to buckle the metal hull plates. The Russians then declared the ship too dangerous to fly. Schwarz returned to Germany and managed to get Carl Berg and the Prussian Airship Battalion to sponsor a similar second ship. This ship, shown in the photos, was 156 feet long with 130,000 cubic feet of hydrogen. Count Zeppelin, who was then working on his own airship design, witnessed the destruction of the Schwarz dirigible and was later accused of stealing part of Schwarz's design, but apart from the fact that they both got their aluminum from Carl Berg, their designs had little in common. *The ship, courtesy Northrop University. The wreck, from* Airships Past and Present, *by Capt. A. Hildebrandt, New York, 1908.*

not yet born when Giffard and Haenlein flew, was growing up. His name was Alberto Santos-Dumont.

His father made a fortune as the first of the great Brazilian coffee planters. Alberto, the youngest of seven children, grew up surrounded by the fascinating machinery of the highly mechanized coffee-harvesting and processing operations.

Alberto Santos-Dumont

I can scarcely imagine a more suggestive environment for a boy dreaming over mechanical inventions. At the age of seven I was permitted to drive our locomobiles of the epoch—steam traction-engines of the fields, with great broad wheels. At the age of twelve I had conquered my place in the cabs of the Baldwin locomotive engines, hauling trainloads of green coffee over the sixty miles of our plantation railway.[2]

While his brothers were riding horseback through the fields, Alberto was reading Jules Verne and filling tiny homemade balloons over an open bonfire and sending them aloft into the tropical night. He sharpened his mechanical skills by dismantling his father's machinery and, like boys the world over, he dreamed of flight.

Alberto Santos-Dumont

In the long, sun-bathed Brazilian afternoons, when the hum of insects, punctuated by the far-off cry of some bird, lulled me, I would lie in the shade of the veranda and gaze into the fair sky of Brazil, where the birds fly so high and soar with such ease on their great outstretched wings, where the clouds mount so gaily in the pure light of day, and you have only to raise your eyes to fall in love with space and freedom. So, musing on the exploration of the aerial ocean, I, too, devised airships and flying-machines in my imagination.

These imaginings I kept to myself. In those days, in Brazil, to talk of inventing a flying-machine, or dirigible balloon, would have been to stamp one's self as unbalanced and visionary. Spherical balloonists were looked on as daring professionals not differing greatly from acrobats; and for the son of a planter to dream of emulating them would have been almost a social sin.[3]

After being injured in a fall, the elder Santos-Dumont sold his plantation and divided the money among his children. It was 1892 when his father gave Alberto half a million dollars and sent him to Paris to get an education. Alberto was eighteen and Paris was the gayest, wickedest, most sophisticated city in the world. It was the Paris of Toulouse-Lautrec and Cézanne, of Victor Hugo and Debussy. It was also, in those last years of the nineteenth century, the center of technology and progress. Young Alberto hired a tutor and began to learn all he could about science and engineering.

He searched for the great aerial cruisers he had read about in Jules Verne, but they were nowhere to be seen. The skies over Paris were as empty of airships as the skies of Brazil.

Alberto Santos-Dumont

To my immense astonishment, I learned that there were no steerable balloons—that there were only spherical balloons, like those of Charles in 1783![4]

In fact, it had been nearly fifteen years since Renard and Krebs flew over Paris and no one had followed them. Alberto would have to be content with ordinary ballooning, but he found that the professional aeronauts all demanded too much money for a flight. Then he picked up a copy of the book *Andrée: Au Pole Nord en Ballon,* by Lachambre and Machuron, the builders of the ill-fated *Ornen.* This led Alberto to the two hearty craftsmen's busy factory. Henri Lachambre had been building balloons since 1875 and was joined in the business by his nephew, Alexis Machuron, a veteran of the French Balloon Corps. They agreed not only to take the young Brazilian for a ride but also to allow him to pilot some of their exhibition balloons in order to gain experience as an aeronaut.

Alberto ordered a specially built balloon much smaller and lighter than any that Lachambre had ever made before. He flew this tiny, one-man balloon in all kinds of weather, even at night—a solitary figure drifting through the darkness.

Alberto Santos-Dumont

Indeed, night-ballooning has a charm all its own. One is alone in the black void, true, in a murky limbo where one seems to float without weight, without a surrounding world, a soul freed from the weight of matter! Yet, now and again there are the lights of earth to cheer one. We see a point of light far on ahead. Slowly it expands. Then where there was one blaze, there are countless bright spots. They run in lines, with here and there a brighter cluster. We know that it is a city.

Then, again, it is out into the lone land, with only a faint glow here and there. When the moon rises we see, perhaps, a faint curling line of gray. It is a river, with the moonlight falling on its waters.

Then, for safety, we throw out more ballast and rise through the black solitudes of the clouds into a soul-lifting burst of splendid starlight. There, alone with the constellations, we await the dawn!

And when the dawn comes, red and gold and purple in its glory, one is almost loath to seek the earth again, although the novelty of landing in who knows what part of Europe affords still another unique pleasure.[5]

In more than one hundred balloon flights, Alberto was gaining the experience he felt would be essential to his next experiment—powered flight. He also became a member of the Paris Automobile Club, driving first a 3½-horsepower Peugeot and then a three-wheeled De Dion, capable of the hair-raising speed of twenty miles an hour. The fast, maneuverable little tricycle cars were very popular with Alberto's young Auto Club friends, and he once rented the local bicycle track for a day and staged a series of tricycle car races that were a great success.

In fact, the motor from his three-wheeled De Dion looked to Alberto like the perfect airship motor. It was small, light, powerful, and relatively dependable. With the aid of a local mechanic he rebuilt it, placing one cylinder on top of the other with a single connecting rod and carburetor. He drew up the plans for an 82½-foot-long gasbag and brought them to Lachambre, who threw up his hands in horror. "He would not make himself a party to such rashness," Alberto recalled and reminded the balloon maker that he had already broken new ground with his tiny spherical balloon and Alberto would, if necessary, build the bag himself. Monsieur Lachambre shrugged his shoulders and went to work.

It was to be the smallest airship capable of lifting Alberto's 110 pounds, his basket, and a motor. The gasbag was of light, varnished Japanese silk. The rudder was of silk stretched on a triangular steel frame. Two sacks of sand suspended from each end of the gasbag on long ropes served in place of elevators. By pulling the

Alberto Santos-Dumont (1873–1932) as he looked in 1903, a wealthy, thirty-year-old bachelor in Paris. Sterling Heilig, a contemporary, described him:

This Brazilian has neither the structure, the complexion, nor the exuberant gestures of the men of his country. He is pale, cold, and phlegmatic, even, if the word may be applied to one so active. In his moments of greatest enthusiasm and of most lively disappointment he is always the same; and he is as free from affectation as a child.

The Century Magazine,
November 1901.

Photo from My Air-Ships, *by Alberto Santos-Dumont, New York, 1904.*

Alberto Santos-Dumont's first airship had a gasbag 82½ feet long and 11½ feet in diameter. Its 6,345 cubic feet of hydrogen could lift only 450 pounds, but that was enough to get the balloon, the sixty-six-pound motor, and Alberto—who weighed 110 pounds—into the air. The ship rose easily to thirteen hundred feet, but on descending, Alberto was unable to fill his air ballonet fast enough to compensate for the contracting gas in the balloon and it folded in the middle. His second ship, a foot larger in the middle, suffered the same fate. *The crash of* No. 2, *from My Air-Ships, by Alberto Santos-Dumont, New York, 1904.* No. 1 *in the air, courtesy Northrop University.*

•

front weight backward, the stern became heavier and the bow rose. By shifting the rear weight forward, the bow went down and the ship descended.

On September 18, 1898, a large crowd gathered at the Jardin d'Acclimatation to witness the first flight. The bag was inflated, the motor started, and with a cry of "Let go, all," Alberto sailed straight into a tree. He had taken off with the wind like a balloon instead of into the wind like a powered aircraft. Two days of repairs and he was back again. This time he started from the opposite end of the clearing, rising on the oncoming wind over the treetops and into the sky.

The ship proved to be maneuverable in every direction, but in his enthusiasm, Alberto climbed higher than he had intended. At thirteen hundred feet he had a magnificent view of Paris but his hydrogen was expanding and escaping through the gas valve. As long as he stayed up there, the long, narrow gasbag remained full and the pressure of the gas kept the bag firm and rigid, but when he started to descend, the gas contracted, leaving the bag partially empty. A smaller air bag or ballonet was sewn into the balloon for just such a situation. An air pump on the motor was supposed to inflate the ballonet with air to take the place of the contracting hydrogen, but the pump couldn't fill it fast enough and the balloon "began to fold in the middle like a pocket-knife."

Alberto Santos-Dumont

I could not think of anything to do. I might throw out ballast. That would cause the air-ship to rise, and the decreased pressure of the atmosphere would doubtless permit the expanding gas to straighten out the balloon again, taut and strong. But I remembered that I must always come down again, when all the danger would repeat itself, and worse even than before, from the more gas I would have lost. There was nothing to do but to go down immediately.[6]

As he started to fall, Alberto saw some boys flying their kites on the grassy slope beneath him. He shouted to them to grab his guide rope and pull it into the wind. As they hauled on the rope, Alberto and his crippled ship settled gently to the ground like a giant kite.

Despite his somewhat unorthodox landing, Alberto was ecstatic. He had controlled his flight in every direction except down. He had flown.

Alberto Santos-Dumont

I cannot describe the delight, the wonder and intoxication, of this free diagonal movement onward and upward, or onward and downward, combined at will with brusque changes of direction horizontally when the air-ship answers to a touch of the rudder. The birds have this sensation when they spread their wings and go tobogganing in curves and spirals through the sky.

"Por mares nunca d'antes navegados!"
[O'er seas heretofore unsailed!]

The line of our great poet echoed in my memory from childhood. After this first of all my cruises, I had it put on my flag.[7]

He made several more flights in his *Airship No. 1* and began work on *No. 2.* He used the same car, engine, and propeller but had Lachambre build a slightly fatter balloon. He also added a larger air pump. On May 11, 1899, he took off into a cold rain squall that cooled the hydrogen faster than his air pump could fill the ballonet and once again the bag began to fold in the middle. A sudden gust of wind blew the ship into the trees. It was a total wreck.

Alberto started immediately on *No. 3.* This time he made the gasbag sixteen feet shorter and twice as fat. This one wasn't going to fold up on him. The only thing salvaged from *No. 2* was the tricycle motor.

He made his first flight on November 13, 1899, testing his steering over the Champ de Mars and then circling the Eiffel Tower before flying to Bagatelle at a speed he estimated at close to twelve miles per hour.

Alberto was soon a familiar figure cruising about the skies over Paris and "Le Petit Santos" became the city's favorite. Even his high collars and specially cut suits became the height of fashion for his young admirers. His wealth and polished manners served him as well in society's drawing rooms as his mechanical skills did in the workshop.

In 1900 Henri Deutsch de la Meurthe, the first petroleum millionaire and a charter member of the French Aero Club, announced a prize of one hundred thousand francs (twenty thousand dollars) for the first aircraft to fly from the club's grounds at St. Cloud around the Eiffel Tower and back again, a distance of nearly seven miles, within a time limit of thirty minutes. Since Alberto was the only one flying at the time, the conditions of the prize were purposely set beyond the capabilities of his current ship in order to encourage others to join in the competition.

His *No. 3* couldn't make the necessary fifteen miles per hour, and Alberto set to work on *No. 4* with a new seven-horsepower engine. The most unusual feature was a bicycle mounted amidships on the keel. Alberto sat on the seat, steered with the handlebars, and started the engine by turning the pedals. But this ship also proved too slow, and a larger, twelve-horsepower Daimler-Benz was installed. The added weight required an extra section inserted into the middle of the gasbag for added lift. He also discarded the bicycle and changed the keel. These alterations turned *No. 4* into *No. 5,* which first flew on July 9, 1901.

After several trial flights, he was ready to try for the Deutsch Prize. The members of the Aero Club's Scientific committee gathered at St. Cloud at 6:00 A.M.

Alberto's *No. 3* was shorter and fatter than his first two ships with little danger of folding up. He even eliminated the ballonet. It was sixty-six feet long and twenty-five feet in diameter with a gas capacity of 17,650 cubic feet. This increased capacity allowed him to use coal gas, the same that burned in Paris's streetlights. It was both heavier and cheaper than hydrogen. *From* My Air-Ships, *by Alberto Santos-Dumont, New York, 1904.*

No. 4 was the airship that flew like a bicycle. The gasbag was ninety-three feet long and seventeen feet in diameter with 14,800 cubic feet. The first three ships used the 3½-horsepower De Dion engine. *No. 4* had a new seven-horsepower Buchet motor. For the first time the propeller was at the bow, but the breeze gave Alberto a cold and the propeller was back at the stern of his next ship.

M. Santos Dumont mounted, alighted, and re-ascended time after time without accessories and as easily and gracefully as a great bird would take wing and come to earth. He flew high, low, in straight lines, and in curves with the wind against him precisely as he willed. He was master of the air as truly as a navigator of a steamship is master of the waves.

The New York Sun,
July 14, 1901.

Courtesy Northrop University.

•

on July 13. At 6:41 Alberto was off. With the wind behind him, he rounded the Eiffel Tower in ten minutes, but now the tailwind became a headwind and his engine began to falter. He reached the starting line in forty minutes, ten minutes too late. Then his engine quit and he drifted backward for a quarter of a mile, ending up in a chestnut tree on the estate of Edmond Rothschild, next door to the home of Isabel, Countess d'Eu, the former imperial princess regent of Brazil. She sent a servant over with a picnic lunch that was delivered by stepladder to her countryman in the tree, directing the disentanglement of his airship. She later sent him a medal of St. Benedict, who protects against accidents.

On August 8 Alberto was ready for his second try at the prize. This time he rounded the tower in nine minutes, but he was slowly losing gas through a faulty valve. As the bag deflated, the support wires went slack and fouled the propeller, ripping the bag. The falling ship caught on the roof of the Trocadero Hotel, leaving Alberto dangling halfway down the side of an eighty-foot light well. The Paris fire department made the rescue.

That evening he gave orders to begin work on *No. 6* and then went out to his usual table at Maxim's where he received a standing ovation.

Twenty-two days later *No. 6* was ready to fly. Alberto and his men had worked day and night to complete it. He was determined to win the Deutsch Prize.

After two more false starts, Alberto finally won it on September 19, 1901. He rounded the tower in nine minutes and started back for St. Cloud. Then the motor began to sputter. In order to adjust it, he had to climb out of the basket and inch his way along the keel, standing on one girder while holding on to the other, with nothing but a single steel pole between him and the streets of Paris a thousand feet below.

The city came to a standstill as all eyes turned upward. Then the engine roared to life again and he raced over the heads of the Scientific Commission at St. Cloud. Alberto shouted down, "Have I won?" The crowd of spectators cried out that he had. All Paris agreed. Only the committee hesitated. Their watches showed that he had missed the deadline by forty seconds.

It took two weeks of meetings and arguments before the committee gave in.

Paris would not allow Le Petit Santos to be denied his prize for a mere forty seconds. He divided the one hundred thousand francs among his workmen and the poor of Paris. The Brazilian government unexpectedly voted him a matching prize, which he kept.

Alberto was now a worldwide celebrity. He spent the winter flying over the Mediterranean as the guest of Prince Albert I of Monaco, who even built him an airship hangar beside the sea. He visited England and then sailed to the United States at the invitation of the St. Louis World's Fair Committee, who asked his advice on the airship races they planned for the 1904 fair. Returning to Paris, he built three more airships including *No. 7,* a racing ship probably capable of speeds up to fifty miles per hour, but since Alberto had no serious competition, he couldn't find anyone to race with. In 1904 he took his *No. 7* back to the World's Fair, but her gasbag was mysteriously slashed and he was unable to enter the competition.

He skipped *No. 8* since he didn't care for that number and built *No. 9,* thirty-six feet long and powered by a three-horsepower engine. It became his personal runabout. He flew it all around the city, stopping at his front door for tea and dropping down on his favorite sidewalk café for an afternoon cocktail, always causing massive traffic jams for blocks in every direction.

His *No. 10,* almost twice as big as any previous ship, was designed to carry ten people. He flew it occasionally but he was becoming interested in heavier-than-air flight. Rumors from America suggested that the Wright brothers of Dayton, Ohio, had already flown, but since no one in America seemed to believe them, no one in Europe did either. Heavier-than-air flight did, however, seem possible, and Alberto decided to achieve it.

He created one of the strangest aircraft that ever flew. But it did fly, first for a few yards on September 13, 1906, and then on October 23 he rose nearly ten feet off the ground and covered a distance of sixty yards. It was universally hailed as man's first airplane flight, an opinion that persisted until 1908 when the Wrights finally arrived in Europe to demonstrate their unquestioned mastery of the air. Their planes, far in advance of anything then flying, quickly established their claim to the first flight back in 1903. It was a bitter blow for Alberto but, as a gentleman, he took

The attempt to win the Deutsch Prize on August 8, 1901, ended with Alberto hanging halfway down a light well in the Trocadero Hotel. The Paris fire department had to make the rescue. It was *No. 5*'s second and last crash. Work began on *No. 6* the next morning. *From* My Air-Ships, *by Alberto Santos-Dumont, New York, 1904.*

•

During his final successful assault on the Deutsch Prize, Alberto had to take time out to adjust his engine. Since it was located amidships while the control car, actually nothing more than a tiny wicker balloon basket, was farther forward, the mechanical adjustment required a certain amount of acrobatic ability. *From* My Air-Ships, *by Alberto Santos-Dumont, New York, 1904.*

no part in the controversy that raged around him. Indeed, there is no record of his ever seeing the Wrights fly. Instead he designed and built his *No. 20,* a small, efficient airplane much like his *No. 9* airship, an aerial runabout that he flew on daily excursions across the countryside. He never patented any of his designs and this plane, the *Demoiselle,* or *Dragonfly,* one of the most stable and reliable of all the early flying machines, was widely copied and flown by others.

With this last triumphant creation, Alberto ended his aviation career, for in 1910 he suddenly gave up flying. At the outbreak of World War I he returned to Brazil where news of the aerial war filled him with sadness and remorse. He became obsessed with the idea that he alone was responsible for the death and destruction raining down on mankind from the skies. He suffered from disseminated sclerosis, a slow, wasting disease that was probably responsible for his withdrawal from aviation and almost certainly brought on his subsequent melancholia. On July 23, 1932, three days after his fifty-ninth birthday, in the last stages of his illness, Alberto Santos-Dumont hanged himself in a house beside the sea.

Once Alberto had shown the way, inventors all over the world rushed to follow his lead. Few, however, were blessed with his methodical approach, mechanical skill, or flying ability. One would-be aeronaut was a fellow Brazilian, living in Paris, Augusto Severo. On May 12, 1902, he and his mechanic, Sachet, made the

ABOVE: *No. 6* ended her distinguished career by falling into the Mediterranean off Monaco. After a number of leisurely voyages out over the sea, Alberto took off on February 14, 1902, only to realize that his ship was not fully inflated. *No. 6* folded up just like his first ships, the gasbag burst, and Alberto settled into the bay. He was rescued by the prince's steam yacht and built his next ship with a chambered gasbag to prevent all the gas from escaping from a single hole. *From* My Air-Ships, *by Alberto Santos-Dumont, New York, 1904.* RIGHT: *No. 9* was a utility runabout designed by Alberto to cruise the boulevards of Paris dropping down on his favorite bistro for an aperitif or off to a friend's house for tea. It was only 36 feet long and 11½ feet in diameter with 7,770 cubic feet of hydrogen, later enlarged to 9,218 cubic feet. The three-horsepower Clement engine, located within arm's reach of the pilot, weighed only twenty-six pounds and gave the ship a top speed of fifteen miles per hour. *From* My Air-Ships, *by Alberto Santos-Dumont, New York, 1904.* BELOW RIGHT: Alberto's *Demoiselle* was small enough for him to carry on the back of his car. Powered by a twenty-four-horsepower Antoinette engine, with a wingspan of 16.4 feet, the *Demoiselle* weighed only 297 pounds and would rise into the air once it had attained a taxiing speed of thirty-six miles per hour. The pilot sat just behind the engine very nearly at ground level. The *Demoiselle* was the lightest, most powerful airplane yet built and was widely copied by other aviators. This photo was taken in November 1908. Two years later Alberto stopped flying and never took the controls of an aircraft again. *From* Scientific American, *December 12, 1908.*

Severo's *Pax* was ninety-three feet long and held 85,750 cubic feet of hydrogen. She had six propellers. A large one at the bow was to push the air aside while a smaller one at the stern drove the ship forward. There was also a ten-inch propeller at each corner of the car for maneuvering. They were all driven by two Buchet engines of sixteen and twenty-four horsepower. Instead of being suspended below the gasbag, the car had a framework that fit into a slot in the bag and extended all the way up to the center of the balloon. *Courtesy Carruthers Collection, Claremont Colleges.*

•

first flight in their airship, *Pax*. Shortly before takeoff Severo was seen sealing up one of his gas valves with wax. Once in the air the ship began to rise too rapidly and its occupants, with little flying experience, became confused and threw out ballast instead of valving gas. The *Pax* with its sealed gas valve rose rapidly to two thousand feet where it burst. Both men died in the fall.

In October of the same year, another experimenter, Baron Ottokar de Bradsky Laboun, and his mechanic, Paul Morin, successfully flew over Paris in an airship of the baron's own design. After a half-hour flight the ship was seen to rise up sharply at the bow. Then the car with the two aeronauts detached itself from the gasbag and fell to earth, killing them both. The car had been attached to the balloon by steel piano wire fitted through eyelets. As the ship stood up on end, the full weight of the car was placed on the lower wires, which simply became unwrapped under the strain. The rest followed and the men were doomed.

While Alberto was winning the Deutsch Prize, two wealthy sugar refiners, Paul and Pierre Lebaudy, were busy building an airship of their own. Their chief plant engineer, Henri Julliot, must have been a little surprised when his employers asked him to set aside his refining machinery and build them an airship, but he was more than equal to the task. After two full years of meticulous investigation and design, Julliot began construction in collaboration with the experienced balloon builder Edouard Surcouf.

The ship they launched on November 13, 1902, was of a new design. A framework of steel tubing built into the bottom of the gasbag made it the first semirigid airship. It was a type that would find increasing favor over the previous nonrigids, for though the new ship retained the interior air ballonet, its metal support made the gasbag much less susceptible to the type of collapse that had plagued Santos-Dumont. It was also hoped that the large flat surface on the bottom of the balloon would act like a giant parachute and slow the descent in case of an accident. The *Jaune* or *Yellow,* as the ship was soon nicknamed because of the bright yellow color of its varnish, was powered by a forty-horsepower Daimler engine driving two propellers that gave it a top speed of twenty-five miles per hour.

The Roze double balloon, the *Aviator*, was built at Colombes, France, in 1901. Its car, propellers, and rudders were located between the two hulls, each of which was 147 feet long, 24½ feet wide, and held 47,655 cubic feet of gas. The total weight of the ship when inflated with lifting gas was to be between one hundred and two hundred pounds, which the two vertical propellers should have easily been able to lift off the ground. They couldn't and the ship never flew. *Courtesy Carruthers Collection, Claremont Colleges.*

•

In a series of test flights out of their hangar at Moisson, some forty miles west of Paris, the Lebaudys' test pilot, George Juchmes, set several endurance records. Then the Lebaudys were ready to give Paris a look at their new ship. On November 12, 1903, with Juchmes at the controls and mechanic Rey along in case of trouble, the *Jaune* set out for the capital. They completed the forty-six mile flight to the Champ de Mars in one hour and forty-six minutes and the ship was put on display in the huge Galerie des Machines.

After nine days on exhibition, the *Jaune* was flown over to the military ballooning headquarters at Chalais-Meudon, where she was to be inspected by Colonel Renard. Everything went smoothly until they reached the broad, tree-studded lawn at Chalais-Meudon. Juchmes was piloting and Rey had stopped the engines when a sudden wind blew the ship into a tree. The envelope exploded but did not burn and the ship fell to the ground in a heap in front of Colonel Renard, Paul Lebaudy, Henri Julliot, Mrs. Juchmes, and Mrs. Rey. Neither aeronaut was injured and the ship was rebuilt with a slightly larger envelope and donated to the government by the brothers as the first ship in the French aerial navy.

In 1906 the government ordered a second Lebaudy ship, *La Patrie,* and the brothers found themselves in the airship construction business. After *La Patrie,* they built *République* and *Liberté* for France and the *Russie* for Russia. The Astra and Zodiac companies were also formed in Paris. Henri Deutsch helped finance the Astra organization, which built the *Colonel Renard, Clement-Bayard, Ville de Paris,* and *Ville de Nancy.*

By the middle of 1909 the French government was heavily involved in airship operations with four military semirigids in service and two more on order. Their only fatal accident occurred on September 15, 1909, when a propeller blade broke off the *République* over Moulins, slicing the gasbag open. The ship fell from four hundred feet killing the four men aboard.

The pioneering dirigible activities being conducted in Paris and Berlin were met with a complete and total lack of interest on the part of British authorities. It was not until 1902 that the first powered airship made its appearance over London, and even then it was greeted with something less than wild enthusiasm.

Scientific American

On September 19 London was surprised to see an airship hovering over its chimneys and spires. The air was apparently quite calm and the ship steadily headed to the northwest, traveling about eight miles an hour. Months ago Londoners heard in a vague way that an English-built airship was in existence, but the matter excited little interest at the time, and latterly was quite forgotten.

The balloon follows the torpedo-shaped construction made familiar by Santos-Dumont, but has more blunted ends. Consequently it has not the graceful lines of its French predecessor. The frame, which bears the aeronaut and the machinery, is constructed of bamboo held taut by piano wire. As seen from the air, it bears some resemblance, in its proportions, to a skeleton canoe.[8]

The ship was the creation of the Spencer brothers, a third-generation family of British balloonists. Their seventy-five-foot-long ship was powered by a 3½-horsepower Simms gasoline engine driving a propeller specially designed for them by Sir Hiram Maxim. On this first flight the ship was piloted by Stanley Spencer, the second of the three Spencer brothers, and covered twenty miles in a little under two hours. A month later at Blackpool, Stanley flew twenty-six miles, but at the end of the voyage he "almost collided with an express train in descending, but escaped by ramming a tree. No serious damage was done."[9] Undaunted, the Spencers continued in aeronautics, launching a larger airship the following year while using their original ship to carry advertising slogans.

In the United States a considerable amount of effort and imagination had gone into the design of flying machines, and dozens of patents were issued, but few airships were built and none flew. Some promoters spent so much energy selling stock in their aerial transportation companies that they had none left for the actual construction.

The first ship to leave the ground in the United States was Frederick Marriott's steam-powered dirigible, *Avitor Hermes Jr.,* which made a brief, unmanned flight near San Francisco in July 1869. After ten minutes of being led around on the end of a rope, the airship was pronounced a complete success and plans were made for a

While Alberto Santos-Dumont was test-flying his *No. 9,* the Lebaudy brothers, Paul and Pierre, seen here in the dark coats with Henri Julliot at the right, were testing their first airship. They called it the *Lebaudy* but everyone else soon nicknamed it the *Jaune (Yellow)* because of the bright yellow coating of lead chromate on the rubberized cotton gasbag. The ship was designed by the Lebaudys' factory engineer, Henri Julliot, who created an entirely new type of airship, the semirigid. He used a metal framework sewn into the bottom of the gasbag to reinforce the balloon and support the weight of the control car and rudder. The *Jaune* was 173 feet long and thirty feet in diameter with 64,800 cubic feet of hydrogen. *Courtesy Carruthers Collection, Claremont Colleges.*

Astra's *Ville de Paris.* The Astra Société des Constructions Aéronautiques was founded by Edouard Surcouf and Henri Deutsch, the man who donated the Deutsch Prize. Their first ship, designed with the help of Colonel Renard, was the *Ville de Paris*, completed in 1904. She was one of the first airships with stabilizing surfaces at the stern. These were actually fabric tubes filled with hydrogen. She was 203 feet long and 34½ feet in diameter with 113,800 cubic feet of gas, powered by a seventy-horsepower Argus engine. *Courtesy Carruthers Collection, Claremont Colleges.*

•

The pedal-driven airship of Charles F. Ritchel had a gasbag twenty-five feet long and thirteen feet in diameter. Ritchel was too heavy, so he hired a pilot for what may have been the ship's only flight on June 12, 1878, when it rose to an altitude of two hundred feet and was pedaled over Hartford, Connecticut, for more than an hour. The ship was then placed on exhibition in Philadelphia. *Courtesy Carruthers Collection, Claremont Colleges.*

larger one. In order to promote stock sales in the new venture, a poetry contest was held, which was won by Bret Harte, a writer whose short stories of the California gold rush, including "The Luck of Roaring Camp" and "Outcasts of Poker Flat," were as popular as those of his contemporary rival, Mark Twain. Harte's winning poem, a parody of Longfellow's "Excelsior," is at least as memorable as the airship it commemorated, and certainly funnier.

AVITOR (An Aerial Retrospect)
by Bret Harte

What was it filled my youthful dreams,
In place of Greek or Latin themes,
Or beauty's wild, bewildering beams?
    Avitor!

What visions and celestial scenes
I filled with aerial machines,
Montgolfiers' and Mr. Green's!
    Avitor!

What fairy tales seemed things of course!
The roc that brought Sindbad across,
The Calendar's own wingèd-horse!
    Avitor!

How many things I took for facts,
Icarus and his conduct lax,
And how he sealed his fate with wax!
    Avitor!

The first balloons I sought to sail,
Soap bubbles fair, but all too frail,
Or kites,—but thereby hangs a tail.
    Avitor!

What made me launch from attic tall
A kitten and a parasol,
And watch their bitter, frightful fall?
                    Avitor!

What youthful dreams of high renown
Bade me inflate the parson's gown,
That went not up, nor yet came down?
                    Avitor!

My first ascent I may not tell;
Enough to know that in that well
My first high aspirations fell.
                    Avitor!

My other failures let me pass:
The dire explosions, and alas!
The friends I choked with noxious gas.
                    Avitor!

For lo! I see perfected rise
The vision of my boyish eyes,
The messenger of upper skies.
                    Avitor!

The British army's first airship, the *Nulli Secundus (Second to None)*, was completed in 1907 by an American, Samuel F. Cody. He was in England trying to sell his man-lifting kites to the War Office. Instead, they asked him to finish their airship that had been started five years earlier with the construction of two fifty-thousand-cubic-foot gasbags. Cody purchased a fifty-horsepower Antoinette V-8 engine and designed the engine bed, propeller drives, and control surfaces. The *Nulli Secundus*'s first flight was made in September 1907 with Cody and two British officers aboard. It lasted twelve minutes. Then the belt driving the ballonet's air fan slipped off and they landed. On her second flight later the same day, the ship dived suddenly from two hundred feet, hit the ground nose first, and bounced back into the air. She flew again in October and achieved a speed of twenty miles per hour. In 1908 she was rebuilt as a semirigid and then dismantled. *Courtesy Cole Airship Collection, University of Oregon.*

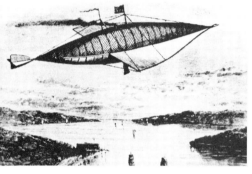

Frederick Marriott was a San Francisco editor and promoter. He envisioned an aerial steam carriage that would be a combination airplane and airship. The large model that he built in 1869 and christened *Avitor Hermes Jr.* was mostly balloon with a couple of winglike appendages, and fell somewhat short of the imaginative drawing in the promotional brochure published by Marriott for his prospective stockholders. The steam-powered model was led around at the end of ropes and is said to have achieved a speed of five miles per hour, although neither engine nor propellers are visible in the photo. The full-sized airship was never built. *The drawing, courtesy Carruthers Collection, Claremont Colleges. The photo of the model, courtesy Marilyn Blaisdell, San Francisco.*

•

The first manned flight in America was made in 1878 in an airship built by Charles F. Ritchel of Corry, Pennsylvania. It was powered by a pedal-driven propeller, the pilot bicycling his way through the air. It was steerable only on very calm days.

After this modest burst of activity, airship construction languished for another quarter of a century until 1903, when news of Alberto Santos-Dumont's triumphs crossed the Atlantic. On October 18, a physician, Dr. August Greth, ascended from downtown San Francisco in a seventy-five-foot-long balloon powered by a six-horsepower gasoline engine. He ended the relatively successful flight by falling into the bay off Presidio Point.

The most successful of the early American airshipmen was Thomas Scott Baldwin. His first job as a circus acrobat led to a trapeze act suspended beneath a balloon, which led to a career as a professional balloonist. Baldwin visited Santos-Dumont in Paris and returned to his home in Oakland, California, to build an airship of his own. On July 29, 1904, his *California Arrow* made its first flight at Idora Park in Oakland before a large crowd. The fifty-four-foot-long ship was powered by a ten-horsepower motorcycle engine built by Glenn Curtiss, soon to become one of the great pioneer airplane designers.

The *California Arrow* was the first completely successful American airship and won all the prizes for flying at the 1904 St. Louis World's Fair. Baldwin, however, was not at the helm. He was too heavy for the ship to lift, and he hired a young balloonist, Roy Knabenshue, as his pilot. Knabenshue's first flight on the *California Arrow* was unscheduled.

Roy Knabenshue

The motor was missing and shaking the frame so much I thought it was going to bounce me off. I yelled, "turn it off" but they thought I said "Let 'er go" and began waving their hats. Then I was in the air headed for a thirty foot fence.

I had to learn to fly that thing and do it pronto. I nearly hit the dome of the Brazilian building, but I finally figured out how to handle it and took it around the ferris wheel.

Then, for no reason, the motor stopped. With all that noise gone, it was just like being in a balloon and I drifted clear across the city of St. Louis and the river and landed in East St. Louis. I hit some bad air currents and some people who saw me said they were amazed at how I maneuvered—I wasn't maneuvering—I was hanging on.[10]

Knabenshue went on to build and fly airships of his own, while Baldwin established a balloon factory and built several small airships including the U.S. Army's first aircraft, an eighty-four-foot dirigible bought by the Signal Corps in 1908.

Baldwin enjoyed a long and successful career in aviation. During World War I he served as the army's chief of balloon inspection and production. He built and flew dirigibles, balloons, and airplanes including one of the first all-metal planes. Of his flying ability, George H. Guy, a contemporary, wrote:

> He has made 3,000 ascensions, and he has never received a scratch. He may rush up into the air at all sorts of speeds, but in descending, one of the great tests of the aeronaut, he settles down to the earth like a lark dropping into a meadow.[11]

Thomas Scott Baldwin died in 1923 in Buffalo, New York, at the age of sixty-eight. Roy Knabenshue also built balloons for the government during the war and died at the age of eighty-three in Los Angeles in 1960.

A considerably less successful aeronaut was John A. Morrell, founder and president of the National Airship Company of San Francisco. His plans called for a fleet of immense dirigibles in transcontinental service, each carrying five hundred passengers. As eager investors rushed to buy stock, he began work on a three-hundred-foot test ship. The gasbag was completed at Berkeley in February 1908,

Thomas Baldwin's *California Arrow* was shown at the 1904 St. Louis Exposition, where it was the only ship to get off the ground. Baldwin had visited Alberto Santos-Dumont in Paris, and the little Brazilian's influence is evident in the ship's design. Alberto never patented any of his ideas and welcomed their use by others. The fact that his ship flew established Baldwin as the country's leading airship builder, and the army awarded him the contract of their first aircraft in 1908. *Signal Corps I*, shown here, was ninety-six feet long, powered by a twenty-horsepower engine built in the motorcycle shop of Glenn Curtiss, who can be seen acting as engineer while Baldwin pilots the ship through its acceptance trial at Fort Myer, Virginia. *Courtesy U.S. Army.*

•

The Morrell airship before takeoff. John A. Morrell envisioned a fleet of airships, each a quarter of a mile long carrying five hundred passengers from San Francisco to New York in a single day. Anxious investors contributed forty thousand dollars and this one-third-size prototype was the result. The Morrell airship was a single, 485-foot-long, nonrigid balloon filled with five hundred thousand cubic feet of illuminating gas and powered by six forty-horsepower automobile engines on a keel made of rope netting covered with mattresses. *From Scientific American, June 13, 1908.*

•

but a storm tore it from its moorings and deposited the wreckage in Burlingame on the other side of the bay. Morrell promptly began construction of an even larger ship, which was completed three months later. The gasbag was 485 feet long and thirty-four feet wide with no support of any kind. Six forty-horsepower automobile engines were slung at intervals along a keel of planks and mattresses suspended beneath the bag.

The first and last flight of the great Morrell airship was made at Berkeley on May 23, 1908. Morrell and eighteen others climbed aboard as the giant gasbag was cast off and rose slowly to three hundred feet.

Scientific American

The ascent was accompanied by the cheers of several thousand spectators. On account of the nose of the balloon being tardily released, the envelope was given an upward inclination toward the rear of as much as 45 degrees, the result being that the gas rushed to this end with great impetus and struck against the top at that point with a pressure of about 30 pounds per square foot, or 30 times more than would be considered safe with a well-constructed balloon. The oiled cloth, of which the envelope was constructed, could not withstand the pressure, and it burst, whereupon the machine fell rapidly to the ground, carrying with it its nineteen passengers, who were tangled in a mass of broken machinery, flapping cloth, and network. The passengers on board the ill-fated craft consisted of the inventor, eight engineers, five valve tenders, two photographers and their assistants, and an aeronaut. Strangely enough, none was killed, six escaping uninjured and several others with slight injuries. The inventor had his right leg broken, but only three men suffered injuries that may result in death.

Morrell says that, though he feels his general theory of the problem of aerial navigation is correct, the ascent was forced on him by the stockholders in the company before he had thoroughly worked out certain principles. Notwithstanding the almost total loss of a machine that cost about $40,000, Morrell says that the company is ready to proceed with the construction of another airship, 750 feet long, 40 feet in diameter, and equipped with eight gasoline engines, operating sixteen propellers and developing nearly 350 horse-power.[12]

Fortunately Morrell never built his second ship and was therefore able to survive his aerial adventures with only a broken leg.

The next notable American airship was that of Walter Wellman. Wellman was a newspaper reporter at a time when reporters were expected to make news as well as write about it. The best-known journalist of this type was Henry Stanley of the *New York Herald,* who led an expedition into Africa to find Dr. Livingstone. The exploits of these journalist-explorers were a guaranteed circulation builder for the paper that could afford to finance an expedition, and best of all, if the undertaking proved successful, the other papers were forced to acknowledge their rival's enterprise by reporting the story.

Few journalists were able to match Stanley's feat in finding Dr. Livingstone in the middle of darkest Africa, but Walter Wellman ran a close second. As a reporter for the *Chicago Herald,* he began his career by locating the spot in the Bahamas where he claimed Columbus first set foot in the New World. He then led two attempts to reach the North Pole by dogsled in 1894 and again in 1899. Both were unsuccessful, and on the second try, Wellman almost lost a leg to gangrene.

The success of the big Lebaudy airships revived Wellman's interest in the Arctic. Surely this was the only logical way to reach the North Pole. Again with the financial backing of the *Chicago Record-Herald,* he ordered an airship built to his specifications in Paris by Louis Godard. The gasbag was 165 feet long and fifty-two feet in diameter with a capacity of over two hundred thousand cubic feet. It was made of two layers of cotton and one of silk with each layer coated with rubber to prevent gas leakage. A thirty-foot steel, wood, and canvas car was slung underneath. Propellers at each end of the car were driven by two motors totaling eighty horsepower. Wellman christened his ship the *America.*

In July 1906, the expedition arrived by steamer at Dane Island off the north coast of Spitzbergen, the same place that Andrée had started from nine years earlier. Wellman's crew of more than thirty workmen immediately set to work unloading the supplies, including thirty sled dogs, 110 tons of sulfuric acid, and seventy tons of iron filings. His carpenters began to build living quarters, a machine shop, and a huge airship hangar, 210 feet long and eighty-five feet high, made of wooden arches covered by nearly an acre of canvas. They took some of their wood from Andrée's balloon shed, still standing nearby. The hangar was not completed until September, too late to inflate the ship and try for the Pole. It was just as well, for when Wellman started up the *America*'s engines, the propellers refused to turn and the transmission came apart.

Returning to Paris, the gasbag was cut in half and an additional twenty-foot section added for extra lift. With 258,500 cubic feet of gas, the *America* was twice as big as the Lebaudy ships and second in size only to Germany's Zeppelins. In Paris Wellman hired Melvin Vaniman, a young man whose previous career included work as a music teacher, guitarist, actor, opera singer, and airplane mechanic. This was his first experience with airships but he seemed to have a natural talent for machinery. He and Wellman proceeded to redesign the *America*'s car and install a new seventy-five-horsepower automobile engine. They also added something they called an equilibrator, a hollow, steel-covered leather tube 120 feet long and six inches in diameter that was to be filled with extra food. It would be dragged beneath the ship like the drag rope on a balloon, inhibiting the ship's rise by adding its own weight to the weight of the ship as it was lifted into the air. It would also slow the ship's descent as its weight was transferred back to the ground. When filled with food it would weigh fourteen hundred pounds. Wellman described it as "ballast

The Morrell airship made her first and last voyage on May 23, 1908, at Berkeley, California, with nineteen men aboard as six thousand people, many of them stockholders, watched. The only man who refused to participate was George H. Loose, the ship's builder. He claimed it was unsafe. *Courtesy Carruthers Collection, Claremont Colleges.*

ABOVE LEFT: Walter Wellman (1858–1934). Few who inspected the *America* disagreed with Wellman's description of her as a stout, well-built airship. It was only Wellman's concept, and Wellman himself, that were in question. *Courtesy Library of Congress.* ABOVE RIGHT: Wellman's airship hangar under construction. The Arctic summer of 1906 saw the erection of a canvas-covered airship hangar at Spitzbergen on Dane Island a few hundred feet from Andrée's starting point. The *America* set out for the Pole the following year. Wellman's critics pointed out that he was attempting the fifteen-hundred-mile voyage to the North Pole and back in a ship that had never been test-flown and at a time when no aircraft of any kind had yet completed an uninterrupted flight of over a hundred miles. *From* The Aerial Age, *by Walter Wellman, New York, A. R. Keller & Co., 1911.*

•

which can be used over and over again without throwing it away."[13]

Returning to Spitzbergen in June 1907, they encountered the worst Arctic storm in thirty years. It continued until the first of September. On September 2, they started for the Pole. Aboard were Wellman, Vaniman, a navigator, ten Siberian sled dogs, provisions for ten months, and fuel for two thousand miles.

Walter Wellman

Assuming the Pole once attained, and the fuel supply exhausted, there is every reason to believe the America could remain in the air, using her equilibrator, several days longer; and in that time there is a large chance that the winds could carry her, as a free or drifting balloon, far toward or perhaps to some land, and any land would mean safety for the crew.

Should this alternative fail, we have not put all our eggs in one basket, nor in two baskets, for there is a third recourse, already spoken of—sledging our way out; and, as shown, we go prepared not only for the summer and autumn, but with provisions enough to enable us to remain out, in case of need, the entire winter, sledging back the following spring, which is the most favorable season for Arctic travel.[14]

Heading north along the coast of Spitzbergen, they flew into a swirling snowstorm. Then they discovered that their compass wasn't working. After two hours in the storm they sighted the coastline through a break in the clouds and landed on top of a glacier, slashed open the gasbag, and waited for their steamer to come and rescue them.

Two years later Wellman tried again. This time the equilibrator snagged on the ice and broke off, whereupon the *America*, suddenly free of fourteen hundred pounds, shot up to five thousand feet losing so much gas that they were forced to land on the water next to a passing ship that towed them back to their camp. When he learned that Commander Peary had already reached the North Pole by dogsled four months earlier, Wellman gave up the Arctic and turned his attention to the first aerial crossing of the Atlantic Ocean.

He persuaded two more newspapers, the *New York Times* and the *London Daily Telegraph,* to join the *Chicago Record-Herald* as sponsors and share the expedition's forty-thousand-dollar cost. Vaniman was sent off to Paris to supervise another forty-three-foot addition to the *America*'s gasbag and the installation of a

The *America* emerging from her hangar.

In seeking the North Pole in an airship, it is no toy that we are playing with. The *America* is no plaything, no fragile, short-lived balloon built to run for a few hours as the wind listeth, and then succumb—but a machine, big and stout, steel-muscled, full-lunged, strong-hearted, built for war, for work, for endurance, able to fight the winds that sentry the Pole and perhaps to defeat them.

Walter Wellman in *McClures Magazine,* June 1907.

Photo from The Aerial Age, *by Walter Wellman, New York, A. R. Keller & Co., 1911.*

•

second eighty-horsepower engine. Meanwhile, Wellman sailed for Africa to report on his old friend, Teddy Roosevelt, on safari.

By the beginning of August 1910, the *America* was ready to be assembled inside a huge wooden hangar near the boardwalk at Atlantic City. It had been built for Wellman by local businessmen interested in seeing their city become the western terminus of future transatlantic aerial traffic. Vaniman had built a new equilibrator with thirty steel cylinders strung on a three-hundred-foot-long steel cable. Each cylinder was four feet long, nine inches in diameter, and held one hundred pounds of gasoline. Forty wooden blocks were tied to the end of the cable. The whole thing weighed two tons. Also to be suspended beneath the ship was a twenty-seven-foot lifeboat carrying food, water, a stove, two bunks, and a radio transmitter.

As Vaniman and his crew struggled to put the *America* together, August turned into September, and while the sponsoring newspapers insisted that Wellman was only awaiting the proper weather conditions to start his epic voyage, the rival papers began to suggest that the huge machine might never get off the ground. They weren't far from the truth. The *America* was proving to be much heavier than expected.

At last on the morning of October 15, 1910, everything was ready and Wellman, Vaniman, four crewmen, and an unexpected cat named Kiddo climbed aboard as Atlantic City's police and firemen walked the *America* out into the fog where a motorboat was waiting to tow her out to the open sea.

Walter Wellman

It was with a keen feeling of disappointment that I looked down and saw only one-tenth instead of one-half of the equilibrator lifted from the sea. But, there was not even a thought of turning back, nor—if the motors started up right—of converting the start into a trial trip. This weakness of the overload was nothing new; we had struggled against it in vain through the weary weeks; it was fundamental and could not be remedied.[15]

The line from the launch was cast off, the engines were started, and they were on their way, they hoped, to Europe. It was the third time the *America* had been off the ground and the first time she had flown with her new engine and expanded gasbag.

As seen from the steamship *Trent,* the *America* was little more than a helpless balloon drifting sideways with the wind, her engines broken into pieces and thrown overboard to keep her from dropping into the sea. The head of the deadly equilibrator can be seen following the ship like a hungry shark. The *America*'s appearance had been changed considerably since her Arctic days, but her control surfaces at the end of the keel were still inadequate for the size of the ship. *Courtesy Library of Congress.*

•

Walter Wellman

All about me were radiant faces—all save Kiddo's, it still a bit sour with strangeness; cats have no imagination, no ken of chemistry and human nature and the history of progress; no vanity in pioneering.[16]

By midafternoon the old engine was running only intermittently and the new one had broken down completely. The ship was unable to rise more than a hundred feet above the sea, and as night approached, the hydrogen contracted in the cool evening air and they had to throw gasoline overboard to stay aloft. In the fog and darkness, they came within inches of ramming the four-masted schooner *Addison E. Bullard.* As Captain Sawyer of the *Bullard* later recalled:

We could plainly hear the steady grind of the machinery and the whirring of the motor, but we could see nothing but the light in the air. It was dark and there was a thick fog. The light came nearer and nearer, and members of my crew said they could hear voices. Then out of the darkness and mist shot a big aerial phantom, as we imagined, going east, and headed directly for the Bullard. The thing was such a big surprise for all hands that we were knocked off our pins. The airship, when almost upon us, rose up higher and shot out to sea. She was probably going 15 miles per hour. The America was less than a hundred feet above the sea, and the topmasts of the Bullard are 110 feet.[17]

The wind was stronger than the single remaining engine, and as each gust hit the great hull, the equilibrator, acting as a two-ton sea anchor, held the ship in place while the wind blew her down almost to the sea. They shut down the useless engine. Now they were a free balloon at the mercy of the wind and the equilibrator, which had started to skip from wave to wave with great shuddering leaps that threatened to pull the *America* apart.

With his ship ready to break up around him, Wellman still had time to imagine even greater difficulties:

I had a particular horror of landing on Long Island. To leave Atlantic City for Europe and pull up somewhere near Montauk or Newport was not to be thought of. Even a holocaust seemed preferable to a fiasco.[18]

By the second day they were dismantling their useless engine and throwing it overboard piece by piece to keep from sinking into the sea. Still there were a few quiet moments as recalled by the navigator, Murray Simon, a merchant marine officer who signed aboard the *America* for a change of pace:

The shadow of the balloon shows up on the surface of the water. It's a delightful, exhilarating sensation, this floating between earth and sky. We hate to think that we are really at the mercy of the equilibrator, and that with a little rough sea we shall be jerked into various stages of nervous collapse.[19]

By the morning of the third day, when they spotted the steamship *Trent,* everyone was ready to give up. As the steamer raced to keep up with the rapidly drifting *America,* Wellman and his crew climbed into the lifeboat and abandoned ship. Even this was not easy, for the equilibrator struck the lifeboat, bruising two crewmen and smashing a hole in the bow. Then the *Trent,* following along at full speed, nearly ran over them, but finally men and cat were safely aboard the steamer watching the *America* drift off into the distance.

Wellman and his crew returned to New York and a hero's welcome. In three days of drift and occasional flight, they had covered slightly over a thousand miles, first in a northeasterly direction along the coast from Atlantic City past Nantucket and halfway to Nova Scotia until the wind changed and blew them southward toward Bermuda, where the *Trent* found them 250 miles offshore, due east of Norfolk, Virginia. Of the 1,008 miles Wellman figured they had flown, three-quarters of them were in directions other than toward Europe. Still, it was farther than anyone had tried to fly in an airship before and deserved a hero's welcome, if not for skill, then at least for daring.

Melvin Vaniman (1867–1912) and Kiddo the cat aboard the *Trent* after their rescue. Vaniman was raised on a farm at Virden, Illinois, studied music in Chicago, and joined a touring opera company as a singer. They went broke in Honolulu, and Vaniman began shooting travel photos for steamship companies, winning a gold medal at the St. Louis World's Fair for his pictures of New Zealand. He became interested in aeronautics while shooting photos from a captive balloon. In France he assisted F. S. Lahm in the construction of an unsuccessful airplane, then he helped Wellman rebuild the *America*. He began work on his own ship, the *Akron*, in 1911. *Courtesy Library of Congress.*

The *Akron* in the air.

America's only airship vanished in a flash of smoke at 6:38 in the morning of July 2d, and with it perished America's only aeronautic engineer with his crew of four men. The accident, although viewed by three thousand spectators along the shore of Atlantic City, will ever remain a mystery; for not a soul aboard the vessel survived. Eyewitnesses of the disaster speak of a wreath of smoke that appeared, followed by a caving in of the gasbag. An instant later there was a loud explosion that burst the envelope, and the car dashed down into the sea, where it fell a heap of wreckage in water a few feet deep.

Scientific American,
July 13, 1912.

Photo courtesy Carruthers Collection, Claremont Colleges.

•

Perhaps the entire operation was best summed up by the rival *Chicago Tribune,* which editorialized:

> We can fully understand why Wellman and his companions embarked on a voyage which for foolhardiness exceeds anything in the history of human recklessness, but what gets us is how a perfectly sane cat ever consented to go.[20]

Wellman gave up flying in all its forms and settled down to a quiet life of book and newspaper writing. He died in 1934 at the age of seventy-five. It is just as well that he retired from aeronautics, for his complete disinterest in test flights would surely have caught up with him sooner or later. The equilibrator was never tried again on any other aircraft.

Though Wellman retired from aviation, Melvin Vaniman did not. He designed a ship of his own and got it built by Frank Seiberling of the Goodyear Tire and Rubber Company, just then starting up in the balloon business. Named the *Akron,* it was 258 feet long, with four hundred thousand cubic feet of gas, and three engines totaling 280 horsepower. Vaniman made several test flights around Atlantic City before starting out for Europe. During one of these tests on July 2, 1912, fifteen minutes after takeoff on a trial voyage, spectators saw the ship burst into flame and fall into the sea. Melvin Vaniman and his four crewmen were killed.

The search for dirigibility led through many false starts, and though the honor of its achievement seems clearly won by Alberto Santos-Dumont, it is an honor some would deny him. Yet the facts are clear. He came to Paris in 1892, a wide-eyed youth of eighteen expecting to see flying machines filling the skies. Instead he found that no one had flown an airship there for nearly fifteen years. He recognized his tricycle engine as the long-sought power plant and set to work building an airship around it. At his retirement ten years later, the skies of Paris and the world were filled with airplanes and airships, most of which were based at least in part on his designs.

Some feel that when a suitable engine was finally available, it was only a matter of time before someone would put it into a successful airship. The same argument prevails in heavier-than-air flight. Many Europeans were thinking about flying, and we should ignore the fact that none of them got around to it until Alberto built a plane and flew it. After all, the critics remind us, it wasn't really a very good airplane—all it did was fly.

The same can be said for Alberto. While others drew up complicated designs and talked about flying, he built aircraft and flew them. It was a job requiring an imaginative engineer, skilled mechanic, and experienced aeronaut. That all these abilities should be found in a single individual was not an accident. His success was the result of long hours in spherical balloons learning to fly plus a willingness to roll up his sleeves and help turn his designs into reality.

Alberto Santos-Dumont

To have been one's self the captain of an ordinary balloon at the very least a dozen times seems to me an indispensable preliminary to acquiring an exact notion of the requisites for construction and handling of an elongated balloon furnished with its motor and propeller.

Naturally I am filled with amazement when I see inventors who have never set foot in the basket drawing up on paper—and even executing in whole or in part—fantastic airships whose balloons are to have a capacity of thousands of cubic meters, loaded down with enormous motors which they do not succeed in raising from the ground, and furnished with machinery so complicated that nothing works! Such inventors are afraid of nothing, because they have no idea of the difficulties of the problem.[21]

Alberto realized what many inventors did not—there was more to flying than simply casting off the lines and sailing away. His advice would be ignored by others at their peril, and to suggest that everyone was ready to fly and Alberto simply happened to be first ignores the fact that, even after he had shown the way, most men still couldn't get the hang of it.

•

The early history of dirigible flight is one of a large number of ideas and a very small number of actual airships. It was much easier to create bold and imaginative designs on paper than it was actually to take wood and cloth and build something. But these three ships were built and one of them actually flew.

•

With the help of young Gabriel Voisin, Alberto Santos-Dumont completed his first airplane in the spring of 1906. The wings were based on Lawrence Hargrave's box-kite designs. The fuselage of the plane stuck out in front with the only moveable control surfaces, a small box-kite, at the bow. It was probably the most unusual and unflyable airplane that ever flew. On October 23, 1906, Alberto lifted it ten feet off the ground and flew for sixty yards through the air. He was carried from the field on the shoulders of the crowd and acclaimed around the world as the first to achieve heavier-than-air flight. *Courtesy U.S. Signal Corps in the National Archives.*

•

3

ZEPPELIN

· THE ·

MAN

· AND HIS ·

AIRSHIPS

If airships are possible at all, then mine is possible.

Count Ferdinand von Zeppelin[1]

The Zeppelins were a family of landed nobility who traced their ancestry back to the Middle Ages. For five hundred years Zeppelins participated in the tangled rivalries of the German kingdoms fighting both for and against Prussia, Austria, Denmark, Sweden, and England. By July 8, 1838, when Count Ferdinand von Zeppelin was born, they had been in the service of the kings of the South German state of Wurttemberg for half a century.

When Ferdinand was two, his father left the royal court for a quieter life managing the family estate at Girsberg near the Swiss border. When the young count was thirteen his mother died and he thought he might study to become a missionary, but his father discouraged this ambition, and by the age of seventeen Ferdinand had decided upon a military career. He entered the military college at Ludwigsburg and at the age of twenty joined the Eighth Wurttemberg Regiment as a second lieutenant. Stationed at Stuttgart he continued his education at Tübingen

OPPOSITE: Lieutenant Zeppelin. The Zeppelins were members of the Junkers class, the landowning aristocracy of Germany. He was the second of three children. His mother, Amalie Macaire d'Hoggeur, was from an old French Huguenot family that fled from persecution in France and settled in Wurttemberg. Though he briefly considered a life in the ministry, the family had a long heritage of military service, and, with his father's encouragement, young Lieutenant Zeppelin began his army career. *Courtesy Northrop University.*

·

· **53** ·

University studying mechanics, economics, chemistry, and history. In the spring of 1859 Wurttemberg and the Southern German Federation joined Austria in a war against France in Italy, but Lieutenant Zeppelin got no closer to Italy than Ludwigsburg, where he spent two years in the engineering section of the quartermaster-general's staff.

When peace returned he spent the next three years traveling in Austria, Italy, France, and England studying each nation and its military organization. In France Lieutenant Zeppelin stayed at the Imperial Palace as the guest of a family friend, the Emperor Napoleon III.

With the outbreak of the American Civil War, Lieutenant Zeppelin applied to the king of Wurttemberg for a year's leave to visit the United States and observe the fighting. Though the young count's father had encouraged his previous journeys, he was not enthusiastic about this one and expressed his doubts in a letter to his son, which serves to illustrate the strong bond of mutual respect between the two men:

> Believe me when I say that despite my grey hairs I am in closer sympathy with your youthful standpoint than many of the younger generation, and you will not be so unjust as to attribute my objections to philistinism, inability to keep up with the times or to understand the spirit and aspirations of youth. But the very fact that I have all my days regarded life in America as quite unworthy of admiration and sympathy and that your choice has fallen upon a country and people whom I have never placed at a high level (perhaps not high enough), since their politics and morality seemed to me to exclude them from playing a worthy part in civilisation or pursuing the divine ideal and mission of human improvement—the fact, in short, that I could never summon up the least enthusiasm for them (a mistake on my part, perhaps) increased my astonishment, my stupor, as I have called it, and led me perhaps too far in search of arguments and warnings. I thought it my sacred duty as your father and as a man of years and experience to save you, if possible, from painful disappointment.
>
> . . . I can only say, speaking as a layman, and deploring on humanitarian grounds the tragedy of a civil war, that the campaign has so far quite failed to command my admiration, perhaps because, from the reports received, it appears to have been conducted in defiance of the rules of international law.[2]

Having expressed his reservations, the father left the final decision up to his son, and Lieutenant Zeppelin sailed from Liverpool for America on April 30, 1863. After landing in New York he arranged passage aboard the French cruiser *Tisiphone,* which was preparing to sail down to Baltimore. A French naval officer recalled the incident some years later:

> As warships, of course, never carry ordinary passengers, it was quite obvious that this young man was a very favored person and this fact became even more obvious to us when we saw with what particular courtesy the captain received him. The young man dined with the captain and it was quite late when he joined the other officers of the vessel in their cabin. He was young and gay and asked whether he might offer his hosts some good Rhine wine which he was carrying in his box. He unpacked twelve bottles of wine and soon all of the company were very merry.
>
> One by one the officers were obliged to leave and go on duty until finally the passenger was left alone with a young midshipman who was not on duty. The two young men drank and talked until dawn. When they had finished all the wine they took a walk around the ship which finally ended on the highest point of the mast: they climbed up to

Lieutenant Zeppelin in the United States. The count was one of a number of European officers who came to the United States to observe the Civil War. With no war of their own at the moment, many paid their own way to America hoping for both adventure and career advancement. When the conflict proved of limited interest, Lieutenant Zeppelin joined two Russian acquaintances in a trip down the Mississippi. They are shown here with their two guides at St. Paul, Minnesota, where Lieutenant Zeppelin (second from right with the rifle) made his first balloon ascent on August 17, 1863, with a German aeronaut, John Steiner, who had also served with the Union army. It was a tethered flight up to seven hundred feet in a balloon filled with coal gas. *Courtesy Northrop University.*

•

prove to each other that they were both entirely steady, despite the wine. The fact that the midshipman could climb the mast did not show any particular prowess for the weather was lovely and the sea was calm. But it was an astonishing feat for the passenger to perform. He admitted to the midshipman that, as a cavalry officer, he had never before had an opportunity to climb a mast, that this was, in fact, his first "ascent" into the spheres above the earth.[3]

After some sightseeing, Count Zeppelin presented his letters of introduction to the Prussian ambassador at Washington, D.C., who arranged for an audience with President Lincoln.

Count Ferdinand von Zeppelin

I had put on frock-coat and top-hat, but the occasion was void of any special ceremony. I was escorted to the President's office in the White House. There rose from behind the desk a very tall spare figure with a large head and long untidy hair and beard, exceptionally prominent cheek-bones, but wise and kindly eyes. During our short talk, Mr. Reed, the private secretary, sat at the desk, while his feet, clad in Turkish slippers and projecting far beyond his trouser-ends, swung to and fro. The President expressed great pleasure at my arrival, approved my purpose and wished me a successful visit.[4]

Lincoln arranged for a pass that would allow the young officer to move freely among the Union armies. This meant that Zeppelin didn't need the letter of introduction to Gen. Robert E. Lee that the general's niece had given him in Philadelphia. He bought a horse from a former colonel in the Prussian Guards Cavalry who was making a fortune selling horses to the government and set out to join the Union army.

Count Ferdinand von Zeppelin

I proceeded by a small steamer to the army on the Potomac. There was very gay company on board, people travelling to spend Sunday with friends and relatives in the army, a curious form of social outing, I thought. Indeed social life altogether seemed to have suffered little from the war, as I had already noticed in Washington. This, no doubt, because the army was a volunteer force and not conscripted. Dancing and gaiety on board were only momentarily suspended as we passed a ship carrying wounded men from the theatre of war.[5]

Though he was supposed to be a neutral observer, Count Zeppelin found himself several times under fire from the Confederates and only with effort managed to restrain his enthusiasm and keep his sword undrawn. After some months of observation he concluded that there was little in the Union army's tactics that could be usefully applied in Europe and he left the army to join two Russians on an expedition down the Mississippi. They eventually reached St. Paul, where Lieutenant Zeppelin made his first balloon ascension.

He returned from America in November 1863 and was appointed to the military staff of King Charles of Wurttemberg. When Prussia attacked Austria in the war of 1866, the other German states supported Austria, and Captain Zeppelin was transferred to the Wurttemberg Division's general staff. Prussia won the war and absorbed several North German states. Wurttemberg remained independent, and three years later the king appointed Captain Zeppelin as military attaché to his son, Prince William. The twenty-one-year-old prince wasn't sure he wanted to be king, and the thirty-year-old captain spent many hours in friendly argument about a prince's duty to his people.

In the summer of 1869 at the age of thirty-one, Count Zeppelin married the Baroness Isabella von Wolff of Livonia. A year later in the Franco-Prussian War, Captain Zeppelin of the Wurttemberg Cavalry Brigade, fighting this time with Prussia, distinguished himself by leading a mounted reconnaissance deep into French territory.

In 1874 he was promoted to the rank of major and given command of the Second Wurttemberg Dragoons. Ten years later he advanced to colonel and was then appointed as military attaché at Wurttemberg's embassy to Prussia in Berlin. In 1887 he became the ambassador.

His three years as ambassador to Prussia, the Kingdom of Wurttemberg's most sensitive diplomatic post, were the years when Chancellor Bismarck was extending Prussia's control over the German states to create a united German Empire. Yet all through this period, though he realized his work was of great importance to Wurttemberg, Count Zeppelin longed to return to his career as a military officer. In 1890 he got his wish. He was promoted to the rank of general but instead of getting the command of a regiment, he was retired. It was an unexpected and bitter blow, but the Prussians were now in control and they weren't interested in putting one of their regiments under the command of an officer still loyal to Wurttemberg, one who had fought against them in the war of 1866. In deference to his position and influence they were obliged to promote him to the rank of general, but then they put him out.

Count Zeppelin had served his country for more than thirty years, and now, just as he reached the pinnacle of his career, it was over. At the age of fifty-two he was too old to start again yet not nearly old enough to be content with the sudden and unaccustomed inactivity of retirement. What was he to do, putter in the garden of the family estate near the shores of placid Lake Constance or walk along the quiet waterfront and drowse away his remaining days in the sun while the rest of the world passed him by? With such a distinguished career behind them, most men would be content to accept retirement, but Count Ferdinand von Zeppelin was not. At the age of fifty-two he set out to invent a practical flying machine.

The idea had been in the back of his mind for many years. It may have been born in far-off Minnesota when he first looked down at the earth from the basket of a balloon. The idea may have come to him at the Siege of Paris as he watched the French balloons sailing high over the guns of his cavalry. Whatever its inception, the idea of flight did not appear in his diary until March 1874, under the title, "Thoughts about an airship":

> The machine must have the dimensions of a big ship. The gas-chambers so calculated as to carry the machine except for a slight overweight. Elevation will then be obtained by starting the engine, which will drive the machine, as it were, towards the upward-pointed wings. Arriving at the desired height, the wings will tend to flatten out so that the airship remains on the horizontal plane. To drop, the wings will be flattened out still further or the speed be reduced. . . .
>
> The gas-chambers should, whenever possible, be divided into cells, which can be filled and emptied separately. The engine must always be able to replace gas.
>
> Parachutes, if they can be used at all, could be attached as part of the ceiling of the passenger compartment and be detachable by the application to them of a person's weight.[6]

It was all there, a large passenger-carrying airship with separate gas compartments, that could be driven up or down dynamically by engine power. Occasional entries in the count's diary over the years show that the idea of an airship never left him. When, in 1884, he read about the flight of Renard and Krebs's *La France,* Count Zeppelin suddenly realized that the French were ahead of Germany in airship development, and he began to consider his ideas more seriously.

La France was the first completely dirigible airship and represented a major advance in the science of aeronautics, but her speed of fourteen miles per hour was still too slow for any but the calmest days. Count Zeppelin felt that most inventors had failed because they made their ships too small. By limiting the size of their gasbag, they limited the size of the engine they could lift, thus cutting down on the amount of horsepower available to drive the ship. A top speed of fourteen miles per

Newly appointed ambassador von Zeppelin from Wurttemberg posed for his portrait in Berlin in 1887. His king had selected him at the age of forty-nine to conduct the sensitive negotiations that would lead to the incorporation of Wurttemberg into Prussia's new German Empire. Ambassador Zeppelin little suspected that in three short years his career would be finished. *Courtesy Northrop University.*

hour was fine in calm air, but in a fifteen-mile-per-hour wind the ship was little better than a free balloon.

What was needed was a very large gasbag capable of lifting more powerful engines that could drive the ship at significantly higher speeds. The problem was that as the gasbag was made bigger, it became clumsy and unstable—like the Morrell airship, for example. Count Zeppelin's solution was to take a dozen or more small balloons and enclose them within a rigid metal framework that was wrapped in a tight fabric cover. By using a series of separate gasbags, the ship could stay aloft even if one or two lost their hydrogen. The outer cover stretched tightly over the framework would give the hull a smooth, cylindrical shape that could be easily driven through the air by means of the powerful engines carried in cars suspended beneath the hull.

This was Count Zeppelin's conception. He had worked it out carefully in his mind during his last years in the army. Now with nothing else to do, he was encouraged by his wife and daughter to complete his plans and submit them to the authorities. In June 1891, he wrote to his friend Count Schlieffen, chief of the general staff:

> You will perhaps remember a conversation we had during a ride in the Tiergarten on the subject of dirigible airships. I did not at the time attempt to put my ideas into practice, as I was too busy to work them out and, besides, it would have worried me to be looked upon, even temporarily, as a candidate for a lunatic asylum.
>
> Now when I have nothing better to do and when public opinion can only hurt me personally, and not any profession in which I am engaged, I have been reverting to those ideas and have given them shape—so far, on paper only.[7]

Little did he suspect how prophetic his words would prove to be or how long the struggle for recognition and support of his ideas would take. For ten long years he worked on his designs in spite of official disinterest and even scorn from many of his former associates in the military and government. "What could an old cavalry officer possibly know about airships?" they asked as they ignored his pleas for an official hearing. Worse yet for the proud old gentleman, he would eventually be openly derided as a fool and a madman. Yet even if he had known what lay ahead, it is doubtful whether he would have changed his course. His duty to his country was clear and he could not do otherwise. It was this sense of duty that he hoped to invoke in the chairman of the Daimler factory as he pleaded for more powerful engines:

> You appear to have less confidence than when I was first permitted to broach my plans to you. That is natural enough and does not surprise me. Once engaged upon the matter, you are influenced by the unfavourable opinion generally passed upon the plan of building airships, by the reports of how hundreds of its devotees, among them highly-skilled technicians, have failed and how millions of money have been swallowed up in it. How then can Count Zeppelin have solved the problem?
>
> I have solved it, not because I knew any more than my rivals, but by the simple, sober thinking of a serious man, whom nature has endowed with common-sense; and by coordinating already established data on the subject, while making use of the latest discoveries and inventions.
>
> I had hoped that you and Dr. Steiner would at least help me on my way towards

To test his motor and propeller system, Count Zeppelin and his engineers took to the waters of Lake Constance. The speed of their boat minus the drag of the water gave them a pretty good idea of the power of their engine and the efficiency of the propellers. The tall young man marked by the number 3 is Ludwig Durr, destined to become the count's chief engineer after engineer Kubler, at the bow of the boat, refused to fly in *LZ-1* without a larger insurance policy. *Courtesy Deutsches Museum, Munich.*

completing a work which would secure for our German Fatherland an advantage that should not be underestimated.

Not for my sake, but for Germany's I implore you to reconsider the matter, before you deliver to my scheme what may be its death-blow.[8]

The fact that he was asking Daimler for the impossible—the technology that he required simply didn't exist yet—failed to deter Count Zeppelin. He plunged ahead confident that invention would soon catch up with his imagination.

In 1895 he was finally able to arrange a hearing by a board of experts appointed by the Prussian War Ministry and, though they approved of his designs in general, they made several specific objections that the War Ministry used to reject the whole plan as being both impractical and too expensive. The charge of impracticality Count Zeppelin firmly rejected. The problem of expense he was only too familiar with, having paid the entire cost of development from his own funds:

If I do not succeed now, there is serious reason to fear that Germany will lose the lead in this invention. There will always be men enough with more technical knowledge than mine; but, if I fail, it would not be so easy to find anyone willing to risk his money on the experiments necessary to satisfy even himself of the practicability of his scheme.[9]

Rejected by the War Ministry and his fortune near exhaustion, still Count Zeppelin persisted. He tried to raise two hundred thousand dollars through a bond issue, but the only response was from a few old friends and the royal family of Wurttemberg. The Prussian War Ministry actively opposed participation in the issue among the military. But just when things looked darkest, the Union of German Engineers responded to the count's request for a critical examination of his plans. Their guarded endorsement persuaded several industrialists to assist him in forming a stock company to build his airship. Even so, Count Zeppelin himself still had to put up half of the money out of his own pocket.

The company was founded in May 1898 as the Gesellschaft zur Förderung der

The first flight of the first Zeppelin airship, *LZ-1,* took place on July 2, 1900. The ship was 416 feet long and 38½ feet in diameter with 399,000 cubic feet of hydrogen in seventeen gasbags. She had a total lift of 27,400 pounds but weighed nearly thirteen tons. This meant that only about fifteen hundred pounds of lift was left for the crew, fuel, and water ballast. The control surfaces consisted of tiny rudders above and below the hull at the bow and on the sides of the hull at the stern. The sliding weight is suspended eighty feet beneath the hull. The *LZ-1* made only eight miles per hour on this first flight but reached seventeen miles per hour on her second flight. *Courtesy Deutsches Museum, Munich.*

•

Luftschiffahrt (the Society for the Encouragement of Aerial Navigation). They built a large, floating construction shed at Manzell on Lake Constance near Friedrich-shafen, and in 1899 work was begun on the first Zeppelin airship, the *LZ-1. LZ* stood for *Luftschiff Zeppelin* (Zeppelin Airship). The first flight took place on July 2, 1900. Ernst Lehmann, who later became one of Count Zeppelin's co-workers, described the scene:

> Although the entire undertaking was regarded as a curiosity—the whim of a retired general who had nothing better to do in his old age—the news spread like wild fire, and many thousands of people were attracted to the lake. They lined the shore like a long black rope and they swarmed aboard steamers and boats. The dockyard motorboat had difficulty in keeping the spectators far enough away not to endanger the ship which was filled with inflammable gas.
>
> At about six o'clock in the afternoon, the float, on which the airship rested, was pushed from the hangar. It looked like a gigantic caterpillar slowly creeping foreward. The crowd was astonished at its immensity and broke out into cries of surprise.[10]

Their surprise was understandable. The *LZ-1* was 416 feet long, the size of an average football stadium. With Count Zeppelin at the wheel and four others aboard, the huge ship rose slowly from the surface of the lake. He steered with a small rudder at the bow and another at the stern. Instead of elevator fins, the *LZ-1* had a 550-pound weight suspended beneath the hull on a cable that was pulled backward to make the ship climb and forward to make it descend. The four propellers were driven by two sixteen-horsepower Daimler gasoline engines.

The first flight lasted eighteen minutes. The sliding weight lever broke, the frame buckled, and the rudder lines fouled. The ship landed on top of a signal stake in the middle of the lake, puncturing a gasbag. After three months of repair work, on October 17, 1990, the *LZ-1* made her second flight. She was aloft for an hour and twenty minutes when the engines stopped and the ship settled slowly on the lake. A mechanic had inadvertently filled one of the fuel tanks with water. Three days later the *LZ-1* made a final flight of twenty-three minutes.

Count Zeppelin's airship had been built and flown. Along with the stock company's original two hundred thousand dollars, the stockholders had put up an additional thirty-seven thousand dollars to finish the ship. Now, that too was spent and the government had shown little interest and offered no contracts. The company's investors were not inclined to continue. The *LZ-1* was broken up and the motors, aluminum, and workshop equipment were sold. The corporation was liquidated and what was left of the enterprise, including the floating hangar, reverted to the sole ownership of Count Zeppelin.

After ten years of constant struggle he had finally seen the realization of his dream. Now he was forced to stand by while his ship was broken up and sold for scrap. He was sixty-two years old and his fortune was gone. His discouragement is evident in this passage from his diary:

> A short spell of rough weather, storm and waves will have rendered my whole stock of material useless. My last trained assistants will have left me. The last sums that I can sacrifice for this purpose will have been spent; old age or death will have set a term to my labours.[11]

This time it was the king of Wurttemberg who came to his aid. As prince he had once been forced to sit and listen to a young army captain lecture him on his duty to his people. Now as king he authorized a state lottery to assist his old friend. It raised thirty-one thousand dollars, and though the Prussians still refused to allow the sale of tickets in the rest of the country, they did present the count with a special grant of $12,500.

The internal combustion engine was rapidly being improved and Daimler was now able to produce an eighty-five-horsepower motor that weighed only eight hundred pounds. That was several pounds less weight and nearly six times more power than the engines in the *LZ-1*. For the new ship, both Daimler and Carl Berg, the aluminum manufacturer, agreed to supply their materials free, but even with this assistance, it was five years before Count Zeppelin was able to raise enough money to start work on his second ship.

On November 30, 1905, the *LZ-2* was ready to be brought out of the floating hangar. As the big ship was pulled out onto the lake, she was caught by the wind and driven ahead of her tugboat. The crew rushed to cut the tow rope but it fouled and pulled the bow of the *LZ-2* down into the water, submerging the keel and breaking the steering planes.

By January 17, 1906, the ship was repaired and they were ready to try again. This time the *LZ-2* rose easily to sixteen hundred feet where she encountered a strong westerly wind. The wind set up a rolling motion that interrupted the flow of benzine and caused the forward engine to stop. The crew brought the ship to a safe landing at Kisslegg, but during the night the storm increased in intensity and the *LZ-2* was beaten violently against the ground and wrecked.

Dr. Hugo Eckener in the Frankfurter Zeitung

The airship lay in front of us like the skeleton of a giant whale. Men worked with axes and saws, cutting it to pieces. . . . As the work of destruction proceeded, the old Count Zeppelin stood upright and calm, occasionally issuing orders. Who can know what it cost the inventor during that sleepless night to make his decision—to order the destruction of the aircraft to which he had devoted a lifetime.[12]

LZ-2 wrecked at Kissleg. After being pounded against the ground several times by the storm at Kissleg, the circular frames of *LZ-2* were bent and broken. As Count Zeppelin watched his ship being dismantled, he learned of his promotion to the honorary rank of cavalry general, which prompted his sardonic remark, "An airshipman without an airship is like a Cavalry Officer without horses, and I am both." *Courtesy Deutsches Museum, Munich.*

•

Once more the king of Wurttemberg authorized a lottery and once more Count Zeppelin began to build an airship. His engineer, Dr. Ludwig Durr, used his own money to set up a wind tunnel to study and improve the new ship's stabilizing surfaces. The *LZ-3* was completed in less than a year and made her first flight on October 9, 1906. She was essentially the same as *LZ-2* with the important addition of horizontal fins at the stern to correct the rolling that contributed to the earlier ship's destruction.

Now the public's attitude began to change. The wreck of the *LZ-2* at Kisslegg had been accepted by most as inevitable, but the news that the old count still meant to carry on was received with amazement. Was this simply a stubborn refusal to face up to failure or was there something more to it? The matter was widely discussed, and when on October 9 and 10 the *LZ-3* easily completed two sixty-mile flights in only two hours, the public finally began to realize what Count Zeppelin had achieved.

The military also began to take notice. Though the general staff still preferred the nonrigid designs of Majors Gross and von Parseval, they did appropriate $125,000 to rebuild the floating hangar on Lake Constance. They also agreed to purchase the *LZ-3* if she could demonstrate her military value by completing a twenty-four-hour flight.

The new hangar was completed in September 1907, and Count Zeppelin then proceeded to fly another series of tests in *LZ-3* that ended with a successful

eight-hour voyage. He managed to postpone the twenty-four-hour flight until the return of better weather in the spring. Knowing full well that the *LZ-3* was not capable of carrying enough fuel for twenty-four hours in the air, he hoped to have a larger ship ready by then to make the flight. Meanwhile the government agreed to put up one hundred thousand dollars to build the new ship and to set aside an additional five hundred thousand dollars to purchase both *LZ-3* and the new *LZ-4* if the twenty-four-hour flight was successfully completed.

LZ-4 was ready to fly on June 20, 1908. With two new 105-horsepower engines and an increased gas capacity of 530,000 cubic feet that gave her over two tons more lift than *LZ-3*, she was ready for the twenty-four-hour endurance flight. With enlarged rudders she showed excellent steering control and a top speed of nearly thirty miles per hour. Count Zeppelin decided to take advantage of the good weather to make a longer voyage across Lake Constance to Switzerland. At noon on July 1, the big ship appeared suddenly over Lucerne as thousands of people in the streets below gazed in amazement at the first flying machine most had ever seen. From Lucerne she cruised to Zurich before returning to the hangar after twelve hours in the air.

The international excitement and acclaim that followed the Swiss flight only served to confirm what a large part of the German public had begun to suspect. The Zeppelin airship was a major German achievement and the old count had created it almost single-handedly in the face of official disinterest and discouragement. A

By the time his fourth airship was completed in the summer of 1908, Count Zeppelin and his engineers had finally evolved an effective though complicated set of stabilizers and control surfaces, especially after the first tests resulted in the addition of the large rudder at the stern. *LZ-4,* shown emerging from the floating hangar, was 446 feet long and 42.7 feet in diameter with 530,000 cubic feet of hydrogen. She had a total lift of 37,038 pounds and weighed 26,445 pounds, which left 10,593 pounds of lift available for crew, passengers, fuel, and ballast. *Courtesy Luftschiffbau Zeppelin, Friedrichshafen.*

week later the count's seventieth birthday became the occasion for an outpouring of congratulations from all parts of the nation including a gold medal presented by the king of Wurttemberg and an honorary doctor's degree from Tübingen, his old university. In response to the official presentation made by a delegation of students, Count Zeppelin noted that it had only taken him ninety-nine semesters after entering the university finally to get his diploma.

Count Ferdinand von Zeppelin

My joy at seeing you is so great that I have overcome the depression which at first filled me at the thought that the honors heaped upon me exaggerate my real achievements. For the work I have done is based only on exact science and did not require from me any great imaginative powers or philosophical speculations. It was never necessary for me to fight for self-confidence and faith for the simple reason that mathematics, logic and practical experiments gave me one proof after another that I was right.

And if a man has this certainty and knows that he will reach his goal, it is not a virtue for him to find the way. I am aware, therefore, that the honors which you and people from other parts of Germany are showing me, are not based on an exaggeration of my personal achievements but that these honors, on the contrary, are directed towards me merely because I am the man who happened to carry out an invention which the entire world had needed for a long time. I am, therefore, filled with hope and gratitude, for I am confident that the invention which a kind Providence permitted me to carry out will become a blessing and an asset to the German Empire.[13]

Many of his friends congratulated him on the successful completion of his long struggle for recognition. Count Zeppelin smiled, thanked them, and kept silent. He had faith in the ultimate triumph of his ideas but he had been at it too long to imagine that all his troubles were over, for he still faced the twenty-four-hour endurance flight, the final test before the army's acceptance of *LZ-3* and *LZ-4*.

They started out aboard *LZ-4* on the morning of August 4, 1908. Count Zeppelin set his course westward along the valley of the Rhine from Lake Constance to Basel. There they would turn north with the river past Strasbourg to Mainz, where they would turn and retrace their route back to Manzell Bay, a total distance of slightly over four hundred miles.

All day long they cruised easily over the river as increasingly large crowds along the banks hailed their progress. Church bells rang, river steamers blew their whistles, and the Rhine bridges were black with cheering people as the huge ship sailed overhead. After eleven hours in the air, engine trouble forced them to land on the river near Oppenheim, a few miles short of Mainz. While the mechanics worked on the motor, a wine merchant gave them a bottle of Niersteiner, which they shared with the count. At 10:30 in the evening a passing Rhine steamer pulled the *LZ-4* out onto the river and they took off again, reaching Mainz at midnight where they turned for home.

Three hours later near Mannheim the balky engine gave out for good with a frozen bearing. Rather than continue into the rising head winds with only one engine, Count Zeppelin decided to land at the village of Echterdingen near the Daimler factory where they could get a replacement. All day the ship lay anchored in an open field guarded by soldiers sent over from Stuttgart. By midmorning a large crowd had gathered as people came from miles around to get a closer look at the great ship. The country roads were jammed and police estimated that fifty

thousand people ringed the field as the wind began to rise and a dark cloud bank rolled in from the southwest. At two in the afternoon the summer storm broke and a sudden gust of wind caught the *LZ-4* sideways, snapped her mooring lines and tossed her high into the air. She smashed into a tree, burst in flame, and fell to the ground a smoking ruin.

The crowd was stunned. Count Zeppelin, who had gone to a nearby inn to rest, was called to the scene of the disaster. The crowd opened to let him pass and stood silently as he looked at the wreckage. He seemed suddenly older and very tired. Without a word he turned and left.

The train ride back to Friedrichshafen must have been sad indeed. All hope of government aid was now gone. His ship had failed in its final test and the War Ministry's five hundred thousand dollars that would have allowed him to continue his work was lost. His own money was spent and his dream was over. Perhaps, he tried to persuade himself, it was for the best. Even with her increased size, *LZ-4* had not been able to overcome the inevitable loss of lift that came with the cooling of her gas at sundown. Several crewmen had to get off at Oppenheim in order to lighten the ship enough to take off from the river. And the engines were still inadequate. With one stopped, the other was not strong enough to drive the ship into even a moderate head wind. Perhaps this final failure was for the best, and yet, he had been so close.

At Friedrichshafen the festive decorations and banners hung at every street corner to celebrate the triumphant return of the airship were quietly removed. Returning to his tiny office, Count Zeppelin barely glanced at the pile of telegrams that littered his desk until his friend, Dr. Eckener, told him what they contained. They had been arriving all morning, money and promises of money from all over

The wreck of *LZ-4* at Echterdingen. Early on the morning of August 5, 1908, Count Zeppelin landed his *LZ-4* in a field near the village of Echterdingen to repair a motor. That afternoon while the mechanics were replacing the engine, a sudden storm caught the ship broadside, snapped the mooring cables, and tossed her into the air. She burst into flame and crashed to earth, a tangled heap of girders. It was this wreck that saved the Zeppelin enterprise. *Courtesy Northrop University.*

Germany. It had started on the field at Echterdingen. Someone suggested a collection for the old count. Others agreed and soon the people were emptying their pockets. One who witnessed the beginning of this extraordinary outburst of national emotion was David Lloyd George, then the British chancellor of the exchequer, who was visiting nearby at Stuttgart.

David Lloyd George

We went along to the field where the giant airship was moored, to find that by a last minute accident it had crashed and been wrecked. Of course, we were deeply disappointed, but disappointment was a totally inadequate word for the agony of grief and dismay which swept over the massed Germans who witnessed the catastrophe. There was no loss of life to account for it. Hopes and ambitions far wider than those concerned with a scientific and mechanical success appeared to have shared the wreck of the dirigible. Then the crowd swung into the chanting of Deutchland uber Alles with a fanatic fervor of patriotism. What spearhead of Imperial advance did this airship portend?[14]

Lloyd George was to become prime minister of England at the end of 1916. By then he would know only too well what it was that he witnessed at its beginnings on the edge of a field at Echterdingen.

The news of the crash spread up and down the Rhine. Where just hours earlier the people had watched with pride and awe as the great ship sailed majestically overhead, they now learned of her fiery destruction, and the impulse to help the old count spread as fast as the news. The passengers and crew of a river steamer collected six hundred marks, a bowling club gave 150 marks, and the newspapers took up the cause. The aldermen of Stuttgart contributed twenty thousand marks and the Mining Association of Essen collected one hundred thousand. All parts of the empire responded with over six million marks ($1,500,000).

In less than a day Count Zeppelin's fortunes had changed dramatically and his dream was now assured. With his newfound wealth he set up the Zeppelin Foundation with himself as director. The foundation's objective was the promotion of aviation, and the count's first grant of three million marks went to establish the Luftschiffbau-Zeppelin (Zeppelin Airship Works), which immediately set to work building a new factory at Friedrichshafen. The War Ministry promised to stand by their original agreement and accept the *LZ-3* and a new ship, the *LZ-5,* for five hundred thousand dollars. In November 1908, Kaiser Wilhelm II came to Friedrichshafen to personally inspect the rebuilt *LZ-3* and bestow the Order of the Black Eagle on Count Zeppelin, whom he called "the greatest German of the century."

The *LZ-3* was taken over by the army in 1909 and designated the *Z-1. LZ-5* was rushed to completion in the spring and, since she still had to complete the War Ministry's twenty-four-hour flight before her acceptance, Count Zeppelin set out on May 29, on what he hoped would be a long voyage. By not announcing his route before takeoff, he planned to take advantage of wind and weather conditions as they developed in order to make the flight as long as possible. The people began to follow the news reports of the progress of the *LZ-5* with even more interest than before, for now she was their ship. Their contributions had built her.

For three hundred miles Count Zeppelin followed a course that took him north and east toward Berlin. When news of the ship's approach reached the capital, a hundred thousand people rushed out to Templehof airfield, the Balloon Corps

On November 10, 1908, Kaiser Wilhelm (left) came in person to Friedrichshafen to present Count Zeppelin with the Order of the Black Eagle, which the count is wearing at his waist on a sash. It was thought that the kaiser might go for a ride aboard *LZ-3,* but he delegated that honor to Prince and Princess Fuerstenberg while he watched from a boat on the lake. *LZ-3* was then accepted by Major Gross on behalf of the German army. *Courtesy Northrop University.*

•

organized a landing crew, and the kaiser and his family hurried out to welcome the airship. Meanwhile, Count Zeppelin, completely unaware of the reception awaiting him and never intending to fly to Berlin in the first place, turned around at Bitterfeld, eighty miles short of the capital, and headed for home.

The kaiser was furious, and all kinds of unflattering stories about the *LZ-5's* airworthiness began to circulate. When it was reported that the ship had run into a pear tree at Goppingen on the homeward journey, the worst rumors seemed to be confirmed. Confidence in the Zeppelin airship quickly returned, however, when the people learned that the *LZ-5* had returned safely to Friedrichshafen in spite of a badly damaged bow. This was exactly the kind of strength the old count had promised for his ships. Only the gasbags at the bow had ruptured. The rest remained intact with enough hydrogen to fly her back to the hangar. A nonrigid or semirigid dirigible would have been destroyed, but the *LZ-5's* rigid frame withstood the crash just as Count Zeppelin said it would.

In spite of the accident, the ship covered 850 miles in thirty-six hours aloft, well over the twenty-four-hour requirement. The flight was universally hailed as a major aeronautical achievement, and the British press was quick to note that the ship had flown far enough to reach London and return. *The American Review of Reviews* called it "the most remarkable flight of man in the history of the world."[15] Even the kaiser was pacified when he learned of the ship's performance, especially after the count promised to bring a Zeppelin to Berlin before the end of the year.

Though public confidence was restored, it would be sorely tried in the future for, as Count Zeppelin was well aware, only his financial problems were solved. The technical difficulties remained and more than once they threatened to put an end to the whole enterprise.

The *LZ-5* was repaired and accepted by the army as their *Z-2*. *LZ-6* was completed in August 1909, and, after a propeller fell off along the way, finally reached Berlin and a tumultuous welcome. *LZ-6* finished out the year with a series of well-received sightseeing excursions for government officials over Lake Constance.

The Zeppelin Company approached the end of 1909 with an excellent public image and a serious problem. Several opportunities for catastrophe had been successfully avoided and the world had finally accepted the practicality of the rigid principle. The problem was what to do with the *LZ-6*. In order to survive, the Zeppelin Airship Works would have to continue to build and improve its ships. It would also have to sell them—but to whom? The army already had the *LZ-3* and *LZ-5* and was not inclined to buy any more. The navy had shown little interest and few other organizations were in a position to purchase and fly a Zeppelin.

The solution first occurred to Alfred Colsmann, the energetic young son-in-law of Carl Berg, the aluminum manufacturer, whom Count Zeppelin had selected as manager of the Zeppelin Airship Works. "Why not take advantage of the current enthusiasm for airships by starting our own airline?" Colsmann asked. Sightseeing excursions would be as popular with the public as they had been with the government officials, and most important, the airline would buy the Zeppelin Company's ships.

On November 16, 1909, Count Zeppelin founded the Deutsche Luftschiffahrts-Aktien-Gesellschaft (German Airship Transport Company), generally and more simply referred to by its initials as Delag. The world's first commercial airline was officially in business. It was six years after the Wright brothers' flight, three years after Alberto Santos-Dumont made the first airplane flight in Europe, and only four months since Louis Bleriot managed to fly a plane across the English Channel.

The mayors of several major German cities joined in founding the company and agreed on behalf of their cities to build a municipal airship hangar. The first to be completed was at Dusseldorf, which received Delag's first airship, the *LZ-7* named the *Deutschland,* which set out for the new hangar early on the morning of June 22, 1910.

Associated Press Night Report

Count Zeppelin was at the helm when the Deutschland left Friedrichshafen at 3 o'clock this morning, and sailed away on the trip that was to mark an epoch in aviation.

The passengers were some of the directors of the Hamburg-American Steamship

It was just before noon on the second day of the flight as the *LZ-5* groped her way through a heavy rain toward the oil refinery at Goppingen where Count Zeppelin planned to refuel. He had stopped the engines and was slowly descending through the rain by valving gas. Suddenly a half-dead pear tree loomed up ahead. Count Zeppelin ordered the helm hard to starboard, the helmsman turned hard to port, and the huge ship drifted straight into the tree, tearing away ninety feet of bow. Men were summoned from Friedrichshafen, and twenty-eight hours later they had the wreckage cut away and the gaping hole sealed over with cloth and reinforced with nearby fir trees. Chief Engineer Durr piloted the ship back to Friedrichshafen at a careful ten miles per hour while Count Zeppelin followed in an automobile in case of further trouble. Despite this difficulty, the 850-mile flight was an aviation record. LZ-5 *on the ground with the tree, courtesy Carruthers Collection, Claremont Colleges. LZ-5 in the air, courtesy Lawrence R. Fredriksen, Costa Mesa.*

•

Company and the German Air Ship Stock Company, joint owners of the dirigible, and guests.

They occupied the mahogany-walled and carpeted cabin situated between the gondolas, from the windows of which they viewed the scenery as the aerial car swept along. Count Zeppelin steered for the greater part of the distance.

The route was via Stuttgart, Mannheim and Cologne to Dusseldorf. It had been carefully marked out in advance for the guidance of the pilot and was followed exactly. There was no air stirring and the Deutschland made her way unhampered through a flood of bright sunshine.

The hour and minute of the probable passing of the various points had been bulletined ahead so that not only the people of the cities on the line filled the streets, but the inhabitants of all the intermediate villages turned out and cheered enthusiastically as

Above: It was the *LZ-6* that finally arrived at the capital on August 29, 1909, as two million Berliners crowded the streets and rooftops and a hundred thousand more gathered at Templehof airfield to greet Count Zeppelin (center left). *Courtesy Northrop University.* Right: The fact that a Zeppelin had yet to make its way to Berlin was a matter of some concern to the Prussians and some humor to everyone else as noted in this cartoon from the Austrian magazine *Kikeriki.* While the kaiser waits forlornly in Berlin (far right), Count Zeppelin sails away over Cologne in his *LZ-5,* the army's *Z-2. Courtesy Carruthers Collection, Claremont Colleges.*

the immense torpedolike structure with its whistling screws drove over their heads at a height of between 200 and 300 feet.

The Deutschland swung gently into her landing here at noon and the multitude surrounding the landing yards shouted a welcome.

The city had been gaily decorated in honor of the event. The promoters of the enterprise were entertained at a public dinner.

Regular trips will be made and many tickets already have been sold for the first few days at from $25 to $50 each. The airship is equipped with a restaurant which will supply the passengers with a buffet service such as is afforded on railroad trains.[16]

The Zeppelin Company hoped that a good performance by the Deutschland would help take the public's mind off the crash of the LZ-5, the army's Z-2, which was blown out of the hands of her ground crew in a storm and wrecked just two months earlier in April. The Deutschland's first six sightseeing flights out of Dusseldorf went smoothly. The seventh, on June 28, was to be a short public relations excursion for twenty newspaper correspondents. They got more of a story than either they or Delag expected. It was printed under the headline, "Pierced by Pines."

Associated Press Night Report

Count Zeppelin's passenger airship Deutschland, the greatest of all the famous aeronaut's models, lies tonight in the Teutoburgian forest, pierced by pine trees, a mass of deflated silk and twisted aluminum.

The thirty-three passengers aboard the airship when it struck the pines after a wild contest with a storm, escaped uninjured, climbing down from the wreck on a rope ladder.

Overtaken by an unexpected storm, the ship was blown off course, and even with all three engines at full speed, the helmsman was unable to hold her into the wind. The Deutschland was driven into the Teutoberg Forest where she came to rest in the treetops thirty feet above the ground. The passengers and crew climbed down safely.

Associated Press Night Report

In the early part of the journey the airship maintained an altitude of about 500 feet, and the passengers enjoying the new sensation expressed contempt for the train rumbling down below and spoke of automobiles as out of date.[17]

A third engine was added to the lengthened LZ-6, and she was pressed into service by Delag to replace the wrecked Deutschland. She began flying out of Baden-Baden but after less than two months, she too was destroyed when, through a mechanic's error, she caught fire and burned in her hangar.

The year 1910, which began with so much promise, turned out to be a disaster. LZ-5 wrecked in April, LZ-7 crashed in June, and LZ-6 burned in September. The only Zeppelin that survived the end of the year was the Army's LZ-3.

The year 1911 didn't start out much better. The LZ-8 was completed by the Zeppelin Company in March, was christened Deutschland II by Delag, and was put into service at Dusseldorf. She managed to make some thirty flights in the two months before she was smashed against a wall by the wind on being brought out of her hangar. She was so badly damaged she had to be junked.

In a little over a year, four new Zeppelins, *LZ-5, LZ-6, LZ-7,* and *LZ-8,* were destroyed, amazingly, with no loss of life. As one spectacular crash followed another, Count Zeppelin saw his dream, once seemingly within his grasp, begin to slip away. TOP: The *LZ-5,* the German army's *Z-2,* met her end on April 25, 1910. She was returning to Cologne in a gale from a military review at Hamburg when she was forced to land at Lemburg for more hydrogen. As two companies of soldiers struggled to hold her, she was carried off by the wind and dumped, a total loss, around a hilltop hotel at Webersburg on the River Lahn. No one was aboard. Scientific American. *May 21, 1910.* BOTTOM: LZ-7, Delag's *Deutschland* was 486 feet long and forty-six feet in diameter, with 670,900 cubic feet of hydrogen. She had a total lift of twenty-three tons and weighed 17½ tons, which left 5½ tons of lift available for fuel, ballast, a crew of nine, and twenty-four passengers. Three 110-horsepower Daimler engines gave her a top speed of thirty-seven miles per hour. She met her end in the Teutoberg Forest on June 28, 1910, with a full complement of newspaper reporters aboard. Again, no one was killed. Scientific American Supplement, *July 30, 1910.*

•

Count Zeppelin's dream was beginning to slip away once more as public confidence evaporated in the face of continuing disaster. Even the directors of Delag were starting to have doubts. They had expected to encounter difficulties along the way as the price of leadership in a new field of endeavor, but the loss of three Delag ships in less than a year was more than even they had bargained for. It was only Count Zeppelin's determination that persuaded them to continue. No one cared to oppose him. Edouard Surcouf, the builder of the Lebaudy airships, summed up the situation when he observed, "In Germany there are no longer friends of the Zeppelin airship, there are only friends of Count Zeppelin himself."[18]

The *LZ-10* was completed and delivered to Delag. On July 11, 1911, she was christened the *Schwaben (Swabia).* This was the ship Count Zeppelin was waiting for. In the *Schwaben,* technology finally caught up with his imagination, resulting in the fast reliable airship that he had dreamed of for so long.

One of the chief differences between *Schwaben* and her predecessors was in her engines, the first Maybach-Zeppelin motors. From the beginning Count Zeppelin

realized that he would need specially designed engines to meet the unique require-ments of his airships and he asked Wilhelm Maybach to make them for him. Maybach together with Gottlieb Daimler had built the first Mercedes automobile. He was well along with his designs when the crash at Echterdingen brought in the money to start an engine factory and the Zeppelin Foundation set up the Maybach-Motorenbau under the direction of Wilhelm's son, Karl Maybach. The *Schwaben's* three 145-horsepower Maybach motors were the result. They weighed seven pounds per horsepower, fifty pounds less per horsepower than the engines of *LZ-1,* and at the same time, they consumed only half as much fuel. They gave the *Schwaben* a top speed of forty-seven miles per hour.

Another improvement was in the control surfaces, which for the first time were all at the stern. But in the opinion of Hugo Eckener, her pilot, there was another more important factor in the *Schwaben's* success, and he attributed it to a source even higher than Count Zeppelin. It was "the wonderful summer of 1911." Five Zeppelins had been overtaken by unexpected storms and destroyed. The lack of

Once, right at the beginning of my service as an airship captain, the presence of a large crowd of spec-tators and a cabin full of influential and important guests tempted me to risk taking the ship out of the hangar with the wind from an un-favourable direction.

Dr. Hugo Eckener,
My Zeppelins
(London: Putnam Co., 1958)

The date was May 16, 1911, and Dr. Eckener's passengers had to climb down to the ground on fire ladders. What was left of *LZ-8,* the *Deutsch-land II,* became part of *LZ-9,* but all the passengers and crew survived.

LZ-10, the *Schwaben,* at 460 feet in length, was twenty-six feet and one gasbag shorter than both *Deutschlands,* but, though she held less gas, she was lighter and could carry 14,300 pounds of useful load, nearly two tons more than the larger ships. Her three new 145-horsepower Maybach engines drove her at a top speed of forty-seven miles per hour, ten miles faster than any Zeppelin had flown before. She was also the first Zeppelin with all her control surfaces at the stern. *Courtesy Luftschiffbau Zeppelin, Friedrichshafen.*

•

reliable weather forecasts would continue to plague airship operations for many years to come, but in 1911, when a long period of good weather was essential to the Zeppelin's survival, they got it.

Dr. Hugo Eckener

Then came that marvellous summer of 1911 with its three months of practically unbroken fine weather, a perfect godsend. No longer were flights daily exposed to the threat of weather disasters. For weeks and months our pilots flew in calm safety and began to understand and master the strange new element. Nature, who "hates man's handiwork," can at times be kind and gentle. But woe to him who disregards her warnings and grows incautious! It was caution which the Schwaben pilots learnt to exercise more and more as public confidence slowly returned. They could not risk losing it again.[19]

In 1911 the *Schwaben* made nearly a hundred flights without a single mishap. She was joined the following year by *LZ-11,* the *Viktoria Luise,* and then by the *Hansa* and *Sachsen.* The cities of Frankfurt, Hamburg, Potsdam, Dresden, Leipzig, Gotha, and Berlin all erected hangars to join those already at Dusseldorf and Baden-Baden.

Even the loss of the *Schwaben* in June 1912 failed to slow the momentum of success. She was returning to Dusseldorf ahead of a storm that caught her on the ground before she could get into the hangar. She was lifted into the air and smashed to the ground twice, then she burst into flame. A spark had ignited the ship's hydrogen, but where had that spark come from? The engines were off. The same thing had happened to the *LZ-4* at Echterdingen. There, the engines were cold, they had been off for ten hours. An investigation showed that the rubber-coated fabric of the gasbags gave off sparks when it was violently torn. All subsequent ships used gasbags made of goldbeater's skin, the intestines of cattle—from the balloon's earliest days the only substance yet discovered that was thin, flexible, and gas tight.

In the last pleasant years before the war, Delag with three ships in service, flew to every part of Germany. Despite the fact that seven Zeppelins had been destroyed, often in spectacular wrecks, no one had been killed. Now with ships flying every day during the warm summer months, the Zeppelin's safety record remained intact and airship travel became an immensely popular, though somewhat expensive, adventure for both German and foreign vacationers alike.

In the summer of 1912 the *Viktoria Luise* was flying between Dusseldorf and Berlin. The four-hundred-mile journey took twelve hours, and in order to land before dark, she started from Dusseldorf at 4:30 in the morning. The early hour seemed to have little effect on business, however, for all flights were sold out a month in advance. An American magazine correspondent joined twenty-three other passengers at the Dusseldorf airfield for the flight to Berlin.

The World's Work

A Zeppelin airship leaves the earth with none of a balloon's soaring motion. It is just like a Pullman train, started without perceptible jar and kept in motion upon a perfect road bed, perfect track, and perfect wheels. We glided up into a southwest wind, and the low-hanging moon showed that we were speeding almost due northward.

After staring down into the fiery blast furnaces of Dusseldorf, they sailed out over the Westphalian countryside as the stars faded in the dawn and the mist fled before the rising sun. Rather than set a direct course for the capital, they headed north for Bremen and Hamburg. Over Hamburg, "The hum of thousands of voices came up to us and could be heard above the clatter of our own motors." As the ship turned southeast to follow the Elbe River toward Berlin, the stewards served lunch.

The World's Work

There was soup, an entree, a roast—all piping hot—vegetables, salad, cheese, and coffee. More of a dinner than a luncheon and all served as though the chef and waiters had the conveniences of a great hotel at their command. The principles of the fireless cooker had been brought into service in preparing the food, the exhaust from the engines being made to supply heat.

After luncheon several passengers dozed comfortably in their armchairs enjoying the sun that shone through the starboard windows. A better place for an afternoon nap than the cabin of a Zeppelin airship cannot be imagined. The drone of the motors becomes a lullaby. There is a sense of motion—swift motion—and yet not even the slightest jar. An almost imperceptible vibration is felt only when a hand is placed on a side wall of the cabin. . . .

Every moment of the voyage was filled with pleasure. We came to earth rested and refreshed, with none of that dusty, worn feeling that fastens upon a person during a railroad trip.[20]

LZ-11, the *Viktoria Luise,* first flew on February 14, 1912. At 486 feet in length with 670,900 cubic feet of gas, she was larger than *Schwaben* and the same size as *LZ-7* and *LZ-8,* the two *Deutschlands.* She was named in honor of Kaiser Wilhelm's only daughter. Here the ship is cruising over the Kiel Regatta. *Courtesy Northrop University.*

•

As the passengers dozed in the warm sunshine or sipped their wine and gazed out the open windows at the unfolding panorama just a few hundred feet below, they were reassured by an occasional glimpse of the ship's crew going efficiently about their business. Some of the serious young men in their crisp Delag uniforms were, in fact, army and navy officers for, by 1912, the Zeppelin organization had begun to train military airship crews.

The crash of *LZ-5* in 1910 left the army with only one Zeppelin, the old *LZ-3.* They ordered a replacement the following year and a third ship in 1912. By the beginning of the war in August 1914, the Army Airship Battalion was flying six Zeppelins plus several smaller Gross and Parseval dirigibles.

The German navy still had no Zeppelins and it took all of the count's powers of persuasion to convince Admiral Tirpitz of their value as long-range scouts with the fleet. The first order for a naval airship was finally placed in 1912. *LZ-14,* the navy's *L-1,* made her maiden flight on October 7, 1912. A week later with Count

Zeppelin in command she made a thirty-two-hour voyage to Johannisthal. A year later while flying over the North Sea toward the island of Heligoland on maneuvers with the German High Seas Fleet, the *L-1* was caught in a violent gale and hurled into the sea. An SOS was transmitted and torpedo boats sped through the storm to the rescue, but after being pounded by the sea for nearly an hour, the *L-1* sank, taking fifteen crewmen with her. The torpedo boats picked up seven survivors. It was the worst aerial disaster in history and the first loss of life aboard a Zeppelin.

A year later the navy's second Zeppelin exploded in midair, killing all twenty-eight aboard. This ship, the *L-2,* featured several innovations in Zeppelin design. The central gangway or keel was put inside the hull and the gondolas were raised up closer to the body of the ship to allow a larger hull to be built within the limited space of the construction shed. This six-foot increase in the diameter of the hull gave it an additional 150,000 cubic feet of hydrogen. With the gondolas up closer to the ship's body, it was possible for the navy to close off the front of the gondolas with windshields. But the windshields created a suction that drew the hydrogen valved from the rising airship down into the gondola where it was ignited by a spark from the engine.

The navy's first two Zeppelins were both lost in the two worst air disasters in history, yet the Zeppelin's military value was now apparent to the naval authorities, and they selected Fregattenkapitan Peter Strasser, an enthusiastic young officer, to replace the former chief of the Naval Airship Service who was killed aboard the *L-2.* Strasser, who had trained aboard the *Hansa,* immediately set to work creating what would become the world's largest airship organization.

The German army, meanwhile, was having much better luck with a larger number of ships. Their only serious difficulty occurred in March 1913, when an inexperienced Zeppelin Company pilot attempted to deliver a new army ship from Friedrichshafen to the Airship Battalion at Metz. The fog closed in covering the ground below and the pilot couldn't tell in which direction the wind was causing his

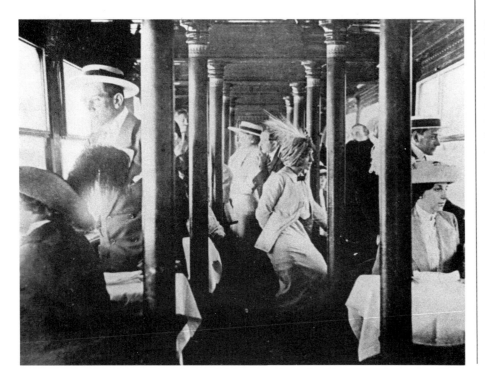

In the four years before the war, the ships of Delag, the world's first airline, flew over one hundred thousand miles carrying 37,750 passengers like these aboard the *Hansa.* They flew mainly on sightseeing excursions as passengers enjoyed an unobstructed view of the countryside a few hundred feet below. The great bulk of the ship's hull overhead kept both wind and rain from entering the open windows. *Photo by Gustav Eyb, courtesy Douglas Robinson.*

LZ-18, the German navy's *L-2,* was the largest Zeppelin yet built, 518 feet long with 953,000 cubic feet of gas and a useful lift of twelve tons. The ship's design featured several innovations. The covered walkway that connected the engine cars on earlier Zeppelins was moved up inside the hull. The engine cars had always been open to allow the slipstream to blow stray hydrogen away from the motors, but the navy felt that the open cars would be too cold on extended North Sea patrols. They enclosed the control car (at the left) with windscreens and also closed off the front of both engine cars. This led to the fatal fire and crash of the ship on October 17, 1913. *Friedrich Moch photo, courtesy Marine-Luft-schiffer-Kameradschaft, Hamburg.*

ship to drift. He continued to navigate by compass and landed when he spotted an airship base through a break in the clouds. It was, unfortunately, the French airship base at the fortress of Lunéville. The French public was just beginning fully to appreciate the awesome military potential of the Zeppelin and now to have one of the giant machines drop right into their midst caused a great sensation.

The Paris Correspondent of the *London Daily Mail*

The maneuver-ground swarmed with people. All Lunéville took a holiday. Every officer in the garrison was there, and many had brought their wives. The people did not say much, but looked at the Zeppelin and smiled. French sappers, holding down the airship, wore a broad grin. The peasants were massed behind and kept up a running fire of chaff.

The bantering note of the crowd turned to real enthusiasm when, at about 10:30, a little point showed in the sky and an aeroplane piloted by a French Army airman from Épinal glided to the ground, skimming low over the top of the Zeppelin. Another machine appeared, and then a third. They came down so close to the airship that their wings almost touched it. Then they flew above its length from stem to stern. Everybody was wild with delight.[21]

It was not delight that animated the Germans when the ship was finally allowed to return after being thoroughly examined by the French. The German press was

unanimous in calling for the Zeppelin commander's court-martial. According to the *Berlin Post,* "It was the unquestionable duty of the senior officer of Zeppelin IV to blow up the airship and all on board."[22]

At the outbreak of war in August 1914, the navy had one Zeppelin in service while the army had six. The three Delag ships were transferred to the army along with their crews, and the world's first airline went out of business. In four years of operation, while the airplane was still considered an interesting toy, Delag ships logged thirty-two hundred hours in the air on sixteen hundred flights covering one hundred thousand miles. They carried 37,750 passengers without a fatality.

Count Zeppelin was seventy-six years old when the war began and was in the process of planning an airship voyage to the North Pole. He and the kaiser's brother, Prince Henry of Prussia, had already sailed by steamer to Spitzbergen and located a base camp. They made several ascents in a captive balloon from Kings Bay and from the pack ice north of Spitzbergen. After spending a month in the Arctic, they determined that only three days out of thirty-three would have been unsuitable for Zeppelin flying.

The plans for a polar flight were cut short by the outbreak of war and, when the old count saw what he felt was a hesitancy on the part of the government in using his airships, he plunged back into the political arena. He was an early advocate of

Count Zeppelin in the Arctic. The outbreak of war interrupted Count Zeppelin's plans for an airship voyage to the North Pole. He and Prince Henry had visited Spitzbergen in June 1910, and made a number of balloon ascensions to test the amount of lift available in the cold weather. They found summer in the Arctic to be generally milder than winter in Germany. *Courtesy Northrop University.*

Above: Staaken R-bomber. In the last years of his life, with his airship organization on a firm footing, Count Zeppelin turned his attention to large airplanes. He contributed, through his Zeppelin Foundation, to the establishment of the Gotha and Dornier airplane companies. He also set up his own company at Staaken near Berlin to develop a series of big, multiengine, all-metal bombers. These planes made several raids on London late in World War I with a dozen or more Staaken and Gotha bombers flying in tight formation using their massed machine-gun fire to protect each other from fighters, just as the Flying Fortresses of World War II were to do over Germany a quarter of a century later. *Official U.S. Air Force photo.* Right: Count Ferdinand von Zeppelin (1838–1917). *Courtesy Northrop University.*

unrestricted aerial and submarine warfare as the quickest way of ending the conflict and he used all his influence to convince the government to become more aggressive in these areas.

With his airships finally accepted by both the army and the navy, he had turned his attention to the airplane. Through the Zeppelin Foundation he assisted both Claude Dornier and the designers of the Gotha bombers. In 1914 Count Zeppelin started a factory at Staaken near Berlin to build his own four- and five-engine bombers, the giant Staaken R-planes.

He was active to the very end when, following an operation, he developed pneumonia. Count Ferdinand von Zeppelin, diplomat, cavalry officer, and aircraft designer, died at Charlottenburg on March 8, 1917, at the age of seventy-nine after one of the most extraordinary careers in modern times.

Between the first flight of his first airship in 1900 and the start of World War I in 1914, Count Zeppelin launched twenty-five giant airships. This amazing level of activity tends to obscure the fact that a number of other aviation pioneers, influenced by the count's failures as well as his successes, were busily creating airships of their own. Some, like the French *Spiess* and the British *Mayfly*, were unsuccessful attempts to copy the Zeppelin. Others, like the German *Gross* and *Parseval* ships, were closer in concept to their French contemporaries and were, for several years, much preferred by the German army over the count's airships.

In 1906, the German general staff, alarmed by the success of the French *Lebaudy*, decided to build a similar semirigid. The job was given to the Balloon Battalion under the command of Captain Gross, who hired Nicholas Basenach, one of Krupp's naval engineers, as his chief designer. Unable to find enough information on the *Lebaudy*, they built a ship of their own featuring a suspended keel with control surfaces at the stern. Designated the *M-1*, she was launched on June 30, 1907, and became the first German army dirigible. Four were built, the last being completed just before the war. *Courtesy Northrop University.*

The *Parseval* airships were direct descendants of the kite balloons first developed by Maj. August von Parseval in 1892. He wanted a dirigible that could support the ground troops and, in case of bad weather, land in a clearing, be folded up, packed into boxes, and carried away on wagons. His first nonrigid was completed on May 26, 1906. Twenty-seven were eventually built. The smallest were 123-foot-long nonrigids that carried three people, while the largest was a 518-foot-long semirigid. They were good ships, and though most were used by the German army, they were also purchased by Austria, Russia, Italy, Japan, and England. *Courtesy Northrop University.*

The *Krell* airship was designed by Otto Krell and built by Siemens-Schuckert around 1912. She was a very large semirigid, 393 feet long with 476,739 cubic feet of gas. Four 125-horsepower Daimler engines gave her a top speed of forty-seven miles per hour. Krell hoped to create a ship as large as a Zeppelin but without the Zeppelin's rigid framework. The savings in weight would then be used for additional load and engine power. His ship proved to be heavier than expected with a disposable lift of only four and one-half tons, and no others were built. *Courtesy Carruthers Collection, Claremont Colleges.*

The *Spiess* airship was France's attempt to build a long-range rigid. She was designed by Joseph Spiess and built by the Zodiac Company at St. Cyr. Her control surfaces were similar to those of *Schwaben* but her framework was of wood. She was 370 feet long and 44.5 feet in diameter with 451,000 cubic feet of hydrogen. She was to be powered by two two-hundred-horsepower Chenu engines, but couldn't lift them both into the air and one was removed. She first flew on March 4, 1913. She was then lengthened by one hundred feet and given three more gasbags, which increased her capacity to 580,000 cubic feet. This enabled her to carry her second engine and reach a top speed of 43½ miles per hour. She made a flight over Paris on December 9, 1913, to great popular acclaim but never flew again and was dismantled at the start of the war.

A series of unique airships was developed in Italy by Enrico Forlanini beginning with this ship, the 132,150-cubic-foot, steam-powered *Leonardo da Vinci*, in 1909. What set Forlanini's ships apart from all others was his use of a series of hydrogen-filled gasbags enclosed within a larger, air-filled bag. The space between the inner gasbags and the outer bag was two inches wide and filled with air that could be pressurized to help maintain the hull's shape at high speeds. This also eliminated the need for air ballonets inside the hull. *Courtesy Stato Maggiore Aeronautica, Rome.*

Dr. Johann Schutte was a professor of naval architecture. With the backing of industrialist Karl Lanz, he established the Luftschiffbau Schutte-Lanz in April 1909. His first airship, the *SL-1,* shown here, was launched on October 17, 1911. She was 432 feet long with 734,500 cubic feet of gas. Two 240-horsepower Mercedes-Daimler engines gave her a top speed of 44½ miles per hour. She was the most advanced aircraft of her day with an internal keel, closed cars, engine-mounted propellers, and a streamlined hull with her control surfaces at the end of stabilizing fins. Her spiraling plywood girders, however, were too heavy and their diamond pattern created too much drag. Subsequent ships used horizontal girders. With the outbreak of war, all German airship patents were shared and the Zeppelin soon became as streamlined as her former competitor. Twenty-one Schutte-Lanz ships were built, all of wood. Strasser disliked them because their plywood girders absorbed moisture over the sea despite all efforts at waterproofing. *Courtesy Northrop University.*

In 1912 the French army ordered a series of large "Grand Cruisers." Each French airship manufacturer would build its own design, but each had to be of at least 700,000 cubic feet—larger than any ship the companies had built before but the equal of Germany's Zeppelins. Lebaudy's semirigid *Tissandier* was launched on October 12, 1914. She was 426 feet long with a volume of 741,500 cubic feet. But seven 120-horsepower Salmson engines could drive her at only thirty-seven miles per hour, and the army rejected her. The photo shows Astra-Torres's *Pilatre de Rozier* launched in January 1915. Her 812,130 cubic foot, nonrigid, trilobe hull was too long to maintain structural integrity and she was later cut in half to make two smaller ships. The Zodiac Company's *D'Arlandes* had the same problem and was also cut in half. Clement-Bayard's nonrigid *General Meusnier* suffered similarly and was sold to Russia but crashed before delivery. *Courtesy Northrop University.*

In 1909 the British Admiralty placed an order with the shipbuilding firm of Vickers, Sons and Maxim for a large Zeppelin-type rigid airship. Designated *Naval Airship No. 1,* she was more generally known as the *Mayfly.* Working to an Admiralty design with only limited information from Germany, Vickers drew upon their submarine building experience, completing the ship in two years at a cost of $205,000. She was 512 feet long with 663,518 cubic feet of hydrogen, powered by two 160-horsepower engines in cars made of Honduras mahogany. She was towed out of her floating construction shed on May 22, 1911, but was too heavy to rise from the surface of the water. She was towed back into the hangar and her external keel and passenger cabin were removed. Three tons lighter, she was being pulled out again on September 24, 1911, when she broke in half. This ended rigid airship development in England for some time. *From* Popular Mechanics, *December 1911.*

4
· T H E ·
AIRSHIP
AT WAR

The authorities on warfare of nearly every great power contend that the destructive power of a fleet of airships in future wars cannot be overestimated. Every country now realizes the potency of this new war weapon, and many of them are systematically preparing to launch into the air a formidable fleet of such craft should trouble arise.

There is much talk at the present time of an unavoidable war between England and Germany within the next few years, and Germany, at least, is consistently organizing a fleet of airships. England's seeming lack of initiative in this new means of warfare has been scored within the last couple of months by such English war experts as Lord Roberts, one of the greatest of that country's generals, and Sir Hiram Maxim, the great inventor. The German Emperor, his army, and his people, have become madly enthusiastic over Count Zeppelin's dirigible airship. The army is proceeding in a businesslike way to perfect its present types of airships and to increase their number. The German is a stolid race, not given to sudden and unwarranted enthusiasms, a fact that leads more than one authority to assert that Germany is confident that aerial war machines will offset the great advantage England has always held in her immense fleet of warships.

Popular Mechanics, December 1909

The military potential of airplanes and airships, so clear to newspaper and magazine writers, was lost on the generals who unexpectedly found themselves fighting a war in the summer of 1914. Even the German army's apparent interest in airships was more the result of Count Zeppelin's persistence, backed by an enthusiastic public opinion, rather than any dedication to aeronautics on the part of the general staff.

Germany's generals were, like their French counterparts, prepared to fight this war just as they fought the previous one, the Franco-Prussian War of 1870. That struggle, more than forty years earlier, had influenced all the military planning that followed. France was determined to recover Alsace and the part of Lorraine lost to Germany. The Germans were equally determined to make

OPPOSITE: By 1916, four factories in Germany were working day and night to build Zeppelins and were launching a new airship every two weeks. This photo was taken inside the hull of the army Zeppelin *LZ-113* before the gas cells were installed, looking forward toward the bow. The man in the foreground is inside the triangular keel standing on the narrow walkway. The next man is sitting on top of the keel. *Georg Blasweiler photo, courtesy Douglas Robinson.*

Soldiers scramble for safety as a U.S. Army kite balloon explodes at Fort Sill, Oklahoma. A spark ignited the balloon's hydrogen as it was being deflated. The inflammability of its hydrogen would prove to be the critical factor in determining the airship's success in World War I. *Courtesy U.S. Army.*

themselves the masters of Europe for good this time. They planned a sweep through Belgium that would carry them to Paris and victory. They would be in Paris in thirty-nine days, then they would turn and crush the Russians before England had a chance to interfere. The whole thing would be over in less than four months.

The Belgians were depending on their impregnable fortresses at Namur and Liège. The French marched into battle wearing bright red trousers while the British Expeditionary Force that sailed across the Channel to their aid included thirty thousand horses and only 125 machine guns. It was to be mounted horsemen against concrete battlements and everyone would be home by Christmas, just as if the Wright brothers and Count Zeppelin had never lived and the world had stood still for forty years.

Neither the airship nor the airplane was included in the battle plans but both were quickly pressed into service as observers—mobile versions of the observation balloon. The first airship to attempt a scouting mission over the Belgian frontier was shot down by French troops. It was, unfortunately, a French airship. Later that same day, a German Zeppelin ventured over the lines and soldiers from both sides joined in shooting it down.

For thirty-five days the German advance across Belgium and into France continued unchecked. The French and British armies reeled before them and the gates of Paris lay twenty miles ahead. Then they reached the banks of the river Marne. The French stood and fought and held. The German advance ended at the Battle of the Marne, and with it ended the dream of a short war. On the banks of that quiet river, now red with blood, began the most savage war man had yet attempted.

As the autumn of 1914 slowly turned to winter and the hopes of victory slipped away, all Europe waited nervously for the Zeppelin raids that they knew were sure to come. Tourists from every part of the Continent had flown in Delag's passenger ships while on summer holiday and had marveled at the power and efficiency of the huge machines as they sailed smoothly over the countryside. Now that war had come, the awful potential of the Zeppelin was all too clear. They watched the skies and waited. Newspaper reports of the largely ineffective airship raids on the forts at Antwerp and Liège only served to heighten the tension. Rumors of sinister shapes lurking in the mountain passes and gliding silently along the fog-shrouded coastline raced through the British population. London began to darken her streetlights and the army dispatched a plane to search the Cumberland hills where a Zeppelin was said to be hiding. Nothing was found and the airships did not come. Where were the Zepps?

The British public would have been even more nervous if they had known of the problem facing their government. The army's Royal Flying Corps had been given the responsibility for the aerial defense of Great Britain. But the army had gone to France and taken all its airplanes with it. In the words of Winston Churchill, the first lord of the Admiralty, "not a single squadron or even an effective machine remained to guard British vulnerable points from German aerial attack."[1]

On September 3, 1914, with many people expecting squadrons of Zeppelins to appear in the skies overhead at any moment, Lord Kitchener, the war secretary,

The flimsy prewar airplanes were of little military value except in their ability to frighten the cavalry's horses. The airship, on the other hand, had already carried thousands of passengers. With the outbreak of war, the world held its breath. Where were the Zepps? But the generals on both sides had no interest in aircraft of any kind and no intention of using them.

asked Churchill if the navy would be willing to take over the aerial defense of the British Isles.

Winston Churchill

I thereupon undertook to do what was possible with the wholly inadequate resources which were available. There were neither anti-aircraft guns nor searchlights, and though a few improvisations had been made, nearly a year must elapse before the efficient supplies necessary could be forthcoming. Meanwhile at any moment half a dozen Zeppelins might arrive to bomb London, or, what was more serious, Chatham, Woolwich or Portsmouth.

I rated the Zeppelin much lower as a weapon of war than almost anyone else. I believed that this enormous bladder of combustible and explosive gas would prove to be easily destructible. I was sure the fighting aeroplane, rising lightly laden from its own base, armed with incendiary bullets, would harry, rout and burn these gaseous monsters.[2]

Churchill's faith in airplanes and incendiary ammunition would eventually prove well-founded. The problem was that few planes and no incendiaries were to be found in England at that time. The Royal Navy began the war with forty airplanes, but only two of them had guns.

On the other hand, the first military Zeppelins built after the start of the war were capable of carrying three tons of bombs at altitudes of nearly ten thousand feet. This was well beyond the range of any gun or plane then in existence. The airplanes in use at the start of the war such as the Farman Shorthorn and the Sopwith Tabloid had a ceiling of around thirty-five hundred feet, more than a mile below the airships. With neither gun nor plane capable of an effective defense, the whole of the British Isles lay open to Zeppelin attack. But the Zeppelins did not come.

With few materials at hand with which to organize a defense, Churchill went on the offense. Less than three weeks after taking over the responsibility for the protection of England, his Royal Navy pilots flying out of Antwerp attacked the Zeppelin bases at Dusseldorf and Cologne. Only one plane managed to find its objective and drop a bomb, which missed the target but did succeed in blowing out every window in the huge Dusseldorf hangar.

The next raid two weeks later on October 8, 1914, was more successful, and the new *LZ-25* was destroyed in her shed at Dusseldorf. The fall of Antwerp to the advancing Germans left the British without an airfield within striking distance of the Zeppelin hangars. That made the next raid somewhat more complicated.

Four new Avro-504 bombers were packed in crates and shipped by boat from England to France where they were carried across country by train to the frontier fortress of Belfort. There they were uncrated and assembled in a French dirigible hangar. By November 14 the planes were ready to go, but bad weather prevented their takeoff. A week later, on November 21, 1914, three of the four planes managed to get into the air and set their course for the Zeppelin Company factory at Friedrichshafen, 120 miles to the east along the German-Swiss border. Each plane carried four twenty-pound bombs. One was shot down but the other two attacked the factory and returned safely to Belfort. There they were dismantled, recrated, and shipped back to England.

In the confusion over the target, the pilots had been unable to determine the effect of their bombs, and it wasn't until several days later that they read an account

of the raid in a Swiss newspaper. It was written by a Swiss engineer working in Friedrichshafen who watched it from his hotel window. He said that the Germans had been taken completely by surprise and a gasworks plus a nearly completed Zeppelin were destroyed. In addition, the Swiss government complained that a Swiss citizen was killed in the bombing. Churchill's reply was short and to the point: "No bomb was dropped on Swiss territory: and if a Swiss was killed in the Zeppelin factory, it serves him right."[3]

The raid on Friedrichshafen was the last to be attempted in the early part of the war. The German advance had captured all the airfields within striking distance of the airship bases, and from those farther away, the weight of gasoline required to reach the targets left little room for bombs. The Zeppelins, on the other hand, had more than enough range to carry a large bomb load to England and return. With little in the way of antiaircraft guns or searchlights to hinder them over their targets, what was holding them back? Where were the Zepps?

Though Great Britain built several small military airships, the war found her with only two dirigibles capable of a military patrol—and neither was built in Britain. One was a German *Parseval* while the other, *Naval Airship No. 3*, was this 230,000 cubic foot French *Astra-Torres* with that company's distinctive trilobe hull. Both ships escorted the British Expeditionary Force across the Channel to France. The *Astra-Torres* remained in service until May 1916, while the *Parseval* served until July 1917. *Courtesy Imperial War Museum, London.*

With only a handful of antiaircraft guns on either side, the men at the front had to improvise, as these German soldiers have done. By digging out around the base of their field cannon, they were able to depress the carriage far enough for high angle and antiaircraft fire. At the start of the war, Germany had a grand total of eighteen antiaircraft guns while England had thirty-three. *From* The Scientific American Supplement, *January 8, 1916.*

•

That question was also being asked in Germany. As German hopes of a quick victory faded, the effects of the British naval blockade of their ports became more noticeable. "Why should the English sit smug and safe on their island while German babies starve?" the press demanded. "Our Zeppelins can carry this war to England. Why do we not use them?" The generals agreed. Only Kaiser Wilhelm hesitated. How could he, the eldest grandson of Queen Victoria, send his Zeppelins against the land ruled by his own royal cousin, King George V?

Killing his cousin's soldiers on the battlefield was a time-honored tradition. Bombing undefended cities was quite another matter. Did the rules of chivalry in warfare still apply? The kaiser's generals argued that with their advance stalled in the west and their coastline blockaded, the rules and restrictions of the past were luxuries they could no longer afford.

In the end, Kaiser Wilhelm unleashed his airships. The distinction between soldier and civilian was about to be laid to rest forever.

On the night of January 19, 1915, the naval Zeppelins *L-3* and *L-4* attacked Yarmouth and King's Lynn on England's Norfolk coast killing four people and injuring sixteen. "Blind, barbarian vengeance," raged the *London Star.* To the *Times* is was "the ruthless and inhuman destruction of the weak and helpless . . . we are confronted with a recrudescence of brutality such as the world has not witnessed for a thousand years." The *Daily Telegraph* branded the airshipmen "common murderers."[4]

With these press notices, strategic bombing was welcomed to the arsenal of modern warfare.

Two months later, just after midnight on March 21, 1915, Parisians were awakened by the crash of falling bombs and the roar of artillery. When it was all over they found that forty bombs had fallen in the city but no one had been killed and only a few were injured. The general feeling next morning was of great relief. The long-awaited raid had finally taken place and it had not been nearly as bad as everyone had feared. The morning papers, in fact, were disappointed that none of the Zeppelins were shot down.

It wasn't until the spring of 1915, nearly a year after the start of the war, that the kaiser allowed his airships to attack the city of London. Even then, he absolutely forbade any bombing of Buckingham Palace, St. Paul's Cathedral, Westminster Abbey, and any museum or government building.

The concept of strategic bombing was brand new. So, too, were the problems of defense against it. Not one of the Allied powers had an airship to match the performance of Germany's Zeppelins. At the start of the war, none of the Allies even had an artillery piece that could be elevated high enough to shoot at an overhead target, and some of the first air-raid casualties were the result of shells falling back to the ground and exploding in the city that fired them.

The defense against the marauding airships was thus left largely to the airplane. But here, too, there were serious problems. The airships preferred to attack at night when the moon was down and their huge forms would be invisible against the black sky with only the blinking out of the stars would mark their passage. Flying an airplane in the daytime was risky enough; few pilots had ever dared leave the ground at night. Now they were ordered not only to fly at night but to fight an experienced enemy as well.

By the end of 1915 most of the defense flyers in Britain were equipped with

B.E.2c biplanes. With an extra gas tank and powered by a ninety-horsepower RAF engine, these planes were capable of a top speed of ninety miles per hour and a ceiling of thirteen thousand feet, although it took them nearly an hour to climb that high.

Their dirt landing fields were illuminated only by drums of burning gasoline, and many a pilot returning from an unsuccessful intercept consumed his slender fuel reserves in a fruitless search for his home base. The first eighty missions flown by British pilots against the attacking Zeppelins resulted in eight crash landings and three dead pilots. No airships were sighted. As late as January 1916, of the fifteen defense planes sent aloft over London one evening, eleven crashed on landing and three more pilots died.

While the defense forces were struggling to develop efficient equipment and techniques, the airshipmen were having problems of their own. The weather over Germany comes from the west. Unfortunately, England is also in the west and information on the kind of weather that was sweeping across the British Isles toward the Continent suddenly became a well-kept military secret. This lack of reliable weather forecasts was to plague German airship operations all through the war. While on a reconnaissance mission over the North Sea, two German naval Zeppelins, *L-3* and *L-4,* were caught in a violent storm and driven onto the Danish coast as one after another of their engines failed. Both ships and four crewmen were lost.

L-47 and *L-46* in a double hangar. Fourteen German airship bases were eventually completed along the Baltic and North Sea coasts with an additional base at Yamboli in Bulgaria. By 1915, work had begun on more than a dozen immense double hangars, each 790 feet long and 197 feet wide, capable of housing two airships larger than any yet built. The *L-47* and *L-46* are in one of the new hangars, Shed III at Alhorn, in the summer of 1917. The hoses on the floor are connected to the nearby hydrogen plant. *Friedrich Moch photo, courtesy Marine-Luftschiffer-Kameradschaft, Hamburg.*

•

The sight of enemy airships hovering unmolested overhead as they slowly and methodically dropped their bombs on English cities was infuriating to the people below. Some said the Zeppelins were so low they could see the faces of the German airshipmen looking down at them. Rioting broke out in the city of Hull after the first airship raid and troops had to be called out to restore order as the citizens demonstrated against their government's inability to protect them from the raiders. *Courtesy Carruthers Collection, Claremont Colleges.*

•

L-10 burst into flames and fell into the sea within sight of its base after being overtaken by a thunderstorm and struck by lightning while valving gas. All nineteen men aboard were killed.

The inflammable hydrogen that lifted them into the air was the airship's greatest weakness and the greatest danger to its crew. Helium, a nonflammable gas only slightly heavier than hydrogen, was found in commercial quantities only in the United States and was not available to Germany.

Besides the danger of instant incineration, this dependence on hydrogen as their lifting gas created all sorts of extra problems for the airshipmen. The Zeppelin carried a machine-gun platform on the top of the ship's hull, but the gunner was able to shoot at enemy planes only when the ship was not releasing gas. Otherwise, the flash from his gun would ignite the escaping hydrogen and set his own ship afire.

When gas was not being released through the valves on the gas cells, however, the ships seemed to be remarkably fireproof. On a raid over the English city of Hull during a thunderstorm, the gunner on top of the hull reported:

A lightning bolt struck the nose of the ship, thirty feet from my post. It almost knocked me down just as I was going to report that there were electrical discharges around me.

Tongues of fire were licking around the muzzles of my machine-guns, and around my head, too. And when I spread my hand, little flames spurt out of my fingertips.[5]

The flamelike electrical discharges are known as St. Elmo's fire. An inspection of the airship showed that the lightning bolt had burned some tiny holes in the canvas cover and melted a spot on an aluminum girder. If there had been any hydrogen outside the gas cells when the lightning hit, the gunner would never have lived to file his report.

In addition to the inflammability of their ships and a lack of reliable weather information, the airship commanders also had considerable difficulty in finding their targets. At a time when night flying was considered a dangerous adventure, they flew their bombing missions only at night when the moon was down. As they hung suspended in the darkness searching the hostile and unfamiliar countryside far below for some sign that would guide them to the objective, they were strictly on their own—no one had ever been there before. More often than not, cloud cover, shifting winds, and the lack of any sort of aerial maps combined to put them far off their course.

What was it like to fly in an airship on a raid against London? In an interview with Karl von Wiegand published in a September 1915 issue of the *New York World,* Kptlt. Heinrich Mathy described a mission:

As the sun sank in the west, we were still a considerable distance out over the North Sea. Below us it was rapidly getting dark, but it was still light up where we were. Off to one side another Zeppelin, in gray war-paint like that of my craft, was visible in the waning light against the clear sky, gliding majestically through the air. A low, mist-like fog hung over the spot in the distance where England was. The stars came out. It grew colder. We took another pull at our thermos bottles and ate something.[6]

A rare picture, the only known photograph actually taken on a raid as a fleet of Zeppelins heads for England on August 9, 1915. The photograph was made by Hans von Schiller aboard *L-11* and shows *L-13* in the middle distance with *L-12* and *L-10* behind her. *Luftschiffbau Zeppelin photo, courtesy Douglas Robinson.*

At a cruising speed of fifty miles per hour, the cold night air whistles through the open windows of the control car. Even the crew's fur-lined flying suits cannot keep them warm. As they approach the English coastline, their running lights are extinguished and only the lights in the compass and engine telegraph glow in the darkness. The roar of the engines is muffled and remote for they are amidships, 150 feet behind the control car.

Kptlt. Heinrich Mathy

Luck was with us. It is a cold, clear, starlit night, with no moon—one of those nights when the distances of objects, in looking toward the sky, are illusive and it is difficult to get the range on a rapidly moving object, altho our instruments tell us exactly how high we are.

The mist has disappeared. Off in the distance we can see the Thames River, which points the way to London. It is an indestructible guide-post and a sure road to the great city. The English can darken London as much as they want; they can never eradicate or cover up the Thames. It is our great orientation-point from which we can always get our bearings and pick up any point in London we desire.

That doesn't mean that we always come up along the Thames, by any means. London is darkened, but sufficiently lighted on this night so that I can see the reflected glow on the sky sixty kilometers away shortly before ten o'clock.

A sudden flash—a narrow band of brilliant light reaches out from below and begins to feel around the sky—a second—third—fourth—fifth—soon more than a score of crisscrossing ribbons ascend.

From the Zeppelin it looks as if the city had suddenly come to life and was waving its arms around the sky, sending out feelers for the danger that threatens, but our impression is more that they are tentacles seeking to drag us to destruction.

Now from below comes an ominous sound that penetrates the noise of the motors and propellers. There are little red flashes and short bursts of fire which stand out prominently against the black background. From the north, from the south, from the right, from the left they appear, and following the flashes rolls up from below the sound of guns.

It is a beautiful and impressive but fleeting picture as seen from above, probably no less interesting from below—the grayish, dim outline of the Zeppelins gliding through the wavering ribbons of light and the shrapnel cloudlets which hang thick.[7]

Kapitanleutnant Mathy had an advantage over most of the other airship commanders. He had visited London before the war and knew exactly where he was as he cruised high above the city. Using St. Paul's Cathedral as a point of reference, he laid a path of destruction from Queen's Square to the Liverpool railway station that left twenty-two people dead and nearly three million dollars in damage. It was the single most destructive raid of the entire war. Mathy became an overnight hero in Germany and among the large communities of German sympathizers in America.

Another airshipman often over England was Oberleutnant Lampel in the army's *LZ-97*.

Oberleutnant Lampel

At high speed we steer for the city, the Commander standing ready on the bombing platform. The electric lamps which he has now switched on glow with a dull, vari-colored light. His hand is on the buttons and levers. "Let go!" he cries. The first bomb has fallen on London! We lean over the side. What a cursed long time it takes between release and

ABOVE: In the control car of army Zeppelin *LZ-38* over England, Hauptmann Erich Linnarz, with the speaking tube to the bomb room in his hand, waits for a course change from his executive officer (left). The engine telegraphs are by Linnarz's head, the rudder man is at the front of the car with the bomb sight to his right, while the elevator man is on the left facing the altimeter with the ballast and gas valve chains above his head. A mechanic climbs down the ladder from the hull overhead. *Painting by Felix Schwormstadt, courtesy Douglas Robinson.* BELOW: Looking forward in the rear engine car of the army Zeppelin *LZ-38* on a bombing raid over England. The mechanics tend their thundering 210-horsepower Maybach while the machine-gunners watch for planes. The engine telegraph is hung from the roof of the car and the radiator can be seen outside above the drive shaft of the starboard propeller. *Painting by Felix Schwormstadt, courtesy Douglas Robinson.*

•

impact while the bomb travels those thousands of feet! We fear that it has proved a dud—until the explosion reassures us. Already we have frightened them; away goes the second, an incendiary bomb. It blazes up underneath and sets fire to something, thereby giving us a point by which to calculate our drift and ground speed. While one of us releases the bombs and another observes results, I make rapid calculations at the navigation table. Now the second incendiary hit is also visible. The flames have scarcely leapt convulsively upward in a shower of red sparks before we hear the shattering report of an explosion, so loud that it is plainly audible above the roar of the propellers. At the same time on come the searchlights, reaching after us like gigantic spiders' legs; right, left and all around. In a moment the bright body of the ship lies in the beams.

"Hard a-port!" The steersman spins his wheel, and in a moment the great ship obeys its helm. We are out of the dazzling rays and once more in the depths of night. But it is no longer pitch dark. The countless beams of searchlights fill the sky with a vivid

Lt. Reginald Warneford's tiny Morane-Saulnier Parasol was a two-seater monoplane developed from a French racing plane first flown in 1912. It was twenty-one feet long, built of wood and linen, with a thirty-four-foot wingspan. An eighty-horsepower, nine-cylinder LeRhone engine gave it a top speed of seventy-six miles per hour. The only armament was six twenty-pound bombs hung beneath the fuselage. The plane's rate of climb was 190 feet per minute, but a Zeppelin could drop ballast and climb at one thousand feet per minute. *Courtesy Imperial War Museum, London.*

light. They have lost us—strike, as it were, wildly past us, catch us once again, go on over us; one remains still, the others hunt around, crossing it or searching along it for the objective, while we steer in quite a different direction.

This mad frolic continues for hours on end. We lose all idea of the passage of time as we fly on, every half a minute releasing another bomb. Every explosion is observed and its position pin-pricked on the map. It is difficult to understand how we manage to survive the storm of shell and shrapnel, for, according to the chronometer, we have spent a good hour under that furious fire. When London lies far behind us, we can still recognize it distinctly; the searchlights are still stabbing the darkness—more than sixty of them—looking for the bird that has already flown. Silence closes in around us, and everything beneath seems stricken with death.[8]

Though the raiding airships were careful to fly well out of reach of the defending airplanes over England, some of the army ships were stationed at bases in Belgium, and there the Royal Naval Air Service hoped to intercept them with a squadron of planes flying out of Dunkirk. It was just past midnight on the morning of June 7, 1915, when Flight Sub-Lt. Reginald A. J. Warneford, flying alone on a patrol just off the coast of Belgium, sighted the unmistakable outline of a Zeppelin in the distance. It was the army's *LZ-37* commanded by Oberleutnant von der Hagen heading back to her hangar at Brussels.

Warneford wheeled his tiny Morane-Saulnier Parasol around and gave chase, but each time he tried to close with the big ship, he came under heavy fire from the machine guns in the gondolas. Warneford had no gun with which to return the fire. After following the airship for more than an hour, he saw it start to nose down toward a break in the cloud cover over Ghent. Warneford moved in above the fleeing ship and dropped one of his twenty-pound bombs. Nothing happened. "I might as well have missed the Mauretania," he said later. He dropped a second bomb and then a third. Suddenly a tremendous explosion shook the sky and tossed his little monoplane high into the air upside down. After regaining control of his plane he looked around for the airship. "I then saw that the Zeppelin was on the ground in flames and also that there were pieces of something burning in the air all the way down."[9]

One man survived the crash of the *LZ-37*. He was the chief helmsman.

Steurmann Alfred Muhler

I was at my elevator rudder, when the observer on the upper platform reported through the speaking-tube: "Airplane two thousand feet aft, above the ship!" We all knew what that meant; the enemy flier was already in the most suitable position for an attack, for we could not repulse him from the control car. Without waiting for the command to do so, the observer on the back of the airship sent a burst of machine-gun fire at the attacking flier. But already I felt a hit. The ship quivered, and my helm turned loosely in the air. It found no resistance—a sign that our steering mechanism had become useless. The control car swayed back and forth as if drunk, and I fell. While I was still trying to get to my feet, the entire crew either jumped or were thrown overboard; at any rate, I never saw them again. The whole immense hull above me was ablaze, instantly becoming a roaring, hissing inferno. Instinctively, I threw myself flat on the floor of the car and clawed the rails, desperately trying to avoid the merciless fire roasting down upon me. I wondered how long it took to fall 5000 feet. I knew this was the end, but I actually welcomed it as preferable to the slow torture of incineration. At last the gondola struck, and everything went black. I regained consciousness in the hospital.[10]

Flight-Lt. Reginald Alexander John Warneford (1892–1915) of the Royal Naval Air Service was twenty-three years old when he shot down the first Zeppelin of the war over Ghent in Belgium. He spent a week in Paris as a national hero and was killed in an airplane accident on his way back to the front. *Courtesy Imperial War Museum, London.*

He had fallen with the flaming ship from five thousand feet, crashed through the roof of a Belgian convent, landed in a bed, and, with only minor injuries, went back to fly again in Zeppelins.

Warneford was forced by a broken fuel pump to land in a field behind German lines where he calmly repaired the line and flew back to Dunkirk. He received Britain's highest decoration, the Victoria Cross, plus France's Cross of the Legion of Honor. After a wild reception in Paris where he was acclaimed a national hero, Warneford picked up a brand-new Henri Farman biplane to deliver to his unit at Dunkirk. Rising to seven hundred feet over the airfield he made a sharp right turn and the Farman's tail snapped off. Warneford was thrown from the plane and killed. He was twenty-three years old.

It may seem strange that Warneford had no machine gun aboard his plane, but at that time the Allies believed the only way to bring down a Zeppelin was by dropping a bomb on top of her. This opinion was due in large part to a clever bit of counterespionage by the Germans. They allowed British agents to "discover" that the hydrogen in their airships was enclosed in a protective envelope of inert gas that would mix with the hydrogen and prevent it from catching fire if an incendiary bullet should pass through it. Though the story was completely false, it delayed the development of incendiary ammunition by the Allies for nearly a year.

But even then, it was not as easy to bring down one of these huge flying firetraps as it might at first appear. One incendiary bullet was not usually enough to do the trick. Pure hydrogen will actually extinguish a flame. It will burn only after it has been mixed with air. The pilot who raked the side of an airship with incendiary fire was liable to cause nothing more serious than a slow leakage of gas from dozens of tiny bullet holes and these were quickly patched in flight by the sailmaker aboard the airship. Only by concentrating a long burst of incendiary machine-gun fire at a single point on the airship's hull could a pilot hope to tear a large enough hole in a gas cell to cause the fatal mixture of air and hydrogen that could then be ignited. And the tiniest flame, once started, sealed the doom of the giant ship and the twenty men who flew her.

As the war entered its third bloody year, the loss of life among airshipmen was still remarkably low. Although twenty-two Zeppelins had been lost, only four crews

The weather and the enemy each took their toll of Zeppelins in roughly equal proportions, and many ships, like the *L-22*, suffered from both.

•

On August 9, 1915, after bombing Dover, Oberlt. Werner Peterson's *L-12* was hit by a single antiaircraft shell that tore open gas cells three and four. As he began to lose altitude, Peterson headed for German-occupied Belgium while his crew jettisoned everything loose. The *L-12* came down in the Channel and was towed to Ostend by a torpedo boat. Half a dozen Royal Navy planes tried to bomb her but they all missed the big target. Shortly after this photo was taken, however, during salvage work, the ship accidentally caught fire and was destroyed. *Friedrich Moch photo, courtesy Marine-Luftschiffer-Kameradschaft, Hamburg.*

•

had gone down with their ships. In spite of the hundreds of reconnaissance and bombing missions that had been flown, less than one hundred men had been killed.

For two full years Zeppelins had ruled the skies. On the eastern front they bombed Warsaw, Salonika, and Bucharest and attacked the rail lines being used by the Russian armies fleeing before Field Marshall von Hindenburg. In the west, the Zeppelins scouted for the High Seas Fleet in the North Sea and cruised over England and France dropping their bombs almost at will.

But the course of the war in the air was due to change. The defense was catching up and the days of the Zeppelin's aerial superiority were rapidly drawing to a close. The first hint of a new element introduced into the air war came at the end of February 1916, when the army airship *LZ-77* was shot down in flames while bombing the railroad junction at Revigny, France. Other ships hit by antiaircraft fire had simply leaked gas and some, with enough hits, had been forced to crash-land. But the *LZ-77* had apparently been hit and burst into flame. The Germans wondered why.

Ernst Lehmann, commanding *LZ-90,* was sent to replace the *LZ-77* on the western front. A week later with seven thousand pounds of bombs aboard, he was heading toward the rail yards at Bar-le-Duc.

Ernst Lehmann

By throttling our motors and concealing ourselves in the clouds, we crossed the front at an altitude of 10,000 feet. I do not know whether we were detected or not, but, at any rate, Bar-le-Duc was not warned and at first greeted us only with a few ordinary shells.

Top: On May 3, 1916, raid on England, Kapitanlt. Franz Stabbert's *L-20* was blown by gale winds across the North Sea to Norway, where she crash-landed in a fjord. Stabbert was repatriated to Germany, where he took command of *L-44* and was lost with all aboard when hit by antiaircraft fire over France on October 20, 1917. *Official U.S. Air Force photo.* ABOVE: Caught by the wind, the *L-22* smashed her bow against the door of the Tondern hangar on April 7, 1916. The triangular patch in the center of the photo is the machine-gunner's post on top of the hull. The ship was repaired, and, a year later on May 14, 1917, she was shot down in flames with all hands by a British flying boat piloted by Lt. Robert Leckie. The *L-22* was the first of several Zeppelins shot down by long-range flying boats introduced in the last year of the war. *Friedrich Moch photo, courtesy Douglas Robinson.*

Though the railway station was an important one, it was small, and since it was well darkened, we had difficulty in finding it. No sooner had the first load of bombs been released, than we were obliged to stop because the LZ-90 had overflown its mark. We circled around and were just making a second attack on the station, which by now was marked by fire, and smoke, when we saw a number of thick yellow rockets coming toward us. They moved fairly slowly, but rose steadily, climbing past our ship, which was then at an altitude of 10,000 feet, and then continuing on still higher!

I ordered full speed ahead, brought the ship to its greatest possible altitude and fled in haste.[11]

Now they knew what had happened to the *LZ-77*. The myth of the fireproof Zeppelin had finally been laid to rest. With the introduction of incendiary ammunition, the hydrogen-filled airships were in serious trouble.

Multiship raids against England had become the rule by the summer of 1916. At two o'clock on the afternoon of September 2, twelve navy and four army airships rose from their bases in northern Germany and set course for London. It was the largest attack fleet of the war. They cruised over the North Sea and arrived off the English coast at nightfall. By midnight they had reached the darkened capital and were preparing to make their bombing runs.

Ernst Lehmann in command of a new ship, the *LZ-98*, was one of the raiders.

Ernst Lehmann

The whole endless sea of houses lay under a silvery fog in which rose up the incessant flashes of explosions and blazing fires. We saw these explosions, but we could no longer see the agents causing them; one by one they had disappeared in the mist. The conical rays of the searchlights passed through each other like bodiless ghosts, and thousands of bursting shells illuminated London like a display of fireworks.[12]

Sir Philip Gibbs, a war correspondent just home from the trench warfare at the western front, was relaxing in his living room when his wife looked up suddenly. "Zeppelins," she said.

Sir Philip Gibbs

[W]e went up to the roof. Fourteen Zeppelins were over London. We could hear very distinctly the throb of their engines. The long white fingers of our searchlights were feeling about the sky, and now and again we could see the silvery gleam of one of these airships. London was quiet and utterly black below us, but there must have been millions of people out-of-doors watching anxiously or fascinated with intense interest.[13]

The airshipmen were not alone in the blazing skies high above the city. Lt. William Leefe Robinson of the Royal Flying Corps was also up there in his B.E.2c biplane.

Lt. William Leefe Robinson

I saw nothing until about 1:10 A.M. when two searchlights picked out a Zeppelin about southwest of Woolwich. The clouds had collected in this quarter and the searchlights had some difficulty in keeping up with the aircraft. By this time I had managed to climb to 12,900 feet and I made in the direction of the Zeppelin which was being fired on by a few anti-aircraft guns, hoping to cut it off on its way eastwards. I very slowly gained on it for about ten minutes—I judged it to be about 200 feet below me and I sacrificed my speed in order to keep my height. It went behind some clouds, avoided the searchlights and I lost sight of it. After about fifteen minutes of fruitless search I returned to my patrol.[14]

The Zeppelin that disappeared into the clouds was probably Lehmann's *LZ-98*, although he was completely unaware of his narrow escape.

Lt. William Leefe Robinson

At about 1:50 A.M. I noticed a red glow in the northeast of London. Taking it to be an outbreak of fire I went in that direction. At about 2:05 A.M. a Zeppelin was picked up over N.N.E. London (as far as I could judge). Remembering my last failure, I sacrificed height (I was still at 12,100 feet) for speed and made nose-down for the Zeppelin. I saw shells bursting and night-tracer shells flying around it. When I drew closer I noticed that the anti-aircraft fire was too high or too low, also a good many rose 800 feet behind—a few tracers went right over. I could hear the bursts when about 3,000 feet from the Zeppelin.

I flew to about 800 feet below it from bow to stern and distributed one drum along it (alternate new Brock and Pomeroy). It seemed to have no effect.[15]

Brock shells exploded, Pomeroy burned. Each drum for Robinson's Lewis gun held forty-seven bullets. The days of darts, grapnels, and air-to-air bombs were over. Killing was becoming efficient.

Lt. William Leefe Robinson

I therefore moved to one side and gave it another drum along its side—without much apparent effect. I then got behind it, by this time I was very close—500 feet or less below—and concentrated one drum on one part underneath. I was then at a height of 11,500 feet when attacking the Zeppelin. I had hardly finished the drum when I saw the part fired at glow. In a few seconds the whole rear part was blazing. When the third drum was fired there were no searchlights on the Zeppelin and no A.A. was firing. I quickly got out of the way of the falling Zeppelin and, being very excited, fired off a few red Very lights and dropped a parachute flare.[16]

Lehmann in *LZ-98* had dropped his bombs on the docks along the Thames and, hidden by clouds at fourteen thousand feet, had broken out of the defense zones ringing the city.

Ernst Lehmann

I looked back in the direction from which we had come and I saw, far behind us, a bright ball of fire. Despite the distance, which I estimated at thirty-eight miles, we knew that the blazing meteor on the further rim of the city could only be one of our airships. The flaming mass hung in the sky for more than a minute; then single parts detached themselves from it and preceded it to the earth. Poor fellows, they were lost the moment the ship took fire.[17]

Millions of Britons witnessed the fiery spectacle. For a year and a half they lived with the fear of the "Zepp nights" when the moon was down and the throbbing of the engines of the unseen invaders as they passed overhead was a prelude to the roar of artillery and the crash of falling bombs. For a year and a half the raiders had come and gone as they pleased, and though the people read newspaper

The German army's *LZ-77* was bombing Revigny on February 20, 1916. It was a clear moonlit night and, with a ceiling over thirteen thousand feet, the ship was safe from French planes and all but the most intensive anti-aircraft fire. The first incendiary shell hit her amidships and she fell in flames. All twelve airshipmen aboard were killed, the first victims of the incendiary artillery shell. *Official U.S. Air Force photo.*

accounts of Warneford's kill in Belgium, here at last was a blazing airship in their own sky over London.

Lt. William Leefe Robinson

Having little oil or petrol left, I returned to Sutton's Farm, landing at 2:45 A.M. On landing I found that I had shot away my machine-gun wire guard, the rear part of the center section, and had pierced the main spar several times.[18]

Robinson was a national hero. He received the Victoria Cross and a seventeen-thousand-dollar reward contributed by British businessmen for the first airman to bag an airship over Britain.

The flames were visible forty miles away and the wreckage fell to earth at Cuffley on the northern edge of London where it continued to burn for two hours. When the remains had cooled enough to be examined, nothing but charred wood was found. At first it was thought that the Germans were running short of aluminum, but then it was discovered that the ship was not a Zeppelin at all, but a Schutte-Lanz, a similar design that used wooden frames rather than duralumin ones.

Sixteen bodies were recovered and given a military funeral despite some public opposition to any sort of honor shown to the "baby killers."

The sight of the blazing ship was a sobering one to all the airshipmen over London that night. They knew that, as the ship caught fire, their doomed comrades had only two choices—both fatal. They could stay with the flaming wreckage and be burned alive, or they could leap out and fall to their deaths, two miles below. The folded parachute became available at about this time but neither Germany nor the Allies adopted it. As Ernst Lehmann explained it, "Since the additional weight was at the expense of fuel and projectiles, we quickly abandoned them again and continued to leave the decision of life or death to our own skill and luck."[19] On the Allied side, the high command felt that pilots equipped with parachutes might be encouraged to abandon their planes before it was absolutely necessary.

Capt. Peter Strasser, the German navy's Fuhrer der Luftschiffe, realized that the improved defenses around London ruled out any airship raids at altitudes of less than fifteen thousand feet. But to achieve this increased height, the older Zeppelins would have to cut their bomb load down to one ton per ship. The risk clearly outweighed the result. His solution lay in the larger and more efficient ships then coming off the Zeppelin Company ways at Friedrichshafen.

On the night of September 23, 1916, ten naval Zeppelins again set out for England. Seven were older ships assigned to targets in the less heavily defended Midlands. The other three were of the new L-30 class and set their course for London. They were 650 feet long and held nearly two million cubic feet of hydrogen. Each carried thirteen hundred gallons of gasoline and four and a half tons of bombs. Six Maybach motors gave a total of 1,440 horsepower and a top speed of sixty-two miles per hour. There were six machine guns in the gondolas plus four more on top of the hull. They also carried life jackets and two life rafts. "These life saving devices, all things considered, were of small practical value, but they may have had some good effect upon morale," says Lehmann.[20]

One of the new ships, the L-31, was commanded by Kptlt. Heinrich Mathy.

Kptlt. Heinrich Mathy

The minutes stretched into hours. My Watch Officer reported a searchlight to the stern; it was evidently newly installed. I marked the discovery on my map and flashed the news out into the fog. Shortly thereafter my Radio Officer intercepted an English wireless message warning London of our approach. The alarm was repeated by a number of stations. The effect was instantaneous. All the villages below us were immediately darkened, and the beams of huge searchlights shot upward to explore the sky. One of the searchlights, further away than the others, caught us. A series of thunderclaps from close by revealed an anti-aircraft battery. The L-31 banked sharply, the rays of the searchlight slid off her, and, although the "Archie" continued to fire, the prey escaped.

At midnight, the three Zeppelins reached the city of London from different directions. The English could darken the metropolis as much as they liked, but they couldn't conceal the Thames. I prepared for the attack. Almost the entire available water ballast was released in order to bring the L-31 as high as possible. A tug on a wire from the control car opened the sliding panels under the ship, where the bombs hung suspended side by side. The Watch Officer reported everything ready; the motors were running full speed ahead. In the dark sky, the searchlights crossed like bared swords.[21]

Fregattenkapitan Peter Strasser was an admiralty gunnery expert before he was selected as Fuhrer der Luftschiffe (airship leader), his predecessor having been killed in the crash of L-2. Strasser took his training aboard Delag's *Hansa* and soon became the driving force behind the German Naval Airship Service.

If a man like Strasser had arrived at his post two or three years earlier, at the outbreak of the war we would have had naval airships of outstanding performance.

Dr. Hugo Eckener,
My Zeppelins
(London: Putnam Co., 1958)

Friedrich Moch photo, courtesy Douglas Robinson.

Heinrich Mathy's *L-31*, flying over the battleship *Ostfriesland*, was the second in a new class of Zeppelin that began to appear in May 1916. They were 650 feet long and 90 feet high, with six 240-horsepower Maybachs and a top speed of sixty-two miles per hour. They had 1,949,600 cubic feet of hydrogen that could lift over seventy tons. Since the ships weighed forty tons, this left thirty tons for fuel, crew, ballast, and five tons of bombs. They carried ten machine guns and could climb to 17,400 feet. *Luftschiff-bau Zeppelin photo, courtesy Douglas Robinson.*

•

Heinrich Mathy (1883–1916) was Germany's greatest wartime airship commander. This portrait of Mathy and his wife, Hertha, was taken on their honeymoon by Maj. Oskar Wilcke at the Zeppelin factory in Friedrichshafen in July 1915. Of his death, his widow said, "He fell in the prime of his life sacrificing it with joy for his country."—C. F. Snowden Gamble, *The Story of a North Sea Air Station* (London, 1928). *Photo courtesy Hertha Mathy, Douglas Robinson Collection.*

Since early afternoon the decoding room at the British Admiralty had been the scene of intense activity. As each enemy airship rose from her base and checked into the radio network, her message was monitored by British listening posts. The course of each ship was plotted as she requested position checks from navigation stations in Germany and as the battle fleet rendezvoused over one of the Channel lightships. Then ground observers followed the drone of the engines as each ship crossed the coastline and flew inland. When it became apparent that they were headed for London, the three flying fields ringing the city were alerted.

Lt. Frederic Sowrey took off in his B.E.2c shortly before midnight. Thirteen thousand feet above the city he met one of the new airships. Two drums of incendiary fire from his machine gun seemed to produce no effect on the huge raider. He loaded his third drum.

Mathy, who had approached from the south and laid a trail of bombs through the heart of London, turned to glance back across the darkened city.

Kptlt. Heinrich Mathy

Suddenly, the sky burst into fire as if a stroke of lightning had split it apart. The L-32, commanded by Naval-Lieutenant Peterson, who was over England for the eleventh time, was overtaken by Fate. We in the L-31 saw the ship catch fire. First the bow burned, and then the flames tongued over the whole envelope. The aft gondola broke off, and the wing cars followed. For eighteen terrible seconds the blazing ball hung like a fateful planet in the sky; then it burst asunder. A glowing mass with a tail of whirling flames fell like a comet on Billerichy, east of London.

Millions of Englishmen witnessed the catastrophe, for the blaze was visible all over London and far into the countryside. The Britons, apparently so even-tempered and composed, broke out into frenzied cheers and danced like mad in the darkened streets. The ships on the Thames sounded their sirens. It was one o'clock in the morning, and noisier than on New Year's Eve.[22]

But the fateful night was not yet over. The third new ship, the *L-33* under Kptlt. Alois Bocker, came under heavy antiaircraft fire and began to lose gas from dozens of hits. She headed out over the Channel but was sinking so rapidly that Bocker turned back and crash-landed a few miles from Colchester. The crew leaped out and tried to set fire to the ship with signal flares but there wasn't enough hydrogen left in the cells to burn. Bocker and his men were captured. Of the three new Zeppelins that attacked London that night, only Mathy in *L-31* escaped—and his luck was running out.

A week later on October 1, 1916, ten naval airships again set out for England. The loss of *L-32* and *L-33* had deeply shaken Strasser, and he ordered his commanders to use extra caution and attack London only under ideal weather conditions. But conditions were far from ideal. The invaders found strong headwinds, squalls, and a heavy cloud cover. Nine of the airships prudently turned off toward the industrial Midlands. Heinrich Mathy headed for London. He had more than a hundred missions to his credit. This was his thirteenth over England.

Four planes scrambled into the air as news of Mathy's approach was flashed across the countryside.

Lt. W. J. Tempest

As I drew up to the Zeppelin, to my relief I found that I was quite free of A.A. fire for the nearest shells were bursting quite three miles away. The Zeppelin was now nearly 12,700 feet high and mounting rapidly. I therefore started to dive at her, for, though I held a slight advantage in speed she was climbing like a rocket and leaving me standing. I accordingly gave a tremendous pump at my petrol tank and dived straight at her, firing a burst into her as I came. I let her have another burst as I passed under her and then banking my machine over, sat under her tail, and flying along underneath her, pumped lead into her for all I was worth. I could see tracer bullets flying from her in all directions, but I was too close under her for them to concentrate on me. As I was firing I noticed her begin to go red inside like an enormous Chinese lantern and then a flame shot out of the front part of her and I realized she was on fire. She then shot up about 200 feet, paused, and came roaring straight down on me before I had time to get out of the way. I nose-dived for all I was worth, with the Zepp tearing after me, and expected every minute to be engulfed in the flames. I put my machine into a spin and just managed to corkscrew out of the way as she shot past me, roaring like a furnace. I righted my machine and watched her hit the ground with a shower of sparks. I then proceeded to fire off dozens of green Very lights in the exuberance of my feelings.

I glanced at my watch and I saw it was about ten minutes past twelve. I then commenced to feel very sick, giddy and exhausted, and had considerable difficulty in finding my way to the ground through fog, and in landing I crashed and cut my head on my machine gun.[23]

Heinrich Mathy was the most daring and successful of all the airship commanders. Tall, slim, and coldly handsome, his popularity among the German people was equaled only by fighter-ace Oswald Boelcke. Mathy, who once told a reporter, "I had much rather stand on the bridge of a torpedo-boat, fighting ship against ship, than to attack a city from the air,"[24] died in flames with his ship and his men over London. He was thirty-four.

Strasser's dream of bringing England to her knees through strategic bombing died with Mathy and his *L-31*. The defense had finally caught up with the Zeppelin.

For three long and bloody years the airship and the airplane had been chasing each other higher and higher into the sky. The airship started the war with a ceiling of sixty-five hundred feet while most planes could not rise above four thousand. Within a few months, improved fighters could climb to sixty-five hundred but the new

Three Zeppelin killers (left to right), Lieutenants Robinson, Tempest, and Sowrey. William Leefe Robinson was born in India, joined the infantry, was wounded, and then took pilot training. After shooting down *SL-11*, he was promoted to captain and given a squadron on the western front. He was shot down and captured in 1917, and died of influenza on December 31, 1918, just three weeks after his release from a German prison camp. Wulstan Joseph Tempest was wounded at Ypres and discharged from the army before he joined the Royal Flying Corps. He was twenty-six when he shot down Heinrich Mathy. Tempest died a year later over the western front. Frederick Sowrey joined the Royal Fusiliers, was wounded at Loos, and transferred to the Royal Flying Corps. He was twenty-three when he shot down the *L-32* and was the only one of the three to survive the war. *Courtesy Arch Whitehouse.*

On September 24, 1916, on a raid over London, the *L-33* was riddled by both airplane and antiaircraft fire. Hydrogen leaked from hundreds of holes and Kptlt. Alois Bocker was forced to crash land his ship at Little Wigborough near Colchester. His men got out safely, but when they tried to destroy the ship, there was barely enough hydrogen left to burn. Bocker and his men were captured by a policeman on a bicycle and the *L-33* was copied by the British in their airships *R.33* and *R.34. Courtesy Imperial War Museum, London.*

•

Zeppelins were capable of altitudes of ten thousand feet. The deadly spiral continued upward until at last the air war was being fought in the bitter cold four miles above the earth. When the airships held the advantage, they could bomb England, France, and Russia at will. When the airplane had the edge, the Zeppelins fell in flames.

In March 1917, the German army gave up their airships in order to concentrate on the development of long-range, multiengine Gotha and Staaken R-bombers. The remaining army Zeppelins were turned over to the Naval Airship Service.

Strasser refused to give up. He was convinced that the new high-altitude ships then coming off the Zeppelin Company's drawing boards would enable him, once again, to carry the war to England. The challenge was clearly up to the Zeppelin Company. Hull girders were redesigned and lightened, engine cars were streamlined, the aft gondola and crew's quarters were eliminated, everything possible was done to reduce weight in order to gain height. Even the machine guns were removed. When the *L-42* was launched in February 1917, she was able to climb to 19,700 feet with nearly two and a half tons of bombs.

At this altitude the airshipmen were once again safe from antiaircraft fire and pursuing planes but they were confronted by even more formidable foes. In the icy air four miles above the earth, water ballast froze, the alcohol solution in the magnetic compasses turned to sludge, and motor oil congealed into lumps that had to be broken up and fed into the engines by hand. Even in their fur-lined flight suits, the men suffered from frostbite as winds of twenty degrees below zero whistled through the unheated ships, and the slightest exertion left them dizzy and gasping for breath in the thin air.

A still greater danger was the inability of German meteorologists to predict the weather at these high altitudes. On October 19, 1917, eleven of the newest Zeppelins set out for England. Good bombing weather had been promised but at twenty thousand feet they encountered gale force winds that drove the giant ships southward across the Channel toward France. Six managed to struggle back to the safety of their bases and one crash-landed behind German lines, but the other four were driven deep into enemy territory as one engine after another failed and froze up. Their mechanics were too exhausted from lack of oxygen to keep them running. *L-44* was shot down by French artillery with the loss of her entire crew. The other three crash-landed in southern France and the surviving crewmen were interned.

England was saved by the storm—for although seventy-three defense planes were sent up, not one was able to climb high enough to intercept the Zeppelins. The only way left to deal with these new high-altitude airships was to destroy them before they left the ground. On July 19, 1918, the *Furious,* a light battle cruiser converted by the Royal Navy into an aircraft carrier, launched the world's first carrier attack against a land target. A squadron of seven Sopwith Camels destroyed two new Zeppelins in their hangars at Tondern near the Danish border.

The bases were not the only victims of the stepped-up offense. Airships on reconnaissance patrol and mine-clearing duty in the North Sea had, for three years, gone about their business undisturbed. Now they came under attack by high-performance seaplanes launched from British tenders as well as by long-range Curtiss flying boats based at Yarmouth.

On August 5, 1918, Strasser again sent five of his "height climbers" against England. The lead ship was to be the newest Zeppelin of all, Kapitanleutnant von Lossnitzer's month-old *L-70.* Her sleek black hull was 694 feet long and enclosed 2,195,800 cubic feet of hydrogen, enough to lift fifty tons into the air. Her seven 245-horsepower Maybach high-altitude engines could be run at full throttle only above six thousand feet and at twenty-one thousand feet they drove the huge ship at seventy-six miles per hour with five tons of bombs aboard. Just as von Lossnitzer was about to cast off, Captain Strasser arrived on the field and climbed aboard.

At eight o'clock that evening three of the approaching Zeppelins were spotted by the Lehman Bank Lightship and the warning was flashed ashore. A dozen planes roared aloft from the Great Yarmouth air station—one of them a DH-4 piloted by Maj. Egbert Cadbury. Behind him in the gunner's seat was Capt. Robert Leckie. Both men had arrived late at the field and headed for the only plane left on the ground. Cadbury was fastest and got the pilot's seat as Leckie scrambled aboard behind him. Each man already had one Zeppelin to his credit and their DH-4 could climb as high as the new airships.

They headed out to sea and met the three incoming Zeppelins at 17,500 feet. The largest of the airships was in the lead.

Maj. Egbert Cadbury

She looked simply immense, as indeed she was, being 300 yards long from stem to stern, and completely blotted out the starry sky above us, and the darkness was only lit up by the barrage of machine-gun fire from her crew and the flashes from our own twin Lewis guns. Bob Leckie gave her a few bursts of fire of tracer bullets, and within a matter of seconds, flames started to leap out from the bows and in an incredibly short time her nose dropped and she went hurtling down, a mass of flames, into the clouds below, where we lost sight of her. Actually, we learned afterwards that she had hit the sea quite

During the war, Oberlt. Freiherr Treusch von Buttlar Brandenfels (seated at right) commanded the German Naval Zeppelins *L-5, L-6, L-11, L-30,* and *L-54.* After the war he became an official in the German air ministry. Lt. Hans von Schiller (left) also commanded a number of airships and joined the Zeppelin Company after the war eventually rising to command of the *Graf Zeppelin.*

Brave, dashing, chivalrous and skillful, they were opposed to us in action, although we were identical in spirit.

C. F. Snowden Gamble, *The Story of a North Sea Air Station*, London, 1928.

Photo courtesy Imperial War Museum, London.

The *L-49* was one of eleven specially lightened ships that attacked England on October 20, 1918, at extremely high altitudes where they ran into a gale that blew them back over France. Four of the eleven crashed, one with the loss of her entire crew. The *L-49* was attacked by French Nieuports and was forced down at Bourbonne-Les-Baines. Her nineteen-man crew was captured and the ship, which landed nearly intact, was carefully copied by the French. Their plans formed the basis for the construction of the U.S. rigid *Shenandoah. Official U.S. Air Force photo.*

•

close to a trawler, eight miles east of Wells, and for hours later the sea was lit up with burning petrol coming out from the sunken Zeppelin. . . .

Unfortunately, our casualties were also heavy as a number of my squadron's officers who also set off in pursuit, failed to return. One pilot at least, as reported by the trawler, evidently mistaking the burning petrol on the sea for the lights of a night landing ground, landed in the sea and was drowned.[25]

It was only by chance that Cadbury and Leckie managed to find a lighted airfield in the fog and land safely. For the destruction of *L-70*, they each received the Distinguished Flying Cross. In a letter to his father, Egbert Cadbury wrote:

Another Zeppelin has gone to perdition, sent there by a perfectly peaceful, live-and-let-live citizen who harbors no lust for blood or fearful war spirit in his soul. It all happened very quickly and very terribly.[26]

Fuhrer der Luftschiffe Peter Strasser went to his death with his comrades aboard *L-70,* the newest and most modern ship in his Naval Airship Service. Three months later the war was over.

Kptlt. Freiherr von Buttlar-Brandenfels

No man is indispensable, at least so people say, particularly in war, but after his death we never succeeded in finding an adequate successor to our beloved Senior Airship Officer.[27]

Was it worth it? Four factories worked around the clock to launch an average of one new Zeppelin every two weeks throughout the four years of the war. One hundred and twenty-eight German airships dropped sixty-two tons of bombs on Russia, fifty tons on France, and 220 tons on England. Twenty airships were lost with their entire crews and 501 airshipmen were killed in action. Did the results justify the effort, expense, and loss of life? Early in the war a British newspaper editor wrote:

> The net result of some half-dozen raids on London has been to unite the public opinion of all England against Germany and to kill some 137 people. During the same period the motor-busses of London have been responsible for 954 fatal accidents. As a military weapon the Zeppelin is far inferior to the omnibus.[28]

The Allied view of the Zeppelin's effectiveness was somewhat influenced by the fact that no Allied aircraft of any kind came close to the range and load capacity of the German rigid airships. Britain's total lack of defensive weapons at the beginning of the war left her wide open to airship attack, but the Germans were equally unprepared, and the great fleets of aerial cruisers that were momentarily expected over England did not, in fact, exist. Half of the German army's six Zeppelins were shot down in the war's first week. Strasser began the war with only one Zeppelin. By the time Kaiser Wilhelm finally decided to unleash his airships, their advantage was already beginning to disappear.

As the world's first strategic bombers, attacking factories and military installations far behind enemy lines, the Zeppelins generally failed. In the beginning there weren't enough of them to do the job and, at the end, they were forced to fly so high that they couldn't locate their targets in the darkness far below. Many German military strategists, including Strasser and Count Zeppelin, also believed that bombing raids on the enemy's cities would destroy the civilian population's will to continue the war. In this they were mistaken. The raids could disrupt England—on the day following an air raid, factory managers found that on the average, 90 percent of their workers came in late and 20 percent didn't show up at all—but there was never any question of the British people demanding a cease-fire as a result of the bombing. The terror of the bombs was real enough, but each burst spread determination, not defeat. It was the theory that was at fault, however, not the Zeppelin, for neither the V-2 rocket of World War II nor the B-52s of Vietnam were able to accomplish the same mission.

On prewar maneuvers in the summer of 1912, the *Hansa* sails with the German fleet. The bombing raids on England tend to obscure the fact that the Naval Airship Service's primary mission was reconnaissance at sea. With Zeppelins dogging their squadrons at the Battle of Jutland and at Sunderland, the British formed a high opinion of the airship's value as a naval scout. In the heat of battle, however, the untrained observers aboard the dirigibles often sent reports that were contradictory or inaccurate. Despite these faults, Admiral Sheer and the other German commanders placed a high value on their airships' ability to protect them from surprise by the stronger British Fleet. *Courtesy Northrop University.*

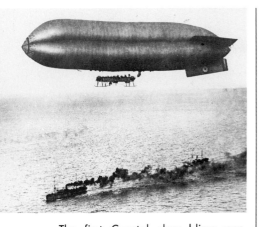

The first Coastal class blimp was launched in September 1915, and thirty-two were built. They were 196 feet long with 170,000 cubic feet of gas in an Astra Torres–type, trilobe gasbag. The Astra Torres method of internal wire bracing produced a more rigid gasbag that could be driven at higher speeds. The ship's car was made by cutting the tails off two Avro seaplane fuselages and joining the back ends together. This produced a car with four cockpits and an engine at each end. Two 180-horsepower Sunbeams were used, one pulling and one pushing. The Coastal blimp could stay in the air for eleven hours and had a top speed of fifty-two miles per hour. *Courtesy Imperial War Museum, London.*

•

The usefulness of the airship for naval reconnaissance is quite a different story. In minesweeping operations and as the eyes of the High Seas Fleet, their unmatched range and endurance were of particular importance.

Adm. Reinhard Scheer

In the beginning of the war, when seaplane-flying was quite undeveloped, they were indispensable to us. Their wide field of vision, their high speed, and their great reliability when compared with the possibilities of scouting by war-ships, enabled the airships to lend us the greatest assistance. But only in fine weather. So the Fleet had to make its activities dependent on those of the airships, or do without them.[29]

The commander of Britain's Grand Fleet, Admiral Viscount Jellicoe of Scapa, agreed with his German counterpart:

The German Zeppelins, as their numbers increased, were of great assistance to the enemy for scouting, each one being, in *favorable weather,* equal to at least two light cruisers for such purposes.[30]

Admiral Jellicoe's successor as commander of the Grand Fleet, Admiral Beatty, was willing to go even further and rate each Zeppelin as equal to five or six cruisers for scouting.

After the defense caught up with the airship and losses began to mount, only the tremendous amount of British equipment and manpower tied down at home for air defense could justify the continuation of the raids. Seventeen thousand men were kept in England for antiaircraft defense, including twelve Royal Flying Corps squadrons with 110 planes, all desperately needed on the western front.

As a weapon of war, the rigid airship was only a qualified success, and its usefulness decreased rapidly as the airplane took its place. The airplane was destined to play a major part in all subsequent conflicts. The airship was not. As Admiral Scheer observed:

We may probably look upon the military career of the airship as over and done with. But the technical side of airship navigation has been developed in such a high degree by our experience in war, that airship traffic in peace times will derive great advantages from it, and the invention of Count Zeppelin will be preserved as a step in the progress of civilisation.[31]

•

The Germans launched ninety-nine Zeppelins during World War I, but they were not the only ships in the sky by any means. They were not even in the majority. France and Italy both built a considerable number of nonrigid and semirigid warships. It was Great Britain, however, as the target of most of the Zeppelin raids and with vital shipping routes to defend, that developed the largest dirigible fleet of any of the Allies. By the end of the war, the Royal Navy had launched 213 blimps, 103 of which were still in service while 23 had been sold to other countries. The number of British airshipmen grew from two hundred in 1914 to more than seven thousand at the war's end and they boasted of never having lost a ship from a convoy under their protection. They flew a total of 88,717 hours, the equivalent of ten years in the air, covered two and a quarter million miles, and lost only forty-eight men in training and combat together.

•

The *SL-3* was one of twenty-one Schutte-Lanz ships flown during the war by the German army and navy. She was launched on February 4, 1915, and was similar to Zeppelins of the same period except for her plywood girders. She was 502 feet long and eighty-one feet high, with 1,143,500 cubic feet of hydrogen. Four 210-horsepower Maybachs gave her a top speed of fifty-two miles per hour. After seventy-one flights, she crashed in the sea off Gotland on May 1, 1916, but all of her crew were rescued. *Official U.S. Air Force photo.*

The British navy's first Submarine Scout blimp was created in February 1915 by hanging the wingless fuselage of a B.E.2c biplane beneath the prewar gasbag. About fifty S.S. blimps were built. They were 143 feet long with sixty thousand cubic feet, a crew of two, and an endurance of eight hours. The ships' seventy-five-horsepower Renault engines gave them a top speed of forty miles per hour. When the engine stopped, as it often did, the mechanic had to climb out on the landing skid to repair it. Then, standing in midair, he had to swing the propeller to start it again! *From* The Scientific American, *June 10, 1916.*

Top: During the war the Italian army used their airships primarily for tactical reconnaissance and as bombers in support of their ground troops. Several were shot down by Austrian planes and by antiaircraft fire. Most Italian airships were semirigids in sizes up to 560,000 cubic feet. At the beginning of 1915, the army had eleven ships in service, eight semirigids similar in design to this 430,000-cubic-foot *M.1* built by the army's Corps of Engineers and three Forlaninis, the largest of which was of 500,000 cubic feet. *Courtesy Stato Maggiore Aeronautica, Rome.* Above: The first North Sea class blimp was completed in 1916 and fourteen were eventually built. They were 262 feet long and sixty-nine feet high with a 360,000-cubic-foot trilobe gasbag that included six air ballonets with 128,000-cubic-foot capacity. Two 240-horsepower Fiat engines gave a top speed of fifty-seven miles per hour. They were the first British blimps with a covered car and carried a crew of ten. A North Sea blimp set a wartime record of four days and five hours in the air without refueling. *Courtesy National Museum of Science & Technology, Ottawa.*

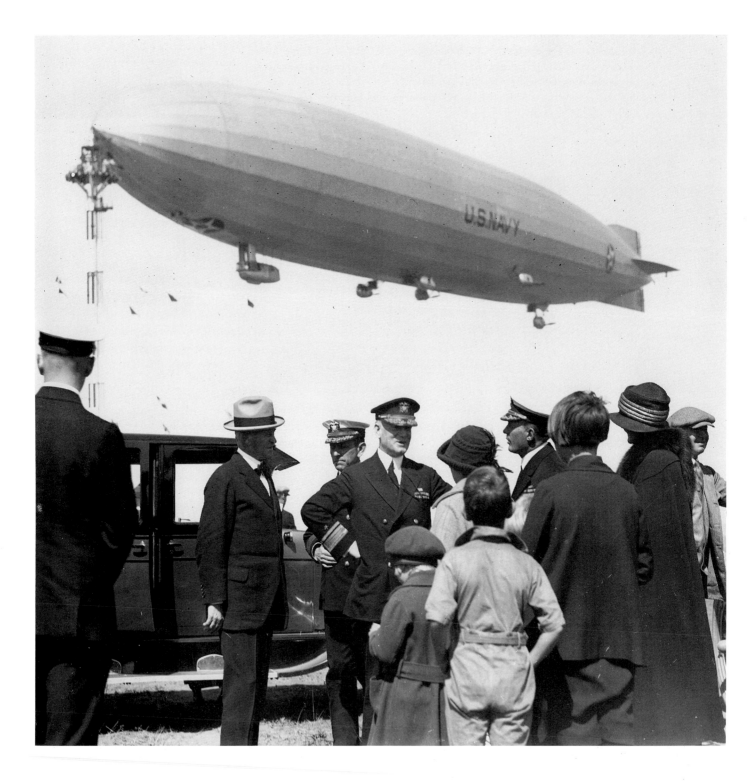

5
· P O S T W A R ·
AIRSHIP
ENTHUSIASM

As a large airship can transport twenty tons or more at a speed of 70 to 90 miles an hour, more points can be reached than would be possible in other ways. In fact, in most places in the United States today, with the roads that we have, it would be impossible to supply an army of any size over them, and as railroads exist only in certain places, airships will be the natural means of supply and should be developed accordingly.

For commercial purposes the airship offers very interesting possibilities. There is no dust or smoke or unpleasant experience in travelling by them. The degree of safety, with the proper ground organization of airship stations, is very good. In fact, the Germans have carried over 200,000 passengers without a fatality.

For communication across the Pacific, or particularly to South America, airships will be a very efficient means of travel.

Brigadier General William Mitchell, Assistant Chief, Army Air Service in
National Geographic, **March 1921**

In the four years of World War I the development of aviation received more money and made more progress than would have been possible in a dozen or more years of leisurely peacetime activity. The commercial potential of the rigid airship for long-distance transoceanic flights was clear to all, and the Germans were just as clearly the masters of the most advanced rigid technology in the world. The Zeppelin had, in fact, already proved her ability to link the continents of the world by air across the great oceans.

On November 21, 1917, a specially lengthened German naval Zeppelin, the *L-59,* had flown to Africa. She carried fourteen tons of ammunition and medical supplies for the German colonial troops fighting in East Africa under the command of Gen. Paul von Lettow-Vorbeck. The *L-59* flew nonstop from Yamboli in Bulgaria to Khartoum in the Sudan, where she received a radio message to end the

OPPOSITE: Rear Adm. William A. Moffett, here at San Diego, accompanied the U.S. Navy's *Shenandoah* on her transcontinental voyage. In 1921 he had been selected to head a new Bureau of Aeronautics created by the navy. Previously, a navy plane's engine came from the Bureau of Steam Engineering, the fuselage from the Bureau of Construction and Repair, while the instruments and pilots were handled by the Bureau of Navigation. *U.S. Navy photo in the National Archives.*

The U.S. Navy blimp *C-5* arrived at Newfoundland on May 15, 1919, after a fourteen-hundred-mile nonstop flight from Long Island. Below her are the three Curtiss flying boats, the largest planes in the navy. The C-class blimps were the best of the early U.S. built nonrigids. The first was launched in the spring of 1918 and twenty were eventually completed by Goodrich and Goodyear for both the army and the navy. They were 192 feet long with 170,000 cubic feet of hydrogen. Powered by two 125-horsepower Hispano-Suiza engines, they cruised at forty-five miles per hour with a top speed of sixty miles per hour and a range of over two thousand miles. *Courtesy Goodyear Tire and Rubber Co.*

•

mission and return to Yamboli. The *L-59* was in the air for four days and four nights and covered 4,225 miles, equal to the distance from Berlin to Chicago. She landed back at Yamboli with enough fuel on board for another 3,750 miles.

With Germany's defeat the Allies saw an opportunity to overtake her lead in airship development, for one of the terms of the peace treaty called for the closing down of almost the entire German aircraft industry.

The rapid wartime development of both airplanes and airships, plus the thousands of people newly involved in aircraft design and construction, was bound to stimulate interest in commercial flying, and the first great challenge in postwar aviation that seemed within reach was the Atlantic crossing. From the tip of Newfoundland jutting more than a thousand miles out into the Atlantic beyond the U.S. East Coast, the powerful westerly winds sweeping out to sea would give an aircraft the extra push needed to carry it all the way to Europe.

The transatlantic flight was made even more attractive in the spring of 1919 when the *London Daily Mail* offered a fifty-thousand-dollar prize for the first nonstop crossing. Within weeks of the announcement, a dozen pilots had gathered at St. John's, Newfoundland, ready to challenge the stormy North Atlantic. Their aircraft included surplus war planes, three brand-new U.S. Navy flying boats, and even a navy blimp.

The first to try were the navy's three Curtiss flying boats, the largest U.S. airplanes yet built. On May 16, 1919, they roared across the surface of Trepassey Bay and lifted into the air headed hopefully for Europe. Two of the planes became lost in bad weather and were forced to land in the Atlantic. The crew of one was picked up by a passing ship while the other taxied and drifted the last two hundred miles to the Azores. The *NC-4*, however, flew all the way, landing at Horta in the Azores the next day after a fifteen-hour flight. She resumed her journey ten days later, arriving in Lisbon on the twenty-seventh and then continuing on to Plymouth, England, covering a total of forty-five hundred miles in fifteen days. The *NC-4* was the first aircraft to fly the Atlantic, although it wasn't exactly nonstop and did not qualify for the *Daily Mail* prize.

Next to try were the British fliers Harry Hawker and MacKenzie Grieve. They started from Newfoundland on May 18, but after fourteen hours and a thousand miles their single-engine Sopwith biplane was forced into the sea with motor trouble and they were rescued by a tramp steamer.

The U.S. Navy blimp *C-5* arrived at St. John's on May 15. The little 170,000-cubic-foot nonrigid would not ordinarily have been considered a serious contender in the race, but the fact that she had just completed a fourteen-hundred-mile nonstop flight from her base at Montauk, Long Island, to St. John's in twenty-six hours meant that she was perfectly capable of flying the nineteen hundred miles to Ireland. While the *C-5*'s two pilots, Lt. Comdr. Emory Coil and Lt. Jack Lawrence, were getting some rest aboard their support ship, the USS *Chicago,* a violent storm came up and tore the blimp from her moorings. The unmanned *C-5* was swept out over the Atlantic at more than sixty miles an hour on her way to Europe—all by herself. She was never seen again.

A month later on June 15, 1919, two RAF flyers, Capt. John Alcock and Lt. Arthur Brown, finally landed nose down in a bog at Clifden, Ireland, after a sixteen-hour flight from St. John's in their twin-engine Vickers-Vimy bomber. They won the fifty thousand dollars and were knighted.

Now it was the rigid airship's turn. The Germans had been preparing for an Atlantic crossing of their own. Though the war was over, the Zeppelin crews were still assigned to their ships and Ernst Lehmann was preparing the *L-72* for a nonstop flight from Germany to New York City and back. His unexpected appearance over the city would create a sensation and demonstrate the Zeppelin's capabilities for commercial transatlantic service, especially when, without landing, he turned around and returned to Germany. Another airship commander, Martin Dietrich, found that his crew wanted to make a similar flight with his *L-71*, except that instead of returning to Germany, they planned to continue on across the United States as far as their fuel would carry them and, when their tanks were empty, land somewhere in Arizona or New Mexico and leave the *L-71* tied to the nearest tree.

Lehmann's *L-72* was in the final stages of preparation when, in March 1919, the Inter-Allied Control Commission heard of the plans and ordered him to stop.

The flights of Lehmann and Dietrich would have been spectacular accomplishments, especially while the airplane was still struggling to complete a one-way Atlantic crossing, and the *L-71* and *L-72,* with a range of more than five thousand miles, had a good chance of success. The airship had come a long way in the nine years since Walter Wellman challenged the Atlantic. The difference between the *America*'s 155 undependable horsepower and the *L-72*'s 1,470 Maybach horsepower, between the *America*'s three tons of disposable lift and the *L-72*'s thirty tons was clearly the difference between failure and success.

With the Germans out of the race, the field was left to England, for though the Zeppelins received the most attention during the war, they were not the only ships in the sky. France, Italy, and England had all developed a considerable airship capability of their own. France alone launched sixty-eight airships of up to five hundred thousand cubic feet. England, however, ended the war with the largest dirigible fleet of all, building more than two hundred airships, 103 of which were still in commission at the signing of the armistice. Most of these ships were nonrigid

Great Britain's rigid airship program got off to a bad start with the collapse of the *Mayfly* in 1911. Two years later when the German army Zeppelin *Z-4* landed by mistake at Luneville, the British got a complete set of photographs from French intelligence, and this became the basis for their next seven rigids. As newer Zeppelins fell into Allied hands, British designs were correspondingly improved. Starting with the *Mayfly*, Britain began work on nineteen rigid airships and managed to get thirteen of them into the air, but every one was a copy of a German original. The first truly original British rigid airship was not built until Barnes Wallis completed his *R.80* in 1920.

•

Though Rigid Airship *No. 9* was Britain's second rigid, she was the Royal Navy's ninth dirigible, which accounts for her misleading designation. She was completed in November 1916, a month after the *Z-4*, her Zeppelin prototype, was dismantled as obsolete. She had 198 hours flying time when she was dismantled in June 1918. *Courtesy Vickers Ltd.*

blimps, but Britain was also the only Allied nation with rigid airships.

Britain's first wartime rigid, after the ill-fated *Mayfly*, was the *No. 9* launched by Vickers Ltd. in November 1916. Similar in size and design to prewar Zeppelins, she was obsolete the day she was completed. By the end of the war England had built nine rigids but only two of them, the *R.33* and *R.34*, were relatively modern ships. Both were copies of the German naval Zeppelin *L-33*, shot down in September 1916 near Colchester. Her crew had tried to set the ship on fire, but so much hydrogen had escaped through the bullet holes that there wasn't enough left to burn. They were interned and the *L-33* was duplicated piece by piece to produce the *R.33* and *R.34*. Both were built with the intention of bombing Germany and were completed just in time for the war's end.

R.34 became the first aircraft to make a transatlantic round-trip. After waiting politely for Alcock and Brown to complete their flight, the *R.34* took off on July 2, 1919, from Scotland with thirty crewmen, a kitten, and a stowaway named Ballantyne. They started out with forty-nine hundred gallons of gasoline weighing 15.8 tons. After meeting head winds most of the way across, they finally landed at Minneola, Long Island, after a 108-hour flight with only enough gasoline left in their tanks for two more hours in the air. As the first to attempt the difficult westward crossing, flying into the wind, they were hailed as the first travelers to arrive in America by air. The return trip made with the prevailing winds took only seventy-five hours. Britain's highest-ranking air officer, Gen. E. M. Maitland, noted a fine bit of flying along the way by the *R.34*'s commander, Maj. G. H. Scott.

Gen. E. M. Maitland

Scott is able by skillful handling to keep the ship in these thick clouds to avoid superheating, at the same time he judges it so nicely that Cooke, standing on top of the ship, is able to get observations with sextant on sun and cloud horizon, the only thing

ABOVE: *R.29* was 539 feet long with 999,000 cubic feet of hydrogen, a total lift of thirty tons, and a disposable lift of nearly nine tons. She was commissioned in June of 1918 and was the only British rigid actually to participate in the war. She attacked three U-boats and caused the destruction of two of them. She was dismantled in October 1919. *Courtesy National Museum of Science & Technology, Ottawa.* BELOW: *R.33* and *R.34* were copies of the German Zeppelin *L-33* that crashed at Little Wigborough in 1916. Both were 643 feet long with two million cubic feet of gas and a disposable lift of 26½ tons. They were powered by five 250-horsepower Sunbeam Maori engines with a top speed of sixty-three miles per hour. Completed in March 1919, they were scheduled to make the transatlantic flight together, but *R.33* was not ready, and *R.34* shown here at Roosevelt Field, Long Island, flew the ocean alone. Eighteen months later she ran into a hillside, was further damaged in a storm, and was dismantled. The airplane was not able to duplicate the *R.34*'s east-to-west Atlantic crossing until 1928. *Courtesy Cole Airship Collection, University of Oregon.*

•

The *R.33* was in service for six years before this incident occurred. She was riding at the high mast at Cardington on April 2, 1925, in preparation for a flight to Egypt to test tropical flying conditions. Her full crew of twenty men was aboard when she tore loose from the mast. The gas cell in her bow collapsed, sealing off the opening and protecting the other cells. Flight Lt. Ralph Booth and his men brought the ship safely back to the hangar at Pulham the next day after a twenty-nine-hour flight. The voyage to Egypt was canceled but the *R.33* was repaired and continued in service until 1928. *Courtesy Radio Times Hulton.*

•

peeping up above the top of the cloud-bank being the top of his head, which is functioning in the same way as a submarine periscope!

What a strange sight it would have been to another passing aircraft to see a man's head skimming along the top of a cloud-bank at forty knots![1]

Meanwhile in Germany sixteen rigids survived the war. Decommissioned and empty of hydrogen, they hung lifelessly inside their gloomy hangars suspended from the ceiling by a network of ropes. Their crews were also standing by in the barracks waiting for the victorious Allies to decide what was to be done with them.

The men of the German High Seas Fleet were also waiting for the Allies to make up their minds. They were interned aboard their ships at the British Fleet's anchorage at Scapa Flow. For seven months they waited. Then they took matters into their own hands. On June 21, 1919, they opened the sea valves and sank the German High Seas Fleet.

When news of the sailors' action reached the airshipmen, they too decided that their ships would not fly for the enemy. Two days after the sinkings at Scapa Flow, airshipmen at Nordholz and Wittmundhaven slipped into the hangars and cut the ropes. Seven Zeppelins including four of the newest crashed to the hangar floors in tangled heaps of worthless junk.

Several Allied nations were counting on German airships to form the beginnings of their own postwar rigid-airship fleets, but of the fourteen ships remaining, half were old and obsolete. That left only seven to be divided up among the victorious Allies. To compensate for their loss they confiscated two small ships built by the Zeppelin Company immediately after the war and rushed into passenger service. *LZ-120,* the *Bodensee,* was only slightly larger than the prewar Delag ships. In three months of operation at the end of 1919, she carried twenty-five hundred passengers in more than one hundred flights between Friedrichshafen and Berlin.

The second passenger ship, *LZ-121,* the *Nordstern (Northstar),* was slightly larger and intended for service between Berlin and Stockholm. It was a bitter blow to the Zeppelin Company when both airships were confiscated to take the place of the ruined warships, but subsequent events would prove that single act of defiance by the airshipmen in destroying their ships would save the Zeppelin Company from extinction.

Under the terms of the Treaty of Versailles, Italy got two naval Zeppelins and the passenger ship *Bodensee.* The *Bodensee* was renamed *Esperia* and flew for several years, but the other two ships were soon wrecked, one after being improperly hung in her hangar. The Italians preferred their own semirigid designs, which they had developed to a high degree during and immediately after the war.

Japan and Belgium each received a Zeppelin, which they dismantled and took home and never got around to putting back together.

France received the last wartime Zeppelin, the *L-72.* They also got the *Nordstern,* which they renamed *Mediterranee* and, after a few flights, dismantled. The *L-72,* on the other hand, was flown to a hangar at Toulon and subjected to an intensive three-year study in preparation for her first flight.

Two naval Zeppelins went to England. One was dismantled and the other was wrecked soon after delivery when she was pulled out of her hangar during a storm to make room for a British ship. The British were not too concerned over the loss for, like the Italians, they much preferred their own rigid designs. The problem was that their designs were actually taken secondhand from captured German Zeppelins.

Toward the end of the war as construction of *R.33* and *R.34* neared completion, more enemy Zeppelins fell into Allied hands, and these were used as the basis for the next British rigids. *R.35* was never completed. *R.36* was damaged after two months of service and never flown again. *R.37* and *R.38* would have to be larger in order to operate successfully across the Atlantic, so they were made fifty feet longer with seven hundred thousand cubic feet more gas capacity than their Zeppelin model.

When the United States offered to buy one of the new ships for two million

The Zeppelin Company was preparing to put the *Bodensee* and *Nordstern* into service between Stockholm, Berlin, and Friedrichshafen when the Allies seized the ships. After her first season, *Bodensee* was enlarged, and both were 430 feet long with 795,000 cubic feet of hydrogen. Four 240-horsepower Maybachs gave them a top speed of eighty-three miles per hour, and they had accommodations for thirty passengers plus a crew of sixteen. The *Bodensee* was rechristened *Esperia* by the Italians and made many flights before she was finally dismantled in 1928. The *Nordstern* was renamed *Mediterranee* by the French, made a few flights, and was dismantled. Esperia, *courtesy Stato Maggiore Aeronautica, Rome.*

R.38 was the largest airship yet built by anyone. At 699 feet in length with 2,720,000 cubic feet of gas, she was 57 feet longer than the German *L-33* and *L-49*; and while based on these ships, her much greater size meant that she was essentially an original design. *R.38* was begun by Short Bros. at Cardington in September 1918, but five months later, after receiving the U.S. offer to buy the ship, the Admiralty nationalized the factory and took over construction. At the end of 1919, the Air Ministry replaced the Admiralty and the Cardington plant became the Royal Airship Works. The *R.38* was completed in June 1921. *U.S. Navy photo in the National Archives.*

•

dollars, the British government accepted, and a crew of U.S. Navy airshipmen sailed for England to begin training in the *R.33* and *R.34* while awaiting the completion of their new ship, the *R.38.*

According to the *New York Tribune,* the *R.38* was "truly an aristocrat of the sky, ranking far above the ordinary navy blimps." Her crew's quarters were even "equipped with comfortable chairs, tables, benches, and a Victrola with a good assortment of records."[2] She was hailed as "America's new Super-Zeppelin"[3] although in truth, with the alterations made by her British builders, there was little of the Zeppelin's structural integrity left in her.

The *R.38*'s first flight was made on June 23, 1921. At half-speed some control wires pulled loose and she had to land. The second trial showed that the rudders and fins were overbalanced and had to be cut down. On the third flight they tried again for a speed run but at two-thirds power, some of the girders amidships buckled and gave way. Repairs were completed and a fourth flight was scheduled for August 23.

The *R.38* took off early in the morning from the airfield at Howden. If all went well she would land at Pulham, refuel, be officially handed over to the Americans, and start for the United States. American insignias had already been painted on her tail. The seventeen U.S. airshipmen aboard under Comdr. Lewis Maxfield were anxious to take charge of their ship and start the voyage home, but General Maitland was determined that everything should be completely satisfactory before the ship was turned over to her new owners. As Britain's ranking air officer he insisted on making this last test flight in person to be sure everything was in good order.

One American who missed the flight was Lt. Comdr. Richard E. Byrd, soon to achieve fame as a polar explorer. He arrived at Howden too late to secure a berth aboard the airship and was unable to talk anyone into changing places. Byrd had to settle for a good view of the takeoff as his friends sailed away into the sunrise.

Lt. Comdr. Richard E. Byrd

How magnificent she looked, the rosy light of sunrise tinting her bright sides a series of soft violet and lavender tints. Officers and observers aboard, lines cast off, she rose slowly and with dignity befitting so huge a craft, sailed away into a cloudless sky.[4]

Forty-four of the most experienced airshipmen of two nations died when the *R.38* broke in half on August 24, 1921, and fell into the Humber River. Designated the *ZR-2*, she was to have been the U.S. Navy's second rigid. The American colors were already painted on her stern in anticipation of the transatlantic delivery flight her new crew would make as soon as the last tests were completed. But in requiring a series of sharp, high-speed turns at low altitude, the British Admiralty wanted a maneuver that German airshipmen had been specifically forbidden to make in their lightly built height climbers, on which the *R.38* design was based. *From Scientific American, September 17, 1921.*

•

After a day-long series of tests over the North Sea, the *R.38* headed for Pulham, but the aerodrome was covered in heavy fog so they turned back out to sea to spend the night. Pulham was still fogged in the next morning and they decided to return instead to Howden.

They had been in the air for thirty-four hours as they approached the city of Hull on the Humber River and began a final speed run. The *R.38* was supposed to make a top speed of seventy miles per hour but so far she had not gotten beyond fifty before things started falling apart. Now with the strengthened frames, it was time for a full-speed trial. Easing slowly up to sixty miles an hour, the huge ship made a series of sharp right and left turns. Slowing her down again to fifty, the captain ordered the rudder hard over and the *R.38* broke in half. The fracture snapped the gasoline lines, spilling fuel over the engines where it ignited setting off the hydrogen in the front half of the ship. It plummeted into the Humber like a blazing comet and sank. The rear section floated more slowly down to the river.

Norman Walker

I was in the lower rudder, and was proceeding back to the tail cockpit for the landing. We were then flying high, 1,500 feet.

I had just reached the cockpit when with a tremendous crash, the girders amidship broke, and the ship split in halves and started to descend towards the river. I cannot describe my sensations but I certainly thought my end had come. I made a rush for the tail to get a parachute, but found two of my enlisted comrades, Harry Bateman and Walter Potter, already there. I knew there was only one chute there for the three of us. Bateman had the chute and jumped, but the chute fouled, and he hung to the tail. Both Potter and I started to run forward for other chutes but just as I got in the keel either the petrol tanks or the hydrogen exploded.

Flames immediately began to sweep the forward part of our half of the ship. What was happening to my comrades in the other half of the ship I do not know. Most of the officers and crew were amidship sitting and lying in bunks when the girders broke. At least one man dropped through the gap, and possibly others did, but probably most of them rolled forward when the nose went down. I ran back to the tail to get away from the fire in the bag. Bateman, Potter and I got into the cockpit. By this time the gas was becoming depleted, and the ship was shooting down rapidly; the forward half of the ship had already beaten us in the mad race for the Humber.

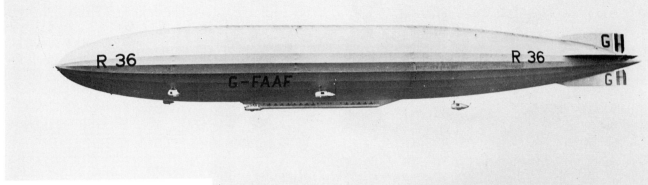

ABOVE: Britain spent more than four million dollars on *R.35*, *R.36*, and *R.37*, but only the *R.36* reached completion. Based on the *L-33* and modified as other Zeppelins were captured, she was launched in 1921 by Beardmore. She was powered by two Maybachs taken from *L-71* plus three 350-horsepower Sunbeams. There were serious proposals for converting her into a commercial ship by adding a fifty-passenger gondola, here drawn onto the ship by an artist. In service from London to India, she could cut travel time from twenty-one days to six, but after the loss of *R.38* she made only a few flights, once directing traffic at Ascot. She was dismantled in 1926, another victim of the *R.38*. *Courtesy Imperial War Museum, London.* BELOW: *R.80* was designed for the Admiralty by Vickers' Barnes Wallis. She was ordered in 1917 as a fast, long-range Atlantic convoy escort. When the government withdrew its financial support from all airship construction in late 1919, Vickers completed the ship on their own. She was 535 feet long with 1,200,000 cubic feet of gas, a disposable lift of nearly eighteen tons, and a top speed of sixty miles per hour. Vickers planned to put her into commercial service carrying thirty passengers from London to Rome via Paris in seventeen and one-half hours, but the Air Ministry took her over as a training ship for the *R.38*'s American crew. She was an excellent ship but after the loss of the *R.38*, she made only a single flight and was dismantled by the government in 1925. *Courtesy Vickers Ltd.*

We could not use the parachute as we were too low, being only a few hundred feet up. I saw we were going to land in the water, and so climbed up on the fabric forward of the tail cup. When I thought we were going to strike, I jumped. I was surprised to find my feet strike bottom and found I was in four feet of water near the shore.[5]

Twenty-year-old navy rigger Norman Walker was the only American to walk away from the wreckage of the *R.38*. Bateman, Potter, and two other Englishmen also survived. All the rest—General Maitland, Commander Maxfield, twenty-six of Britain's most experienced airshipmen, and sixteen of America's—died in the wreck. The crash of the *R.38* with forty-four lives made it the worst aerial disaster in history, and the loss of so many of the best airshipmen of both nations would continue to cast a tragic shadow over airship development in Britain and America for years to come. It signaled the end of rigid development in Britain for several years. In terms of the history of lighter-than-air flight, the loss of the *R.38* may have been the most costly of them all.

The French were as enthusiastic as the British had been about the peacetime potential of the rigid airship, but the French chose to approach the problem much more cautiously. Rather than rush into the construction of new ships, they planned to use their German Zeppelins, the *Nordstern* and *L-72,* which they renamed the *Dixmude,* as flying test vehicles to study thoroughly every aspect of rigid construction and handling. They were especially interested in establishing an airship route between France and her colonies in Africa. The crash of the *R.38* only served to convince them of the soundness of their cautious approach.

For two full years after the *R.38* went down, the *Dixmude* sat inside her hangar at Toulon while her French crew under Comdr. Jean du Plessis de Grenadan carefully examined every inch of her intricate structure. They disassembled each of the airship's six engines a hundred times until at last they felt ready to take her out and fly.

On August 2, 1923, the *Dixmude* emerged from her hangar for the first time in three years, and a week later she flew to Corsica. The defects shown up during this flight required three more weeks of adjustment and, on August 30, the *Dixmude* took off on her second flight. Writer Maxime Baze, aboard as a passenger, looked down on Toulon as night fell.

Maxime Baze

The harbor of Toulon, in which a squadron was anchored, showed in magnificent outline, with all its lights burning. Searchlights reached for us and discovered us in the sky. I had the impression, over that illuminated harbor surrounded by the mists of the city, of an immense casket suddenly opened to show a glittering cluster of pearls.

We gained the open sea. One by one the lighthouses appeared. The one near Planier, which sailors ordinarily can not see more than 70 miles, followed us for almost 36 hours.

The Dixmude pointed toward Barcelona. In the midst of the sky, a tempest suddenly arises, a clattering storm. Our wireless telegraph apparatus was put out of commission. With admirable coolness and presence of mind, the officer-aeronauts fought against the elements. Rain beat on the ship. A motor stopt, the most important, that one in the bow nacelle; a second stopt, also, then a third. No one was discouraged. The mechanicians, suspended in the void, made necessary repairs. Officers, tied in their places, regulated the equilibrium. By transferring six men from one end of the fuselage to the other, the Dixmude was saved, and, at daybreak we looked down on the Balearic Islands.

After flying over Ibiza in the Balearics, they continued on to Algeria on the north coast of Africa.

Maxime Baze

The "White City," extending below our feet presents an unforgettable picture. The Dixmude, once more under control, is obedient to those who sail her. The dirigible rises, dips its prow, turns upward again, maneuvers to the right, performs evolutions to the left. The Algerians look up at us, entranced. The citizens have climbed upon their

LZ-114, the German navy's *L-72*, is shown on July 12, 1920, as she departed Germany for France where she was rechristened the *Dixmude*. She was 660 feet long with 2,400,000 cubic feet of hydrogen, a top speed of eighty miles per hour, and a ceiling of 25,300 feet. As a specially lightened, high-altitude bomber, she was not intended for extended flight at lower altitudes, but the French were seriously considering airship service between Paris and their African colonies and they used their Zeppelins, the *Dixmude* and *Mediterranee*, to test the possible routes. *Friedrich Moch photo, courtesy Douglas Robinson.*

•

terraces, have filled the squares, and are spread out over all the roads. The tramways are blocked, and no vehicles can move anywhere in the city. Thousands of admiring looks, and some possibly a little anxious, are fixt upon the Dixmude.[6]

They cruised over Carthage the next morning, then Tunis and Bizerta, before turning once more northward over the Mediterranean to Sardinia, Corsica, and back to Toulon, a total distance of eighteen hundred miles.

This flight was just a warm-up, however, for the next one in September, a record-setting four-day, forty-five-hundred-mile voyage over much the same route. Starting again from Toulon they crossed the Mediterranean to Oran, then sailed down the North African coast to Bizerta. Turning north toward Sardinia they met a storm that blew them all the way back to North Africa. There they set out once more across the sea, crossing the French coast at Nice, then flying on to Paris before returning to Toulon.

The flight received worldwide acclaim. Only the Germans persisted in pointing out that the *Dixmude* was originally built for very high altitude flying and her structure, purposely made as light as possible, was not really designed for the turbulent air of lower altitudes.

On December 18, 1923, the *Dixmude* set out once more in quest of even greater honors. With forty crewmen and ten observers aboard, they followed much the same route as before, dropping postcards over Gafsa, Tozeur, and Bizerta. For three days all went well. On the fourth day the radio operator on an Italian steamer intercepted what he thought was a distress call from the airship. Nothing more was heard. A week passed without a sign of the *Dixmude*.

Then on December 29, some fishermen hauling in their nets off the southwest coast of Sicily brought up the body of du Plessis de Grenadan, the *Dixmude*'s commander. Several villagers then recalled seeing a very bright light in the sky early on the morning of the twenty-third over the stormy channel between Sicily and Tunis. Some weeks later a few bits of charred wreckage were found in the same area—nothing more. Even the ship's homing pigeons failed to return, leading authorities to suspect that the ship had been struck by lightning while valving gas. Nothing else seemed to explain her sudden and almost total disappearance.

The loss of the *Dixmude* brought an end to rigid airship development in France. Only a few small nonrigids and semirigids continued to be built by the Zodiac Company until France was overrun by the Germans in World War II.

The United States entered the postwar period with a great deal of interest in rigid airships but no experience. The only ships the United States had flown during the war were blimps. Yet many military men including Gen. Billy Mitchell, the assistant chief of the Army Air Service, and Adm. William Moffett, the chief of the navy's Bureau of Aeronautics, were convinced that large dirigibles would be useful in patrolling America's broad ocean frontiers.

Congress divided the responsibility for U.S. airship development between the armed forces, with the navy getting the rigids while the army took over the nonrigids. Construction of the first American rigid airship began in 1920 at the Naval Aircraft Factory at the Philadelphia Navy Yard. The design was based on plans drawn up by the French from a captured German Zeppelin, the *L-49*. While this ship was being built, the navy arranged for the purchase of the *R.38* from Great Britain and the army bought a large semirigid from Italy. With three large airships, the United States would be able to test and compare each type before deciding which features were most desirable for future American-built ships.

The loss of the *R.38* with seventeen navy airshipmen was a serious blow to the U.S. dirigible program, but before the end of the year, the army's Italian-built semirigid arrived. In November the *Roma* was assembled, inflated with hydrogen, and made her first flight.

The Italians had built a number of semirigids and the army hoped to take advantage of their experience, but just as the *R.38* turned out to be an untried modification of the successful *R.34*, the *Roma*, too, was something brand new. She was 410 feet long and held nearly 1,200,000 cubic feet of gas—the largest semirigid ever built—certainly far from a proven design.

She had successfully completed twenty-two flights in Italy, but on her third U.S. test flight from Langley Field, Virginia, to Washington, D.C., she was overtaken by strong winds and her performance prompted some unfavorable comment from her new army crew, most of whom had to return to Langley Field by train.

Lt. Clifford Smythe wrote to his father, "The dirigible seemed sluggish and slow to respond to the controls. While she ended the trip all right, she disobeyed her rudder several times in a way that was alarming." It would be, Lieutenant Smythe concluded, "criminal negligence to fly her again without changes in her construction."[7] Sgt. J. M. Beall was even more emphatic. "This ship is a death trap," he wrote to a friend. "It's going down one of these days and only three or four of us are coming out alive."[8]

Early in February 1922, the army replaced the *Roma*'s original Ansaldo engines with more powerful Liberties, and on February 21, she started out on her first trial flight with the new engines. Twenty-five minutes into the test, just after a speed run, a cable at the stern supporting the rudder assembly appeared to give way and the whole box-kite-like structure slipped sideways, making the ship uncontrollable. The *Roma* flew straight into the ground from a thousand feet up, striking some high-tension wires that ignited the ship's hydrogen. Eleven of the forty-five men aboard survived. Thirty-four did not. The dead included Lieutenant Smythe and Sergeant Beall.

It was the second airship disaster in six months: first the *R.38* with the loss of seventeen Americans, then the *Roma* and thirty-four more dead, and almost the entire loss of life in both cases occurred when the hydrogen caught fire. Two days after the *Roma*'s crash, the Washington correspondent of the *New York World* reported, "there is in storage in Texas more than enough helium to have inflated the bags of the Roma."[9]

Of all the earth's elements, only two are lighter than air. One is hydrogen, the other is helium, and though helium is the heavier of the two, it has one great advantage over hydrogen. It won't burn.

Helium was first discovered in 1868 as an unknown element in the spectrum of the sun. Twenty-seven years later it was found on earth in small amounts in the atmosphere and in the volcanic fumes issuing from the mouth of Mount Vesuvius. In 1903 it was found to be a part of the natural gas pumped from a well in Dexter, Kansas. World War I intensified the global search for helium but no other nation could find enough of it to fill their balloons and airships. It was only after joining the Allies in 1916 that the United States learned of the military value of this nonflammable lifting gas that only the United States seemed to possess in commercial quantities. In 1917 the Bureau of Mines began producing helium at three installations around Fort Worth, Texas. The first shipments of the strategic gas were ready to be sent overseas just as the war ended.

Now the nation learned that while thirty-four men were burning to death aboard the *Roma*, there was enough helium sitting unused in storage tanks in Texas to fill the ship. The military authorities protested that, with their limited congressional appropriations, they couldn't afford to buy the gas from the Bureau of Mines. For while hydrogen could be inexpensively manufactured anywhere in the world, helium could only be extracted from the natural gas by freezing it to 328 degrees below zero. By 1920 the Bureau of Mines was producing it for a little less than ten cents per cubic foot. It cost seventeen thousand dollars to fill the *Roma* with hydrogen. The same amount of helium would have cost $120,000, more than the army said it could afford.

The public outrage was reflected in the press. "Congress and the military authorities are busily shifting the responsibility to one another for our failure to develop and utilize our huge sources of this gas," editorialized the *New York Globe*. "The country has had quite enough needless slaughter of American men through failure to provide a sufficient factor of safety."[10] The *New York Herald* wrote,

The *Roma* was designed and built by a team of Italian army engineers under the direction of General Crocco, the builder of Italy's first semirigid back in 1907. But with a length of 410 feet and a gas capacity of 1,200,000 cubic feet, the *Roma* was twice the size of any previous semirigid. She was completed on March 1, 1920, but the war was over and the government apparently had no further use for her. She was sold to an Italian businessman who planned to fly her as a one-hundred-passenger commercial ship, but when the U.S. army offered him $185,000, he accepted and the *Roma* was disassembled and shipped to Langley Field, Virginia. *Courtesy Stato Maggiore Aeronautica, Rome.*

"Between August and February, all the grim lessons purchased in England at the price of 44 lives were forgotten. This ought to be a lesson; if we can't afford helium, we can't afford dirigibles."[11]

It was an outcry that the authorities could not ignore. No American airship ever again flew with hydrogen.

Now the United States was left with only one big airship, the *ZR-1*, being assembled at Lakehurst. The navy originally intended to buy two ships from England, but after the *R.38* disaster they turned to the only other organization with rigid airship experience, the Zeppelin Company.

Since Germany was prohibited from building aircraft by the Treaty of Versailles, the Zeppelin factory at Friedrichshafen, where thirteen thousand people once worked around the clock creating the ships of war, was reduced to making aluminum pots and pans.

The Allies had decided that Germany owed the United States eight hundred thousand dollars in war reparations. Payment was originally to be made in military airships but these were destroyed by their crews. It was then that Hugo Eckener, who became president of the Zeppelin Company after Count Zeppelin's death, saw an opportunity to stay, at least temporarily, in the airship business. Bypassing the two governments involved, he took his proposal directly to the U.S. Military Commission in Berlin. Would the United States be interested in receiving a brand-new Zeppelin instead of the eight hundred thousand dollars in cash? The navy jumped at the chance and Congress and the War Department agreed. Only England and France, the United States' wartime allies, seemed hesitant to give their approval, for though they were no longer interested in rigid ships of their own, they were still not too

The *ZR-1*, the *Shenandoah*, was a copy of the German *L-49* forced down in France in 1918. A complete set of plans were made by the French and passed on to the United States. The design was completely wind tunnel–tested and a thirty-five-foot hull section and an extra gas cell were added to compensate for the use of helium and for the additional weight of stronger girders than those in the high-altitude *L-49*. The *Shenandoah* was 680 feet long and 78 feet in diameter, with 2,115,000 cubic feet of helium. She had a total lift of sixty-two tons and weighed forty tons, which left twenty-two tons for useful lift. She was powered by six three-hundred-horsepower Packard engines. *Clements photo, courtesy Goodyear Tire and Rubber Co.*

On January 16, 1924, the *Shenandoah* was moored to the high mast at Lakehurst in a test of her ability to ride out the stormy weather she might find in the Arctic. With inadequate vents in her tail fins, she was hit by a sharp blast of wind at seventy-five miles per hour and the sudden unequal air pressure blew in her top fin cover. With the fin gone, she pitched sideways and the next blast tore her from the mast, ripping out her mooring winches and collapsing her two forward gas cells. Her crew returned the ship safely to Lakehurst the next morning. *Courtesy Cole Airship Collection, University of Oregon.*

•

pleased to see another nation receive a new Zeppelin. Finally after protracted negotiation they reluctantly agreed only after the United States promised never to arm the ship or to use it for military purposes.

The contract for the construction of the *LZ-126* was signed in June 1922, just in time to stop the Inter-Allied Aeronautical Commission from dismantling the big shed at Friedrichshafen.

While the *ZR-3* was being started in Germany, the *ZR-1* was completed and brought out of her hangar at Lakehurst, New Jersey. Like the British *R.38*, the *ZR-1* was a copy of a German naval Zeppelin with an extra thirty-five-foot section added in the middle for more lift. Unlike the ill-fated *R.38,* however, the *ZR-1's* designers had made extensive stress tests and strengthened the entire framework. The ship's first flight was made on September 4, 1923. A month later the *ZR-1* was officially christened the *Shenandoah, the Daughter of the Stars.*

She was the first rigid airship built in America, the first to be flown by Americans, and the first ever to fly with helium. Yet in spite of her experimental nature, the Navy Department was preparing to send the *Shenandoah* on a voyage to the North Pole. A series of mooring masts were being constructed at various points along the route and, as a final test of her ability to withstand bad weather, the ship was scheduled to spend several days moored outdoors to the high mast at Lakehurst. The wintry gales that swept across New Jersey were considered at least the equal of anything she would meet in the Arctic.

Standing watch aboard a ship at the mooring mast was one of the least popular of an airshipman's duties. The crew was required to stand regular watches and actually to "fly" the ship, constantly adjusting the ballast and trim as changes in wind and temperature altered the balance of the ship as she rode a hundred feet above the ground with her nose locked into the mast. Unlike the smooth sailing of free flight, a ride at the mast could be very uncomfortable in heavy weather as the ship pitched and rolled with every gust.

For four days the *Shenandoah* endured icy blasts of up to sixty miles an hour without difficulty, but just at sunset on the evening of January 16, 1924, the storm increased in intensity and a seventy-mile-per-hour gale wrenched the ship from the mast and blew her across the field. As soon as they realized what was happening, the men in the control car rushed to dump ballast and the huge ship bounded over the tops of the trees and disappeared into the stormy night.

Twenty-one men were aboard the ship when she tore loose including a sailor delivering a load of sandwiches from the mess hall. Lt. Comdr. Maurice Pierce was the senior officer, but the man who immediately took charge was Capt. Anton Heinen, a World War I Zeppelin Company test pilot brought to the United States by the navy to train American airshipmen. The little German had already impressed the men with his crisp, no-nonsense manner and encyclopedic knowledge of airships.

One engine had been idling as the ship rode at the mast. Now Lieutenant Commander Pierce ordered all six to full power while Heinen turned the ship's tail into the wind to protect the damaged bow where the two forward gas cells had ripped open as the mooring winch and nose cone tore away.

Radio operator J. L. Robertson had been repairing the ship's transmitter when the wild ride began, and despite the fact that parts were scattered all over the room and his tool box flew out the window, he had the set assembled by 9:00 that evening and succeeded in contacting station WOR in Newark, which informed him that the

Shenandoah was then directly over the city. WOR cancelled its regular programs and began relaying weather information and position reports to the stricken ship as thousands of listeners tuned in to the real-life drama taking place in the howling gale high overhead.

For eight hours the *Shenandoah*'s crew struggled to return their crippled ship to Lakehurst. Though he had no official status, Captain Heinen took charge and skillfully brought the ship slowly back to her base. As their instructor and the man who had supervised the ship's construction, few of those aboard questioned his authority, especially after he gave a junior officer the choice of obeying his orders or being thrown overboard.

At 2:30 the next morning the *Shenandoah* was safely back in her hangar. Everyone praised her strength in weathering the gale, but the fact that she had torn loose from the mooring mast gave Navy Department officials second thoughts about the polar flight, especially after the loss of the *Dixmude* only two weeks earlier.

By the time Lt. Comdr. Zachary Lansdowne arrived at Lakehurst in February to take command of the *Shenandoah*, the North Pole flight was off. In its place, however, was a transcontinental voyage scheduled for the fall of 1924 to make use of the mooring masts already erected at Fort Worth, San Diego, and Fort Lewis, Washington.

On October 7, 1924, the *Shenandoah* cast off at Lakehurst bound for Fort Worth by way of Baltimore, Washington, Atlanta, and Birmingham. Rear Adm. William Moffett, chief of the navy's Bureau of Aeronautics and an enthusiastic advocate of rigid airships, was aboard as an observer.

By 1924 the cost of helium was down to five and one-half cents per cubic foot but it still cost over one hundred thousand dollars to fill the *Shenandoah* and the navy was forced to develop special flying techniques to conserve the precious gas.

The *Shenandoah*'s triangular keel ran along the bottom of the hull from bow to stern beneath the gasbags. It was illuminated by daylight coming through the translucent outer cover. In the dark of night, however, the narrow catwalk must have seemed a perilous place to a visitor, for a single misstep could send him plunging through the canvas outer cover to his death far below. Yet the surefooted airshipmen rarely gave a second thought to their precarious perch as they went about their business inside the huge hull. The fuel tanks in the background could be cut loose if the ship had to be lightened quickly. *Clements photo, courtesy San Diego Aero-Space Museum.*

•

Crossing the Rocky Mountains they actually had to fly down into Dragoon Pass with the sheer canyon walls towering up above the ship on both sides. At a higher altitude they would have lost too much helium through gas expansion. Down in the mountain pass they risked losing only their lives.

After refueling at San Diego the *Shenandoah* flew up the Pacific Coast to Fort Lewis, Washington. They arrived at 8:15 in the morning and were forced to wait all day until the cool evening air contracted the helium enough to allow them to land without valving gas.

From Fort Lewis the *Shenandoah* turned and retraced her route back to Lakehurst, covering a total of more than nine thousand miles in nineteen days. The only civilian on the flight was Junius Wood, a writer for the *National Geographic* magazine. Though the naval airshipmen had grown accustomed to their routine aloft, Wood found it an awesome experience to be cruising through the dark of night on the huge ship a half mile above the earth.

Junius Wood

White running lights were on the forward and aft gondolas, green lights on the two starboard cars, and red on the two on the port side. Within, all was dark, except for a moment on the bridge or for the glow from electric torches in the long tunnel in the keel, as men passed back and forth, changing watch in the engine cars, measuring fuel tanks, inspecting motors and gas bags, and performing other tasks which required constant vigilance. . . .

In the dark the long keel is eerie with phosphorescent figures and letters, which glow from every latticed frame or piece of emergency gear, with lights which flash in the distance and disappear and lights which suddenly appear from nowhere, while one fur-padded form leans at a danger angle and another passes on the ribbon of a runway.[12]

While the *Shenandoah* was still on the West Coast, the navy's second airship, the *ZR-3*, arrived at Lakehurst after her transatlantic delivery flight from the Zeppelin

Halfway through her nine-thousand-mile transcontinental flight, the *Shenandoah* cruises over Los Angeles as an army biplane flies up to greet her. The propeller at the rear of the control car, shown in earlier photos, is no longer there. The Packard engine has been removed to save weight, and the ship is flying with only five motors. The control car was originally separated from the hull to give the propeller room to turn. With the engine removed, the navy planned to attach the car directly to the hull. *Courtesy Historical Collection, Security Pacific National Bank, Los Angeles.*

•

factory at Friedrichshafen. The navy had prepared for any emergency with cruisers on station along the route and emergency landing fields set up at Boston, Mitchell Field on Long Island, Langley Field in Virginia, and Parris Island, South Carolina. They also requested all amateur radio operators to clear the airship's frequencies while monitoring them in case of trouble. Fortunately there was none. The five-thousand-mile transatlantic flight went smoothly and the *ZR-3* arrived safely at Lakehurst after an uneventful eighty-one-hour voyage, and the second crossing of the Atlantic from east to west by an aircraft. When the *Shenandoah* returned from her transcontinental flight on October 25, the two ships were docked side by side in the huge Lakehurst hangar. A month later the *ZR-3* was christened the *Los Angeles* by Mrs. Calvin Coolidge.

As the first Zeppelin to be built in five years, the *Los Angeles* represented a considerable advance over any other airship. Since the Allies would not allow the Zeppelin Company to build a warship, the *Los Angeles* was essentially a passenger craft that happened to belong to the U.S. Navy. Her cabin was considerably more luxurious than the *Shenandoah*'s, resembling a Pullman sleeping car. There were five compartments, each with large windows and two six-foot upholstered seats that made into upper and lower double beds. Curtains separated each compartment

The *ZR-3* circles Berlin's Brandenburg Gate in this composite stereoscopic view representing the start of her transatlantic delivery flight. Begun on October 12, 1924, it was crucial to the Zeppelin Company's survival. The *ZR-3* was their 116th airship, the first to be launched in five years and the first to attempt the Atlantic. The U.S. Navy's contract order had saved their factory from destruction, but the *ZR-3*'s failure over the ocean would be the end of their dream of a fleet of transatlantic passenger liners. Five master airship pilots manned the bridge while the cruisers *Detroit* and *Milwaukee* waited offshore in case of trouble. *Courtesy Cole Airship Collection, University of Oregon.*

from a central corridor. Forward on the left in place of the sixth compartment was the radio room and forward of that was the control car.

The navy now had two airships but helium enough for only one. The *Los Angeles* crossed the Atlantic filled with hydrogen. The *Shenandoah* was hung up in the hangar and her helium pumped into the *Los Angeles.* Early in 1925 she made two trips to Bermuda, where she moored to the airship tender *Patoka.* In May she flew to Puerto Rico. In June engine trouble forced her to turn back from a tour of the Midwest. While the *Los Angeles* received a thorough overhaul, her helium was transferred back into the *Shenandoah,* which was then scheduled to complete the interrupted Midwestern flight, including visits to several state fairs and a landing at the new airship mast Henry Ford had erected at Dearborn, Michigan.

Zachary Lansdowne was born in Ohio. As commanding officer of the *Shenandoah* he knew only too well the unsettled weather conditions she would meet over the Midwest in the summer. He asked that the flight be postponed, but the most the Navy Department would agree to was a two-week delay. The navy had few opportunities to show off its vessels in the Midwest and, as a result, the people in that part of the country sometimes wondered if their tax dollars were well spent on cruisers and battleships. It was an attitude reflected by many of their representatives in Congress. The *Shenandoah* was as big as a battleship and, better yet, she could sail the skies of the Midwest. She would draw huge crowds to the state fairs, and successful fairs often produced happy politicians, which couldn't hurt the navy at appropriations time.

At sunset on the evening of September 2, 1925, the *Shenandoah* cast off on her goodwill trip. In the two years since her launching she had made fifty-six flights covering twenty-five thousand miles. This one, scheduled to last five to six days, would be her fifty-seventh and Lansdowne's last before his regular rotation back to sea duty.

An hour and a half out of Lakehurst headed due west, she was greeted by the auto horns and factory whistles of Philadelphia. The air was still warm at midnight as she glided effortlessly over the Alleghenies near Somerset. At 3:00 A.M. the watch officers in the darkened gondola saw the first flashes of summer lightning, behind them in the east, then ahead in the west and northwest. Meeting rising headwinds at twenty-five hundred feet over Cambridge, Ohio, Lansdowne ordered the ship down to twenty-one hundred feet. The lightning was moving closer. At 5:08 the ship began to rise.

Few people were outside at that hour of the morning. Those who were saw the great ship in silhouette against the pale moonlight and high above her a strange rolling cloud beginning to form.

The men in the darkened control car now caught sight of the violent line squall coming into being high over their heads. To Lt. Comdr. Charles Rosendahl it looked as if "this new cloud was either coming toward us or building up very rapidly."[13] Then Chief Rigger Allen at the elevator wheel reported the beginning of the ascent, "She's rising at two meters per second and I can't check her, sir," he said quietly. Lansdowne ordered more speed from the engines and a down angle of eighteen degrees on the bow. Yet despite the added tons of power downward, the rise continued. Lansdowne sent men scrambling up the ladder into the hull to remove the covers that prevented the automatic valves from opening. The *Shenandoah* shot up through her pressure height at thirty-eight hundred feet and continued on—despite

five minutes of gas valving from the control car—to sixty-two hundred feet. There she paused and then started down.

"We shot down at a terrific rate of over 1,400 feet per minute for perhaps over two minutes," Rosendahl recalled. "My eardrums felt ready to burst!"[14] Lansdowne ordered the ballast dumped and four tons of water poured from the hull. Half a mile down, the descent ended and a second ascent began, even more violent than the first. Rosendahl was on his way up the ladder from the control car into the hull to prepare to drop fuel on the next fall. There was no ballast left.

Lt. Comdr. Charles Rosendahl

Just as I stepped upon the rungs of the ladder, the ship took a very sudden upward inclination that seemed to me very much like the beginning of a loop in an airplane. The angle was greater than any I'd ever experienced before in an airship. The control car was not an integral part of the hull for having once contained an engine, it was suspended below the ship by wooden struts and wires. As I climbed up the ladder, I heard the snapping of struts. . . . The control car then seemed to lag behind the sharp upward thrust of the bow.[15]

The wooden struts were torn loose. All that held the control car to the hull were the control cables connecting the steering wheels to the rudders and elevators at the stern. Ten men were in the car. As the cables began to give way, Col. G. C. Hall and Lt. Joseph Anderson, the aerologist, scrambled up the ladder into the hull. Commander Lansdowne and seven men remained at their posts in the doomed car.

The *Shenandoah* and *Los Angeles* rest side by side in the hangar at Lakehurst. The *Los Angeles* on the right is empty and suspended on cables from the hangar roof, while the *Shenandoah* is filled with helium and ready to fly. The difference in the shape of the two hulls is apparent here, for though the *Los Angeles* was twenty-two feet shorter than the *Shenandoah*, she was twelve feet wider, and this extra width gave her half a million cubic feet more gas. *Courtesy San Diego Aero-Space Museum.*

Lt. Comdr. Zachary Lansdowne took command of the *Shenandoah* in February 1924. He was scheduled to return to sea duty after the flight of September 2, 1925. Lansdowne was one of the navy's most experienced airshipmen and in 1919 had accompanied the British *R.34* on her transatlantic flight as a guest of the Admiralty. *Official U.S. Navy photo.*

•

Lt. Comdr. Charles Rosendahl

I had gone but a short distance along the keel when there was a terrific clashing, metallic din and a combination of noises easy to remember, more than difficult to forget. The bottom panel of the outer cover and several of the transverse structural members of the flat keel were cut loose along one side, as the control wires from aft carrying the free control car like a plummet, tore along the bottom before they pulled out completely. The keel walkway, thus left unsupported along one side, effectively impeded passage except by laboriously crawling around amidst wires and through the structure outboard of the keel. And whether it occurred simultaneously I cannot say; but my next recollection is that of standing there looking aft, faced with the unbelievable vision of the rest of the ship floating rapidly away from me and downward into the dull gray light of the breaking dawn. It was preceded and accompanied by that unmistakable "cry" of metal under severe stress—this time really distress. It was as though a thousand panes of glass had been hurled from on high to pavement beneath.[16]

The tortured *Shenandoah* gave way at frame 130, about two hundred feet from the bow. "It was as though the ship had been held up at each end and then struck on top with a giant's hammer and twisted by the snout at the same time," Rosendahl said. With the struts gone, the weight of the control car pulled the cables loose at the stern and dragged them along the keel until they came free, then car and cables plummeted to earth carrying Lansdowne and seven others to their deaths. The bow with Rosendahl and six men aboard drifted for twelve miles before they were able to valve gas and bring it safely to earth. The remainder of the hull, nearly five hundred feet of it, broke in two again. The stern with eighteen men fell slowly to the ground and all survived. Machinist Ralph Jones was at his post in engine car 3 when the bow of the ship broke off.

Ralph Jones

I looked out and saw half of her float away. I said, "Well Jones, you might as well sit here and let it happen; you can't do any good by moving away." So I sat tight by my engine and closed my eyes. First thing you know, I was walking around on the ground. Then she blew away again, and there I was alone in the field.[17]

The men in engine cars 4 and 5 ahead of Jones were not so lucky. Their section of the ship supported only by two torn and nearly empty gasbags fell rapidly to earth dragged down by the weight of the engines. At the last minute the two cars pulled away and the top part of the section containing the crew's quarters and galley landed more softly. All four mechanics were crushed in the two engine cars, but the ship's cook stepped out of his galley, hailed a car, and went to town to notify Lakehurst of the crash.

It was nearly seven o'clock in the morning when Rosendahl finally brought the two-hundred-foot bow section down—almost on top of Ernest Nichols's three-room house.

Ernest Nichols

I was in the house when my neighbor called up on the telephone and said an airship was headed for my house and that I had better stop it. I ran out and here it came right through our orchard, headed straight for the house.

It sure enough was coming right toward my house. I looked up and there was my oldest boy—I have six boys and one girl—sticking his head out of the up-stairs window. I

knew I had to stop that thing or the house would be smashed and my kids would be killed. Then, too, I heard the fellows up there [inside the bow] yelling, "Grab hold! Grab hold! Turn her south!"

So I grabbed hold of the cable that was hanging down and drew it around that fence post. The post snapt right off. I grabbed the cable again and threw it around that old maple stump. The stump had two prongs on it and I thought sure it would hold but it didn't. By that time the nose was so close to the ground the underside had me backed up against the fence and I had to run. I was headed away from the house then but it knocked off the top of that shed and the wheel on that well and then bowled over that grape arbor. I kept following it and finally threw the cable around that tree.

All that time I didn't know what the thing was. I didn't know it was so big. Why, it's over 190 feet long.

Soon my kids came running out and we helped tie it up. Then the men began climbing out. Even then it didn't stay where it was, for we had to tie it again several times during the day and the men borrowed my shotgun and punctured the gas-bags.[18]

The nearest town was Sharon, Ohio, eighty miles east and a little south of Columbus. As nearby farmers rushed to aid the survivors, others came to loot. By nightfall the wreckage was stripped of everything that could be moved. Only bare and twisted girders remained of the once-proud *Daughter of the Stars*. Zachary Lansdowne had fallen less than a hundred miles from his boyhood home, a victim of the violent summer weather he knew so well.

On September 2, 1925, two navy airplanes fell into the sea while attempting the first flight from California to Hawaii. The next day fourteen men died with the

The *Shenandoah* had her fatal meeting with the line squall over Ava, Ohio, at 5:30 on the morning of September 3, 1925. Her control car, engine cars 4 and 5, the crew's quarters, and the tail section shown here all landed within two miles of each other. Eighteen men walked away from the tail section while four survivors rode the crew's quarters to the ground. The forward third of the hull maintained most of its buoyancy and drifted to earth twelve miles away with Rosendahl and six others aboard. Twenty-nine men survived. Of the fourteen dead, two fell out where the hull broke open, four were killed in the section dragged down by the forward engine cars, and Commander Lansdowne with seven others died in the control car. *Official U.S. Air Force photo.*

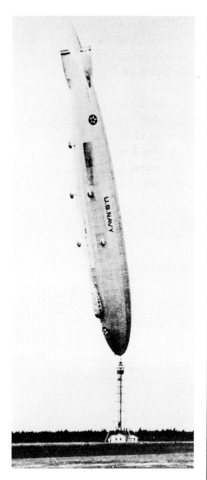

On August 25, 1927, the *Los Angeles* was moored to the high mast at Lakehurst with a crew of twenty-five aboard preparing to take off on a training flight. A cold breeze struck the tail of the ship, giving it added buoyancy, and it slowly began to rise. Crewmen grabbed for the nearest girder as tools, spare parts, and everything loose slid down the keel and through the outer cover. At the top of her ascent, the ship turned gracefully in a half circle and started down, descending until she was once more riding parallel to the ground on the other side of the mast. Construction of a low mooring mast was completed forty-five days later. *Courtesy Jack R. Hunt.*

•

Shenandoah. It was too much for an army colonel at Fort Sam Houston, Texas. On September 5, he issued a seventeen-page statement to the press that would lead to his court-martial. The colonel's name was Billy Mitchell and his outspoken criticism of military aviation policies had already cost him both his job as assistant chief of the Army Air Service and his temporary rank of brigadier general.

Col. William Mitchell

I have been asked from all parts of the country to give my opinion about the reasons for the frightful aeronautical accidents and loss of life, equipment and treasure that has occurred during the last few days. This statement therefore is given out publicly by me after mature deliberation and after a sufficient time has elapsed since the terrible accident to our naval aircraft, to find out something about what happened.

About what happened, my opinion is as follows: These accidents are the direct result of the incompetency, criminal negligence and almost treasonable administration of the national defense by the Navy and War departments.[19]

He went on to charge that aviation policy was being dictated by army and navy officers who knew nothing about flying, that fliers were not allowed to criticize their equipment, that the planes for the Hawaiian flight were untested, and that the *Shenandoah* was overweight and had no business flying on a publicity tour.

Mitchell was court-martialed and convicted of insubordination and disrespect of his superiors. He was suspended from rank, duty, and pay for five years. But he achieved his purpose. The army and navy found that their aviation policies were also on trial in the spotlight of public opinion.

Mitchell's was not the only voice raised in protest, however. An even more authoritative statement was issued by Anton Heinen, the German Zeppelin commander who had saved the *Shenandoah* when she was blown away from her mooring mast.

Capt. Anton Heinen

I worked on that ship long before she was completed. We submitted her to tests more rigid than any to which German-built Zeppelins had ever been subjected. The Shenandoah was perfect in every respect, but 16 valves were included for a purpose in the original design. They were for an emergency. It may not have been necessary to use them once in ten years, but it was for just an emergency as occurred Wednesday morning that they were intended.

Soon after I was apprised of the disaster I went to the air station at Lakehurst and there I learned what I had already surmised. Within the last three months eight of the 16 valves had been removed from the gas envelopes of the ship. What was the result? When she was lifted suddenly to great height the gas expanded and burst the frame. And where would the breaks naturally come? Just aft of the forward engine where the envelopes are largest. Any schoolboy could tell that.

The alterations to the ship were designed as a measure of economy to save helium. It was poor economy for it wasted the most precious material aboard—14 human lives. They say I am crazy and seeking publicity because I speak the truth. I could have taken the Los Angeles filled with hydrogen on that same morning and followed in the wake of the Shenandoah and brought her through without the slightest danger.[20]

Though the navy still had the *Los Angeles* hanging empty in the big hangar at Lakehurst, all their helium had been carried off in the thunderstorm over Ohio. Half

In 1931 the Allies removed their restrictions on the *Los Angeles'* use as a military airship and, for the first time, she joined the fleet on maneuvers off the west coast of Panama. Here she is moored to the airship tender *Patoka*, converted from a fleet oiler by the addition of the mooring mast on her stern. The *Shenandoah* and the *Akron* also moored to the *Patoka. Courtesy Goodyear Tire and Rubber Co.*

•

a year would pass before they could get enough gas to inflate and fly her.

Once airborne, however, the *Los Angeles* proved her worth. For the next eight years she flew all over the United States and, in 1928, completed the first nonstop flight to the Panama Canal. In 1931 the Allies finally lifted their restrictions on the *Los Angeles'* use as a military ship. She returned to Panama and participated for the first time in fleet maneuvers. Flying from the airship tender *Patoka* she put in 275 hours scouting over fourteen thousand miles.

The *Los Angeles'* perfect performance year after year did much to restore the public's confidence, but the six years 1919 to 1925 were costly ones for those who believed in airships.

These years were costly not so much in terms of ships, though the loss was great (the *R.38, Dixmude, Roma,* and *Shenandoah*), for it would later be argued that with the exception of the semirigid *Roma,* these were all old ships built from outdated designs left over from the war. The true cost was in men and in time, and here the loss was enormous: Edward Maitland, Lewis Maxfield, du Plessis de Grenadan, Zachary Lansdowne, and 150 of the most experienced airshipmen of three nations. This was the loss that could not be made up, the loss that would be most keenly felt in the ambitious airship programs that were to come, a loss that in England and even in America might have changed the future.

The loss in time was more difficult to assess. The Allies hoped to overtake the German lead in rigid airship technology by confiscating their ships at the end of the war, but there was no way they could take over the Germans' long years of experience and the subtle, almost instinctive feel for airship flying that the Germans had acquired, often at great cost, in both peace and war.

In the end the Allied effort came to nothing, and worse, their best men died while the Zeppelin Company spent six years making pots and pans. The Zeppelin Company that could have built a dozen modern airships built only one, the only rigid airship to survive this period of intense and futile effort—the *Los Angeles,* one of the two most reliable airships that ever flew.

The years 1919 to 1925 were a crucial period in the development of the rigid airship—a period of great loss—while the airplane, the airship's ultimate rival, continued to catch up.

The possibilities of the all-metal airship have intrigued lighter-than-air designers since before the first metal ship was built by David Schwarz in 1894. An outer cover made of metal would be gastight, thus eliminating the need for interior gasbags while opening up more of the hull for lifting gas. The weight saved plus the added gas would more than make up for any increase in the weight of a thin metal cover in place of a fabric one, and the metal cover would last much longer. The problem was to make a metal outer cover that was gastight, strong enough to maintain its shape, yet still light enough to fly. In the late 1920s two metal airships were actually built, the first since Schwarz's attempt a quarter of a century earlier.

The *City of Glendale* was designed and built by Thomas B. Slate in Glendale, California, in 1929. She was 200 feet long, 59 feet in diameter, with 330,000 cubic feet of hydrogen. She was built in this hangar set over a depression dug into the ground so that the hull fit snugly into the round construction space. The corrugated hull was of .011-inch-thick duralumin coated with aluminum to prevent corrosion. *Courtesy Historical Collections, Security Pacific National Bank.*

The duralumin was formed into long strips. A single strip extended all the way from bow to stern and was riveted to interior support rings by men working on a platform cut to the shape of the hull, halfway up the side of the hangar. As each corrugated strip was set in place and crimped to the adjoining strip, the entire hull was rotated downward so that the next strip could be set in place. One hundred and fifty-eight strips completed the hull. *Courtesy Historical Collections, Security Pacific National Bank.*

Less than a year after construction began, the *City of Glendale* was ready for this lift and trim test on January 6, 1929, when she rose fifty feet into the air at the end of ropes. When she next emerged from her hangar on December 17, 1929, with engines in place and ready to fly, the crewman monitoring her pressure gauges stepped out to have his picture taken, the sun expanded her hydrogen, popping a seam, and she was walked back into her hangar never to emerge again. *Courtesy John W. Underwood, Glendale, California.*

Thomas B. Slate, standing in his elevator, invented a successful carbon dioxide refrigeration system and put the money from that into his airship. He is holding the radial-bladed blower that, when mounted at the bow of his ship and driven by a thirty-six-hundred-horsepower steam turbine inside the hull, was to force air away from the bow and create a vacuum into which a propeller mounted at the stern of the passenger car would drive the ship, thus eliminating air resistance. *Courtesy Historical Collections, Security Pacific National Bank.*

Slate predicted that the *City of Glendale* would be able to lift a payload of five tons, including forty passengers and a crew of five. Her two engines would drive her at a top speed of nearly one hundred miles per hour and she would cruise at eighty-six miles per hour. He also devised this system of two elevators that would carry passengers up to the ship while she remained aloft. But further investment dried up in the depression and the *City of Glendale* was eventually broken up for scrap. *Courtesy the* Glendale News Press.

Of history's three metal airships, the last was the one that flew. Ralph Upson left Goodyear in 1920 and, with Carl B. Fritsche, established an airship company in Detroit backed by money from the auto industry. They landed a million-dollar navy contract to build a metal blimp. Designated the *ZMC-2 Metalclad*, her hull was aluminum-coated duralumin rolled to .0095 of an inch. *Courtesy Northrop University.*

The *ZMC-2*'s technical committee included Charles F. Kettering, director of General Motors Research Laboratories, and W. B. Mayo, chief engineer of the Ford Motor Company. The *ZMC-2* made her first flight on August 19, 1929, with five people aboard. She was 149.5 feet long with 202,000 cubic feet of helium. She remained in navy service for twelve years, successfully completing 752 flights. Fritsche and Upson drew up plans for a much larger ship but the navy did not buy it. When war broke out in 1941 the *ZMC-2* was too small for antisubmarine patrols and she was dismantled. *Courtesy Northrop University.*

6
· TO ·
· THE ·
ARCTIC

Why should anybody want to go to a place where somebody else has been?[1]

Roald Amundsen

At the age of fifteen Roald Amundsen decided to become an explorer. Though this ambition is common in young boys, in Roald's case it led him to embark upon a program of physical and mental conditioning that eventually carried him to the South Pole.

He took up soccer and cross-country skiing to build up strength and endurance. He spent as much time as possible outdoors and left his bedroom window open wide all night, even in winter, a considerable accomplishment in Oslo, Norway. Because he felt that military training would be useful to an explorer, he concealed his nearsightedness in order to pass the physical.

In reading the journals of previous Arctic expeditions, he noted that the division of authority between the explorer and the captain of the expedition's ship was a frequent source of conflict, and young Amundsen determined that he would command his own vessels. After his enlistment in the army was completed, he spent six years as an able-bodied seaman, rising to the rank of mate before passing the examination for a captain's license.

OPPOSITE: Amundsen and a dog team. Amundsen's original goal had been the North Pole, but on learning that Peary had reached it, Amundsen headed south. With him he took a hundred of Greenland's best sled dogs, and these were to provide his margin of success. He and his men wintered on the ice at the Bay of Whales and set out for the Pole on October 19, 1911: five men, four sledges, and fifty-two dogs. They covered the 1,860 miles to the South Pole and back in ninety-nine days. *Courtesy Norsk Polarinstitutt, Oslo.*

·

This portrait of Amundsen was made when he was in his thirties, probably soon after he became the first man to sail the Northwest Passage from the Atlantic Ocean to the Pacific across the top of the North American continent. He and six companions set out from Norway aboard their seventy-two-foot fishing smack, *Gjoa*, on June 16, 1903, and sailed into San Francisco Bay in October of 1906, three years and four months later. *Courtesy Norsk Polarinstitutt, Oslo.*

•

After a course in magnetic science at Hamburg's Deutsche Seewarte and at the observatories at Wilhelmshaven and Potsdam, Amundsen bought a seventy-two-foot fishing boat, and in 1903, at the age of thirty-one, one step ahead of his creditors, sailed off on his career as an explorer. On that first voyage he achieved a four-hundred-year-old dream of man: he found the Northwest Passage and sailed his tiny ship from the Atlantic to the Pacific across the frozen top of North America.

In 1911 Amundsen became the first man to reach the South Pole, racing eight hundred miles across the Antarctic continent by dogsled. He and four companions arrived at the Pole after a fifty-five-day march from the coast. They got there just a month ahead of Robert Falcon Scott, and while the Scott expedition starved to death on the return journey, Amundsen and his men survived by eating their sled dogs.

It had taken Amundsen sixteen years to prepare himself for his chosen profession, but that long apprenticeship had paid off in a surprisingly short time. He was thirty-one years old when he set out to explore the polar regions, and before his fortieth birthday he had achieved worldwide recognition as one of the greatest explorers of all time, with major discoveries at the two ends of the earth.

With both the North and South poles now attained, Amundsen was convinced that the only practical way to continue scientifically exploring the polar regions was by air. Aircraft, however, would require more money than he could raise. Amundsen was not a wealthy man. He had been forced to finance his expeditions by writing books and giving lectures. He was, in fact, deeply in debt and had resigned himself to spending the rest of his life working to pay off his creditors. It was at this, the lowest point in the great explorer's life, that a young American named Lincoln Ellsworth asked to speak to him.

Ellsworth was an experienced outdoorsman with a wealthy father and a great interest in Arctic exploration. It was a fortuitous meeting. Ellsworth had the desire and the money, Amundsen the desire and the experience. The two men became great friends.

In 1925 they organized a six-man expedition and attempted to reach the North Pole in two Dornier-Wal seaplanes. When engine trouble forced one plane down on the ice 150 miles short of the Pole, the other landed beside it and Amundsen, Ellsworth, and their men spent the next twenty-four days hacking a runway out of the shifting ice that would be long enough to allow the single remaining plane to take off with both crews aboard. The heavily loaded ship cleared the jagged ice ridges at the end of the runway with only inches to spare, but even as he flew homeward, Amundsen was planning his next aerial assault on the Arctic, this time by airship.

His goal lay beyond the Pole, the huge unexplored region between the top of the world and the coast of North America, a great empty spot on the map where many believed another continent might lie. Amundsen's plan was to fly the twenty-two-hundred miles from Spitzbergen to Alaska. But the airplane had not been the answer. One engine had failed and they had gone down. Fuel had taken the place of survival equipment and still there wasn't enough fuel. They lost their way in the fog, and if the fog had outlasted the fuel, they would have been in even greater difficulty. To reach the Pole and beyond, Amundsen needed to carry a heavy load a long way. He needed an airship and the airship he wanted could be purchased for seventy-five thousand dollars.

Though the Dornier-Wal flying boats were German, they had been built in Italy to circumvent the Allied prohibition on German aircraft construction. In Italy Amund-

sen met Col. Umberto Nobile, head of the Italian government's aircraft factory, and had flown in Nobile's newest creation, the *N-1,* a 345-foot semirigid airship.

Now the *N-1* was for sale and Lincoln Ellsworth agreed to put up the money to buy her. When the Italian government learned of Amundsen's plans, they offered to give him the *N-1* free of charge if he would make the expedition under the Italian flag. Amundsen refused.

Roald Amundsen

I had not the slightest intention of permitting my dream of seventeen years to be fulfilled under any other flag than that of my native land. I had spent a lifetime learning the art of Polar exploration. I had carried the Norwegian flag through the Northwest Passage and to the South Pole. Nothing could induce me to make the first Arctic Ocean crossing under any other.[2]

Instead, Amundsen and Ellsworth, acting through the Aero Club of Norway, bought the *N-1* and contracted with Nobile to be their pilot. As the man who designed the airship, supervised her construction, and had flown her for hundreds of miles, he was the obvious choice for such a hazardous undertaking. From the very

Umberto Nobile (1885–1978) was born in Lauro near Naples. As an engineer on the Italian army's aeronautical staff, he assisted in the design of the army's military airships, the *Roma* and the *SR-1* purchased by England. By 1925 he had advanced to the rank of colonel and had completed work on his N-class of semirigid dirigibles. His tiny terrier, Titina, accompanied him everywhere, even to the North Pole. *Courtesy U.S. Information Agency in the National Archives.*

•

beginning, however, there was a difference of opinion as to Nobile's role in the expedition. According to his contract with the Aero Club, Nobile believed he was to be an equal partner in the "Amundsen-Ellsworth-Nobile Polar Expedition." Amundsen, on the other hand, saw his role in quite a different light.

Roald Amundsen

Ellsworth's financial assistance had made the flight of 1925 possible and would make the flight of 1926 possible. Ellsworth and I had been congenial companions in danger and in achievement. I was delighted to share the national honours with my beloved American friend. I did not intend, however, to share them with the Italians. We owed them nothing but the opportunity to buy and pay for a second-hand military dirigible. I was very glad to be able to hire the Italian officer who had constructed and piloted this ship. But the expedition was Ellsworth's and mine. It was our idea. It was financed with our money, and it would be made in a craft which we had bought and paid for.[3]

This initial misunderstanding between Amundsen and Nobile was never resolved and eventually led to serious problems. It may have been that the two men were of such different temperaments that each was simply unable to comprehend the viewpoint of the other. A suggestion of this gap between the austere northerner and the hot-blooded southerner can be found in their attitude toward dogs. Nobile took his tiny terrier Titina with him wherever he went. She crossed the Arctic Ocean with him even though he had to admit that "Titina thoroughly disliked flying."[4] He even took her to the White House where, in the excitement, she wet on President Coolidge's rug. Amundsen's appreciation of dogs, on the other hand, was on a much more utilitarian level. He used them to pull the sleds on his dash across the Antarctic continent to the South Pole. But as the supplies were consumed and the sleds became lighter, the dogs turned from power sources into food sources. "On December 19 we killed the first dog on the homeward trip," he noted in his diary. "This was Lasse, my own favorite dog. He had worn himself out completely and was no longer worth anything."[5]

Though this is a minor point, it serves to illustrate the deep differences in temperament and outlook between these two men that would finally erupt into bitter hatred.

The *N-1* was renamed the *Norge (Norway)* and Nobile set to work tearing out the ship's paneled bedroom, bathroom, and kitchen to make way for more fuel tanks. Other members of the expedition set sail for the island of Spitzbergen where they were to erect a special roofless hangar at Kings Bay, the starting point for the voyage to the Pole and beyond.

Before the twenty-two-hundred-mile flight across the Arctic Ocean could begin, however, the *Norge* would have to complete the forty-five-hundred-mile journey from Rome to Kings Bay, and for this purpose, hydrogen, supplies, and spare parts were shipped north to points along the route.

On April 10, 1926, the *Norge* set out from Rome. Nobile scheduled his first stop at the British airship base at Pulham, fourteen hundred miles and thirty-two hours flying time away. From there, it was fourteen hours to Oslo and seventeen more to the big Russian airship hangar at Gatschina, just outside Leningrad. There they were forced to wait for three weeks while a blizzard delayed the completion of the hangar at Kings Bay. Finally everything was ready and the seventeen-hundred-

The Norge was 348 feet long and sixty-two feet in diameter, powered by three 250-horsepower Maybach engines with a top speed of seventy-one miles per hour. Before her polar voyage could even begin, she had to complete the forty-five-hundred-mile flight from Rome to Spitzbergen. This in itself was a major undertaking for so small an airship, and its successful completion was a tribute to Nobile's skill, for neither Amundsen nor Ellsworth was among the twenty-one people who made the flight. *Courtesy Stato Maggiore Aeronautica, Rome.*

•

mile flight from Gatschina to Spitzbergen was made in just under two days with a refueling stop at the tiny Norwegian village of Vadso on the shores of the Barents Sea.

Nobile and the *Norge* arrived at Kings Bay on May 7, 1926, where Amundsen and Ellsworth were waiting. Also at Kings Bay, the island's only port with a loading dock, were Lt. Comdr. Richard E. Byrd and Floyd Bennett of the U.S. Navy with their big Fokker trimotor monoplane, *Josephine Ford.* No one had been to the Pole since Peary first reached it by dogsled seventeen years earlier. Now, three expeditions, including that of Capt. George Wilkins at Point Barrow, Alaska, were after it. Byrd was first. On May 9, he and Bennett took off, flew to the Pole, and returned in fifteen hours.

Now it was Amundsen's turn. Three days later on the morning of May 11, 1926, the *Norge* was ready to be cast off and rise into the clear blue Arctic sky.

Lincoln Ellsworth

The idling engines were shut down completely; and at 8:55 A.M. Nobile shouted in Italian from his window: "Let go the ropes!" An instant later Riiser-Larsen repeated the order from his side in Scandinavian, and slowly and without a sound the great airship began to rise.

The morning had brought a flat calm, and our ascent was almost perpendicular. Nobile dumped more sand, and the movement accelerated. It was so smooth, so even, as to suggest planetary motion. We were not rising; we were poised, and the world was falling away from us as if lowered by hydraulic power. The walls of the fjord leisurely went downward past us. Familiar faces, uplifted toward us, grew indistinct and then unrecognizable. From behind the fjord mountains rose up, glaciers and infinite snow fields glittering in the sun. Kings Bay became a toy town set in an immense white plain.

Then came a phenomenon for which we were not prepared. Swarms of gulls and other polar birds flew out from their rookeries in the cliffs to inspect this huge new cousin in the air. The air vibrated with thousands of flashing wings and shrill, excited cries. In the stillness of our cabin we could hear the roaring of the Josephine Ford far below, as Byrd and Bennett took off to bear us company during the first stage of our journey.

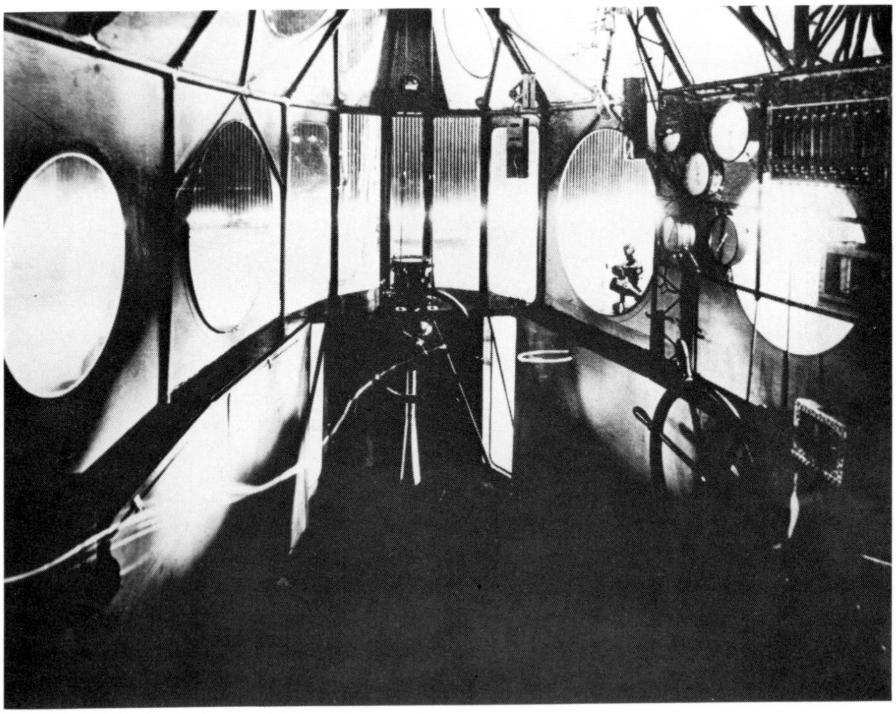

The *Norge* was a semirigid airship with a metal keel on the underside of the gasbag that extended all the way from bow to stern. The control car, shown here, and the three engine cars were built into this keel. The top of the control car opened directly into the hull where 645,000 cubic feet of hydrogen were contained in ten separate gas compartments. *Courtesy General Umberto Nobile, Rome.*

•

We rose above the fjord, and once more the North spread out under our eyes. The Byrd plane climbed up to us, its engines scaring away our feathered escort. Signal bells rang, and the engines started. With the dignity of an ocean liner, the ship came around, headed for the mouth of the bay. There we turned northward to maneuver for the meridian of the Kings Bay wireless station, which we were to follow to the North Pole.[6]

In addition to seven tons of gasoline, the *Norge* was loaded with rifles, sleds, tents, and enough food and supplies for fifty days. The crew consisted of Nobile and five Italian mechanics, Amundsen and seven Norwegians, Ellsworth the lone American, and Dr. Finn Malmgren, a Swedish meteorologist. Altogether there were sixteen men and Titina.

With such a mixed crew the language barrier presented some problems.

Umberto Nobile

In the control cabin of the Norge the official language, so to speak, was English; but there were times when English did not suffice to make my orders clear, and then I spoke Italian. In moments of crisis, when there was not an instant to lose, and orders had to be executed immediately, my Italian must have been accompanied by very expressive gestures; otherwise, I cannot explain how I managed to make myself understood.[7]

Whatever his language, each man on board seemed to share in the curious feeling of exhilaration combined with great calm known to all aerial explorers as the uncertainty and confusion of long months of preparation finally come to an end. Ahead only two possibilities remained—success or failure. The morning was clear and calm with the temperature at twenty-three degrees.

Lincoln Ellsworth

Two hours after leaving Kings Bay we found ourselves over the pack ice. What weather! The sun shone brilliantly out of a sky of pure turquoise, and the whale-like shadow that

Lt. Comdr. Richard E. Byrd and Floyd Bennett flew to the North Pole on May 9, 1926, in their Fokker trimotor. They returned to Kings Bay and a hearty embrace by Amundsen and Ellsworth. Each group offered friendly assistance to the other while insisting to reporters that they were not in a race to reach the Pole. Both groups realized that they would have to go to the other's aid if anything went wrong. In fact, the unexpected competitors represented an added safety factor. *Courtesy Library of Congress.*

•

our airship cast beneath us trailed monotonously across a glittering snow field, unbroken, save where wind and tide had rifted the icy surface into cracks and leads of open water. As we cruised, three white whales darted under the protecting shelf of an ice floe, frightened at the sight and noise of the weird monster that took to the air instead of the sea, and sent up columns of spray that reflected the bright sunshine. As we approached latitude 83½ degrees, the snow-crowned peaks of Spitzbergen merged into the deepening blue of the southern sky, losing their identity; and all signs of life vanished.[8]

Sixteen and a half hours of steady flight at nearly fifty miles per hour brought them to ninety degrees north latitude, the top of the world. Night had been left far behind, and though it was 1:30 in the morning, the summer sun bathed the endless ice in bright sunlight. Hjalmar Riiser-Larsen, the navigator, had been at the window with his sextant since 1:10. As the sun's disk slowly covered the instrument's bubble, he cried out, "We're here, we're over the North Pole!"

They circled around and brought the *Norge* down to six hundred feet. Amundsen dropped the Norwegian flag, Ellsworth the American and Nobile the Italian flag. Then Nobile dropped the flag of Rome, the parchment of the Royal Geographical Society, the ensign of the Aero Club, the banner of his ground crew, and finally a Fascist banner.

Roald Amundsen

Ellsworth and I had each, of course, brought a flag to be dropped overboard as we crossed the Pole—Ellsworth the Stars and Stripes and I the national flag of Norway. In keeping with Nobile's injunctions, we had each brought a little flag not much larger than a pocket handkerchief. As we crossed the Pole, we threw these overboard and gave a cheer for our countries. Imagine our astonishment to see Nobile dropping overside not one, but armfuls, of flags. For a few moments the Norge looked like a circus wagon of the skies, with great banners of every shape and hue fluttering down around her. Nobile produced one really huge Italian flag. It was so large he had difficulty in getting it out of

Amundsen rests in the back of the *Norge* control car as they head for Alaska. Amundsen readily admitted that his was the easiest job of all on the epic three-day journey. He was there to look for undiscovered land. During his three winters with the Eskimos on the Northwest Passage, he had adopted their loose reindeer skin clothing, far lighter, warmer, and more flexible than the best Europe had to offer. This too, contributed to his success at the South Pole. *Courtesy Library of Congress.*

•

the cabin window. There the wind struck it and it stuck to the side of the gondola. Before he could disengage it we must have been five miles beyond the Pole.[9]

Ellsworth celebrated his forty-sixth birthday at the North Pole with toasts to his continued good health drunk in egg punch. Now every direction was south and the largest empty spot left on the map of the world lay before them as they set their sun compass for Point Barrow, Alaska, fifteen hundred miles away. Admiral Peary thought he had glimpsed a distant snow-covered mountain range beyond the Pole. Dr. Harris, the eminent tidal expert with the U.S. Coast and Geodetic Survey, thought they would find a continent there. Amundsen hoped at least for islands.

For two days they flew onward into the unknown. The desolate ice pack stretched to the horizon, its surface broken only by the great cracks or leads that open and close in the ice as it floats on the restless sea. Their greatest danger was the fog that closed in around them freezing to the metal parts of the ship in layer upon layer of ice that broke off and fell into the propellers where, with a loud report, it was hurled through the fabric hull. But Nobile had foreseen this danger and had strengthened the area around the propellers in order to protect the gasbags inside.

Umberto Nobile

We had been in the air for 32½ hours. The cabin was horribly dirty. The dozens of thermos flasks heaped on the floor, near the little cupboard where we kept the charts and navigation books, presented a particularly sad spectacle: some of them empty, others overturned, others broken. Coffee and tea had been spilt everywhere, and all over the place were the remains of food. In the midst of all this mess there stuck out picturesquely Amundsen's enormous feet, with his grass-stuffed shoes, his diver's gaiters and red and white gloves.[10]

They had brought lunches packed for them by the wife of the coal mine superintendent back at Kings Bay. But with the temperature inside the ship at fourteen degrees, the hard-boiled eggs had frozen solid like small round stones, impossible to eat. The sandwiches had also frozen but were still edible, though the bread squeaked as they chewed it.

On the morning of the third day they sighted land. A few solitary Eskimos on the barren Alaskan coast for years afterward told the story of a great flying whale or perhaps the devil himself who came roaring down on them out of the north that morning.

They had been in the air for two days and nights with little sleep. For another day and night they were forced to struggle southward against dense fog and gale force winds of seventy miles per hour that caused them to lose their way. Finally on the morning of May 14, the weary men sighted a small cluster of houses and landed. They were at Teller, a tiny settlement of fifty-five surprised inhabitants sixty miles north of Nome. The *Norge* was quickly deflated, dismantled, and later shipped back to Italy in crates.

The news of their safe arrival was flashed around the world and the voyage of the *Norge* was universally hailed as a major achievement. "If Commander Byrd's flight was a lyric of the air," exclaimed the *New York Herald Tribune,* "the non-stop passage of Captain Amundsen from Spitzbergen to Alaska is an epic."[11] Ellsworth summed up their feelings with these words:

To those of us who made that first crossing of the Polar Sea it will ever be life's peak, for, in all human experience, never before had man traveled so fast and so far into the realm of the unknown. There is an indefinable something about such an experience, where illusion and reality are hauntingly intermingled, that may well color one's whole sentiment of existence ever after.[12]

Not until the space age did man again travel "so fast and so far into the realm of the unknown" and it may be that only the first astronauts who walked upon the moon can really know what Ellsworth and the others experienced.

It seemed the crowning achievement of Roald Amundsen's long career as an explorer. The conquerer of the South Pole had become the first man to visit the two ends of the earth and proved that no continent intruded into the frozen sea that floated around the North Pole. His pioneering work with airplanes and airships had added a new dimension to exploration. A hard day's journey into the unknown could now be made in less than an hour, but Amundsen himself found these new ways less to his liking than the old. He confided to his friend Ellsworth that he planned to retire.

Lincoln Ellsworth

It wasn't his game, he told me—he guessed he was too old to learn. He was born of an age when, out of the sheer urge for bodily effort, men traveled forth afoot, if need be, to explore the yet untrodden.[13]

The voyage across the polar sea would have been a fitting climax to Amundsen's career, but as the press clamored for more information and Nobile began to telegraph details of the flight, the bitter rivalry between the two men started up in earnest.

Amundsen, with little money of his own, was forced to rely on newspaper and magazine articles, books, and lectures to finance his expeditions. He had signed exclusive contracts with a number of publishers before the voyage but now rival publishers were besieging Nobile with requests for articles. Amundsen was furious. At a final meeting in Nome when Nobile pressed his claim as an equal in the leadership of the expedition, Amundsen lost his temper.

Roald Amundsen

When, in his peroration, he grandiloquently shouted, "I have given my life to this expedition—I had the whole responsibility of the flight," anger got the best of me. For this strutting dreamer, this epauletted Italian, who six months before had had no more thought of Arctic exploration than he had of superseding Mussolini as the Chief of State, to be shouting this kind of presumptuous nonsense in my face, with my thirty years of labour and achievement in the Polar regions, and to be claiming an equal share with us in the conception and execution of the transarctic flight, with his silly talk about giving his life to the expedition and having the whole responsibility of it—all this was too much for me to stomach. With furious indignation, I reminded him now in no uncertain tones of the pitiable spectacle he would have presented on the Polar ice if the Norge had by chance been forced down, and pointed out how preposterous would have been his claim to effective leadership under those conditions. And in heated tones that carried finality I reminded him, for the last time, that Ellsworth and I were the leaders of the expedition, that we should never recognize his right to claim a major share in its achievement, and that we would prevent him, if we could, from writing anything about it except what his contract permitted him to write about the technical aspects of the flight.[14]

After taking a steamer from Nome to Seattle, the members of the expedition went their separate ways. Amundsen returned to Norway. Nobile, on the other hand, began a triumphal tour of the United States that ended with a reception at the White House where Titina favored President Coolidge's rug. The two men never met again. Now they continued their bitter feud from the lecture stage and in print as each wrote books and articles castigating and belittling the achievements of the other. One example is Nobile's article in the August 1927 issue of the *National Geographic*:

I conceived the idea of preparing and effecting an Italian Polar expedition with a dirigible, and by June, 1925, my plan had already taken shape in its main lines. We would start from Spitzbergen in order to explore all that Polar zone within a radius of 600 to 900 land miles. I did not contemplate a mere run to the Pole, but a campaign of exploration, taking advantage of favorable weather conditions prevailing from May to September. We would, in this manner, have effected a fanlike series of explorations from our island base.

While this Italian project was ripening, Captain Roald Amundsen asked to meet me.

In our interview he explained his idea to use a dirigible to cross the Arctic from Spitzbergen to Alaska. His idea was conceived independently of mine, but after mine.

We soon came to an accord, under the terms of which I assumed the whole responsibility for the technical preparation for the expedition. This was effected in Italy under my direction and responsibility.[15]

For his part, Amundsen in the August 1927 issue of *The World's Work* issued the serious charge that three times during the flight of the *Norge*, Nobile seemed to be "standing in a sort of daze"[16] with the wheel in his hand as the airship sped toward the ice and only the quick action of others in pushing Nobile aside and grabbing the wheel saved them all from certain destruction.

Nobile retaliated in the January 1928 issue of the same magazine:

The flight over the Arctic Ocean from Spitzbergen to Alaska was like a pleasure trip to Amundsen, or very nearly one. When I met Amundsen he said to me:

"I want to get from Kings Bay to Point Barrow across the North Pole. Can you take me there?" I answered:

"Yes, it is possible. I also have thought and desired what you propose. There are enormous difficulties to be overcome, but I will overcome them."

This was about all there was to the conversation. Shortly afterwards, Amundsen went on a six months' trip to the United States and on ending the tour he came nonchalantly to Spitzbergen to take-off. I gave him the only comfortable easy-chair we had on board. After three or four days of navigation I disembarked him at Teller. A pleasure trip, more or less, for Amundsen. On my part, however, the flight was the materialization of a long and hard task, both in study and work—the supreme test of a will after years and years of training and experiment.

At the Academy of Science of Leningrad the night before the Russia-Spitzbergen crossing—actually the most dangerous phase of our flight—I made the following statement: "Our undertaking is twofold: an expedition of exploration, for which I give the credit to Amundsen, and an aeronautical feat, planned by us Italians, for which I assume all responsibility."

All this has never been denied. After the flight, however, when it was seen that the exploration expedition had practically failed because of Amundsen's absolute indifference toward his part of the work, the incredible happened: Amundsen attempted to usurp the merit for the aeronautical feat! The attempt was not easy of performance. The dirigible was of Italian make, all the work of preparation for the flight was done by Italians, all the responsibility borne by Italians.[17]

A good deal of this discussion now seems a little foolish. Who had the idea first? Who dropped the largest flag? Did Amundsen sit down more than Nobile? There was only one question raised in the controversy that turned out to be of critical importance. It was the question of Nobile's ability as an airshipman. Was Nobile a competent pilot? Amundsen says not, but as we have seen, his judgment was not entirely objective where Nobile was concerned. On a number of occasions Nobile exhibited great skill in handling the *Norge,* and even Amundsen had to admit that in the extremely difficult landing at Teller, without benefit of a ground crew, Nobile handled the ship perfectly. Furthermore, the successful completion of the eight-thousand-mile voyage from Rome to Alaska has to stand as a major achievement in aviation history and here again, the credit belongs entirely to Nobile.

Yet the charges, mostly made by Amundsen in the heat of anger, remain. They would be of little interest were it not for the shadow they cast over the extraordinary

After the successful flight of the *Norge*, Nobile was promoted to the rank of general by Benito Mussolini, who is here at the left admiring a reluctant Titina. After the loss of the *Italia*, however, the Fascist government was quick to join in the condemnation of Nobile, though it continued to defend the actions of the two naval officers Mariano and Zappi. *Courtesy General Umberto Nobile, Rome.*

events that were to follow, for two years later Umberto Nobile returned to the Arctic, but this time his expedition ended in disaster and death.

Nobile, now promoted to the rank of general, had been fascinated by the vast Arctic wilderness and he was determined to return, this time at the head of an expedition unquestionably his own.

Mussolini donated the military dirigible *Italia,* a sister ship of the *Norge,* and allowed the city of Milan to pay all the expedition's expenses. A navy ship, the *Città di Milano,* was ordered north to Spitzbergen to serve as a base of operations. This time, Nobile hoped to make a series of flights to explore the uncharted coastlines of Greenland, Siberia, and Canada plus, if all went well, a landing at the Pole.

Umberto Nobile

To tell the truth, so far as scientific observations were concerned, the Norge expedition had not done much. The hazardous nature of the crossing from Spitzbergen to the American coast, starting from Rome with such a small airship, had obliged us to concentrate our attention on the aeronautical problem, at the expense of the purely scientific side. The new expedition, on the other hand, would be able to boast of being the first scientific aerial exploration of the Arctic. [18]

All five of the *Norge's* Italian crewmen volunteered to return with Nobile to the Pole. Three officers were selected from the Italian navy, all trained navigators and two with airship experience. Three more airshipmen and two journalists rounded out the crew. Dr. Aldo Pontremoli, professor of physics at the University of Milan, was in charge of the scientific observations assisted by Dr. Francis Behounek, the director of the Prague Wireless Institute, and Dr. Finn Malmgren, a professor at the University of Uppsala, who was serving again as meteorologist as he had aboard the *Norge.* This time the crew would consist of sixteen Italians, one Czechoslovak, and one Swede, plus, of course, Titina. The only member of the expedition with Arctic experience was Malmgren.

The *Italia* set out from Milan early on the morning of April 15, 1928. Nobile chose to fly the more direct route across Central Europe by way of Vienna and Breslau to Stolp, Germany, where they remained for seventeen days awaiting the *Città di Milano's* arrival at Spitzbergen. The final leg of the voyage was by way of Stockholm and Vadso to Kings Bay, where they arrived on May 6, after another extraordinary flight, this time of thirty-three hundred miles from Milan to Spitzbergen.

The first voyage of exploration was made on May 11 toward the unmapped Siberian islands of Severnaya Zemlya, but it had to be cut short due to bad weather. The *Italia* returned to Spitzbergen after eight hours. Four days later the weather cleared and they set out again for Severnaya Zemlya. This flight covered twenty-four hundred miles in sixty-nine hours, just under three days in the air.

Two weeks later at 4:28 on the morning of May 23, 1928, the *Italia* started for the North Pole. Sixteen men and Titina were aboard. Eighteen hundred pounds of food and survival equipment were suspended evenly along the metal framework of the keel. In the cabin were two waterproof sacks of supplies that could be dropped at the Pole if they were able to carry out their plan to land three men there.

After reaching Cape Bridgman on the north coast of Greenland, they set their course for the Pole. The fog that had plagued them since they reached the pack ice began to clear and a brilliant sun flooded the frozen ocean below.

F.C. D. 10394
ITALIA

Umberto Nobile

With the blue sky above, the radiant sun lighting the inside of the cabin, and the wind astern increasing our speed, the journey to the Pole proceeded in joyous excitement. All on board were happy, and contentment shone from every face. . . .

Meanwhile the Naval officers were making their solar observations. We were getting nearer and nearer to the goal, and the excitement on board was growing.

Twenty minutes after midnight, early on May 24th, the officers who were observing the sun with a sextant cried: "We are there!"[19]

A cloud bank was rolling in making a landing impossible, but Nobile brought the ship down to 450 feet and they dropped the Italian flag, the banner of the city of Milan, and a large wooden cross given to them by Pope Pius XI.

Umberto Nobile

We were all moved: more than one had tears in his eyes. Zappi cried: "Long live Nobile!" I was grateful to him, as I was to Malmgren, when he came and said, clasping my hand: "Few men can say, as we can, that we have been twice to the Pole."[20]

After sending radio greetings to Mussolini, the Pope, and King Victor Emmanuel, they left the North Pole at a little after two o'clock on the morning of May 24 and headed for Spitzbergen. For thirty-one hours they flew into twenty- to thirty-mile-per-hour head winds that cut their airspeed in half. At 9:25 on the morning of May 25 the elevator jammed. They were at an altitude of 750 feet and Nobile ordered the engines stopped while repairs were made.

The *Italia* at Kings Bay. The *Italia* was the same size as the *Norge* with the same engine power, lift, and range. She, too, completed a major voyage just to reach the starting point for her polar flights. First she flew 1,250 miles from Milan to Stolp, Germany, now Slupsk, Poland. Then it was 1,200 miles to Vadso, Norway, on the Barents Sea, and finally 850 miles to Kings Bay. The large oak cross given to Nobile by Pope Pius XI can be seen hanging from the keel just in front of the forward engine cars. The *Città di Milano* is just beyond the tiny Kings Bay coal-mining community. *Courtesy Stato Maggiore Aeronautica, Rome.*

Thousands of pounds of gasoline had been consumed since the takeoff and they had been flying with the bow downward, using the air pressure on the top of the hull to help keep the ship from rising, but with the elevator jammed, there was a danger of flying down into the ice. Now with the engines stopped, the *Italia* began to drift up into the cloud layer. A sharp kick freed the elevator wheel but Nobile ordered the mechanism dismantled and checked. At a height of twenty-seven hundred feet they broke through the clouds into bright sunshine. At thirty-three hundred feet the wheel was reassembled and the engines started up again.

While they were above the clouds the navigators had taken their position from the sun and discovered that they were a little over a hundred miles northeast of Kings Bay, only three or four hours flying time away. Once they got below the cloud layer again, they should sight the islands to the northeast of Spitzbergen within a few minutes.

At their original altitude of 750 feet the *Italia*'s hydrogen was cold and dense but because of the tons of fuel consumed, the ship was light, flying dynamically to stay down. With the engines stopped, the *Italia* had risen and the gas expanded with the altitude. When they broke through the cloud layer into the sunlight, the heat of the sun added to the expansion of the gas. As the ship continued to rise there was a serious danger that the hydrogen would fill the hull and be blown off through the safety valves. At thirty-three hundred feet Nobile started down.

He wanted to get below the clouds again where he could see the ice. That was the only way he could be sure of his speed and drift, but when the *Italia* plunged into the cloud layer, she lost the sun's rays and her hydrogen began to cool. As they went lower in the clouds the gas continued to cool and lose lift, but when they caught sight of the ice at nine hundred feet, Nobile later recalled, the *Italia* was still light and flying dynamically to stay down.

The first sign of danger came suddenly from the man at the elevator wheel. "We're heavy!" he shouted. The ship was down eight degrees at the stern and falling. Nobile ordered the third engine started and the other two to full speed. Now the stern was down by twenty degrees as the engines strained skyward. But still they fell. Extra fuel had been put aboard at takeoff in place of ballast, and now most of that fuel was gone and there was no ballast left to throw over to lighten the ship. A crash was inevitable and Nobile ordered the engines stopped to lessen the danger of fire.

Umberto Nobile

There was a fearful impact. Something hit me on the head, then I was caught and crushed. Clearly, without any pain, I felt some of my limbs snap. Some object falling from a height knocked me down head foremost. Instinctively I shut my eyes, and with perfect lucidity and coolness formulated the thought: "It's all over!" I almost pronounced the words in my mind. . . .

When I opened my eyes I found myself lying on the ice, in the midst of an appalling pack. I realized at once that others had fallen with me.

I looked up to the sky. Towards my left the dirigible, nose in the air, was drifting away before the wind. It was terribly lacerated around the pilot-cabin. Out of it trailed torn strips of fabric, ropes, fragments of metal-work. The left wall of the cabin had remained attached. I noticed a few creases in the envelope.

Upon the side of the crippled, mutilated ship stood out the black letters ITALIA. My eyes remained fixed on them, as if fascinated, until the dirigible merged in the fog and was lost to sight.[21]

The jagged pack ice had sliced the cabin open. Nobile, Titina, and eight men were dumped out into the snow. The stern engine car was torn off and the mechanic crushed to death. Then, two tons lighter, the shattered hull of the *Italia* rose into the sky and drifted off into the mist. Six men were still aboard.

With a broken leg and, he feared, internal injuries, Nobile lay down and prepared himself for death. After a half-hour, finding himself still alive and beginning to feel better, he took charge of the survival attempt. One of the sacks of food and equipment intended for use at the Pole had fallen with them onto the ice, as had the auxiliary radio transmitter.

There was nothing to do but settle down on the ice and wait for rescue. Both Nobile and Natale Cecioni, one of the mechanics, had broken legs. The others were bruised but not seriously injured. They had a tent that they dyed red for better visibility, one sleeping bag, and a pistol from the supply sack as well as 280 pounds of pemmican and chocolate, enough food to last for forty-five days. Some cans of gasoline and all their navigation instruments had also fallen from the ship. They would be able to chart their exact position on the drifting ice and transmit it to the *Città di Milano* back at Kings Bay.

Prior to their departure they had arranged with the ship to monitor the thirty-two-meter wavelength at fifty-five minutes past each odd-numbered hour, but when it became apparent that the airship had gone down, the *Città di Milano* stopped listening for the prearranged signals. The explanation later offered by the ship's captain for this unusual behavior was that when the *Italia*'s radio messages stopped, they naturally assumed that the radio operator was dead. They thought perhaps he had stuck his head out of the window and been struck by the propeller of the generator.

So while the men on the ice were transmitting an SOS every two hours, the *Città di Milano* was not listening. Instead, they were preparing to search for the missing airship in the area directly to the north of Spitzbergen. Nobile and his men learned of the search from the news broadcasts transmitted by the powerful shortwave station at San Paolo, Italy, but when the sun came out and they were able to find their position, the castaways discovered that they were a hundred miles to the northeast of the area to be searched. They had crashed almost within sight of North East Land on the opposite side of Spitzbergen from Kings Bay and the *Città di Milano,* and by the third day on the ice they found to their dismay that their ice floe was drifting rapidly to the southeast, even farther away from the search area. The pack ice carried them twenty-eight miles in three days to within sight of the islands off the coast of North East Land.

The first bit of good luck occurred on the sixth day, when Malmgren was able to sneak up on an inquisitive Polar bear and kill him with three pistol shots. This added four hundred pounds of fresh meat to their food supply.

As the days wore on and their hopes of rescue began to fade, some of the men decided to set out across the ice for help. Nobile wanted them to stay together and put their trust in the radio, but their signals still went unanswered and the drifting ice had carried them to within ten miles of Foyn Island, which beckoned invitingly on the horizon. From there it might be possible to march around North East Land to Cape

North, where they heard on the radio that the Norwegian sealing ship *Hobby* was headed. It was finally decided that three men should go for help while the rest remained at the tent. Malmgren, who knew the ice, would take two of the naval officers, Adalberto Mariano and Filippo Zappi, with him. On the seventh day they set out.

On the tenth day the castaways' radio call was finally heard, not by the *Città di Milano* a hundred miles away at Kings Bay, but by a young Russian amateur radio operator at Archangel, twelve hundred miles away. Four days later the *Città di Milano* also began to receive their transmissions and they were able to send out their exact position. They were found—but not yet saved.

Meanwhile, the ships and planes of six nations were mobilizing to search for the lost airship. Italy dispatched three planes to assist the *Città di Milano* while France sent three steamers and two planes. Finland responded with a steamer and two airplanes, Sweden with two ships and three planes, Russia with two icebreakers and a seaplane, and Norway with four ships and three planes along with her best Arctic pilots, Luetzow Holm and Hjalmar Riiser-Larsen, Nobile's old shipmate aboard the *Norge*. Roald Amundsen volunteered to lead the search.

Two more weeks were to pass before the Norwegian sealer *Hobby* was able to break through the ice to Cape North, close enough to launch the first two planes. On June 17, they flew to within two miles of the castaways without seeing them. Three times the planes returned and three times, despite signal flares and Very lights, they flew past without seeing the tiny tent in the endless desert of jagged ice.

On the twenty-sixth day after the crash, Maj. Umberto Maddalena, piloting an Italian flying boat with a receiving set aboard, was guided to the tent by radio from the ice. Maddalena dropped 660 pounds of supplies and returned with another plane two days later, again guided by the radio, with more supplies. Later that same day two Swedish planes circled over the tent and dropped food and survival gear. Then on the thirtieth day on the ice, the two Swedish planes returned and one landed. It was piloted by Lt. Einar-Paal Lundborg.

Lt. Einar-Paal Lundborg

Nobile wore no hat. The upper part of his body was clothed in a gray knitted jacket. His legs were encased in light gray sports trousers. On one foot he wore a light summer shoe, on the other a stocking and reindeer sock. Around his broken leg was wound a gray puttee.

I hurried up to him. He offered me both hands and drew me down to him in a strong embrace. I told him who I was and that I had come to take them all away from their involuntary stay on the ice.

I asked General Nobile to be the first. I told him I couldn't take more than one this time, because my mechanic was with me. I assured General Nobile that I would return soon alone, and then would be able to take two at a time.

General Nobile pointed to Cecioni, a fine, big powerful fellow of typical Italian appearance. He sat immediately next to the General, making a stretcher from bits of the crusht gondola of the *Italia*. By means of this he was to be helped along, as both his legs were broken.

"I have decided on another procedure," said General Nobile. "First Cecioni, then Behounek, Trojani, Viglieri, Biagi and, finally, myself."

I asked the General to alter this order so he could go with me immediately.

Lt. Einar-Paal Lundborg was a pilot with the Swedish government's rescue expedition. They had chartered two ships, the steamer *Tanja* and the Norwegian whaler *Quest*. The *Tanja* carried two Hansa-Brandenburg float planes and this ski-equipped Fokker. A Junkers trimotor seaplane, another Swedish plane, and a Finnish plane flew up to join them. After rescuing Nobile, Lieutenant Lundborg returned, flipped his plane, and spent the next twelve days with the castaways. The people in this photo are from the *Krassin*. Courtesy Norsk Polarinstitutt, Oslo.

•

I considered his presence on land extremely desirable for the management of relief work, particularly in case I couldn't carry all to safety that night.

After a short discussion with the others, General Nobile accepted my proposal and asked me to wait until he had time to get ready.

Nobile's dog, Titina, which since my arrival in camp had successfully attempted to make friends with me, didn't appear to question whether it was to go along or not. It was first to be taken up into the machine.

The leave which General Nobile now took of his comrades was more than pathetic. He embraced and kissed each one, and appeared to give encouraging words to all of them.[22]

The fateful decision was made and Nobile was lifted aboard the Swedish plane and flew off, leaving his men behind.

Umberto Nobile

My eyes travelled in search of the tent, but at first I could not find it. Schyberg [Lundborg's co-pilot] pointed it out to me—a wretched little object, a scrap of soiled material, almost invisible against the whiteness of the ice. There was an ache at my heart as I thought of my comrades still there on that one tiny piece of ice lost among so many others. The only sign of life was the festoon of white and red flags hoisted on the wireless mast.[23]

When Lundborg flew back to rescue the others, his ski-equipped Fokker flipped over on the ice breaking a wing and he, too, joined the castaways.

Back at Spitzbergen the rescuers had sent for some smaller ski planes that would be able to land safely at the tent. Meanwhile, all hopes turned to the ten-thousand-ton Russian icebreaker *Krassin*. She reached Spitzbergen on June 30 but broke a propeller blade while trying to push through the heavy ice off Cape North.

The *Krassin* reached the tent on July 12, 1928. Three hours earlier the ship had picked up Mariano and Zappi and learned of Malmgren's death. The tent is at the left, the antenna mast for the all-important radio at the right. *Courtesy Norsk Polarinstitutt, Oslo.*

•

On the forty-third day the Swedes again landed on the ice and rescued Lundborg but the landing was dangerous and they did not return for the others. On the forty-seventh day a plane from the *Krassin* sighted three men on the ice, two standing and one lying down. After radioing the men's position, the plane became lost in fog and crash-landed on North East Land. The *Krassin* pushed ahead and reached the men's position on the forty-ninth day. It was Mariano and Zappi, the officers who started out with Malmgren to march to land. But where was Malmgren? The two Italians said that he had died a month earlier. He had made them dig a shallow trench for him in the ice, laid down in it, and insisted that they continue on without him.

Now the *Krassin* pushed on to the tent reaching it three hours later on the evening of July 12, forty-nine days after the crash of the *Italia*. With the castaways saved, the next task was to rescue the rescuers. Captain Sora of the Italian Alpine Forces had set out with two Norwegians to try to reach the tent by dogsled, but one Norwegian became ill and was left behind on North East Land while the other two went on and ran out of food on Foyn Island. They were spotted there by the *Krassin* and brought off by a Finnish and a Swedish airplane while their companion walked back to the Norwegian whaler *Braganza*. The *Krassin* then continued on to rescue the five Russians whose plane had crash-landed earlier.

Now only the six men who had drifted off in the hull of the *Italia* remained to be rescued. While the *Krassin* was still at the tent, Nobile tried to get planes to search to the east where some of his men reported seeing a column of smoke a half hour after the airship drifted away. It could have been a signal fire or the smoke from the burning hydrogen. The *Italia* carried nearly a ton of food and survival equipment away with her. The men who remained aboard had only to open the valves or slash the gasbag in order to bring the ship down. Did any of them survive the landing? The question was never answered for the planes were not sent out. The search was ended.

A storm of controversy immediately engulfed the expedition and, strangely enough, the abandonment of the search for the men aboard the *Italia* was only a minor part of it. Had the expedition been properly planned? What happened to Malmgren? Why was he left to die in an ice trench while his two companions continued on to safety? But the biggest question concerned Nobile. How could he allow himself to be rescued before his men? "Were the laws of the air less chivalrous than the laws of the sea?" wondered the *New York Times*.[24]

While there was considerable discussion as to where the blame for the tragedy should fall, the press was unanimous in hailing the hero of the affair.

The *New York World*

Where airplanes equipped with pontoons and radio, airplanes of all sizes and designs, handled by the best pilots of Europe, had managed, after weeks of labor, to bring one of the Italia's crew to safety, the Krassin, a mere ship, rescued seven, and then turned around and rescued some would-be rescuers.

Airplanes and wireless played a part, but the actual hero of the rescue was the strong vessel built to dispute the right of way with icebergs. And, while six other nations contributed their share, the glory of the exploit belongs to Russia.[25]

Some publications, however, took a slightly narrower view of the entire operation.

The World's Work

If Fascism wishes to advertise its cause by hurling heroic ventures into the unknown, and if Communism wishes to reply by sending out ice-breakers and aviators to the rescue, the world must rejoice that the argument is on a heroic level. But it is to be hoped that future Arctic explorers will profit by the mistakes of Nobile's party. The cause of aviation is not advanced by recklessness.[26]

Meanwhile, the Fascists were taking their own shots at Nobile. *Il Corriere Padano,* the newspaper controlled by Italo Balbo, the Italian air minister, even went so far as to print the story that Nobile had really broken his leg while running to the rescue plane!

Mussolini sent a special train to pick up the survivors but orders were also sent that Nobile should grant no interviews or reply to any of the charges being made against him in the newspapers. At Narvik, Norway, where they boarded the train, a large crowd watched them silently, but as the train passed down the length of Sweden and the people saw the exhausted condition of the men, they began to realize the tremendous ordeal they had suffered through, and the crowds became larger and friendlier at each stop. In Italy, Mussolini had ordered cordons of police to keep the people away from the train but at every station they broke through and filled the coach with flowers. At the end of their journey in Rome, Nobile and his men were mobbed by a wildly cheering crowd of two hundred thousand.

Eight months later an Italian board of inquiry found General Nobile completely responsible for the loss of the *Italia* and the deaths of his men. He resigned his commission and left Italy in disgrace. He went first to Russia as an advisor to their airship program and then to the United States. He returned to Italy in 1945 when his former titles were restored.

There was one more life claimed by the ill-fated *Italia.* Roald Amundsen was not a part of the expedition. He and Nobile were still bitter enemies. Yet when he heard that the *Italia* was down, Amundsen offered his years of Arctic experience to the search. On June 18, he left Tromso, Norway, with five others aboard a French seaplane. They were never heard of again.

A writer for the *Schenectady Union-Star* may have said it best:

Surely if it is sublime to lay down one's life for a friend, how much greater is it to lay it down for an enemy.[27]

Roald Engelbregt Gravning Amundsen (1872–1928), the White Eagle of Norway. *Courtesy U.S. Information Agency in the National Archives.*

POSTSCRIPT

General Umberto Nobile died in Rome on July 30, 1978, at the age of ninety-three. Until the end of his life, he continued to take an active interest in history's judgment of his two extraordinary Arctic voyages. He personally supplied the following comments for this book. Some of them are taken from his memoirs previously published in several languages but not as yet in English.

The Flight of the *Norge*

In this enterprise there was glory for everyone. First and foremost for Amundsen, who had initiated it and been its leader; for me, who had built, prepared, and tested the airship, trained the Norwegian crew members, established the bases along the European route, commanded the airship during 171 flying hours, over a distance of thirteen thousand kilometers; for the Aeroclub of Norway, which had helped to prepare these bases and assumed responsibility for the financial part of the expedition; for Ellsworth, who had given such a generous contribution in money; for Riiser-Larsen and all the other members of the crew. . . .

Things being so, it might have been expected that the men who side by side had shared the same risks and the same emotions of so great an adventure would have remained bound together forever by reciprocal respect and friendship. Unfortunately this did not happen. A dispute arose between Amundsen and me, and I must explain how it developed, and what were the causes.

Quarrels after polar expeditions having members of different nationalities have often arisen in the past, but they have seldom assumed a form as acute as in our case. I think the reason was partly due to the nature of the expedition, but also to the fact that Amundsen, with his mentality, his rough, strong character, averse from all sentimentalism, was so unlike me that we might have almost come from two different planets. To make matters worse, he and I never had the chance to get to know each other. Amundsen had nothing whatever to do with the work of preparing the flight. After our conversation in Oslo in the summer of 1925, we had no further opportunity of discussing it. We only saw each other twice in Rome; at the end of August 1925 when he came to sign the agreement with the Italian government, and in March 1926, when we formally took over the airship—two brief encounters, during which we merely exchanged a few polite remarks.

One document relating to the expedition was of decisive importance, the agreement signed by Amundsen and Ellsworth in Rome in March 1926 in which it was stated that, "In recognition of what the Italian government and Nobile had done for the expedition, it would assume the name 'Amundsen-Ellsworth-Nobile Transpolar Flight.' "

In his book of memoirs, *My Life as an Explorer,* Amundsen, speaking of this decision, writes that it had been taken "solely to gratify Italian national pride" and adds: "No publicity would be given to Nobile after we had got the *N-1* out of Italy." In fact, in the book that he wrote in collaboration with Ellsworth, *First Crossing of the Polar Sea,* he makes no mention of the official name of the expedition.

For Amundsen, the Rome document was a pure formality, useful to satisfy Italian national pride, but valid only up to the moment of the handing over of the airship by the Italian government. . . .

During the whole flight I had no occasion to speak to him or Ellsworth, since I had to concentrate my whole attention upon controlling the airship, amid the difficulties and dangers that arose, especially on the last day.

Only at Teller, after the landing, did Amundsen and Ellsworth speak to me, thanking me profusely, and yet the next day, both of them, accompanied by Wisting and Omdal, left for Nome, without saying goodbye to me.

At Nome . . . meeting Ellsworth on the street, I pointed out to him that he and Amundsen, by publishing independently their account of the journey, as they were doing, were breaking one of the fundamental clauses of our agreement. He asked me to come and talk to Amundsen about it and we went together to the Log Hut.

Amundsen gave his own account of this interview, omitting among other things one essential point: that, at the end of our talk, he and Ellsworth, faced with the agreement that had been signed at Oslo, admitted that I had right on my side. "You are right," said Amundsen, and invited me to write at once the aeronautical account of the expedition, which he would add to his own report and send to the *New York Times* signed by all three of us.

Satisfied and reassured, I set to work at once to put my notes in order, and when they were ready I told Ellsworth, who promised to arrange a second meeting with Amundsen. But I heard no more from either of them. When I happened to meet Ellsworth at the wireless station, I remonstrated with him and he went with me to talk to Amundsen.

This second and last discussion was extremely unpleasant. At first, Amundsen seemed embarrassed and replied evasively to my request that he should do what had been arranged at the previous meeting, but he finished by telling me bluntly that neither he nor Ellsworth intended that I should write the aeronautical part of the report. Then I lost my temper, expressing my indignation at this open violation of the undertaking they had given. This is what Amundsen in his book calls my "emotional oration."

Today I am convinced that the real cause of the very strange behavior of Amundsen toward me, unworthy of a gentleman, is to be found in his financial difficulties, which tied him strictly to Ellsworth and constrained him to do everything to meet the wishes of his backer. If the book published by him and Ellsworth had included my name on the title page, as had been stipulated in our contract, that would have enhanced rather than diminished Amundsen's prestige. But no doubt the person who objected to this was Ellsworth, who believed that the fact of having contributed money toward the expedition entitled him to regard the *N-1* as a taxicab and her commander as its driver.

Dropping the Flags at the Pole

After I had dropped the Italian flag, I ordered Alessandrini to bring me three small pennants weighing altogether less than seventy or eighty grams. One of them had been given to us by the governor of Rome at a solemn ceremony in the capital. Another one had been handed over to me by the workers of the military factory where the airship had been built and prepared for the polar flight.

The three pennants were kept in a pocket of the inside cover of the pilot's cabin, from which they were extracted one by one and dropped overboard. This very simple operation is thus described by Amundsen:

> Imagine our astonishment to see Nobile dropping overside not one, but armfuls, of flags. For a few moments the Norge looked like a circus wagon of the skies, with great banners of every shape and hue fluttering down around her.[28]

A highly picturesque, amusing, but truly fantastic description.

The Crash of the *Italia*

As a matter of fact, nobody knows the real cause of the sudden heaviness of the airship. Many hypotheses have been formulated (see, for instance, the chapter "The Causes of the Catastrophe" in my book *With the Italia to the North Pole*, pp.

182–90), but nobody can say which of these is the true one.

In recent years, the meteorological services of the Italian air force have made an extensive research into the weather conditions on that day in the region where the catastrophe occurred, coming to the conclusion that the most probable cause of it was that the airship was suddenly overtaken by a warm, moist front.

No doubt, if this occurred, the cause of the sudden heaviness would be explained. This hypothesis is acceptable, but there is still no proof of it. The heaviness might also be explained by a sudden split in the envelope due to the long struggle against the storm. One or the other of these causes is probably the true explanation.

The Rescue from the Ice by Lundborg

I have always resented having to discuss this episode because it is near to my honor, and because it is in the category of actions in which every critic is a hero, even if he sits in an armchair.

Unfortunately, the wreck of the *Italia* was caught up, both in Italy and in other European countries, in the political passions that were developing and were to lead to the Second World War.

The criticism aimed at me was sparked off by a communiqué from Stefani, the official Italian press agency, in which they repeated the news already given by the Swedes but added that the reasons why I had been brought off first were not known. This hypocritical remark was enough.

My action was compared with that of the captain who is first to leave his sinking ship. The *Italia* was wrecked it is true, but I and nine of my men were spilled out on the ice, while the wreck lay somewhere unknown, with the remaining six members of the expedition. My duty was plain: It was to organize the diverse forces and nationalities engaged in the attempt to rescue the men in the tent, the three who had left to walk over the pack ice to land, and the six who had been carried away in the mortally wounded airship.

The End of the Search

You are quite right in calling attention to the fact that it is surprising so little public indignation was aroused by the apparent indifference to the fate of the men remaining aboard the *Italia;* but this was deliberate on the part of the Fascist chiefs, who wished to get rid of Nobile and had no interest whatever in the members of his expedition.

The responsibility for not having allowed this search, which I myself had requested for the remains of the airship, just when it could have been made in the best possible conditions, rests entirely with Romagna, the commander of the *Città di Milano*. At my request, Swedish planes were ready to reach the spot where the *Krassin* was, but Romagna ordered the immediate return of the *Città di Milano* with the rescued Italians, and the end of rescue operations.

The End of the Story

It has been very bitter for me to go back over this painful and acrimonious dispute. I do not know how better to conclude my account of the *Norge* expedition than by quoting what Odd Arnesen wrote in his book *Roald Amundsen, as I Knew Him.*

On the evening of 26 May, 1928, at Oslo, Amundsen was seated at a banquet given by the Geographical Society in honor of Wilkins and Eielson, who had arrived in Norway, after flying an aeroplane across the Arctic ice cap, from Point Barrow to the northern coast of the Svalbard. Together with Amundsen there were Otto Sverdrup, Gunnar Isachsen, Tryggve Gran, and others. Suddenly a telegram arrived. Congratulations for the guests? No, it was a telegram of very few words announcing the disappearance of the *Italia.* The men present at the banquet all had great experience in Arctic matters, and had often looked death in the face. There was a silence, the telegram was read. The faces of the men around the table showed how deeply they were moved. Later on, during the ceremony, Amundsen was asked whether he would be prepared to take part in any rescue action for the Italian castaways. "Right away!" those were the terse words that Roald Amundsen pronounced, and the people present at the feast said that they had never seen him look so handsome, with his virile, deeply lined face and shining hair.[29]

So, with the brief words spoken that evening, a strong and brave man had signed his own death warrant. A few weeks later, he disappeared into the polar sky, to enter the world of legend.

**General Umberto Nobile
Rome, 1975**

This photograph of Gen. Umberto Nobile was taken in February 1975, on his ninetieth birthday. *Italfoto, courtesy General Umberto Nobile, Rome.*

•

7
HUGO ECKENER
· A N D   T H E ·
GRAF ZEPPELIN

If one took a balloon of any type and flew it in conditions of complete calm, say in an enclosed space, a certain forward motion could always be achieved by means of a propeller, and consequently, a certain manoeuvrability by means of a rudder. In the open air, of course, such a balloon would be swept away by the smallest breath of wind. This seems to be what was happening to the Zeppelin airship yesterday; an air current of strength 1 on the Beaufort scale would have carried it merrily off. However ingenious the design of the aircraft may be, one thing stands out clearly—either the four propellers must be made considerably bigger and more effective, or their rate of revolutions must be increased by using more powerful engines. [1]

The second flight of *LZ-1* as reported by Dr. Hugo Eckener
in the *Frankfurter Zeitung*, October 1900

In the history of lighter-than-air flight there is one ship that showed the way, one ship that flew longer, farther, and with less mishap than all the others put together. From polar exploration to transatlantic passenger service, from weekend excursions to a round-the-world voyage, the *Graf Zeppelin* did them all. And she handled them so smoothly, so effortlessly that it seemed as if the airship's future was at last secure. She made it look easy and she even made a profit.

They called her a lucky ship. But the *Graf Zeppelin*'s luck was not born of chance, it came from the man who flew her, a man who left nothing to chance. Hugo Eckener was probably more closely attuned, both by training and by temperament, to the unique world in which an airship moves than any man has been, either before or since.

He was born August 10, 1868, in Flensburg, a north German town just a few miles from the Danish border. A Baltic fjord links Flensburg with the sea, and young

Opposite: The *Graf Zeppelin* cruises near Hammerfest, Norway, in July, 1930. As a prelude to a planned Arctic expedition, the ship made charter flights to Norway and Iceland. Here the *Graf Zeppelin* passes over the coastal fjords before crossing the Barents Sea to Spitzbergen. *Courtesy Carruthers Collection, Claremont Colleges.*

Dr. Hugo Eckener joined Count Zeppelin in January 1906 as a part-time publicity writer. Five years later he was in command of Delag's *Deutschland II.* The results of that command can be seen in the photo of *Deutschland II* on page 73. From this inauspicious beginning, Eckener went on to become the world's most experienced airshipman flying Delag ships before the war and training airship commanders during the war. Here in the control car of the naval training ship, *L-6,* during a visit from Count Zeppelin, are (left to right) Hauptmann Kuno Manger, Dr. Hugo Eckener, Count Zeppelin, Hermann Kraushaar, and Rudolph Wesphal. *Friedrich Moch photo, courtesy Marine -Luftschiffer - Kameradschaft, Hamburg.*

•

Hugo became an expert small-bodt sailor. His father owned a cigar factory but died when Hugo was only twelve. He excelled at school and eventually graduated with one of the first doctorates in psychology from Wilhelm Wundt's pioneering Institute for Experimental Psychology at Leipzig. Eckener then spent a year in the army and was discharged with the rank of sergeant. At the age of twenty-nine he married and went off to Egypt on a five-month honeymoon. In 1899 Dr. Eckener and his new wife settled down in Friedrichshafen, where he started to work writing a textbook on political economics, another of his many interests.

Of course no one could live long in the small town of Friedrichshafen without becoming aware of the activities of old Count Zeppelin banging away inside his huge shed floating out on the lake. Eckener had written occasional articles for the *Frankfurter Zeitung,* and in the fall of 1900 the newspaper asked him to cover the second flight of *LZ-1.* A regular reporter had been sent to cover the first ascent, but it had been unpromising and the paper hesitated to spend much money reporting the second attempt. Eckener watched the flight and wrote the article. He noted that several rather serious problems would have to be overcome before Count Zeppelin's airship could be of any practical value.

It was nearly six years before Count Zeppelin was ready to try again with *LZ-2,* and once more the *Frankfurter Zeitung* asked Eckener to go out to the lake and take a look.

LZ-2 did even worse than *LZ-1* and Eckener reported as much. But this time, Count Zeppelin chose not to ignore the generally unfavorable article by the young psychologist and part-time newspaperman.

Hugo Eckener

[A]s I was working in the garden, our maid came to me, quite excited, to say that Count Zeppelin was ringing the doorbell. I told her to invite the Count inside and show him into the living-room, where I would join him immediately. I pulled off my working-smock, tried to make myself presentable for the prominent visitor, and went into the room. Here I found the old gentleman in meticulously correct morning clothes, with a silk hat and yellow gloves, the courteous and distinguished aristocrat which he was at all times.[2]

Count Zeppelin sat down and proceeded to explain exactly what he felt had gone wrong with *LZ-2* and how he proposed to correct it in *LZ-3.* Eckener was so impressed by the old gentleman that he volunteered to help write his news and publicity releases. It was a spur-of-the-moment offer on Eckener's part, inspired more by the force of the count's personality than by confidence in his ideas, but Count Zeppelin quickly accepted. Without realizing it, Hugo Eckener had just changed the course of his life.

Count Zeppelin was not a technician, yet he had an extraordinary ability to seek out the engineers and designers who could turn his ideas into reality. For the most part, the men he gathered around him at the very beginning were still with the Zeppelin Company thirty years later. Their knowledge and experience placed the German airship industry far above any other in the world. Now once again, Count Zeppelin had gone out of his way to recruit a part-time newspaper writer and doctor of psychology who was to become the premier airship commander of all time.

What were the special qualities that would serve Eckener so well in his new role? To understand these, we must look closely at the airship. It is first of all, a creation of technology. Not only is it one of the largest machines ever built, it is also one of the most complicated, requiring of its creators the most precise knowledge of stress, lift, and pressure. In an age before computers, the airship's designers and draftsmen spent thousands of hours figuring the stress on every inch of its miles of delicate metal and wire framework. They had to develop the lightest, strongest, and most flexible metals and the lightest, most powerful engines of their day.

The airshipman then, had to be a technician, a master of stress analysis and pressure gauges. But he also answered to a much older influence, for his traditions and terminology came from the sea. His helmsman steered to port and starboard. His engines answered to "full ahead" and "slow astern." In most countries, the airshipman wore a naval uniform and his ship was most at home flying over the ocean. Yet his command was not as close to the superdreadnought navy of the 1920s as it was to the earlier days of sail. The airshipman cruising high above the sea watched wind and weather as closely as those who, in times past, sailed under canvas upon the sea.

The ideal airshipman, then, must be master of the most advanced technology of his day as well as the older arts of wind and sea. Eckener picked up the technology as he went along. The more subtle responses to the forces of nature had been his since boyhood when he sailed the Baltic in his tiny boat. He became an expert in the fledgling science of meteorology, and to his training in economics and psychology he added an unexpected flair for showmanship. But of all the qualities that Hugo Eckener brought to the control car of his Zeppelins, the most important was an inflexible concern for the safety of his ship. No detail was too insignificant to escape his notice and he never hesitated to change to a safer flight plan even though it meant leaving kings and princes standing on the ground waiting in vain for his arrival.

Eckener took his first airship ride aboard *LZ-3*. He wrote occasional newspaper and publicity articles until Delag was formed in 1909, then he went to work full-time for the new company. When Delag's first passenger ship, *Deutschland,* was wrecked in the Teutoberg Forest and her captain fired, the question arose as to who would fly the next ship. Someone mentioned Eckener's name and he suddenly found himself in command of an airship.

At the start of World War I, Eckener's attempt to enlist as a naval Zeppelin commander was rejected. He was too important to risk at the front. He spent the war years training hundreds of new airship officers. By the war's end he was director of the Zeppelin Company as well as its most experienced pilot.

Dr. Ludwig Durr joined Count Zeppelin in 1899 at the age of twenty-one. He stepped into the chief engineer's job when the count's previous engineer refused to fly in his own creation, *LZ-1.* The count fired him on the spot and hired the intense young man who devoted the rest of his life to the Zeppelin organization, exercising complete engineering control over all subsequent airships. With Eckener flying the ships that Durr built, the Zeppelin Company had an unbeatable combination. *Courtesy Northrop University.*

With the signing of the Treaty of Locarno in October 1925, the Allies finally lifted the restrictions on German aircraft construction. Now the Zeppelin Company had permission to build their own airships again; all they lacked was the money. The work on the *Los Angeles* had enabled them to keep their best designers and construction personnel together, but there had been no profit involved, and the manufacture of aluminum pots and pans had barely generated enough to pay the rent. There was nothing left over with which to finance the construction of a new airship. Eckener estimated that it would cost a million dollars.

The Zeppelin Company's most valuable asset was still the German public's immense pride and faith in their airships. They had come to the old count's aid at Echterdingen—perhaps they would respond once again. Eckener and his senior airship commanders, Lehmann, von Schiller, Flemming, Wittemann, and Pruss, launched a lecture tour that took them to every corner of Germany. Their appeal was a success and the Zeppelin-Eckener Subscription Fund soon stood at $750,000. The German government, encouraged by the enthusiastic public response, agreed to contribute the remaining $250,000.

On July 8, 1928, Count Zeppelin's daughter, Hella, the Countess von Brandenstein-Zeppelin, christened *LZ-127,* the *Graf Zeppelin.* The ship that bore his name was launched on the ninetieth anniversary of Count Zeppelin's birth. She was 775 feet long, one hundred feet wide, and held 3,945,720 cubic feet of gas. Not all of this was hydrogen, however, for nearly a quarter of the *Graf Zeppelin's* hull was filled with Blaugas, a special gaseous motor fuel. Since Blaugas weighed the same as air, there was no change in weight on a long flight as fuel was consumed. With 25 percent less hydrogen, the ship had 25 percent less lift, but this was almost exactly offset by the thirty-two tons of gasoline she didn't need to carry.

Though the *Graf Zeppelin* had nearly twice the gas capacity of the *R.34* and was over a hundred feet longer than the *Los Angeles,* she was still, in Eckener's opinion, the smallest possible ship that could safely fly in transatlantic passenger service. Without enough money to build a new construction shed, Dr. Ludwig Durr, the Zeppelin Company's chief engineer, had been forced to create the best design within the limits of the space available inside the old shed. By moving the control car farther forward than normal onto the curve of the bow, he kept it from adding to the height of the ship. This allowed him to squeeze a 113-foot-high airship into a 114¼-foot-high construction hangar.

Hugo Eckener

Perhaps these enforced limitations also had their advantages, for we had to confess that while we were convinced that the Zeppelin could operate in any kind of weather, we lacked experience of how matters would go in the air above the ocean. Thus the Graf Zeppelin became a training-ship with a pioneering mission, not only for airships but also for all kinds of flight above the oceans. This was especially true of navigation, which was still in its infancy.[3]

Though the designers had been forced to compromise, the workmen had not. The *Graf Zeppelin* sailed through her trial flights without even a minor structural defect coming to light. Her top speed proved to be eighty miles per hour and her thirty-three tons of useful lift was slightly more than expected.

On September 18, 1928, she set out on a thirty-six-hour endurance trial.

The *Graf Zeppelin* under construction. The Zeppelin Company's *LZ-127* was built of duralumin, an alloy of aluminum and copper, with the strength of mild steel and only one-third of its weight. The improved duralumin in the *LZ-127* was 20 percent stronger than that used in *LZ-126*, the *Los Angeles*. The new ship had a total lift of ninety-four tons and weighed sixty-one tons, which left thirty-three tons available for useful lift. Five 530-horsepower Maybach V-12 engines gave her a top speed of 79.6 miles per hour and, at a cruising speed of seventy-one miles per hour, she had a range of eighty-four hundred miles. *Courtesy Cole Airship Collection, University of Oregon.*

•

Eckener laid out a flight plan that would give them maximum public exposure—from Frankfurt to Mainz, Cologne, and Dusseldorf, then out over the North Sea to spend the night. The next day they flew over Hamburg, Kiel, and, finally, Berlin. The German people had put up the money and they deserved a look at their airship.

It was four years since a German Zeppelin had cruised over a German city. The people were ecstatic. All along the way they jammed the streets and rooftops for a glimpse of their ship. After all, they asked, who had a better right? Not once, but twice when the banks, the financiers, even the government had turned their backs, it was the people who had come forward. Each man with his small contribution had a part in this great ship, a ship unmatched by any other country, that now would carry the German flag to every corner of the world. Long humbled in defeat, the pride of the entire nation focused once again on a Zeppelin.

But the *Graf Zeppelin* had been built to prove the airship's worth in regular transatlantic passenger service. The sooner she started with it, the sooner they would have their answer. It seemed feasible. The British airship *R.34* had successfully crossed from England to America and back. Charles Lindbergh had even flown from New York to Paris all alone in his *Spirit of St. Louis*. These aerial pioneers had

The *Graf Zeppelin (Count Zeppelin)* was christened on July 8, 1928. Three months later, after attracting huge crowds on a half-dozen German trial flights, she set out for America.

In this vast monster of the atmospheric deeps, . . . the public despite the tragedies that have punctuated the history of the dirigible, feels a strange confidence. Its bulk, its shining majesty of line and contour, which satisfies so generously one's instinctive conception of an airship—and, of course, its ability to remain afloat without momentum—inspire faith.

New York Herald Tribune,
October 1928

Courtesy Lufthansa Airlines.

conquered the Atlantic. They were the trailblazers. But to fly it on a regular schedule, carrying passengers and freight, was quite another matter.

On October 11, 1928, the *Graf Zeppelin* set out on her seventh flight. If all went well, it would take her across the Atlantic to America. She carried forty-three crewmen and twenty passengers. Each passenger had paid three thousand dollars for a one-way ticket. Hugo Eckener was at the helm.

In mid-Atlantic they met a storm front, a towering wall of blue-black clouds lying in wait across their path and stretching from horizon to horizon. It advanced toward the speeding airship with lightning flashing on every side. There was no way around, they would have to go through.

Hugo Eckener

I was already fully convinced that the ship could survive even very bad weather structurally intact, and also that squalls over the sea were not as violent as above the overheated land. But this was still only a theory.[4]

As the ship plunged into the storm front, her nose dipped, then bounded into the air, dumping everything onto the floor with a crash that was lost in a clap of thunder. Then the *Graf Zeppelin* leveled out and sailed serenely on as her passengers picked the breakfast dishes out of their laps.

She had not gotten through untouched, however. The fabric was ripped from the underside of the port stabilizing fin. Eckener's son Knut and three others volunteered to climb into the fin to repair the damage. The engines were slowed and they scrambled out onto the exposed girders with nothing between them and the icy Atlantic a thousand feet below. The squall had dumped several tons of rainwater on the huge hull and now with her engines slowed, the ship lost most of her dynamic lift and began to settle slowly toward the sea. As the men worked feverishly retying the cotton cover to the framework, the ship sank lower and lower. Finally Eckener could wait no longer. Less than three hundred feet above the sea he ordered the engines speeded up, the men scrambled out of the fin, and Eckener drove the ship back up to fifteen hundred feet. Then he slowed the motors and the men climbed out onto the exposed girders again. For three anxious hours the work continued until the job was completed and they could resume their journey.

After flying safely through one more line squall, they crossed the U.S. coastline at Cape Charles, Virginia, then flew to Washington, D.C., and New York City, which came to a complete standstill as millions of people stopped to watch the giant Zeppelin circle overhead. Then Eckener turned toward Lakehurst where thousands more were waiting.

After a flight of 111 hours and 45 minutes, they landed to a riotous welcome. All America had been following the progress of their voyage. It had been front-page news since their departure. The anxious moments over the ocean only served to heighten the excitement of this first commercial crossing of the Atlantic by air. Eckener's explanation that the torn fin demonstrated not the weakness of the airship, but rather the ease with which it could be repaired in flight, was enthusiastically accepted. Eckener and his crew were given a triumphant ticker tape parade down Broadway and were even invited to breakfast with President Coolidge.

On October 29, the *Graf Zeppelin* left Lakehurst for the return flight to Friedrichshafen. The passenger section was sold out and hundreds had been turned away. The weather maps showed good weather all the way across the North Atlantic. They didn't show the large cold air mass that was pushing its way down from the Arctic. By the time the *Graf Zeppelin* met it two hundred miles out at sea, it had created a full-fledged hurricane with winds of seventy miles per hour that drove the struggling ship stern first, all the way back to Newfoundland. With the ship's engines driving into the gale at fifty miles an hour, they were actually flying backward at twenty miles per hour. Once Eckener realized what was happening, he changed course to take advantage of the storm winds, which pushed them to Friedrichshafen in seventy hours, a day and a half less than the flight out.

It had been an eventful first voyage. Serious and unexpected hazards had been placed in her way and the *Graf Zeppelin* had overcome them all. She had taken the worst the North Atlantic had to offer and sailed through relatively unscathed. Transatlantic airship service was a reality.

Once again a Zeppelin had captured the world's imagination. She was front-page news in every corner of the globe. Her achievement, the opening of a commercial air route across the ocean, certainly merited the response. But there was something more in the great outflow of excitement and enthusiasm that was to accompany the *Graf Zeppelin*'s every voyage. In Germany it was personal pride

The *Graf Zeppelin* was the most successful airship ever built, with a million-mile safety record. Yet she was actually a compromise design. She was not nearly as large as the Zeppelin Company wanted to build, but with no money for a new construction shed, she was the largest ship that could be built in the old shed. Eckener felt that she was the smallest ship that could safely be put into commercial transatlantic service. *Courtesy Luftschiffbau Zeppelin, Friedrichshafen.*

•

and a sense of national vindication, but no such sentiment can explain the rest of the world's interest.

Part of it was man's pride in his technology, his ability to overcome the forces of nature and span the oceans. But Hugo Eckener saw his Zeppelins as filling a more basic need. The doctor of psychology had considered the question carefully.

Hugo Eckener

I always felt that such effects as were produced by the Zeppelin airship were traceable to a large degree to aesthetic feelings. The mass of the mighty airship hull, which seemed matched by its lightness and grace, and whose beauty of form was modulated in delicate shades of colour, never failed to make a strong impression on people's minds. It was not, as generally described, a "silver bird soaring in majestic flight," but rather a fabulous silvery fish, floating quietly in the ocean of air and captivating the eye just like a fantastic exotic fish seen in an aquarium. And this fairy-like apparition, which seemed to melt into the silvery blue background of sky, when it appeared far away, lighted by the sun, seemed to be coming from another world and to be returning there like a dream—an emissary from the "Island of the Blest" in which so many humans still believe in the inmost recesses of their souls.[5]

The *Graf Zeppelin*'s premier season had been a success. For the first time since 1914, a German airship was again the leader in commercial aviation. Now, while Zeppelin technicians gave the ship a thorough inspection and winter overhaul, Eckener and his staff began to plan their 1929 season.

Eckener knew that his dream of a worldwide commercial Zeppelin network depended on building confidence with both the public and the financial community. He would have to prove his ship's safety and dependability under all kinds of flying conditions. He would also have to keep the *Graf Zeppelin* on the front page. He had captured the public's interest with the transatlantic flight but he knew how quickly their attention could be diverted to other amusements.

In March he scheduled a Mediterranean flight for German government and aviation officials. Who would be able to resist a sunny Mediterranean cruise after a northern European winter? He would then fly once more to America just to show how easy it was. And finally, as a grand climax to the 1929 season, Eckener would sail the *Graf Zeppelin* all the way around the world!

The Mediterranean flight was a great success. With the president of the Reichstag and the minister of transport among the dignitaries aboard, they cruised over Rome, Naples, Capri, Crete, and Cyprus to Jerusalem where they descended to one thousand feet below sea level over the surface of the Dead Sea. After a three-day voyage, the sightseers returned to Friedrichshafen and winter.

Years later during World War II, Eckener recalled his flight over the Dead Sea and surprised a gathering of U-boat commanders with the statement that he had sailed further beneath the surface of the sea in his Zeppelin than they were able to go in their submarines.

The Mediterranean cruise had been pleasant and uneventful. The first Atlantic crossing of the 1929 season was quite a different story. They set out from Friedrichshafen on May 16 with twenty passengers, forty crewmen, and Suzie the gorilla traveling as cargo.

Eckener followed the valley of the Rhone across France to the Mediterranean and then turned southwest along the coast of Spain toward Gibraltar. In the passenger lounge the tables were being set for lunch when an engine stopped. The *Graf Zeppelin* often cruised on only four motors to save fuel and the loss of an engine barely slowed her down. That evening the last warm rays of the setting sun flooded the dining room as the Spanish coastline slipped into shadow far below and the second engine stopped.

Now his margin of safety was gone and Eckener knew he would have to turn back, but with only three engines, the ship's speed was cut to fifty-five miles per hour and she turned to face head winds of up to fifty miles per hour. Morning found them back near the French coast. In eight hours they had gained only two hundred miles. As they struggled toward the mouth of the Rhone they met the full force of the mistral, the cold, dry wind that sweeps down the river valley from the North Sea. By two o'clock that afternoon they were only a hundred miles inland. Then the third engine quit and, five minutes later, the fourth. One motor remained and the insistent fury of the mistral began to drive the huge ship stern first down the valley toward the sea.

As Eckener searched the terrain below for a sheltered place large enough to crash-land his ship, a message crackled over the wireless. It was from the French Air Ministry. "Airship hangars at Cuers and Orly available for your use."[6] Cuers, the naval airship base a few miles outside Toulon, was ninety miles downwind of them, their last hope before being swept out to sea. In an only partially controlled drift, Eckener guided his stricken ship over the base and valving gas, descended into the waiting arms of a French naval landing crew who walked the ship into the hangar.

The French were not fond of Zeppelins. Too many had brought terror and death to France in the last war. They placed strict controls on all the *Graf Zeppelin*'s flights over their territory. Eckener had already complained in the press that the late

The *Graf Zeppelin*'s control car and passenger rooms were in a single gondola, ninety-eight feet long and twenty feet wide. The control car was at the front with the navigator's chart room behind it. Next was the radio room with the galley beside it; followed by the large combination lounge and dining room. Behind the lounge were ten passenger compartments, five on each side of a central corridor. Each compartment had an upper and lower berth that folded into a couch in the daytime. The washrooms and toilets were at the end of the gondola.

•

ABOVE: The navigation room. *Courtesy Deutsches Museum Munich.* BELOW: The combination passenger lounge and dining salon. *Luftschiffbau Zeppelin photo, courtesy Douglas Robinson.*

arrival of French overflight permission had delayed the start of the current voyage by a full day. But in the emergency, France had saved his ship.

Once safely inside the hangar with the passengers sent off to nearby hotels, Eckener ordered his exhausted men into the ship's lounge, opened up the best champagne, and threw a party. He even invited Suzie the gorilla.

Propeller coupling failure was found to be the cause of the breakdown. Six days later new mountings were installed and the *Graf Zeppelin* returned to Friedrichshafen. Four of the five engines had been slightly altered by the ship's chief mechanic and all four had given out. A minor adjustment had resulted in near tragedy. Now the scheduled around-the-world flight became especially important. Eckener needed a spectacular success to offset what could only be regarded as a rather spectacular failure. He needed to prove the basic soundness of his ship in a dramatic way. He needed the round-the-world flight.

Graf Zeppelin stateroom made up for the daytime. *Luftschiffbau Zeppelin photo, courtesy Douglas Robinson.*

•

Hugo Eckener

It was the task of the commercial department of the Zeppelin Company to demonstrate the usefulness of the Zeppelin under all conditions throughout the world and to obtain experience in all its zones. How better could this be done than in a flight around the world? At the same time this would provide a brilliant testimonial of the endurance and operational radius of the ship, and would promote propaganda for the cause throughout the world. And the flight seemed technically feasible, for if necessary we could use two intermediate bases: the airship hangars at Lakehurst and at Kasumigaura near Tokyo.[7]

The *Graf Zeppelin* would feel right at home in the hangar at Kasumigaura, for it was another German hangar, dismantled by the Allies and shipped to Japan along with a wartime Zeppelin as part of Japan's share of the war reparations.

If a round-the-world airship flight seemed technically possible, economically it was not quite so simple. The most expensive part of the preparations would be the shipment of the airship's special gaseous fuel to Japan—883,000 cubic feet of Blaugas would have to be shipped in steel containers to Tokyo by freighter along with several technicians to supervise the ground arrangements for the ship's landing. Eckener estimated that the whole flight would cost at least $250,000. Where would the money come from?

Here is where Eckener the economist-journalist-publicist-showman took over from Eckener the psychologist-corporation executive-airship commander. He sold the exclusive world press rights to the flight, excluding Europe, to William Randolph Hearst for $100,000. Then he sold the European rights to three German newspapers for $12,500. That took care of half the expenses. He then arranged for an issue of special Zeppelin postage stamps to pay for the other half. That, plus the paying passengers at $2,500 each, would give him a profit of $40,000. Hugo Eckener had not studied economics for nothing!

The next question to be settled was the route. The *Graf Zeppelin* had been designed primarily for over-water flights with a normal cruising altitude of twelve hundred feet. She was certainly capable of flying much higher but when she did, she lost gas, and less gas meant less lift was available for passengers, cargo, or fuel. It would definitely be safer to chart a low-altitude course around the mountains.

There was a water route to Japan—through the Mediterranean, the Indian Ocean, and the China Sea—but this was nearly nine thousand miles long and there

The *Graf Zeppelin*'s seven-thousand-mile voyage from Berlin to Tokyo set a nonstop long-distance record that stood for more than a quarter of a century until it was broken in 1957 by another lighter-than-air craft, a U.S. Navy blimp. Here the *Graf Zeppelin*'s shadow glides silently over the vast wilderness of forest and swamp in Siberia's Yenisei River Basin. *Courtesy Zeppelin Museum, Friedrichshafen.*

•

was a possibility of typhoons in the China Sea. The most direct route lay over the plains of Central Russia to Lake Baikal, through the Amur River valley to Manchuria, and across Northern China to Japan. This was three thousand miles shorter, but it was subject to fog and heavy rain, especially in the Amur valley. Eckener finally chose a slightly longer overland route that would take him five hundred miles farther north over Siberia to Yakutsk on the Lena River and across the five-thousand-foot-high Stanovoi Mountains to the Sea of Okhotsk and Japan. All things considered, this route seemed the safest, since the only serious obstacle, the mountains, would be encountered at the very end of the flight when the ship would be less heavily laden, having consumed several tons of motor oil along the way.

The agreement with Hearst stipulated that the flight must begin and end in the United States, so on August 1, 1929, the *Graf Zeppelin* left Friedrichshafen for Lakehurst. There she took on twenty passengers, including Lt. Comdr. Charles Rosendahl and two Hearst reporters, Lady Drummond Hay and Karl von Wiegand. On August 7 she took off again for Friedrichshafen on the first leg of the world flight.

At Friedrichshafen she picked up a Russian government official and then set out on the longest part of the journey, the seven thousand miles across Europe and Asia to Tokyo.

The endless wastelands of Siberia made a profound impression on Eckener. He described the experience in a speech to the National Geographic Society as he accepted their Special Gold Medal.

Hugo Eckener

We flew hundreds of miles over uninterrupted stretches of these swamps. We then saw small pools, one after another, followed by more or less large lakes. These were connected by strips of swampy land. Then came low, swampy woods extending for many miles. The whole region gave the impression of a dreadful waste, uninhabitable for man or beast, where there were not even waterfowl.

In grotesque contrast to all the deadly silence, the airship sailed, its cabins lighted, its care-free occupants dining and enjoying themselves; and yet, if for some reason it had been necessary to land in these swamps, escape from those black-green waters would not have been possible.

We flew over that dread waste the whole night, from seven in the evening until nine o'clock next morning, and it was with sensations of relief that we finally hailed the broad Yenisei River, which, notwithstanding its loneliness and remoteness, seemed to us like a safe street that would lead us again to towns and people.

The banks of the river extended endlessly, a monotonous waste, not a house, not a settlement in sight, not a boat on the broad, powerful stream to enliven the picture. After about an hour, a small village of a few huts appeared on the left, and at the right was Imbatsk, for which we had been looking.

Our appearance might have impressed as an inconceivable miracle the inhabitants, who begin and end their lives here, far from the outer world. Perhaps we frightened them, for we could not see anyone emerge from the houses. Three or four animals drawing carts ran away.[8]

Finally the desolate reaches of Siberia lay behind and a single mountain range remained between the *Graf Zeppelin* and the sea. All the maps Eckener had consulted before departure stated without conviction that the peaks of the Stanovoi mountains were probably no higher than five thousand feet. If they encountered fog there, Eckener planned to ascend to six thousand as an extra margin of safety. Now the foothills of the Stanovois rose before them into a clear blue sky.

Hugo Eckener

The mountains became more abrupt and awesome, partly covered with woods, partly barren and rising to magnificent peaks. We tried to find our way, if possible, over lower ridges, but soon had to ascend to 3,600 and 3,900 feet. More and more ridges of mountains towered before us and we had to go up to 4,500 and 4,900 feet.

Finally, following a deep-cut valley, we arrived at the last ridge immediately before the Okhotsk Sea, which we had to pass at a height of 5,500 feet. We flew as close as possible, clearing the ridge by only about 300 feet. Steep walls of rocks at both sides were even 600 to 1,000 feet higher still. Therefore we should really have attained an elevation of 6,200 to 6,500 feet to have crossed the Stanovoi Mountains safely. We blessed our good fortune which gave us clear weather for this part of the trip.[9]

A quarter of a million Japanese turned out to welcome the *Graf Zeppelin* to Tokyo as she landed and refueled for the first nonstop flight ever attempted across the Pacific. The seven thousand miles from Friedrichshafen to Tokyo had taken less than a hundred hours. Now Eckener caught the tail of a typhoon to speed him on his way across the Pacific, covering the fifty-four hundred miles from Tokyo to San Francisco in sixty-eight hours.

The riotous welcome accorded the great ship as she sailed in over the Golden Gate put a severe strain on the descriptive powers of the *New York Times'* special correspondent:

In silver silhouette against the blue sky of a perfect San Francisco late afternoon, Dr. Hugo Eckener's world-circling leviathan of the air dipped and curtsied for an hour this evening for the awe and delight of hundreds and hundreds of thousands of San Francisco's citizenry and their guests. . . .

The tens upon tens of thousands of automobilists, parked in their cars for miles along the ocean beach, the Skyline Boulevard, Golden Gate Park and the Presidio, received the first view of the graceful, steadily oncoming monster of silver sheen,

The *Graf Zeppelin* made a late afternoon landfall over San Francisco thus completing the first nonstop flight across the Pacific Ocean. With the help of a typhoon, she had flown the fifty-four hundred miles from Tokyo in sixty-eight hours for an average speed of nearly eighty miles per hour. In contrast, the first transpacific passenger flights of Pan American Airlines' *China Clipper* six years later would average only thirty-four miles per hour when all their refueling stops were included. And the first *China Clippers* of 1935 could carry only twelve passengers while the *Graf Zeppelin* carried twenty. *Courtesy San Diego Aero-Space Museum.*

•

burnished at times to russet by the rays of the declining sun, as it advanced steadily toward the Golden Gate.

With the first radio messages factory whistles, sirens, automobile horns and the noise-making equipment of the Fire Department added their combined diapason of reverberation to roar upward to merge with the roaring of the motors of the Zeppelin and the snappier punctuations of the convoying airplanes from the army, navy and newspapers that buzzed and circled around the transpacific guest like bees around some gigantic floating comb. One could count these convoy planes into three figures. . . .

Throughout the entire downtown area every roof and balcony and window giving any vantage point whatsoever was thronged with watchers, who remained until the last flick of the giant air fish's tail moved with stately, even motion on into the west.[10]

After making her landfall over the Golden Gate the *Graf Zeppelin* cruised down the California coast to Los Angeles, where she landed for refueling. Halfway down the coast she flew over William Randolph Hearst's magnificent castle at San Simeon. It was night and the place was in darkness as she approached. Suddenly a switch was thrown and all the turrets and spires were bathed in light as the ship sailed over.

Eckener was quite concerned about crossing the desert beyond Los Angeles. The hot air rising from the surface would decrease the lifting power of his hydrogen. To compensate, he shipped seven of his forty-man crew from Los Angeles to Lakehurst by plane, thus giving him nearly half a ton more lift.

He needed it—but not for the desert. Though the takeoff was scheduled for midnight, a crowd estimated by police at half a million had gathered to witness the great event. When Eckener discovered that there was not enough hydrogen at the field to fill the gas cells completely, he sent for more but no truck was able to get through the gigantic traffic jam that stretched for miles in every direction. Finally he decided to take off anyway. The airfield was ringed with high-tension wires and the *Graf Zeppelin* cleared them with only inches to spare, leaving a trail of canned peas, tea, and cases of ginger ale, all jettisoned at the last moment to gain the last precious inches over the deadly wires.

The historic round-the-world voyage was successfully completed when the *Graf Zeppelin* touched down at Lakehurst at 8:13 on the morning of August 29. Three weeks and twenty-one thousand miles earlier, she had taken off from the same spot headed in the opposite direction.

Once again Eckener and his men were feted as heroes. They were given their second ticker tape parade down Broadway and were received by President Hoover at the White House.

Then they flew back to Friedrichshafen, thereby completing the round-the-world flight that began in Germany as opposed to the one that began and ended in the United States. But the American press couldn't resist pointing out that the German world flight took twelve hours longer than the American one. The *Graf Zeppelin* had circled the globe in slightly less than three hundred hours in the air at an average speed of 70.7 miles per hour.

The world flight was a resounding success. The last lingering doubts about airship travel vanished overnight as investors besieged the Zeppelin Company with offers of enough money to build and fly ships to every corner of the earth. A week after the flight, former Democratic presidential candidate Al Smith announced that a Zeppelin mooring mast would crown the summit of the Empire State Building, which

his company was then constructing. The days of privation and compromise were over. At last the money was at hand to build a fleet of luxurious passenger airships that would make the *Graf Zeppelin* seem primitive by comparison.

The future of commercial airship travel was assured. The success for which they had worked so long had finally arrived. Nothing could stop them now. It was a heady two months. The world flight ended at Lakehurst on August 29, 1929, two months to the day before Black Tuesday, when the stock market began its fifty-billion-dollar slide.

The future of the airship, so near at hand, evaporated along with the speculators' paper profits, and six long years were to pass before Eckener would be able to scrape the money together to build the first true commercial Zeppelin, the *Hindenburg*. And while the airship was marking time for lack of money, the airplane was catching up. An airship would never be moored to Al Smith's mast at the top of the Empire State Building.

Still, things could have been worse. Though five thousand banks would go out of business by 1933, the bankers all insisted that the economy was fundamentally sound and President Hoover said that prosperity was just around the corner. If 1929 had been a bad year for the stock market, it had been a great year for the *Graf Zeppelin,* and there were still more than enough people who could afford to fly in her. She went into the hangar for a winter overhaul, and Hugo Eckener began to lay his plans for the 1930 season.

Thus far their flights had been stunts designed primarily to catch the public's

At Los Angeles the *Graf Zeppelin* made her first landing since Tokyo. Dr. Eckener is climbing down the ladder. The control car, navigation room, and radio room are in front of the door, the lounge behind it. The three tiny fish-shaped objects beneath the radio room are antenna weights, reeled out in flight to improve reception. The air-driven propeller beside the radio room powers the generator. The big dome beneath the car is a shock-absorbing bumper. *Courtesy Historical Collection, Security Pacific National Bank, Los Angeles.*

•

attention and demonstrate the airship's capabilities. The world flight had firmly established the *Graf Zeppelin*'s all-weather reliability. Now it was time to cash in on that hard-won reputation. It was time for the *Graf Zeppelin* to stop wandering about the world and settle down on a nice, scheduled, commercial route where she could make some money.

Eckener had the ideal route in mind. A large number of Germans had settled in South America. They had gone into farming, opened small businesses, or established branches of European firms—and they had prospered. But the only direct service between Germany and South America was by boat, which took two weeks or more. It seemed like the perfect market for the *Graf Zeppelin,* and Eckener began to look for a way to finance a trial flight.

Raising money early in 1930 was not the easiest thing to do, and when the German government turned him down, Eckener went to an unlikely source, the United States Post Office. The world's stamp collectors had furnished half the money for the world flight and now, through a special U.S. stamp issue, they financed the *Graf Zeppelin*'s first voyage to South America.

On May 18, 1930, she left Friedrichshafen bound for Brazil, where landing rights had been secured at Recife. Along the way, she stopped off in Spain at Seville to pick up mail and extra passengers. In spite of warnings of torrential tropical rainstorms that would drive the ship down into the sea, Eckener did not believe the southern ocean could be any worse than the cold and stormy North Atlantic and, in fact, the endless expanse of sun-swept sea appeared specially designed for the *Graf Zeppelin*. After an effortless crossing she refueled at Recife, then cruised twelve hundred miles along the lush tropical coast down to Rio de Janeiro. From there Eckener charted a course north to Lakehurst, flying by way of Natal, Brazil, where he dropped a bouquet of flowers on a monument to Alberto Santos-Dumont.

It was a touching and appropriate gesture, for though Alberto Santos-Dumont in his last years felt himself personally responsible for the destruction and death inflicted by airplanes and airships in the war, so too, in the last years before his death in 1932, his eyes now filled with tears of pride at the news of the peaceful accomplishments of the *Graf Zeppelin*.

After the flight from South America to Lakehurst, they took on new passengers and returned across the North Atlantic to Friedrichshafen. The great triangular voyage had carried them fifteen thousand miles over three continents. It convinced Eckener of the feasibility, both aeronautic and economic, of the South American route. But before the *Graf Zeppelin* settled down into routine commercial service, there was one last excursion he wanted to make.

Count Zeppelin had talked about it. He and Prince Henry of Prussia were almost ready to go when the war broke out. Andrée tried it, so did Wellman, Amundsen, and Nobile. Even the U.S. Navy had planned to send the *Shenandoah* to the Arctic. What was it about the polar regions that held such fascination for airshipmen? Perhaps it was the fact that there seemed no other logical way to explore this terrifying wilderness of ice and snow. Whatever the lure, Hugo Eckener was not immune.

The record of his predecessors was not encouraging. Andrée vanished, Wellman failed, Nobile began in success but ended in failure and disgrace. Even Amundsen was lost there in an unknown grave. Still Eckener was determined to take the *Graf Zeppelin* to the Arctic.

When Al Smith announced that Zeppelins would soon be picking up passengers from a mooring mast atop the Empire State Building, then nearing completion, an enterprising newspaper photographer anticipated the great event by superimposing this image of the *Los Angeles* onto the mast. All of the grand schemes born of the *Graf Zeppelin*'s successful world flight soon disappeared, however, in the depths of the depression. *Courtesy Culver Pictures.*

•

The idea was first suggested to him by Fridtjof Nansen, the famed Norwegian statesman and polar explorer. As a statesman, Nansen helped secure Norway's independence from Sweden and won the Nobel Peace Prize for his work in repatriating prisoners after World War I. As a scientist and explorer, he spent two years drifting with the Arctic ice pack in his tiny ship *Fram* and had driven to within 272 miles of the Pole by kayak and sled before being forced to turn back.

In 1928 Nansen founded the International Association for Exploring the Arctic by Means of Airships and he invited Eckener to join. A year later Nansen died and Eckener was elected president of the association in his place. As president, he felt somewhat obligated to attempt a flight.

Like everything else he undertook, Eckener approached the Arctic carefully and methodically. First he accepted two charter flights that would serve as tests of Arctic flying conditions. The first on July 8, 1930, was a seventy-hour cruise almost to Spitzbergen. The second, ten days later, was to Iceland.

The crossing of the equator aboard a cruise ship is a great event, with King Neptune and his court coming aboard to initiate the passengers into his select company. But when the *Graf Zeppelin* crossed the equator on her voyages from Friedrichshafen to Recife, it was Aeolus, king of the winds, who presided over the ceremonies, for it was to his realm rather than to Neptune's that the dirigible belonged. Each initiate received this certificate. *Courtesy Cole Airship Collection, University of Oregon.*

•

Hugo Eckener

Our intention of making an Arctic flight was considered a great risk by many people, including meteorologists and airship experts. Firstly, they believed that fog, clouds, and snow would greatly hamper and endanger navigation over the Polar Seas. Secondly, they considered that the danger of "icing up" of the airship was a very serious threat. Both opinions are wrong. Concerning the alleged navigational difficulties, the testimony of Polar experts, such as Nansen, Amundsen, and Wilkins, with whom I discussed this question, was that the Polar region generally is less covered by low cloud and fog than, for example, Central Europe and North America in the autumn and winter.[11]

As for the problem of icing, Eckener had already gained considerable experience during the war when his ships were forced to fly all winter through freezing North Sea storms. He wasn't worried.

Hugo Eckener

I know of no case where Zeppelins during the first World War were endangered by icing, although very often during winter cruises thick, clear ice would form on braces, struts and wires. One Zeppelin was lost in the winter of 1916 on the Russian Baltic coast through being weighted down by snow during a snowstorm. But in this case the commander had tried for a long time to find his hangar in a blizzard, and finally the ship was so heavily loaded with snow that she became too weighty, and sank to the ground. Had she gone a few hundred feet higher, where the snow was drier and would have been blown away by the slipstream, the ship could have been kept in the air and, when the weather cleared, could have found her hangar.[12]

Satisfied by the trial flights that there were no special problems to be overcome, Eckener sent the *Graf Zeppelin* in for her winter overhaul and turned to the one problem that was always with him—money. The distinguished members of the International Association for Exploring the Arctic by Means of Airships were rich in polar experience and scientific knowledge, but short on cash. Who could he get to pay for the Arctic expedition?

William Randolph Hearst had been contacted but was not enthusiastic. Then Sir Hubert Wilkins, a well-known Arctic explorer and a member of the association, came up with an idea. He would take a submarine under the ice to the Pole, bore up through the ice to the surface where the Zeppelin would be waiting to exchange mail and passengers. This Hearst liked. The contract he offered to Eckener read:

> If the airship and the submarine succeed in meeting at the North Pole and in exchanging passengers and mail, the Hearst Corporation will pay $150,000 for reporting rights on board the airship. If the airship and the submarine merely succeed in meeting at the North Pole, the Hearst Corporation will pay $100,000. On the other hand, if there is merely a meeting somewhere in the Arctic, the Corporation will merely pay $30,000.[13]

Hugo Eckener

I freely admit that I had little confidence in this agreement even with respect to the third contingency, but I signed it, for it gave our flight tremendous advance publicity, and this had an effect on the sale of stamps to collectors. And so I was able to finance the flight, at least to a large extent.[14]

Wilkins obtained an obsolete U.S. Navy submarine and sailed it to Trondheim, Norway, for refitting and repairs, but the sub turned out to be in poor condition and the repair work took so long that Eckener was forced to go ahead without Wilkins. With no submarine to accept the mail, Eckener was in danger of losing his stamp money, and he turned to the Russian government for help. They were already planning a scientific expedition to Franz Josef Land aboard the Soviet icebreaker *Malygin,* and Eckener arranged to meet the ship there and exchange letters. The *Graf Zeppelin* carried 650 pounds of mail, which was traded for 270 pounds carried aboard the *Malygin.* This paid for the flight.

With a full load of scientists and equipment, the *Graf Zeppelin* took off from Friedrichshafen on July 24, 1931. After a stop at Berlin they headed for Leningrad. At the Russian frontier a flight of Soviet airplanes gave them an official escort—and made sure they didn't fly over any Russian fortifications. At Leningrad the ship was refueled while the Russians loaded her with caviar, hams, and extra Arctic survival equipment—just in case.

The expedition's fifteen scientists were under the direction of Russian Arctic expert Prof. R. L. Samoilovich and included German, Swedish, and Russian meteorologists, physicists, biologists, geographers, and aerial surveyors. Two Americans were also on board, Coast Guard Lt. Comdr. E. H. (Iceberg) Smith and Lincoln Ellsworth, the wealthy explorer who had accompanied Amundsen and Nobile on the flight of the *Norge.*

They spotted the *Malygin* off Franz Josef Land and landed on the water nearby among the drifting ice floes. A boat loaded with mail put out from the icebreaker.

Hugo Eckener

As the boat approached, we recognized General Nobile, the commander of the Italian airship, Italia, wrecked the year before. In the spring Nobile had offered to accompany me as a "Polar expert" when he heard of our plans. I declined with thanks, for we did not intend to accumulate experiences on a cake of ice. So he had gone with the Malygin, perhaps in the rash hope of finding traces of his comrades possibly carried off to Franz Josef Land with the wreck of the airship. Doubtless he would gladly have come on board the Zeppelin, and I would gladly have let him come for the rest of our flight; but something happened which made me decide to take off as soon as possible.[15]

In spite of her sea anchor, the *Graf Zeppelin* had started to drift toward the nearby ice and was in danger of hitting it. As soon as the mail was loaded, Eckener dumped ballast and took off without inviting his visitors aboard.

Eckener's treatment of a fellow airshipman seems a little harsh, but he had apparently sided with his friend Roald Amundsen in the controversy that followed the flights of the *Norge* and *Italia.* He believed that the *Italia* had crashed because of an error by Nobile, and Hugo Eckener had little sympathy for anyone who he thought had mishandled an airship.

The *Graf Zeppelin* continued on, mapping and photographing the uncharted areas of Franz Josef Land, the Taymyr Peninsula, and Novaya Zemlya. Then she returned home by way of Leningrad and Berlin, landing back at Friedrichshafen exactly one week and 8,142 miles after her departure.

In August she flew again to South America and back. She made two more South American crossings in September and October.

In 1932 the *Graf Zeppelin* flew to South America nine times. In 1933 she made nine more flights carrying four hundred passengers. The number of crossings was

By 1931 the *Graf Zeppelin* was ready to settle into scheduled passenger and cargo service, and the four-thousand-mile flight from Central Europe across the South Atlantic to Brazil was the perfect route. In the next five years she made fifty-eight round-trip voyages to South America carrying more than twenty-five hundred passengers, who must have enjoyed an extraordinary adventure from Rio de Janeiro to the castles on the Rhine, seen almost at eye level as the ship cruised down in the river valleys and through the mountain passes. Best of all from Eckener's point of view was the fact that the *Graf Zeppelin* had no competition. The only other aircraft flying the South Atlantic were either French mail planes on the much shorter route from Dakar in Africa to Natal, Brazil, or the German Condor mail planes operating from catapult ships stationed off the coast of Africa and near the Brazilian island of Fernando do Noronha. *Courtesy Luftschiffbau Zeppelin, Friedrichshafen.*

Dr. Hugo Eckener (1868–1954), the world's premier airship commander. *Luftschiffbau Zeppelin photo, courtesy Douglas Robinson.*

•

increased to twelve in 1934 and sixteen in 1935, carrying five hundred and 720 passengers respectively. In 1936 the *Hindenburg* joined her on the South American run, and together they carried fifteen hundred passengers, the *Graf Zeppelin* making twelve crossings while the *Hindenburg* made seven.

By 1938 the *Graf Zeppelin* had flown over a million miles on 590 flights that took her to London, Cairo, Helsinki, Stockholm, Rome, Moscow, and all around the world. She had crossed the ocean 144 times, and carried sixteen thousand passengers and 275 tons of mail and freight. She had spent 17,178 hours—almost two years—in the air. And all this without an accident, without an injury of any kind. The *Graf Zeppelin* was truly a "lucky ship." But her luck came from the man who flew her, and Hugo Eckener saw to it that as little as possible was left to luck.

Hugo Eckener

To pilot an airship is to a great degree a matter of character. One should be able to say "no" frequently, and that is often more difficult than to say "yes." It is particularly difficult when a continuous series of splendid successes can be anticipated, and a refusal may be interpreted as a lack of self-confidence and courage.

Once, right at the beginning of my service as an airship captain, the presence of a large crowd of spectators and a cabin full of influential and important guests tempted me to risk taking the ship out of the hangar with the wind from an unfavourable direction. I paid for my weak-kneed decision by damaging the ship so badly that she had to be almost completely rebuilt, and thereafter was cured of such impulsive acts.[16]

From then on, Eckener never hesitated to refuse any request that might involve even the slightest danger to his ship. He had postponed the *Los Angeles'* delivery flight to the United States for a full day despite the fact that thousands of people were waiting to see the takeoff. When the *Graf Zeppelin* arrived in the U.S. he received dozens of invitations to visit cities in the Midwest. Important passengers were lined up with their money in hand, but one look at the unsettled weather conditions in that part of the country in late October convinced Eckener to return to Germany.

On the pre-Arctic charter flight to Spitzbergen they were within sight of the island when the fog began to close in. The cold fog could cause dangerous icing on the ship and also prevent them from getting a good navigation fix on the island before starting back across the sea to Norway.

Hugo Eckener

It became clear to me that Spitzbergen would be entirely covered with fog in less than the hour it would take us to arrive there. So I decided to turn back. Naturally the news of this decision caused great disappointment, not to say indignation among the passengers, and I was fiercely attacked later on this account in a Swiss paper by a particularly dissatisfied gentleman. But I had my own good reasons, which I did not want to communicate to the passengers, in order not to disturb them.[17]

Eckener was also criticized in the press when, on the Arctic flight, he saw his ship drifting toward the ice and took off, leaving Nobile and the others from the *Malygin* behind, despite the fact that they had been promised tea aboard the airship. Then, once again, on the round-the-world flight:

Hugo Eckener

The Russian representative on board came to me in the control car to emphasize the absolute necessity of flying over Moscow. He apparently was instructed to demand this; for in Moscow, as he said, "hundreds of thousands were awaiting expectantly the appearance of the world-famous Zeppelin," and the Government had led them to expect it. I still hesitated to give a definite promise, for I first wanted to look at the evening weather report, since the morning report indicated uncertain weather conditions over southern Russia. When the evening report was received, it showed that a low-pressure area had developed north of the Caspian Sea, causing strong easterly winds as far north as Moscow. We would have to be prepared for head winds if we flew by way of the capital, while I had every right to expect calm air or even favourable westerly winds on a route laid out more to the north. What to do?

It was clear to me that it would be "politically" desirable not to vex and disappoint the Muscovites. On the other hand, navigational considerations obliged me to use the weather situation to the best advantage, for the journey was long and our fuel supply limited. . . . It was a fundamental principle with me to take navigational considerations into account first of all, even if political or other disadvantages might ensue. Therefore I decided to steer to the north and to leave Moscow on our right. The Russian Government representative was furious and almost threatening, but it availed him nothing. While the inhabitants of Moscow were vainly keeping watch on their roofs for our ship, the latter was continuing her progress in steady flight to the northeast.[18]

Even with his highly developed sense of public relations on behalf of airship travel, Eckener refused to allow anything to come before the safety of his ship. But his position was unique. He was captain of the *Graf Zeppelin* and director of the Zeppelin Company. No one told him what to do—there was no higher authority looking over his shoulder second-guessing his decisions. Other airship commanders were not so fortunate. Zachary Lansdowne, for instance, did not want to take the *Shenandoah* on her fatal flight, but he had to follow orders and hope for the best. Eckener would simply have refused and, in fact, did refuse to fly over the same area under similar unfavorable weather conditions.

Other airship commanders would find themselves in Lansdowne's position. Few would be in Eckener's. The luck of the *Graf Zeppelin* was Hugo Eckener.

Dr. Hugo Eckener noted that seven of the *Graf Zeppelin*'s historic voyages were made possible only through the interest and assistance of the world's stamp collectors. The world flight and the expedition to the Arctic were both largely financed by the sale of special Zeppelin stamps. The first crossing to South America in May 1930 was financed entirely by a special issue of the U.S. Post Office that raised one hundred thousand dollars for the flight. Today, Zeppelin stamps such as these issued by the United States, Russia, Germany, and Brazil are a valued part of many stamp collections. Even more highly regarded are the envelopes with both stamps and postmarks that tell the stories of the historic flights they made. The one shown here was carried to the Arctic and transferred between the *Malygin* and the *Graf Zeppelin* in 1931. *Stamps and cover, courtesy Jerry Clark, Costa Mesa.*

•

8

· T H E ·

BIG SHIPS

Thus, it would seem that now airships are at last "on their feet" in this country, in spite of opposition and prejudice arising largely from uninformed persons. It can be safely asserted that no one who has ever flown in a rigid airship or who has studied them with an open mind, can see anything but great possibilities in the type. I lack the words to describe the moments of despair that those of us connected with these early days of our airship project have endured. Older officers in the service have told me of the similar difficulties through which even such now firmly recognized and established types as destroyers, submarines and airplanes had to fight their way for recognition. Yet in spite of the antagonism, obstacles and difficulties that have often made some of us wonder whether or not to continue the struggle, airships have not only survived but will eventually triumph effectively. Perhaps the restricted patronage of airships has been a blessing in disguise. Airships owe their recognition and status in this country, to only a few persistent invincible believers and doers, headed by Admiral Moffett.

Lt. Comdr. Charles Rosendahl[1]

The year 1924 marked the beginning of what can be called the golden age of airships. It started when the British government authorized the construction of two giant passenger ships. At five million cubic feet each, they were to be twice the size of any airship yet built.

A year later in 1925 the Allies lifted the ban on German aircraft construction and the Zeppelin Company began planning the *Graf Zeppelin*. In 1926 the United States followed the British with the announcement of two new 6,500,000 cubic foot naval airships, and the contract was awarded the following year to a new corporation formed by two of the most experienced airship builders in the world, the Goodyear-Zeppelin Company of Akron, Ohio. The *Graf Zeppelin* was launched in 1928 and began her series of successful voyages culminating with the world cruise of 1929, the same year that Britain's *R.100* and *R.101* were completed and work began on the first of the new U.S. Navy rigids. In 1930 the *R.100* successfully crossed the Atlantic to Canada and back.

OPPOSITE: The first flight of the *R.101* on her first day out of the construction shed took the big ship to London where the public had been waiting for a look at her ever since work began five years earlier. She received an enthusiastic reception as she cruised over the heart of the city toward St. Paul's Cathedral at the left. *U.S. Information Agency photo in the National Archives.*

•

There were, of course, setbacks along the way—the loss of the *Shenandoah* in 1925 and Nobile's *Italia* in 1928—but these only served to prove the case for larger, more efficient ships. The *Italia* was a small semirigid while the *Shenandoah* was a copy of a captured World War I Zeppelin, obsolete the day her keel was laid. Many airshipmen argued that the tragedies of the *R.38, Dixmude,* and *Shenandoah* could all be traced to the practice of using outdated Zeppelin designs. The time had come, they said, to put the modern technology of the 1920s to work creating the safer and more efficient airships that were possible only with greater size.

As the announcement of one new airship program followed another, as success followed upon success, the public, governments, and airshipmen alike were swept up in an ever-growing wave of enthusiasm. Even the most skeptical had to admit that with three great nations, England, Germany, and the United States, all deeply committed to rigid airship programs, the golden age of the airship had at last arrived.

Britain's decision to abandon airship construction after the crash of the *R.38* in 1921 was unpopular with the Dominions and the Admiralty. The men who administered the far-flung empire saw the airships as the only practical means of rapid mail and passenger service. The travel time from Singapore to England could be cut from twenty-four days by steamer to eight days by airship, and the voyage from Canada or Egypt could be cut from six days to two and a half. The admirals looked to the airship as a solution to a shortage of both light cruisers and cash. It could perform most of the duties of a light cruiser at considerably less cost, and an airship built large enough to carry airplanes would be much less vulnerable to attack than the German navy's World War I Zeppelins had been.

In 1922 Comdr. Dennistoun Burney combined the Dominion and Admiralty requirements into a single proposal to restart the rigid-airship construction program. They would build six five-million-cubic-foot ships over a period of several years with the first, a passenger ship, going into service between England and Egypt. The plan was approved by the government in 1923, but before the contract could be awarded, the Conservative party lost the election and a new Labor government came into power.

The Laborites were equally enthusiastic about airships but they questioned the Conservatives' plan of awarding the contracts to private industry. They decided instead to authorize the construction of only two ships, one to be built at Cardington by the government, the other by the Airship Guarantee Corporation, a subsidiary of the Vickers Company, at Howden. The organization that did the best job would get the contract for the remaining four ships.

It was to prove to be a fateful decision, and having made it, the Labor government soon found itself voted out of office again.

Samuel Hoare, the Conservative government's air minister, had approved the original plan for six airships. Now he was back in office but with a completely different plan to administer, one that was too far along to change. The difficulties started almost immediately.

Sir Samuel Hoare

[T]he number of experts who knew anything about airships could be counted on two hands. Even at the end of the war it was very small, and since then, it had been diminished by the irreparable loss of Brigadier Maitland and his crew in the disaster that destroyed the R.38 in the Humber on August 24, 1921. There were really not enough skilled men in the following years to divide between two widely separated efforts of construction. There was the further disadvantage that the small and separated groups were apt to look with suspicion and sometimes jealousy at each other's work. As the construction progressed, what was no doubt intended as friendly competition tended to become a hindering rivalry. I tried my best to hold the balance between the two centers of construction, but it was not an easy task. . . .

For the next five years there was scarcely a day on which awkward problems connected with the double programme did not arise. Throughout these months of controversy I greatly missed the guidance of some expert and experienced mind. If Brigadier Maitland had lived, I should have had it.[2]

The tragic shadow of the R.38 continued to fall across Britain's airship program. All of the most experienced airshipmen that were left were hard at work on the Vickers Company's R.100 at Howden or the Air Ministry's R.101 at Cardington. There was no one left with enough experience to supervise and coordinate the two efforts, no one with the experience and detachment to judge the work being done, no one to realize that mistakes were being made.

As work began on the R.100, Vickers hired a bright young airplane engineer away from the de Havilland Company and made him their chief calculator. Despite his talent as an engineer, he was destined to achieve fame in a very different field where, under the name Nevil Shute, he was to write such best-sellers as Pastoral, Trustee from the Tool Room, and On the Beach.

He began work in the design section under Barnes Wallis, chief designer of Vickers's wartime rigids and the R.80. But as for himself and the other young engineers, Shute had to admit, "few of the rest of us had ever seen an airship, much less flown in one."[3]

All but one of Britain's wartime rigids had been built by either Vickers, Beardmore, Short Bros., or Armstrong, Whitworth. The one exception was designed and built by a staff of Air Ministry engineers after the government had nationalized the Short Bros. factory at Cardington. Their ship was the R.38, and the official inquiry into her crash uncovered the fact that her designers had never calculated any of the stress factors that their ship would encounter in flight.

Nevil Shute

On taking up my new job I spent many hours in reading old reports and records to find out what had been done in the field of airship calculations before, and when I came on the report of the R.38 accident enquiry I sat stunned, unable to believe the words that I was reading. I had come from the hard commercial school of de Havillands where competence was the key to survival and a disaster might have meant the end of the company and unemployment for every one concerned with it. It was inexpressibly shocking to me to find that before building the vast and costly structure of R.38 the civil servants concerned had made no attempt to calculate the aerodynamic forces acting on the ship, and I remember going to one of my chiefs with the report in my hand to ask him if this could possibly be true. Not only did he confirm it but he pointed out that no one had been sacked over it, nor even suffered any censure. Indeed, he said, the same team of men had been entrusted with the construction of another airship, the R.101, which was to be built by the Air Ministry in competition with our own ship, the R.100.[4]

The *R.100* was 709 feet long and 130 feet in diameter, with five million cubic feet of hydrogen in fourteen gas cells. She had a total lift of 156 tons and weighed 102 tons, leaving fifty-four tons for disposable lift. The two men standing on top of the nearest circular frame give an idea of the hull's immense size. It clears the top and sides of the construction shed by only a few feet. *Courtesy Vickers Ltd.*

•

As the two groups set to work they found that they had very little in the way of background information to use as a guide. Their previous ships had been copied from wartime Zeppelins and now even these models would have to be discarded.

Nevil Shute

From the start it was evident that it would be necessary to depart entirely from the Zeppelin design since this ship was to be more than twice the size of any airship that had flown before, and to attempt to build an airship from first principles alone, guided only by sound theory and calculation, and by the use of the most up to date aeroplane practice where that was applicable.[5]

The problems were enormous and the engineering and design phases alone took well over two years. Construction materials had to be selected, engines designed, and girders tested. It was a little like starting on a skyscraper without ever having built a house. For two and a half years the two competing design teams struggled at reinventing the airship, and though the two groups were working to the same set of specifications, and Cardington and Howden were only 150 miles apart, the men never met to exchange ideas.

Nevil Shute

In the five years that were to elapse before either airship flew neither designer visited the other's works, nor did they meet or correspond upon the common problems that each had to solve. Each trod a parallel road alone, harassed and overworked. . . . If the Cabinet Committee wanted competition they had got it with a vengeance, but I would not say that it was healthy.[6]

Though the ships they were building were to be essentially the same in size, load capacity, and speed, the working conditions of the two construction groups were quite different. The Vickers Company took the job at a fixed price. They agreed to produce an airship for $1,750,000. The more money they spent on experimentation, the less profit would be left over when the job was done. They therefore set about their work in a no-nonsense, almost Spartan manner.

Nevil Shute

Excluding hand tools, there were not more than a dozen machines employed in the construction of R.100. Economy was the paramount consideration in the shop equipment. A bitter little tale went around at Cardington, where they had everything they cared to ask for, to the effect that R.100 was getting on rather more quickly now that one of us had bought a car and lent the tool kit to the workshops.[7]

At Cardington, on the other hand, a considerable amount of basic research was being carried out. Special engines were being designed and a full-size hull section was constructed and hung in place above the floor of the hangar for test purposes. They even spent a good deal of time and money designing and building their own gas valves. The Vickers group simply bought a set of valves from the Zeppelin Company. Besides being time-consuming, Cardington's program of basic research had another disadvantage, for though research money was fairly easy to obtain, the government expected its expenditures to bring results. This made it much more difficult to discard an unsuccessful experiment and begin again from a different angle.

The Vickers group found it easier to change their minds when it looked as if something wasn't going to work out. With less money invested, they had less to lose by starting over. Their selection of airship engines serves as an example. They started by trying to build a new type that would run on kerosene mixed with the ship's hydrogen. When that proved impractical, they switched over to the special diesels that the government was developing at Cardington for R.101. When these appeared to be too heavy, they changed again to Rolls-Royce airplane engines, which turned out to be completely satisfactory. But the government engineers, with a considerable investment of taxpayers' money in their own special diesels, found it easier to justify a little more money to try to improve them, than a lot more money to junk them and start again.

To gain public support for the expensive program, the Air Ministry's press department began issuing glowing descriptions of the wonders of airship travel.

The *New York World*

Passengers will be able to take their meals in a sumptuously appointed dining room, as undisturbed and at ease as if they were travelling on a sixteenth-century French river barge.

Concerts and entertainments such as are given on the big ocean greyhounds will be staged in the dining saloon. And motion pictures will be thrown on a small screen while the ship is speeding through the air at eight-five or ninety miles per hour. Solid protections against the wind's velocity will render air travellers almost unaware of the great speed at which they are travelling and the sensation will be merely one of gently floating on the ether like the legendary Thief of Bagdad on the Magic Carpet in the Arabian Nights.[8]

Statements like these served primarily to make the British public even more impatient to see their airships completed. As the years dragged on and the

The tiny figure of the workman seated at the right gives an idea of the *R.100*'s size. He is lacing the outer cover to the framework. Strips of fabric will be glued to the girders to fill the gaps between the panels. Both design teams had used a minimum of longitudinal girders to save weight and simplify their stress calculations, but this meant that the unsupported fabric panels were much larger than those of other ships. On *R.100* the outer cover took on a wave pattern at high speeds. On *R.101* it gave way in long tears. *Courtesy* Radio Times Hulton, *London.*

The *R.101* was brought out of her construction shed on October 14, 1929, and moored to the high mast at Cardington. In its pastoral setting, this was the only large mooring mast in England. Four of the ship's five engine cars can be seen here, including the stern engine that was to be used exclusively for reversing. The control car is very small and can be seen amidships between the front and rear engine cars.

•

expenditures mounted, it was Samuel Hoare, the air minister, who was left to hold off the critics.

Sir Samuel Hoare

In the meanwhile, the House of Commons was clamouring for quick results. Burney's very active propaganda made many members expect to see the two airships in the air within a few months. Year after year, therefore, for the whole length of the Parliament, I had to meet a full scale attack whenever I introduced the Air Estimates. "When are you going to bring your two old horses out of the stable?" "What have you to show for the hundreds of thousands of pounds that you are spending every year on them?" My only answer was to play all the possible variations on Asquith's "Wait and see" and to report that the experiment was a very new one, and must be given time.[9]

R.101 was finished first. Early on the morning of October 14, 1929, she was brought out of her hangar after five long years of design and construction. Dawn was just breaking and thousands of spectators lined the road leading to the airfield.

The *Philadelphia Inquirer*

There was a hush for a moment, and then there was bedlam. The thousands lifted up their voices in mighty cheers. The giant apartment-house of the skies, lit up by row on row of electric lights, seemingly stretched back into infinity, was revealed in all its silvery magnificence.[10]

As the four-hundred-man ground crew walked the huge ship toward her mooring mast, the *Philadelphia Inquirer*'s correspondent reported, "a man on horseback dashed to and fro, keeping grazing sheep and cattle away from the dirigible." The *R.101*'s first flight was made later that same day with fifty-one people aboard. They flew from Cardington to London and received an enthusiastic ovation as they cruised over Buckingham Palace and the House of Commons. The round-trip covered two hundred miles and was pronounced a complete success by Maj. G. H. Scott, the *R.101*'s commander:

Maj. G. H. Scott
I am delighted with the ship. It has been perfectly satisfactory in every way. Everything has gone perfectly. The ship has been extremely easy to control. We have had excellent weather, but the ship gives every promise of being extremely airworthy also in high winds.

While over London I could clearly hear the whistles of boats on the river and of railway locomotives. The ship is remarkably quiet, and in the passenger quarters the sounds from the ground could easily be heard above the hum of the engines.[11]

As they cruised over London, uniformed stewards served luncheon in the spacious dining room. The menu started with soup, then went on to roast mutton in onion sauce, fresh vegetables, dessert, coffee, and beer. The ship's designer, Lt. Col. Vincent Richmond, was also reported to be very pleased with her performance.

Lt. Col. Vincent Richmond
The only noise was a curious sound, rather of a hissing character. So quiet was it that it was possible to speak to a friend across the wide lounge without the voice being raised more than a little. We had a magnificent view from the big windows beside the promenade at each end of the lounge.[12]

Shortly before *R.101* was completed, the Conservatives were voted out of office again and the Labor government took their place. Sir Samuel Hoare, who had supervised the construction of the two ships for five years, was replaced as air minister by Lord Christopher Thomson, the man largely responsible for the original plan to build one private and one government airship. Thomson was so proud of the *R.101* that when elevated to the peerage—the only way to keep him in the government after he lost two elections—he took as his title, Lord Thomson of Cardington, the home of the Royal Airship Works. He went along on the ship's second flight.

Lord Thomson of Cardington
I have never had such a pleasant experience. There is a feeling of complete detachment and security. I have never been as comfortable on any ocean vessel, and the motion is comparable to that of a river steamer, only the airship is not so noisy. I prefer this very much to heavier-than-air transport. I like to walk about and stretch my legs. I like to look at the view and see it; and in this ship there were always fifty acres of country to be seen

The *R.100* was powered by six 670-horsepower Rolls-Royce Condor engines. Two engines were mounted in each of three power cars and drove propellers at both ends of the car. She proved to be very fast with a top speed of eighty-one miles per hour, well above the seventy miles per hour called for in the government specifications. At this speed, however, her outer cover took on a curious wave pattern. Since it didn't seem to cause any serious difficulties, the problem was solved by simply not flying the ship faster than seventy miles per hour. *Courtesy Wide World Photos.*

•

The passenger accommodations aboard *R.100* were on two decks above the crew's quarters on a third lower deck. The dining salon, shown here, seated fifty-six and had windows on each side. The divided stairway at the left led up to the lounge, which also featured large view windows. The staterooms for one hundred passengers were located on both decks. All the uncomfortable-looking models in this publicity photo are Vickers employees and include Nevil Shute standing on the stairway at the left. *Courtesy Vickers Ltd.*

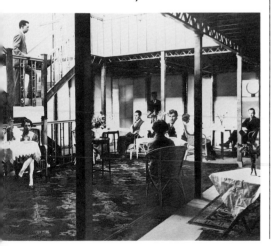

or a fine direct view downward of a city. Near Northampton, for instance, we saw a pack of foxhounds running over country, and also saw the fox, from a height of 1,500 feet.[13]

According to all the newspaper accounts, the *R.101* was proving to be an excellent ship, but even before her launching, Shute and the men at Vickers began to hear disquieting rumors about her.

Nevil Shute

Early in the design our calculations had disclosed a curious aerodynamic feature in the stability of these huge ships; not only could they both easily be steered by hand without the assistance of a servo motor, but no balance area was required upon the rudders although they were over a thousand square feet in area. At a comparatively late stage in the design we learned on sure authority that R.101 not only had balanced rudders but had servo motors fitted at great weight and cost to assist the helmsman in the steering of the ship. Out flared our inferiority complex; we suspended work on the rudders and spent three days in checking through our calculations to find our mistake. At the end of that time we knew that our figures were correct, and we were left dumbly staring at each other. Either these ships could be steered by hand or they could not; it was impossible that we could both be right. There must be something in this that we did not understand.

The engine installation was another one. An airship requires engine power to go astern to check her way as she approaches the mooring mast and in R.100 we had arranged for two of our six engines to drive their propellers through a reversing gearbox for this purpose. As R.101 approached completion we were astonished to hear that her reversing propellers had proved a failure, and in consequence four of her five engines were arranged to drive ahead and the fifth one would go astern. The fifth engine apparently was to be carried as a passenger on all her flights solely for the purpose of going astern for a minute or two at the start and finish of each flight, and with its power car it weighed over three tons. Again we were left staring at each other, speechless. It is the greatest mistake to underrate your competitor, and in spite of their past record it was incredible to us that our competitors should perpetrate such childish follies. There *must* be something in this that we did not understand.[14]

R.100 was completed by Vickers a month after *R.101* but another month was to pass before the wind died down enough at Howden to allow her to be walked out of her hangar. At dawn on the morning of December 16, 1929, a dead calm was predicted and five hundred soldiers arrived to bring her out of the shed. The *R.100* cleared the hangar doors with two feet on either side.

With both ships now finished and in the air, it was possible to compare them. The rumors about *R.101* were true. She had servo motors on her rudders and carried one engine just for backing up. And in spite of the optimistic newspaper accounts, she had another far more serious problem. The *R.101* was much too heavy. Her hydrogen could lift 148 tons, but *R.101* weighed 113 tons. That left only thirty-five tons of disposable lift for crew, passengers, supplies, cargo, and, most important of all, fuel. She would need to carry more than twenty-five tons of diesel oil for her voyage to Egypt. Without more lift, *R.101* could not carry enough fuel to go anywhere.

Both ships were supposed to lift sixty tons. *R.100* came closest with a disposable lift of fifty-four tons. Her five million cubic feet of hydrogen, slightly more than the *R.101,* could lift 156 tons while the ship weighed only 102 tons.

R.101 was eleven tons heavier than *R.100* and most of this extra weight was in her engines. Diesels were used because the fuel is much less flammable than gasoline, but the diesels chosen were giant Beardmores, originally designed to power Canadian railway locomotives. The five of them together weighed seventeen tons, nearly twice as much as the *R.100*'s nine tons of Rolls-Royce airplane engines.

There was only one solution. After all unnecessary equipment, including the servo motors, was taken off, the *R.101* would have to be cut in half and an additional gasbag inserted in the middle. The added hydrogen would raise her available lift to 49.3 tons, still five tons less than *R.100,* but since *R.101*'s diesel engines consumed less fuel per hour, the weight difference between the two ships on a long flight would be nearly equalized.

The *R.100* was flown down to Cardington for her trials. With the two ships docked side by side in the big hangar, the men from Vickers finally had a chance to get a good look at the competition.

Nevil Shute

We put the ship into the shed that evening, "put her back in the box" as someone irreverently described the operation. Here she stayed over Christmas while we sorted out her teething troubles, berthed in her shed beside R.101. Some of us had seen R.101 before she flew; we now had a good opportunity to examine her in her completed state. We found her an amazing piece of work. The finish and the workmanship struck us as extraordinarily good, far better than that of our own ship. The design seemed to us almost unbelievably complicated; she seemed to be a ship in which imagination had run riot regardless of the virtue of simplicity and utterly regardless of expense.[15]

R.100 completed her final forty-eight-hour acceptance flight at the end of January 1930. Then while *R.101* was being sliced in half, *R.100* flew to Canada. Early on the morning of July 29, she slipped from the mooring mast and set out on her eighth voyage—thirty-three hundred miles across the North Atlantic to Montreal. All went smoothly until they arrived off the mouth of the St. Lawrence River, a few miles from Quebec. There they encountered severe turbulence that tore the fabric on three of the four fins. Shute and other crewmen had to climb out into the fins to repair the damage. Between Quebec and Montreal they met a line squall that tossed the ship three thousand feet up into the air but made only two more small rips in the fin covering.

They reached Montreal's St. Hubert airport at dawn and moored to the high

In the control car of *R.100,* the rudder man stood at the front while the elevator man was on the right rather than the left as in German airships. Each man had a large altimeter at his station as well as a microphone for communication with the navigation room. *U.S. Information Agency photo in the National Archives.*

As the *R.100* approached the high mast at Montreal's St. Hubert Airport in the first light of dawn, she became the fourth airship to fly the Atlantic. She followed the *R.34, Los Angeles,* and *Graf Zeppelin,* but the *R.100* made the fastest crossing of all, completing the 3,364 miles from Cardington to Montreal in three days, four hours, and fifty-one minutes. *Courtesy Vickers Ltd.*

•

mast. The flight had taken seventy-eight hours and they still had five tons of fuel left. A hundred thousand people turned out to view the ship as she rode at the mast. The outer cover was repaired and *R.100* made a short side trip to Ottawa, Toronto, and Niagara Falls before returning to Montreal. As they were landing, the reduction gear on one engine gave way and could not be repaired in Canada. They decided to return to England on only five engines. The *R.34* and *Graf Zeppelin* had already proved that the prevailing winds made the eastward crossing of the North Atlantic much easier and faster than the westward crossing, so they anticipated no trouble. After twelve days in Montreal they set out on August 13 for the return to England, landing safely at Cardington on the sixteenth after an uneventful 57½-hour flight.

At five million cubic feet, the two British airships were by far the largest ever built, but just as they were being completed, the United States began work on two even larger ships. Three weeks after the *R.101* was launched and two weeks before the completion of *R.100,* Adm. William Moffett officially started construction of the U.S. Navy's 6,500,000-cubic-foot *ZRS-4,* the *Akron.*

One of the major factors in Britain's decision to restart her rigid-airship program was the Admiralty's concern over their shortage of fast scouting cruisers. If Britain's admirals were concerned, America's should have been panic-stricken, for at the end of World War I the U.S. Navy didn't possess a single modern cruiser. They had enough capital ships, but without squadrons of fast cruisers to search for

the enemy's fleet in the vast reaches of the Atlantic and Pacific, their battleships were seriously handicapped.

America's naval planners arrived at the same conclusion as their British counterparts: airships could fill the need for scouting cruisers. After studying the performance of Germany's wartime Zeppelins, a board made up of the navy's senior flag officers found them "so remarkable that it is most necessary for the Navy of the United States to develop dirigibles of this type as soon as possible."[16] The recommendation was signed by Adm. George Dewey, the hero of Manila Bay and the only man to achieve the rank of admiral of the navy.

The navy's rigid airship program got off to a bad start with the loss of their first two ships, the *Shenandoah* and the British-built *R.38.* Only the *ZR-3,* the German-built *Los Angeles,* remained, and she was too small for the kind of long-range over-sea operations that the navy had in mind. As the years passed, however, the navy found itself with too many priorities and too little money from a budget-minded Congress. One of the airship's strongest advocates eventually became Rear Adm. William A. Moffett, the chief of the navy's Bureau of Aeronautics. As he testified during the Navy Board hearings of 1926:

When I first came in contact with rigid airships I couldn't see anything to them. I couldn't see that they were any good as a means of scouting or transportation; you couldn't get it going when you wanted it; you couldn't get it out of the hangar. Lansdowne came to me. I listened to him very carefully. At first, I refused to have anything to do with it. I listened to Lansdowne's arguments and he persuaded me. . . . It is a noteworthy thing that every officer who has anything to do with these ships . . . is in favor of them and thinks they will be of great value to the Navy.[17]

Admiral Moffett wasn't willing to spend any of the money that his Bureau of Aeronautics had earmarked for airplanes but he thought the other admirals ought to give up some of their cruiser appropriations to buy airships. The other admirals didn't think much of that idea but they were perfectly willing to accept any new money that Congress might be persuaded to appropriate specifically for rigid-airship construction. Congress, unfortunately, wasn't interested.

Now the admirals found themselves faced with a new problem. They were in a struggle with the army for control of military aviation. Congress had given exclusive control of the United States' rigid-airship development to the navy. But the army was beginning to complain that under the navy's control, nothing was being developed. Even those admirals who cared least for rigid airships were unwilling to allow the army to take the program over by default. To hand the army a vehicle capable of flying thousands of miles out to sea would be a serious blow to navy prestige. More importantly, it could lead to a curtailment of naval aviation and the establishment of a separate air force just as the navy was starting to develop the aircraft carrier. All the admirals agreed, rather than see army dirigibles patrolling their sea lanes, the navy would have to build rigid airships.

The Lighter-Than-Air Design Section of Admiral Moffett's Bureau of Aeronautics under Comdr. Garland Fulton had begun preliminary planning for two large modern airships in 1924. The two five-million-cubic-foot ships then being started by the British seemed to be about the best size although, since the U.S. ships would be filled with helium rather than the lighter hydrogen, they would have to be of six-million-cubic-foot gas capacity to achieve the same amount of lift. The new ships should also be able to fit inside the eight-hundred-foot-long hangar at Lakehurst.

The wreck of the *Shenandoah* in 1925 added another specification to the design. The *Shenandoah* had been built with wire-braced frames in the Zeppelin manner and she had broken apart. What was obviously needed for these larger ships, the navy thought, was the stronger and heavier rigid frame, the type being developed by the British government in their *R.101*. To offset the added weight of these stronger frames, the specification for the new ship's gas capacity was increased to 6,500,000 cubic feet.

Though the plans for the projected *ZRS-4* and *ZRS-5* were begun in 1924, the money for them was not forthcoming until 1928 when Congress finally appropriated two hundred thousand dollars—hardly enough to fill a ship with helium, let alone build it. It was enough, however, to allow Admiral Moffett to start looking for a contractor.

He did not have to look far. The only serious candidate for the job was the Goodyear-Zeppelin Corporation of Akron, Ohio. This organization, two-thirds of which was owned by the Goodyear Tire and Rubber Company and one-third by the Zeppelin Company, was formed in 1924 when Dr. Karl Arnstein and twelve Zeppelin company engineers arrived in America after completing work on the *Los Angeles*. With the Allied ban on German aircraft construction still in effect at that

The idea of a military airship launching her own defense planes had intrigued designers ever since World War I, and a considerable amount of experimentation had been conducted. The British launched planes from their *No. 23* and from the *R. 33*. The U.S. Army experimented with blimps like the *TC-7* shown here, while the navy launched planes from the *Los Angeles*. By 1924 the navy had decided to put airplanes aboard their next rigid airships. *Courtesy San Diego Aero-Space Museum.*

•

time, there seemed no other way that the Zeppelin Company could remain in the airship business. When the Allied restrictions were lifted the following year, the Zeppelin Company found itself in business on both sides of the Atlantic.

On October 6, 1928, the navy signed a contract with the Goodyear-Zeppelin Corporation for the construction of two 6,500,000-cubic-foot airships, the first for $5,375,000 and the second for $2,450,000. There was one unique idea incorporated into the plans for *ZRS-4* and *ZRS-5* that set them apart from all other airships ever built. It was a feature that the navy had written into the specifications way back in 1924. Each of these ships was to carry four airplanes. They were to be flying aircraft carriers, capable of launching and retrieving planes in flight. The British had already experimented briefly with airplanes released from the *R. 33*, and the U.S. Army had tested a trapezelike hook-on device with one of their blimps. Further tests using a trapeze suspended beneath the *Los Angeles* proved that it was actually easier to hook a plane onto a flying airship than it was to land it on the ground.

The Goodyear-Zeppelin Corporation's first job was to build a hangar in which to build the airships. Even the hangar had to be aerodynamically designed and wind tunnel tested to prevent dangerous air currents from building up around its huge corners. Construction of the hangar took nearly a year and was almost completed on November 7, 1929, when Admiral Moffett officially started work on *ZRS-4* by driving a golden rivet into her main frame. The *R.100* was completed a month after the *ZRS-4* was begun and seven months later she flew to Canada and back.

With the return of the *R.100* from her transatlantic flight in August 1930, the airship had arrived at the pinnacle of her long years of development. *R.100* was a success and her sister ship was preparing to fly to India. The *Graf Zeppelin* had sailed all the way around the world, the *Los Angeles* was continuing her years of trouble-free operation, the navy's huge new dirigible was under construction in Ohio with a second ship ready to be started, and, finally, the Zeppelin Company was completing the plans for two new transatlantic airships, the most luxurious yet conceived.

In the United States two corporations were formed to plan American airship routes across the Atlantic and the Pacific. Their boards of directors read like a *Who's Who* of American business. The International Zeppelin Transport Corporation was headed by Col. E. A. Deeds of the National City Company, P. W. Litchfield, president of the Goodyear Tire and Rubber Company, and J. C. Hunsaker, vice-president of the Goodyear-Zeppelin Corporation. Its board of directors included Dr. Hugo Eckener, Roy A. Hunt, president of the Aluminum Company of America, J. A. Rafferty, president of the Carbide & Carbon Chemical Corporation, Frederick Rentschler, president of United Aircraft & Transportation, and Charles F. Kettering of General Motors.

They had already pinpointed routes and flying times, and selected a terminal site between Philadelphia and Richmond for the American end of the transatlantic service. The European terminal would be in the Rhine Valley midway between Berlin and Paris. The eastward flight was scheduled for fifty-eight hours in summer when the ships could fly the shorter northern route and sixty-four hours in winter when they flew a more southerly course. The westward voyage was scheduled for between seventy and eighty hours, with an 80 percent on-time projection. The Zeppelin Company would operate the European terminal while the American organization ran the U.S. terminal. An equal number of German and American airships would fly the route.

In the Pacific a second corporation, the Pacific Zeppelin Company, was planning routes from the West Coast to Honolulu, Manila, and Yokohama. The directors of the company included Edward P. Farley of the American-Hawaiian Steamship Line, R. Stanley Dollar of the Dollar Lines, W. P. Roth of the Matson Navigation Company, Juan Trippe, president of Pan-American Airways, J. A. Talbot, chairman of Western Air Express, Clarence H. Cooke of the Bank of Hawaii, Kenneth Kingsbury, president of Standard Oil of California, Walter Dillingham of Hawaii, and Herbert Fleischhacker of San Francisco.

The airship voyage to Hawaii was scheduled for thirty-six hours while the return to the mainland would take forty-eight hours. The flight from California to Manila via Hawaii would be made in six days and the return by way of Japan would take two days longer.

Why were the presidents of Pan-American, Western, and United serving as directors of an airship corporation? The fact is that in 1930 commercial service by airplane across the oceans seemed a long way off. The first plane flight from California to Hawaii had taken place only three years earlier in 1927, and as yet, no plane had been able to fly back to the mainland against the wind. The *Graf Zeppelin,* on the other hand, had already carried paying passengers all the way from Japan to California. The westward crossing of the Atlantic by plane had first been achieved in 1928, though the *R.34* did it nine years earlier and the *Los Angeles, Graf Zeppelin,* and now the *R.100* easily made the same flight.

In the 147 years since the Montgolfiers' first balloon, the airship had never been so close to success as it was in August 1930. No one could know, but the dream of rigid airships had gone as far as it was to go. For now it was time for the *R.101* to fly to India.

An imperial conference was scheduled for October 1930. The premiers of all the dominions of the British Empire would be gathered together in London. What better opportunity to demonstrate the new government-built airship? The premiers of

Australia and New Zealand would travel by steamer for six weeks to reach England. Lord Thomson planned to fly to India in *R.101* and return in a matter of days just as the conference began its discussion of aviation matters. It would be a major triumph for the airship—and for Lord Thomson. Some said it might even lead to his appointment as the next viceroy of India.

But *R.101* was in trouble. Even before the Canadian flight of *R.100*, intermediaries for the government engineers at Cardington approached the Vickers group with the suggestion that perhaps they should postpone the long flights of both ships for a year on the grounds that they were still in the experimental stage.

Nevil Shute

Perhaps if we had realized at the time how very, very bad their ship was, how real the danger of complete disaster if they started for India, we might have taken a different attitude to this approach. Their own secrecies concealed the real facts from us; we guessed that their ship was a bad airship, but we did not know the whole story. We brushed aside this approach, perhaps roughly. We said that our ship was perfectly capable of flying to Canada; the Canadian flight was a part of our contract and it was necessary for us to do it. Again, the bitter competition between the staffs loomed large. A heavy loss had been made upon the construction of R.100. If this was to be recouped from future airship contracts, ours must be the organization to carry on the work and they must give up. We would complete our contract and prove the efficiency of R.100 by flying to Canada; they could please themselves whether they flew to India or not.[18]

Exactly how bad was *R.101*? A few years earlier in the construction program, an Air Ministry press release stated:

If British designers had been content to follow closely the Zeppelin system of construction as practiced in 1924, the new airship would have been finished long since; instead they proceeded to tackle the problems involved on new lines.[19]

But each new innovation, each proudly announced departure from basic Zeppelin design, resulted in a major weakness in the ship. *R.101* was the only airship ever built of steel. The others were all of duralumin which, though not as strong, is much lighter. *R.101* was also the first ship with rigid frames. The Germans used a single ring supported by internal wiring. In *R.101* three rings were bound together to form a single rigid frame. This too was stronger than usual and three times heavier. Both the gas valves and the system of wires that held the gasbags in place were specially developed and patented by Col. Vincent Richmond, the ship's chief designer, but his valves, mounted on the sides of the gasbags rather than on the bottom, were too sensitive and opened whenever the ship rolled. His wiring system worked well until he loosened it in order to increase the volume of the gasbags. Then the bags began to chafe against the ship's girders despite the hurried addition of four thousand special protective pads.

To compensate partially for the heavier frames, fewer longitudinal girders were used in both *R.100* and *R.101*. This allowed stress calculations to be made more easily but it also left large sections of the outer cover unsupported.

Nevil Shute

In both ships the outer cover was the main weakness. Extended flight trials were to prove that our outer cover on R.100 was just good enough for the service demanded of it, but only just.[20]

On October 1, 1930, the *R.101* was brought out of her hangar, forty-five feet and one gas cell longer than when she went in. Originally she had a total lift of 148 tons and weighed 113 tons. That left her with only thirty-five tons of disposable lift, not enough to carry fuel to India, let alone passengers. The extra gas cell increased her capacity by 600,000 cubic feet to 5,500,000. That, plus the removal of every pound of excess weight, increased her disposable lift to 49.3 tons. She was essentially a brand-new airship. *Courtesy Flight International, London.*

•

In the seven weeks following her launching, *R.101* made seven flights for a total of seventy hours in the air, all in good weather. The enthusiastic public statements issued by Colonel Richmond and Major Scott gave no hint of the serious problems they had uncovered, but on November 30, 1929, they took their ship into the hangar, where she remained until the following June while more than five tons of costly equipment, including her servo motors, were ripped out to give her more lift. Even the glass in her windows was replaced with lighter Plexiglas.

They had already decided to cut the ship in half and add an extra gasbag, but the *R.101* was scheduled to appear at the Royal Air Force display at Hendon on June 28, and rather than risk any complications, they decided to postpone the operation until after the air show. As the ship was riding at her mast after being brought out of the hangar, her outer cover gave way in two long tears, which were quickly sewed together for her appearance at the show.

At the end of July 1930, while *R.100* was flying to Canada, *R.101* returned to the hangar where she was cut in half and forty-five feet of hull and an extra gasbag were added to her middle. Her engines were also reworked so that all five drove forward and two could be stopped, adjusted, and then started up in reverse.

An examination of the outer cover showed that it was rotting away where the adhesive on the reinforcing tapes had reacted with the dope on the fabric. This was caused by another of the government engineers' innovations—they had doped the outer cover before it was stretched over the framework instead of afterward as was usually done. Now crews of men had to work around the clock stripping off and replacing the acres of rotting fabric. The work continued all through August and into September. On their return from Canada, the *R.100*'s commander, Squadron Leader Booth, showed a piece of the old cover to Shute.

Nevil Shute

It was ordinary outer cover, linen fabric, silver doped on a red oxide base. On the inner surface two-inch tapes had been stuck on with some adhesive, evidently for strengthening. I didn't know what I was expected to say, and turned it about in my hands, and suddenly my hand went through it. In parts it was friable, like scorched brown paper, so that if you crumpled it in your hand it broke up into flakes. I stared at it in horror, thinking of R.100. "Good God," I said. "Where did this come from?"

"All right," said Booth, "That's not off our ship. That's off R.101."

"I hope they've got all this stuff off the ship."

He smiled cynically. "They *say* they have." [21]

The two months of feverish alteration were completed on September 25, but a crosswind prevented the undocking. Finally at six o'clock on the morning of October 1, 1930, the *R.101* was walked out of her hangar. Now 777 feet long with reworked engines and a new outer cover, she was in essence a brand-new airship.

Through all the long months of increasing difficulty, Lord Thomson never wavered from his intention to fly in *R.101* to India and return in time for the imperial conference. He did agree, however, to move the date of his return back from October 16 to October 20. He would allow Richmond and Scott to take as long as necessary to get their ship in order—as long as they flew him to India and back within the next nineteen days.

The crew immediately set out on a sixteen-hour test flight, returning to Cardington on Thursday morning, October 2. An oil leak in one of the reworked engines caused it to be stopped and, in case the other reversing engine was similarly affected, it was run at half-speed. A full-power test was therefore impossible and there was no time for any more test flights. All the next day, October 3, was spent in provisioning the ship and making last-minute preparations for receiving the important passengers. At 6:30 on the evening of Saturday October 4, 1930, in the face of a gathering storm, the *R.101* slipped from her mooring mast for the last time, bound for India.

Yet even in the last frantic hours before departure when the ship's dangerously overloaded condition must have been apparent to all—even then—there was time for one last insane gesture. They pumped nine tons of unnecessary fuel aboard—nine tons more than *R.101* would need to reach safely her first stop at Ismailia, Egypt! There Thomson planned to give a formal dinner aboard the airship for the high commissioner of Egypt and various British and Egyptian officials. The ship was scheduled to remain at Ismailia's high mast for only twelve hours, not long enough for both a state dinner and a complete refueling. By carrying nine extra tons of fuel from England they would save half their refueling time in Egypt and the dinner guests would not be bothered by the smell of diesel oil.

Compared to the fueling decision, the matter of the carpet was of minor importance. In order to impress the dinner guests it was decided to cover the entrance corridor and lounge with pale blue carpet. The corridor was six hundred

The wreck of *R.101*. Of the fifty-four men aboard *R.101*, six survived. The official inquiry concluded that the ship's outer cover may have given way at the bow, allowing the wind to tear open the forward gas cells. This loss of gas caused the dive reported by the survivors. The ship was heavy and the rain added extra tons of water to her outer cover. She could not rise more than a few hundred feet above the ground and the loss of lift at the bow dropped her nose onto this gently rising hillside near Beauvais in the north of France. Then she burst into flame. *Courtesy Wide World Photos.*

•

feet long and the lounge was the size of a tennis court. The carpet added another two or three tons to the heavily laden ship.

Two last-minute decisions and twelve tons were added to *R.101*—the margin between life and death for fifty-four people and no one seemed to notice. No one seems to have complained, not the director of airship development, not the assistant director, the flight director, or the chief inspector, not the ship's captain or any of his officers. Lord Thomson's dinner party added twelve tons and the men who should have known better did nothing, and all of them were flying on *R.101* to India. Perhaps they were simply past caring.

As the huge ship rose sluggishly from the mast, her commander, Flight-Lt. Carmichael Irwin, ordered an up angle on the elevators and all engines to half-speed. Irwin, one of the most experienced airship commanders in Great Britain, had reported to his superiors that he did not feel the *R.101* was capable of making the flight to India. He was overruled.

Up on the luxurious promenade deck, Sir Sefton Brancker, the director of civil aviation, watched with mixed emotions as the lights of the field disappeared into the gathering darkness. Only two days earlier he had faced Thomson with his doubts about *R.101*'s airworthiness. "If you're afraid to go—don't!" Thomson had replied. "There are many others who will jump at the chance!"[22] Brancker accepted Thomson's challenge. Now in the darkness he wondered again if he had made the right decision.

Of all the men aboard that night, only Lord Thomson seemed completely at ease. He had risen to his present station by taking chances. Here was one more that gave promise of carrying him even farther. The prize was the viceroyalty of India, and Lord Thomson of Cardington trusted to his luck to see him through. Rather than wait for the Air Ministry's inspectors, he had issued *R.101*'s certificate of airworthiness himself, just two days earlier.

With a single sixteen-hour test flight in her new configuration, with chafing gasbags, unreliable valves, inadequate engine power, and a suspect outer cover, with neither a high-speed test nor a single hour in rough weather, the overloaded *R.101* was flying into a rising gale sweeping in over France. She would need more than Lord Thomson's luck to see her through.

The huge ship reached London at 8:00 P.M. The people looking up into the driving rain from the streets below saw the red and green running lights and a row of lighted windows turning slowly south toward Paris. *R.101* left the coast at Hastings on course for the mouth of the Somme, sixty miles across the Channel. The crossing took two hours. At midnight the ship's radio operator transmitted:

To Cardington from R.101, 24.00 GMT. 15 miles S.W. of Abbeville. Average speed 33 knots. Wind 243 degrees, 35 miles per hour. Altimeter height 1,500 feet. Air temperature, 51 degrees Fahrenheit. Weather—intermittent rain. Cloud nimbus at 500 feet. After an excellent supper our distinguished passengers smoked a final cigar, and, having sighted the French coast, have now gone to bed to rest after the excitement of their leave-taking. All essential services are functioning satisfactorily. The crew have settled down to watch-keeping routine.[23]

R.101 had never flown in such bad weather before. As she rolled and pitched in the storm, her gasbags surged against the girders and their sensitive valves snapped open to exhale the precious hydrogen. Then, perhaps, the outer cover began to give way.

Few people were out in the wind and rain that night but fifty-seven-year-old Alfred Rabouille had rabbit snares to set. It was 2:00 A.M. Sunday morning when he heard the sound of engines above the howl of the wind.

Alfred Rabouille

I clearly saw the passengers' quarters, well lit and the green and red lights on the right and left of the airship. Suddenly there was a violent squall. The airship dipped by the nose several times and the fore part crashed into the north-west edge of the Bois des Contumes. There was at once a tremendous explosion, which knocked me down. Soon flames rose into the sky to a great height—perhaps 300 feet. Everything was enveloped by them. I saw human figures running about like madmen in the wreck. Then I lost my head and ran away into the woods. [24]

It was four minutes past two when Joe Binks climbed down the narrow ladder of the after power car to relieve engineer Arthur Bell at his station beside the thundering Beardmore diesel.

Joe Binks

As he was speaking, we both noticed that the ship went over at a surprising angle, but quickly righted herself again.

We were making 65 knots at this moment, when an order came through to slow down the engines. Immediately afterward the nose dipt, and we got a second order to shut off the engines.

We had hardly done so when we struck something. We could hardly believe it was the ground, as we had no idea we were so near earth. But there was not time to think of that, as the forward engines exploded as we crashed to earth, and waves of flame came rushing aft.

At the same time water began pouring into the cabin. We thought at first the airship was in water; but a second later, we saw it was coming from the tank overhead, which had broken and was flooding down on us.

We crouched in the cabin, away from the heat and flames. Then, seeing the water cutting a way for us right through the body of the ship, we dropt down and found that our part of the ship was some feet above the ground. So all we had to do was roll over and over in the wet grass, with wet handkerchiefs over our faces, to get away from the flames.

Bell and I thought, at first, of helping to save others, but we saw in a flash that there was no chance for those forward, as the ship, by this time, was a mass of solid flame in which they were imprisoned. [25]

Bell, Binks, and four others survived. All the rest died.

Their bodies were returned to England aboard a destroyer. The funeral procession from Westminster Hall was two miles long. Half a million people turned out to view it. It was the kind of demonstration usually reserved for the death of kings.

Back at Cardington the *R.100*, a perfectly sound, two-million-dollar airship, was broken up and sold for scrap. She brought $2,500.

R.100 being dismantled. After the *R.100*'s successful return from Canada, she never flew again. She was put into the hangar at Cardington and remained there for a year after the crash of *R.101*. Then she was dismantled. A steamroller flattened her girders so they could be taken away by truck and melted down. The ship that took five years and two million dollars to build was sold for scrap for twenty-five hundred dollars. *Courtesy Cole Airship Collection, University of Oregon.*

9
THE END
· OF THE ·
DREAM
· OF RIGID ·
AIRSHIPS

In 1908, when I told a school friend, a chemist, that I had decided to join the Zeppelin enterprise, he stared at me in horror and cried, "That's terrible! Hydrogen and petrol, the two most treacherous substances in existence! I would never want to have anything to do with either of them! How can you meddle with these explosive substances?"[1]

Hugo Eckener

It is difficult for us today to understand Britain's reaction to the crash of *R.101*. In this modern age we have become accustomed to air disasters with high loss of life. Forty years ago such losses were not yet commonplace, but even so, there must have been something more than the horror of needless death to cause a country to abandon a major aircraft program completely and junk a perfectly good airship. More men had died in ship sinkings and mine explosions than aboard *R.101*, yet ships still sailed and miners still dug in the earth. What was different about the airship?

There were critics who contended that the future of aviation lay with the airplane. Though it had yet to carry a single paying passenger across any ocean, it would soon, they said, replace the airship. The fact that dozens of airplanes fell out of the sky for every dirigible that crashed did not seem to bother them.

OPPOSITE: The christening of the *Akron*. On August 8, 1931, twenty-one months after Admiral Moffett officially began construction by driving a golden rivet, the *Akron* was christened by Mrs. Herbert Hoover as a crowd estimated at half a million jammed the city of Akron, Ohio, to witness the great event. Lieutenant Commander Rosendahl and the ship's crew stand at attention just in front of the control car. Six weeks later the *Akron* was ready to fly. *Courtesy Goodyear Tire and Rubber Co.*

Inside the *Akron*'s hull. Most rigid airships had a single triangular keel running the length of the hull. It strengthened the framework and served as a passageway for the crew. When they started building larger ships, the Zeppelin Company added a second axial keel straight through the middle of the ship for extra strength. In the *ZRS-4* and *ZRS-5*, the navy went a step further with three keels. One can be seen here at the top of the hull while the other two run along each side of the airplane hangar at the bottom. This left the bottom of the hull free for the hangar door opening. Notice the depth of the rigid frame just in front of the partially opened gas cell. *Courtesy San Diego Aero-Space Museum.*

•

Perhaps it was a difference in expectation. Perhaps no one really expected the fragile-looking airplanes to be safe, while the airship's immense silver body, on the other hand, appeared to be the very essence of power and stability. She seemed to inspire confidence in all who saw her. The spacious lounges, the paneled dining rooms, and promenades looked so solid and secure. When an airplane went down, it merely confirmed one's worst suspicions, but the failure of an airship was a failure of trust—a confidence betrayed.

The *R.101* disaster was the first serious setback in the development of the new generation of large rigid airships that began back in 1924. The momentum that had been built up over the previous six years would carry the airship programs of the United States and Germany on in spite of this loss, and if the new ships were successful, then the end of Britain's participation would have little effect. It was just that the crash of one ship placed a greater burden on those which were to follow. Because one had crashed, the rest would have to be better. Their chance of failure was diminished by the failure of *R.101.*

Ten months after the *R.101* burned on a hillside in France, the U.S. Navy's *ZRS-4* was christened by Mrs. Herbert Hoover. The new ship was named the *Akron* in honor of the city where she was built. On September 23, 1931, under the command of Lt. Comdr. Charles Rosendahl and with 113 men aboard, she made her first flight. Then, for her forty-eight-hour endurance trial, she covered two thousand miles from Akron to St. Louis, Chicago, Milwaukee, and then back to Akron. She was officially commissioned as a naval vessel at Lakehurst on Navy Day, October 27, 1931.

In addition to her great size and new role as a flying aircraft carrier, the *Akron* featured several other innovations. With the use of nonflammable helium, it was now possible to put her eight 560-horsepower Maybach engines inside the hull. This gave the ship a more streamlined shape and eliminated the drag of external power cars. It also gave the mechanics more room to work. The propellers were mounted on twenty-foot booms that could be rotated ninety degrees downward to drive the ship straight up or, when the engines were reversed, straight down.

The gas valves were placed on top of the gasbags, but in case of trouble they could be easily reached from a gangway that ran all the way along the top of the ship just beneath the outer cover. For the first time a satisfactory substitute had been found for goldbeater's skin. The U.S. Bureau of Standards had developed a gelatin-latex mixture that, when applied to cotton cloth, produced a material both lighter and more impervious to gas than the traditional cow's intestine.

Like the *Shenandoah*, the *Akron* featured an extensive water recovery system that could collect more than a pound of water from the engine exhaust for every pound of fuel burned. By creating water ballast as the ship flew along, it was not necessary to valve expensive helium to compensate for the weight of fuel used on long flights. Once again, as in the *Shenandoah,* the expense of helium was to be a major factor in the day-to-day operation of the *Akron.*

Another departure from previous airship technology was in the *Akron*'s specially strengthened frames. The Goodyear-Zeppelin Corporation had offered a design featuring conventional wire-braced frames, but the navy preferred a second design using rigid frames similar to those being developed for the British *R.101*. With the collapse of the *Shenandoah*'s framework still fresh in their memory, the navy's engineers decided that the new larger ships required the new stronger frames.

One final innovation was in the *Akron*'s tail structure. In all previous Zeppelins the girders inside one fin continued all the way through the hull and into the fin on the other side. The girders supporting the rudder fins met those supporting the elevator fins in a cruciform or cross shape inside the hull. This was eliminated in the *ZRS-4* and *ZRS-5*. Their fins were simply bolted onto the frames, which, being stronger, were able to withstand the tremendous air pressures that played across the huge fins' surfaces.

As the *Akron* completed her trials, she was found to be eleven tons heavier and four miles an hour slower than planned. But even with this overweight, she still had a disposable lift of seventy tons, twenty tons more than *R.101*. The *Akron*'s speed was raised to her specified eighty-three miles per hour when new adjustable-pitch, three-bladed propellers were added in 1933.

She was the largest airship yet built and the first to launch and retrieve airplanes. She was only the second rigid ship built in the United States and the third to be flown by U.S. naval airshipmen. Under these circumstances one might expect that the *Akron* would be regarded primarily as an unproven, experimental aircraft. This was not the case. Five million dollars of taxpayers' money had been spent in the middle of a depression and results were expected—by the public, by the Congress, and especially by those admirals who would have much preferred to see the money spent on surface ships or even on airplanes. The *Akron* was not to be allowed a period of trial-and-error experimentation to work out the inevitable problems that occur in every prototype. Time was running out for rigid airships. The *Akron* could not afford to make mistakes.

On January 9, 1932, a little more than two months after being commissioned and before her trapeze and airplanes were installed, she went to work with the Scouting Fleet off the coast of Georgia. Her assignment was to locate the enemy fleet. She found it on the second day of the exercise, seven hours ahead of her own scouting cruisers, but her success was tempered by the fact that she had sailed right over the same fleet a day earlier without seeing it, even though a dozen of the *Akron*'s lookouts were scanning the horizon. The enemy, meanwhile, had her in sight for twenty minutes.

She gave a second less-than-memorable performance a month later on February 22, as she was being brought out of her hangar at Lakehurst to take the members of the House Committee on Naval Affairs for a ride. A sudden gust of wind snapped the restraining cables at the stern and, as the Congressmen watched in amazement, her tail fin was dragged across the ground, bending the girders and ripping her outer cover to shreds. Nobody got a ride that day and the *Akron* spent the next two months in her hangar being repaired. When she emerged on April 28, her trapeze was finally in place and she was ready to begin her intended career as a flying aircraft carrier.

Ten days later she was on her way across the country to San Diego where she was to rejoin the Scouting Fleet in the Pacific for more maneuvers. The three-day flight was made with only minor delays due to fog and thunderstorms over Texas. At eight o'clock on the morning of May 11, the *Akron* was ready to land at Camp Kearny in San Diego. One of the ship's officers climbed aboard a plane and flew down to supervise the landing crew, but instead of the disciplined, experienced sailors he expected, he found hundreds of brand-new recruits from the nearby training station.

The tail fin construction. In German-built airships the girders supporting the tail fins extended all the way through the hull and out into the fin on each side. In order to save weight, these cruciform girders, named for the cross formed where they met inside the hull, were eliminated in the *Akron* and *Macon*. Their huge fins, each weighing twenty-seven hundred pounds, were simply bolted to the tail frames. Since these were the stronger, rigid frames, it was found that they could accept the extra load that the single ring frames could not. *Courtesy Goodyear Tire and Rubber Co.*

A rare sight—two American rigid airships, the *Los Angeles* and the *Akron*, in the air together over Washington, D.C. The *Los Angeles* was decommissioned soon afterwards. The *Akron* was 785 feet long with 6,500,000 cubic feet of helium. This gave her a total lift of 201 tons. She weighed 131 tons, which left a disposable lift of 70 tons for fuel, ballast, crew and five airplanes. She was powered by eight 560-horsepower Maybach V-12s. Her top speed of 79 miles per hour was below the 83.3 miles per hour that was called for in her contract. *Courtesy Goodyear Tire and Rubber Co.*

The cross-country flight had consumed thirty-five tons of gasoline. The exhaust condensers had been unable to replace completely the lost weight with water, and unless Lieutenant Commander Rosendahl could land early in the morning when his helium was still cool, his ship would be several tons light, but as his officers struggled to maneuver the inexperienced ground crew, the hours passed and the sun began to warm the gas, increasing its lift. It was nearly noon before the recruits had the mooring lines at the bow firmly in hand but by then it was too late. The gas had warmed and even the power of the engines driving straight downward could not force the ship to the ground. They would have to release some of their precious helium—there was no other way to bring the ship down. Rosendahl gave the order to valve gas but something went wrong and five tons of water ballast were dumped by mistake. Officers in the control car and on the ground shouted the command to let go all lines as the ship shot skyward—and all but three men let go. They were carried aloft clinging to the mooring lines.

As the landing crew and spectators watched in horror, the three tiny figures dangled beneath the huge ship. Then one let go and fell to his death. Another followed. The third, eighteen-year-old Bud Cowart, held on for an hour before he could be winched safely aboard.

Bud Cowart

Aw, I just hung on. Part o' the time I sat down and then I'd stand up on the toggle knotted in the rope. I saw the other fellows fall and it didn't make me feel any too good, but there was nothing I could do about it—'ceptin' to hang on tighter. I wouldn't do it again for love or money.[2]

The *Akron* was not moored to the Camp Kearny mast until seven o'clock that night. A simple landing operation had been turned into a nightmare because of the navy's reluctance to lose any of its valuable helium. Two men died, and, in the end, so much helium was valved anyway that the *Akron* didn't have enough left to join the fleet on maneuvers. There was no helium at San Diego to replace the loss. Only after unloading two airplanes and a dozen men did Rosendahl feel he had enough lift to make the five-hundred-mile flight up the coast to the new airship base at Sunnyvale just south of San Francisco, where more gas was stored.

From Sunnyvale the *Akron* made a series of public relations flights cruising as far north as Bellingham, Washington. She also moored to the mast of the *Patoka* in San Francisco Bay before rejoining the Scouting Fleet in an exercise off the coast of Mexico's Baja California. Though Rosendahl was ordered to fly once more without his airplanes, the intensive drilling of his crew was beginning to pay off as they located the enemy fleet several times. The enemy cruisers launched catapult planes and claimed to have downed the big ship by machine-gun fire and dive-bombing. Though no one had ever tried to shoot down a helium-filled airship, the British experience against World War I Zeppelins suggested that attacking a fireproof airship would not be as easy as the navy pilots seemed to believe.

Adm. Arthur Willard commanding the Scouting Force was only mildly impressed by the *Akron*'s performance. Though he felt that "under most conditions a dirigible is a most efficient scout, insofar as making the first contact is concerned," he thought that the airship would be immediately shot down. He was willing to concede, however, that "the sacrifice of a dirigible under these conditions may well be worth the information gained."[3]

With this considerably qualified success under her belt, the *Akron* returned across the continent to Lakehurst by way of the mooring mast at Parris Island, South Carolina. She was forced to release her two planes over Arizona in order to gain enough altitude to cross the mountains. Without compasses, the two airplane pilots were forced to follow the railroad tracks all the way back to Lakehurst.

For the next nine months the *Akron* completed a number of training and test flights. Her full complement of airplanes was finally delivered in June of 1932 shortly after her return from California, and, as the testing continued, the men of the *Akron* finally began to realize the potential of the ship they flew—an aerial aircraft carrier that, with her planes as distant outriders, could patrol far beyond her own horizon. There was even the beginning of the idea of a flight control officer aboard the airship plotting the courses of the distant planes, sending them on wide scouting sweeps away from the ship and directing them back again by radio as the ship herself flew onward or changed course at more than seventy miles per hour.

The *Akron*'s potential was being tentatively grasped, if not by the admirals, at least by the trapeze pilots and some of the airshipmen, but its full realization depended on equipment not yet fully developed—direction finders, homing devices, and more powerful radios. In the meantime the *Akron* flew to Cuba and Panama in search of new mooring sites. On each of these flights she landed at Opa-Locka, Florida, just south of Miami, where Admiral Moffett's Bureau of Aeronautics hoped to develop a second East Coast airship base far from the icy winter storms of Lakehurst.

On March 11, 1933, *ZRS-5,* the *Akron*'s sister ship, was christened by Mrs. William A. Moffett with the name *Macon,* after the largest city in the district of

As a captain, Admiral Moffett commanded a battleship and won the Medal of Honor at Vera Cruz. He was promoted to rear admiral in 1921 and selected to head the navy's newly formed Bureau of Aeronautics. For more than ten years he was deeply involved in the development of all phases of naval aviation, especially large flying boats and aircraft carriers. But he seemed to have a special interest in airships and often flew aboard the *Shenandoah, Los Angeles*, and *Akron. Courtesy Goodyear Tire and Rubber Co.*

The wreckage of the *Akron* was located twenty-seven miles southeast of Barnegat Light in 105 feet of water with the top of her hull eighty feet beneath the surface. Here her lower fin is being brought up. In terms of loss of life, the crash of the *Akron* was the worst air disaster yet to occur. In the twenty-one months since her launching, she had made seventy-four flights and had seventeen hundred hours in the air. She flew with the fleet only twice, neither time with her airplanes. The navy blimp *J-3* took off at first light the next morning to search for survivors and crashed in the same storm, killing two of the nine aboard. *Courtesy Wide World Photo.*

•

Georgia's Carl Vinson, the chairman of the House Committee on Naval Affairs; certainly as good a reason as any for naming an airship. Admiral Moffett gave a short speech in which he envisioned the day when even larger ships carrying a dozen airplanes would serve as the eyes of the fleet.

Admiral Moffett was scheduled to retire at the end of the year after twelve years as chief of the Bureau of Aeronautics. Though he was a little concerned about the length of time it was taking the airship to find her place in fleet operations, he still felt she could serve an important function in the overall picture of naval aviation that he had worked so hard to develop.

Three weeks after the *Macon*'s christening, Admiral Moffett was at Lakehurst to fly once more aboard the *Akron*. It was to be a few days' cruise off the New England coast calibrating new radio direction stations. Lieutenant Commander Rosendahl had completed his tour of duty aboard the *Akron* and returned to sea. His place was taken by Comdr. Frank McCord, a twenty-year naval veteran with two years' service on the *Los Angeles*.

They cast off from the mast at 7:30 on the evening of April 3, 1933, and disappeared into a low mist. Four hours later the *Akron* was fighting for her life in the middle of one of the worst Atlantic storms of the decade.

There was no hint of it on their early evening weather maps, but at a half-hour past midnight on the morning of the fourth, they found themselves surrounded by flashing lightning and howling winds. From her cruising altitude of sixteen hundred feet the *Akron* was beaten down by a series of violent downdrafts until her tail fin struck the surface of the sea. The huge ship struggled to rise again but her tail was held fast and she began to sink.

The crew of the German tanker *Phoebus,* plowing through the storm-tossed sea, saw what appeared to be a row of lights falling from the sky. They changed course and fifteen minutes later were surrounded by floating bits of wreckage and the strong smell of gasoline. Lowering a boat they found four men clinging to the wreckage. One died aboard the tanker, leaving only three survivors of the *Akron:* boatswain's mate Richard Deal, aviation metalsmith Moody Erwin and Lt. Comdr. Herbert Wiley, the ship's executive officer. Seventy-three others drowned in the icy waters.

Lt. Comdr. Herbert Wiley

The elevator man reported several times that the ship was falling, and I heard the report 800 feet. By this time the bow of the ship nosed to about 20 degrees, but even then we were falling quite rapidly. In the fog nothing could be seen. I asked the altitude and the answer was 300 feet. I gave the order to stand by for a crash, and the signal was rung to the engine cars. Then we hit. We had, as I remember, a list to starboard—my side of the car—and water, I remember, rushing in my window carried me out of the other window—the window the captain was standing by.

I tried to swim as rapidly as I could to get from under the ship, and finally I came to the surface. I could see the ship drifting away from me when the lightning flashed. The bow was pointed up in the air and the whole structure was a general wreck. I saw two lights on what I thought was the stern, and looking to the side of them I saw the lights of a ship. I also thought I could see the glare of the Barnegat lighthouse.

I swam toward the ship and after about ten minutes found a board about three feet square which I clung to the rest of the way. I saw several men in the water, but none very close that I thought I could help.

When I got about 400 yards from the ship, the wind changed and the waves began hitting me in the face instead of rising from behind me. The captain put his ship broadside to the sea and it floated down toward us. I think he had heard the cries of some of the men in the water. I swam easily to the steamer, and they threw a life-ring to me and hauled me aboard.[4]

Two weeks later a fishing trawler snagged her nets on the wreckage lying on the bottom in 105 feet of water, thirty-five miles east of Atlantic City—the final resting place of the *Akron* and most of her crew. Four bodies were recovered from the control car. One of them was Rear Adm. William A. Moffett. He is buried at Arlington National Cemetery.

In nearly two years of operation the *Akron* had worked with the fleet only twice. Three other scheduled appearances had been canceled, first by a damaged fin at Lakehurst, then by the loss of helium at San Diego, and finally by Rosendahl's reluctance to accompany the fleet on its long voyage from the Pacific to the Atlantic through the Panama Canal. It is little wonder that many officers looked on the airship as a most unreliable member of the fleet's air arm. Even on the two occasions when the *Akron* did show up, she was without her airplanes and was forced to operate as a direct observer, just as airships had done fifteen years earlier in World War I. When her full complement of planes was finally delivered in June 1932, the men of the *Akron* began to work toward the concept of a flying aircraft carrier, but by then their time had run out.

Now the *Macon* was left to carry on alone. She had to develop an entirely new concept in aviation and justify her existence to a skeptical navy. And her time, too, was short. She made her first flight on April 21, 1933. With new propellers and a different radiator installation that produced less drag, her top speed proved to be eighty-seven miles per hour, four miles per hour faster than the *Akron*.

On October 12, her trial flights completed, the *Macon* left Lakehurst bound for Sunnyvale on the West Coast. She left the decommissioned *Los Angeles* alone in the big hangar. The *Macon* would never return.

On her arrival at Sunnyvale, now renamed Moffett Field, she was almost immediately ordered out to join in fleet maneuvers. Her debut was not encouraging. In the first eight hours of the exercise she was "shot down" twice. One who fully appreciated the seriousness of the *Macon*'s position was Rear Adm. Ernest King, Admiral Moffett's successor as chief of the Bureau of Aeronautics. In a letter to Admiral Halligan he wrote:

This is to be a critical year for airships. We have only one airship. We must not be reckless, but if airships are to justify themselves, the Macon has got to show more than she has shown.

I am trying to keep an open mind on the airship question, but the more I see of airships the more I can visualize a useful field for them in searching operations, especially in conjunction with their airplanes, provided we can get the airships to perform.

. . . [T]his letter is a personal plea for (a) wider operation of the Macon directly with the Fleet and on additional problems which might be framed to suit her special characteristics; (b) a square deal all around for the Macon during this crucial year, so that at its conclusion when we come to total up the ledger, no one may say she has not had a fair test.[5]

Admiral King got started in aviation at the age of forty-seven when he assumed command of the navy's first aircraft tender, the USS *Wright*. He also served as

Gen. Billy Mitchell. Six weeks after the loss of the *Akron*, a joint congressional committee was convened to examine the causes of the crash and all phases of the United States' lighter-than-air program. Everyone even remotely connected with the airship was invited to testify. All the navy brass, from the chief of naval operations on down, gave at least qualified support to naval airships, especially as potential long-range scouts. But in the sixteen days of testimony, one voice stood out for its emphatic and unqualified support of airships. It was the voice of a civilian—Billy Mitchell, once the chief of the Army Air Service:

The airship is not particularly vulnerable to attack. It can remain aloft for long periods of time. It can go from one place on the earth's surface to any other place on the earth's surface with an enormous load of military weapons and return. It has great potentialities against ships on the surface of the water, and it can sink anything on the top of the water or under the water. As far as airships are concerned with relation to heavier than air, we can use them as mother ships, not only for carrying other airplanes but for repairing other airplanes and for refueling other airplanes. In other words, if we intend to send a fleet of ships across the Pacific Ocean we can attend them with airships and use them as an auxiliary to airplanes or we can act directly with airships, using gliding bombs, air torpedoes, or other airplanes.

Official U.S. Air Force photo.

•

ABOVE: The *Macon* flew with her planes from the very beginning, and her crew was just starting to come to grips with their potential for long-range reconnaissance over a wide area while being directed by radio from the airship. Here two of her planes approach the *Macon*'s trapeze, which has been lowered to retrieve them. What look like rows of windows up the side of the *Akron*'s hull are the condensers for her water recovery system. On a long voyage an airship becomes lighter as her engines burn tons of gasoline. To compensate, a hydrogen-filled ship can release gas, but the *Akron* was filled with expensive helium. To save it, the navy devised a way to condense water from the engine exhausts, recovering a pound of water for every pound of gasoline burned. Thus the ship stayed in equilibrium without valving helium. The system was heavy and the hull-mounted condensers slowed the ship down, but this was a price the navy was willing to pay to save helium. *U.S. Navy photo, courtesy Naval Air Station, Moffett Field.*
RIGHT: The *Macon* approaching the mast. The *Macon* was christened by Mrs. William A. Moffett on March 11, 1933. The ship was exactly the same size as the *Akron* with a few improvements. She was several tons lighter, which meant that her disposable lift was increased to eighty tons. With a top speed of eighty-seven miles per hour, she was 7.5 miles per hour faster than the *Akron*, thanks to new three-bladed propellers and a cleaner hull mounting for her water recovery condensers. Here, the *Macon*'s two front propellers have been rotated to help push her down to the mooring mast. *U.S. Navy photo in the National Archives.*

Admiral Moffett's assistant and as captain of the aircraft carrier *Lexington*. In World War II he was to become chief of all U.S. naval operations, but in 1933, like Admiral Moffett and others before him, Admiral King was looking beyond the airship's admittedly unsatisfactory performance and had become intrigued by her potential. Unfortunately, few other naval officers were willing to make the effort, and the senior officers with airship experience who could plead the airship's cause with their Naval Academy classmates and comrades in the councils and wardrooms of the fleet—those officers who could use their rank, influence, and experience to work out the techniques for the airship's proper utilization with the fleet—those men were gone—killed aboard their airships. Promising young men like Lewis Maxfield, Emory Coil, and Valentine Bieg never became senior officers. Their careers ended with the *R.38*. Zachary Lansdowne, Lewis Hancock, Jack Lawrence, and Regg Houghton died in the *Shenandoah*. Now Moffett, McCord, and seventy-one more airshipmen were gone with the *Akron*. The *Macon* was left with very few friends in high places.

After several inconclusive exercises off the California coast, the *Macon* was ordered to fly across the country to join the fleet maneuvers in the Caribbean. On April 20, 1934, she left Moffett Field for Opa-Locka, Florida. While flying through the Sierra Diablo mountains near Van Horn, Texas, a strong gust of wind hit the ship broadside, snapping two girders in a tail frame supporting the rudder and elevator fins. The frame was temporarily patched in the air and they continued on to Opa-Locka, where a team of Goodyear-Zeppelin technicians arrived to repair the damage. As the work went on at the Opa-Locka mast, a series of torrential tropical rainstorms drenched the ship, hordes of rattlesnakes emerged from the surrounding swamps, and a crowd of owls tried to nest among the gasbags. The last owl was evicted over Jamaica as the repaired ship flew to join the fleet off the Panama Canal.

On returning to Moffett Field the command of the *Macon* passed to Lt. Comdr. Herbert Wiley, one of the oldest surviving airshipmen, with service aboard the *Shenandoah, Los Angeles,* and *Akron.* After the crash of the *Akron* he had rejoined the fleet as navigator aboard the cruiser *Cincinnati.* He knew at first hand of the fleet's low regard for airships and he was determined to bring the *Macon* up to her full potential.

Wiley started by developing the long-range search techniques of the trapeze planes with the aid of newly developed direction finders and radio homing equipment. To test his new methods he planned to find and intercept the cruiser *Houston,* which was carrying President Roosevelt through the Panama Canal to Clipperton Island and Honolulu. Using newspaper accounts of the president's departure time as a guide, Wiley's navigators plotted the *Houston*'s probable course and speed across thirty-five hundred miles of empty Pacific, and the *Macon* cast off on what was scheduled as a training cruise.

Just before noon on July 19, 1934, the lookouts aboard the *Houston* were startled to see two tiny fighter planes circling overhead, a thousand miles from the nearest airfield or carrier. A few minutes later the *Macon* pushed her way through the clouds and launched a plane that dropped a bundle of the previous days' San Francisco newspapers for the president. Roosevelt was delighted. The fleet's admirals, taken completely by surprise, were furious. "We considered it a publicity stunt and that he [Wiley] had no business doing it," fumed Admiral Standley, the chief of naval operations.[6] But Admiral King of the Bureau of Aeronautics was not nearly as upset. This was the kind of scouting the *Macon* was supposed to do, the kind he had ordered Wiley to develop.

Wiley followed this first success by intercepting the fleet on its return to the West Coast and then by finding and rescuing two downed fliers during the next exercise. Things were looking up, but so far fleet maneuvers had been conducted close to the coastline where the *Macon* was at the mercy of short-range land-based planes. Now Admiral Standley agreed, at Admiral King's urging, to allow the *Macon* to operate between the West Coast and Hawaii where she would finally get a chance to fly as she was intended, in long-range reconnaissance. The navy's General Board even recommended the addition of a second rigid airship to the fleet.

It might have worked, but the *Macon* still carried in her tail the weakened frame that had given way in the mountains over Texas. It had been temporarily repaired at Opa-Locka and the work of permanent reinforcement was going on at Moffett Field while the ship continued to participate in maneuvers. It was one of the frames to which the fins were bolted.

Lt. Ward Harrigan, the *Macon*'s senior heavier-than-air pilot, lands on the airship by latching his skyhook onto the ship's trapeze. The yoke will be lowered to steady the plane's fuselage as the trapeze swings it up through the T-shaped hangar door in the bottom of the *Macon*'s hull. The insignia on the plane's side shows a big trapeze aerialist catching a little one. They were quite literally, "The Men on the Flying Trapeze." The navy tested several different hook-on planes before selecting these Curtiss F9C-2s, originally designed as small, carrier-based fighters. Their most important feature was their ability to fit through the *Macon*'s hangar door. After July 1934, the F9C-2s flew from the airship with their wheels removed and an extra gas tank in their place that increased their range by 50 percent. *Courtesy Goodyear Tire and Rubber Co.*

A Sad Home Coming!

"A sad homecoming!" The *Macon* made only fifty-four flights in her brief career. She was christened on March 11, 1933, and crashed in the Pacific just twenty-three months later on February 12, 1935. She survived two months longer than the *Akron*, but neither ship lived to celebrate a second birthday. Shortly after the loss of the *Macon*, the big airship base at Sunnyvale was traded away by the navy in exchange for three army posts. Moffett Field did not return to navy control until 1942, when Japanese submarine activity along the Pacific coast forced its reactivation as a blimp base. *From the* San Francisco Chronicle, *February 14, 1935.*

•

On February 12, 1935, the *Macon* was returning from a fleet problem off the coast between San Diego and Santa Barbara. Spirits were high. They had done a good job and the prospects in Hawaii were even better. The repairs were almost completed; only the top fin remained to be reinforced.

At five o'clock that evening they were cruising at fourteen hundred feet, approaching Point Sur, just south of Monterey. The last of the planes had been recovered and drawn up into the hull. They were less than two hours from Moffett Field. Wiley ordered five degrees left rudder. Just as the coxswain turned the wheel, a sharp gust of wind struck the ship and she rolled violently to starboard.

At Point Sur, lighthouse keeper Thomas Henderson was watching the *Macon* through his binoculars. He saw her stern dip sharply as the leading edge of her top fin lifted away from the hull. Then the fin literally disintegrated before his eyes, leaving the rudder post and rudder standing alone.

As the fin and part of the frame carried away, the three stern gasbags were ripped open and 20 percent of the *Macon's* helium poured out through the hole left by the fin. The stern began to sink and crewmen rushed to cut the slip tanks loose as Wiley ordered the release of all ballast aft of amidships. The vision of shipmates aboard the *Akron* falling into the sea was still fresh in the men's minds but the *Macon* was not falling, she was rising. Eighty percent of her helium was still intact, but sixteen tons of fuel and water had been dumped and the engines, still running at seventy miles per hour, began to drive the ship upward as the stern sank downward.

The *Macon* survived her brief fall. Her rise would prove fatal. Within two minutes of the break, she rose from sixteen hundred feet to her pressure height of twenty-eight hundred feet. The helium expanded to fill her remaining gasbags completely and now every additional foot of altitude meant the loss of vital lift through the gas valves.

For eight minutes she rose. Then at 4,850 feet the *Macon* slowed to a stop and started down. It was not a wild, plummeting fall into the sea, for more than half her helium was still aboard. The descent from just under a mile in the air lasted twenty-five minutes, yet there was absolutely nothing anyone could do to stop it.

They hit the sea at 5:40. The life rafts were already inflated and every man had on his life jacket. Forty minutes later the *Macon* slipped beneath the gentle waves. At 7:00 the cruisers *Richmond* and *Concord* were picking up survivors. Eighty-one were saved, two were lost—radio operator Ernest Dailey and Florentino Edquiba, a Filipino mess steward.

The U.S. Navy's experiment with rigid airships was finished. The decommissioned *Los Angeles* back at Lakehurst was taken out for an occasional unofficial flight, but in 1940 she was dismantled and her duralumin melted down for airplane parts.

Did the rigid airship really have a place in the prewar navy, or were the efforts of Admirals Moffett, King, and so many other officers and men doomed to failure from the very beginning? Were the millions of dollars wasted? Were the lives thrown away? Or could the rigid airship have played an important role for the navy and the country? What if an airship had been flying distant reconnaissance out of Hawaii in the early days of December 1941? The facts are inconclusive and we can only guess at what might have happened. The proof lay in 105 feet of water off Atlantic City and at the bottom of the Pacific off Point Sur, and for most men in the navy and in Congress, that proof was conclusive.

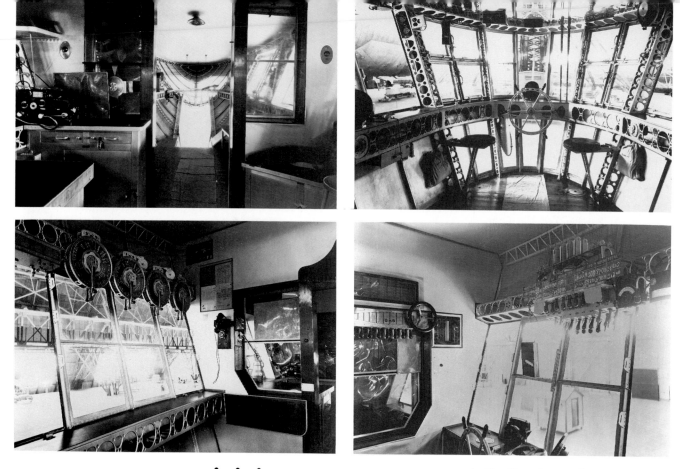

• • •

While the efforts of others were ending in disaster and death, Hugo Eckener and the *Graf Zeppelin* sailed serenely on. They were circling the globe as the *R.101* was being completed; they were preparing for the Arctic voyage when she crashed. They carried four hundred passengers to South America the year the *Akron* went down and 720 the year the *Macon* was lost. While other nations spent millions trying to improve on Zeppelin design, the Zeppelin Company was struggling desperately to scrape enough money together to build a new ship of its own.

Adolf Hitler became chancellor of Germany on January 30, 1933. The previous government had been able to offer only limited assistance to the Zeppelin Company, but Eckener suspected that the Nazis, with their highly developed sense of propaganda, would be much more likely to appreciate the publicity value of successful German airships.

Eckener was correct. On March 25, 1935, Air Minister Hermann Goering formally organized the Deutsche Zeppelin-Reederei, the German Zeppelin Transport Company. Controlling interest and half the stock in the new concern went to the government's Lufthansa Airline in exchange for the $2,200,000 necessary to build a new passenger airship. For its share, the Zeppelin Company contributed the *Graf Zeppelin* to the new organization. Air Minister Goering pledged his full support to the development of both airplanes and airships, but when Eckener invited the former World War I fighter ace up for a ride in the *Graf Zeppelin*, "he vehemently declined."[7]

For seven years the *Graf Zeppelin* had served as a test vehicle to determine the most favorable design for the first true transatlantic passenger Zeppelins. Now with a new construction shed and government financial aid, work could finally start on those ships. Hugo Eckener and his engineers decided that the new craft would need an additional ten miles per hour in cruising speed over the *Graf Zeppelin*'s seventy-

The *Macon*'s control car was fifty feet long with the bridge at the front, a combination radio room and navigator's chart room in the middle, and the gangway leading to the ground at the back. The top-left photo is taken looking past the chart table in the left foreground to the radio at the left to the lowered gangway through the open doorway in the center of the picture. The rudder wheel is at the very front of the control car as seen in the top-right photo. The bottom two photos show the port and starboard sides of the bridge just forward of the navigation/radio room. The four engine telegraphs in the left photo relay signals to the eight engines. In the right photo, the elevator wheel is at the right with water ballast and fuel tank release handles above it. *Official U.S. Navy photos, courtesy Naval Air Station, Moffett Field, California.*

•

The *Hindenburg* emerging from her hangar. After the *Graf Zeppelin*'s triumphant world flight in 1929, the financial future of commercial airship travel seemed assured, but all the plans evaporated with the stock market crash. The depression helped bring the Nazis to power in Germany and the Nazis brought financial aid to the airship. But the Zeppelin Company had lost precious time as well as the controlling interest in their organization. Here the *Hindenburg* emerges from the new construction shed at Friedrichshafen, dwarfing the smaller hangar at the left where the *Graf Zeppelin* was built eight years earlier. *Courtesy Luftschiffbau Zeppelin, Friedrichshafen.*

•

four miles an hour. This would cut half a day off the travel time to Rio or North America. It would also require double the *Graf Zeppelin*'s horsepower and 50 percent more fuel capacity. For greater safety they intended to use diesel engines instead of gasoline and, if it was available, helium rather than hydrogen. In place of the older ship's twenty passengers, they planned to accommodate fifty in considerably more luxurious surroundings. To meet all these requirements they would need twice the gas volume of the *Graf Zeppelin*. They would need a seven-million-cubic-foot airship.

The Zeppelin Company had skipped construction of *LZ-128* in order to start the new ships *LZ-129* and *LZ-130*. Work began in 1934. The two 804-foot ships were only twenty-nine feet longer than the *Graf Zeppelin,* but with a maximum diameter of 135 feet, they held nearly twice as much gas and could lift a 110-ton load. Four Daimler-Benz diesels developed forty-two hundred horsepower and a top speed of eighty-five miles an hour. The passenger accommodations included a dining room, reading room, bar, smoking room, and two promenade decks. There was even a specially built metal piano weighing only 112 pounds.

The first ship was to be placed in service on the North American run, with ten flights scheduled for the spring and summer of 1936. For this the Reederei would need permission to use the landing facilities at Lakehurst, and only President Roosevelt could authorize the use of a U.S. government installation by a private commercial enterprise. In February 1936, Eckener sailed for America to see the president.

Roosevelt expressed interest in the project, although as a former small-boat skipper, he told Eckener of his doubts about the feasibility of maintaining a schedule across the stormy North Atlantic. With the president's approval, the secretary of the navy, Admiral Leahy, ordered 250 men assigned to the nearly deactivated naval station at Lakehurst.

By the beginning of March 1936, the newly christened *Hindenburg* was ready for her first trials. At the end of the month, on March 31, she was scheduled to start on her first commercial flight to Rio, but now the already complex technical problems inherent in the launching of a new ship were further complicated by political difficulties.

The Nazis were not fond of Hugo Eckener. He had refused them the use of the Zeppelin Company hangar for one of their early rallies and had even been seriously suggested as a candidate for president of Germany against Paul von Hindenburg in order to forestall Hitler's rise to power. Though he declined to run against the old field marshal, Eckener's popularity and often loudly expressed anti-Nazi opinions did little to endear him to the new regime. They took advantage of their controlling interest in the Reederei to move him upstairs to chairman of the board and install the less-outspoken Ernst Lehmann in his place as director.

Eckener was not pleased with the new arrangement. Even at the age of sixty-seven he had no intention of retiring. How could he leave his Zeppelins in the hands of others at this critical stage of their development? The fact that Lehmann was the company's most senior airship commander with twenty-five years in Zeppelins made no difference to Eckener. The inevitable clash of personalities was not long in coming.

The occasion was the German national election of 1936. The Propaganda Ministry demanded that the Reederei send the *Graf Zeppelin* and the *Hindenburg* on a four-day campaign flight. Since the government was half-owner of the ships, Eckener could not refuse the request, although he declined to participate in person. As the *Hindenburg* was being walked out of the hangar in a gusty wind, her lower fin was damaged and two hours of repairs were required.

Hugo Eckener

I was naturally very angry over this incident, which could easily have turned out much worse and involved taking a chance with the new ship. In a rage, I went to Captain Lehmann, who was responsible for bringing her out, and said to him, "How could you, Herr Lehmann, order the ship to be brought out in such wind conditions? You had the best excuse in the world to postpone this idiotic flight; instead you risk the ship merely to avoid annoying Herr Goebbels. Do you call this showing a sense of responsibility towards our enterprise? What do you want to do with it?"

Herr Lehmann assured me that he could repair the damage, temporarily, in two or three hours and could then take off after the Graf Zeppelin.

With bitterness, I answered his remark heatedly: "So, is that your only concern, to take off quickly on this mad flight and drop election pamphlets for Herr Goebbels? The fact that we have to take off for Rio in four days and have made no flights to test the engines apparently means nothing to you!"[8]

The conversation was overheard and reported to Propaganda Minister Goebbels, who promptly banned any further mention of Eckener in the government-controlled press. As far as most Germans were concerned, Hugo Eckener suddenly ceased to exist. Meanwhile the *Graf Zeppelin* and the *Hindenburg* spent four days and three nights cruising over the countryside broadcasting speeches and dropping leaflets as 99 percent of the German people cast their ballots in favor of Hitler's policies. At a voting booth aboard the *Hindenburg,* 104 votes were cast for the Fuhrer—none against.

The *Hindenburg* then set out for Rio as scheduled on her first commercial flight. She went, as Eckener feared, without a high-speed engine trial. Just past the Cape Verde Islands one diesel gave out with a broken wrist pin. They continued on to Rio on the three remaining engines with only a slight reduction in speed. There the damaged engine was repaired as well as possible and put back into service at half-power.

The return flight was without incident until they again reached the vicinity of the Cape Verde Islands. First they encountered stronger-than-usual head winds, then

The *Hindenburg* was 804 feet long and 135 feet in diameter, with 7,062,150 cubic feet of hydrogen. She had a total lift of 240 tons and weighed 130.1 tons, which left a useful lift of 109.9 tons. On transatlantic flights she carried sixty-four tons of diesel fuel and 3.3 tons of motor oil. She was powered by four eleven-hundred-horsepower Daimler-Benz diesels with a top speed of 84.4 miles per hour. At her cruising speed of seventy-eight miles per hour, she had a range of 8,420 miles. On the *Hindenburg*'s maiden flight, Dr. Eckener turned to his companions in the control car and said, "Gentlemen, at last we have built a real airship." *Courtesy Luftschiffbau Zeppelin, Friedrichshafen.*

The Nazis insisted that Ernst Lehmann take Eckener's place as director of the Zeppelin Company, a move that Eckener resented. Lehmann was, however, an experienced airshipman who commanded army Zeppelins during the war and had been connected with the Zeppelin Company for many years. He sometimes entertained his passengers on the concertina after dinner, and he was more diplomatic than Eckener in dealing with the realities of life in Nazi Germany. *Courtesy San Diego Aero-Space Museum.*

•

another wrist pin gave way. With one engine broken down and another on half-power, Eckener knew that the pins in his two remaining engines were likely to be similarly affected. He had no choice. He throttled them back in the hope of relieving the strain. The *Hindenburg's* air speed fell to sixty-three miles an hour, but the trade winds blowing against her at thirty-one miles per hour cut her ground speed to thirty-two. They had fourteen hundred miles yet to go. If one more engine failed, their speed would drop to zero.

Hugo Eckener

Beneath us the open sea, to starboard the wastes of the Sahara Desert, and 75 people in the ship! . . . I contemplated steering close to the African coast, so that, in case of emergency—meaning failure of another motor—the ship could be promptly set down on land in the desert, before the trade wind should blow us out to sea. This would certainly mean the loss of the ship. I confess that I have hardly ever experienced so much mental torture as in those hours of vacillation and perplexity. The picture in my mind's eye, which I considered very possible, was of a crowd of 75 people filing through the blazing sands of the Sahara towards a native settlement, provided, I hoped, with food and water salvaged from the airship.[9]

The safest course of action would be to turn around and run with the wind back to Rio even though it would then be weeks before replacement parts and mechanics could be shipped across the South Atlantic from Germany to fix the engines. Eckener had only one chance to complete the voyage successfully. He had to find an altitude where the northeast trades were not blowing. The *Hindenburg* was too heavily loaded to rise into the prevailing westerlies that blow above the trade winds, but at thirty-six hundred feet he found a twenty-mile-per-hour crosswind that allowed them to make eighty miles an hour toward Gibraltar and safety.

With her engines repaired and the wrist pin problem corrected, the *Hindenburg* made ten flights to the United States in the summer of 1936 plus six more voyages to Rio de Janeiro. The first flight to Lakehurst took two and a half days. The return trip with fifty-five passengers took just two days, one hour, and fourteen minutes. In her first year of commercial service the *Hindenburg* carried more than fifteen hundred transatlantic passengers and twenty tons of mail and freight.

She had been built with sixteen tons of extra lift in anticipation of the day when she would be filled with heavier helium, but since none was obtainable, the Reederei decided to use part of this extra lift to increase the ship's passenger capacity from fifty to seventy. All ten flights from the United States had been completely sold out and the *Hindenburg* had paid 80 percent of her first year's expenses from receipts. The twenty additional berths would allow her to break even in her second season. The next ship, *LZ-130,* was being built to accommodate one hundred passengers, while the *LZ-131* would be designed for 150. It was clear that two ships flying the same route and sharing the expenses of landing fields and administration would make a profit.

The financial community again began to show an interest in the Zeppelin. Perhaps it really was true that only the Germans possessed the knowledge and experience to build successful rigid airships. They had, after all, been flying commercial Zeppelins since 1909 and, after millions of passenger miles, they had yet to lose a single passenger. The *Hindenburg's* success and obvious profit potential led to the founding of the German-American Transport Corporation with plans to put four Zeppelins into weekly service across the North Atlantic. Two ships would be built and flown by Germans and two by Americans.

The *Hindenburg* began her 1937 season in the middle of March with a flight to Rio. The United States and Germany had approved a May-through-November schedule of eighteen round trips between Frankfurt and Lakehurst. At eight o'clock on the evening of May 3, the *Hindenburg* cast off from the newly completed Rhein-Main World Airport eight miles south of Frankfurt, and turned toward the Atlantic. Aboard were thirty-six passengers and sixty-one crewmen. Twenty of the crew were young airshipmen on a training flight. Max Pruss, a wartime airshipman and veteran of twenty-six years in Zeppelins, was in command. Zeppelin Company director Ernst Lehmann was also along for the ride.

One of the passengers was Margaret Mather, a diminutive single woman who had already flown in airplanes over the Mediterranean, the Greek Islands, the Dolomites, and throughout Europe and North Africa. As an accomplished world traveler, Margaret Mather was daunted only by the stormy North Atlantic where even the most luxurious accommodations aboard a fast passenger liner were of little consolation to a person prone to seasickness. She eagerly seized the opportunity to fly aboard the motion-free *Hindenburg*.

Hindenburg poster.

Europe by Air in 2½ days via the *Hindenburg* of the German Zeppelin Co. Staterooms with running hot and cold water: $400 including berth, meals, tips; regular schedule May to October.

Newspaper ads in New York, San Francisco, and Los Angeles, 1937.

Photo courtesy San Diego Aero-Space Museum.

•

Margaret Mather

It had rained on and off during the day, and was still drizzling as we crossed the brief space which separated the Zeppelin from the hangar. In spite of this there were many spectators, including a band of little boy Nazis who had been allowed to come quite near to inspect the ship.

I followed the other passengers up the narrow gangway and was taken to my cabin, which was very tiny but complete, with washstand and cupboards and a sloping window. After a hasty look I went above to watch the casting off. . . .

The little boy Nazis scurried over the field as we slowly rose. It was an indescribable feeling of lightness and buoyancy—a lift and pull upward, quite unlike the take off of an airplane. . . .

All the passengers were hanging over the windows, trying to get a glimpse of the Rhine. We were sailing along rapidly through the dusk, guided by beacons, which flashed from hill to hill. We passed hamlets and villages gleaming jewel-like in the darkness, and came to a great spreading mass of lights, which someone said was Cologne, and suddenly we were looking down at the cathedral, beautifully clear and dark amid the glow.[10]

At a late supper of salad, cold meats, and freshly baked biscuits, Mather found herself seated next to Captain Pruss, who ate quickly and returned to the control car. It was still early in the season and he knew there would be storms and bad weather ahead.

Margaret Mather

I was tired and glad to go to bed. My bunk was narrow but most comfortable and furnished with fine linen sheets and soft light blankets. The walls of my tiny cabin were covered with pearl-gray linen. It was charming, and I spent most of the following day there, glad to rest and to look through my sloping window at the angry waves, whitening the sea so far below.

At the German end of her run, the *Hindenburg* was docked in the big hangar at the new Rhein-Main World Airport just outside Frankfurt. She wears the Olympics symbol on her hull in honor of the 1936 games held in Berlin.

•

We flew high above the storm, but a strong head wind buffeted and delayed us. It sounded like surf, but the ship sailed calmly through it. If one looked attentively at the horizon the slightest variation from the horizontal was perceptible, but there was no feeling of unsteadiness. I told Captain Pruss how much I was enjoying the trip, what a wretched sailor I was on the sea; he was pleased but assured me that it was one of the worst trips he had made. The wind grew stronger and the second night the captain did not go to bed at all, but still one felt no motion, though the wind beat like waves against the sides of the ship. It was almost uncanny.[11]

The most experienced airship passenger aboard the *Hindenburg* was Leonhard Adelt, a writer who was collaborating with Ernst Lehmann on a book about his

Zeppelin experiences. Adelt and his wife, Gertrude, were flying as guests of the Reederei.

Leonhard Adelt

Our trip on the Hindenburg in May was the most uneventful journey I ever undertook in an airship. Visibility was bad, and we had barely glimpsed the North Atlantic before we had crossed it. Passengers spent their time reading, addressing postcards in the writing room, discussing Germany's problems in the smoking salon. In the reading room the Doehner children played games while their mother crocheted. The ship glided as smoothly through the black storm clouds as though it were a calm, moonlight night.

On the third day we sighted Newfoundland. Binoculars and cameras appeared, and my wife's delight grew when the white dots along the coast turned out to be icebergs. The captain ordered the ship to fly low and steer toward them. Very slowly we passed over the most beautiful, which looked like a magic marble statue. The sun came out and laid a double rainbow around the airship.[12]

After another night in the air and a leisurely breakfast, the *Hindenburg* arrived over Boston.

Margaret Mather

All the ships in Boston harbor saluted us and as we flew over the suburbs we saw cars draw up by the roadside and their occupants leap out to gaze at us. Airplanes circled about us and one or two accompanied us on our way. It was delightful to look down on the gardens. Yellow forsythia was in bloom, and some sort of trailing pink; the grass plots were vivid green, and we saw apple trees in blossom and woods full of dogwood and young green leaves. Our passing frightened the dogs, who rushed to their houses, and caused a great commotion in the barnyards—especially among the chickens and pigs; the latter rushed desperately to and fro, and seemed absolutely terrified, and the chickens fluttered and ran about in proverbial fashion. Cows and sheep did not notice us much.[13]

Over New York City the ship came down so low that the passengers could see the news photographers atop the Empire State Building taking their pictures. Leonhard Adelt saw the Statue of Liberty at the edge of the city, "small as a porcelain figure."[14] The landing at Lakehurst was scheduled for 4:00 P.M. but dark rain clouds were hovering over the field and Captain Pruss turned back toward the coast to wait until the storm front drifted past. At 6:30 tea and sandwiches were served by the stewards as the passengers watched deer bounding through the pine woods along the New Jersey coastline.

Commander Charles Rosendahl

As the thunderstorm passed and the rain practically ceased, I sent a radio message to Captain Pruss recommending that he come on in and land. Hence, at about 7 P.M., the Hindenburg came into view and passed over the station on a northerly course at an altitude of 500 or 600 feet to have a look at surface conditions. After circling, the Hindenburg came back over the station, adjusted her trim and static conditions by valving hydrogen and dropping ballast in perfectly normal fashion, headed into the wind, descended to about 200 feet altitude, backed down on her engines to check the headway of the ship, and at 7:21 dropped her manila landing ropes to the ground. The ground crew at once grabbed the ship's landing lines, connected them to the

It took just thirty-two seconds from the time the first tiny flame was seen at the top of the hull in front of the tail fin until the *Hindenburg* lay a smoking ruin on the ground. Thirty-six people died in the wreck: twenty-two crewmen, one member of the ground crew, and thirteen passengers. Sixty-one passengers and crewmen survived. ABOVE PHOTO, *courtesy Wide World Photos.* OPPOSITE ABOVE PHOTO, *Official U.S. Air Force photo.* OP-POSITE BELOW PHOTO, *courtesy Wide World Photos.*

•

corresponding ground lines and began the operation of hauling them taut as the first step in the landing maneuver. From the very nose of the ship, the steel mooring cable by which the ship was to be pulled in to its connection on the mooring mast, began to make its appearance. Following the passage of the thunderstorm, the wind had become light and variable, scarcely two miles per hour velocity on the surface and only some six knots at the ship's altitude.[15]

The rainy weather and long delays had discouraged most spectators, but a few hundred still waited in the gathering dusk together with the reporters and cameramen covering the ship's arrival. Herbert Morrison, a radio announcer for WLS in Chicago, was making a transcription of the event for later broadcast.

Herbert Morrison

It is practically standing still now. The ropes have been dropped and they have been taken hold of by a number of men on the field. It is starting to rain again. The rain had slacked up a little bit. The back motors of the ship are holding it just enough to keep it —
— It's burst into flame! Get out of the way! Get this, Charley, get out of the way, please! It is bursting into flames. This is terrible! This is one of the worst catastrophes in the world! The flames are 500 feet into the sky. It is a terrific crash, ladies and

gentlemen. It is in smoke and flames now. Oh the humanity! Those passengers! I can't talk, ladies and gentlemen. Honest, it is a mass of smoking wreckage. Lady, I am sorry. Honestly, I can hardly — I am going to step inside where I can't see it. Charley this is terrible. Listen, folks, I am going to have to stop for a minute because I have lost my voice.[16]

Leonhard Adelt

With my wife I was leaning out of a window on the promenade deck. Suddenly there occurred a remarkable stillness. The motors were silent, and it seemed as though the whole world was holding its breath. One heard no command, no call, no cry. The people we saw seemed suddenly stiffened. I could not account for this. Then I heard a light, dull detonation from above, no louder than the sound of a beer bottle being opened. I turned my gaze toward the bow and noticed a delicate rose glow, as though the sun were about to rise. I understood immediately that the airship was aflame. There was but one chance for safety—to jump out. The distance from the ground at that moment may have been 120 feet. For a moment I thought of getting bed linen from the corridor in order to soften our leap, but in the same instant, the airship crashed to the ground with terrific force. Its impact threw us from the window to the stair corridor. The tables and chairs of the reading room crashed about and jammed us in like a barricade.[17]

Margaret Mather

I was pinned against a projecting bench by several Germans who were thrown after me. I couldn't breathe, and thought I should die, suffocated, but they all jumped up.

Then the flames blew in, long tongues of flame, bright red and very beautiful.

My companions were leaping up and down amid the flames. The lurching of the ship threw them repeatedly against the furniture and the railing, where they cut their hands and faces against the metal trimmings. They were streaming with blood. I saw a number of men leap from the windows, but I sat just where I had fallen, holding the lapels of my coat over my face, feeling the flames light on my back, my hat, my hair, trying to beat them out, watching the horrified faces of my companions as they leaped up and down.[18]

Leonhard Adelt

"Through the window!" I shouted to my fellow passengers, and dragged my wife with me to our observation window.

. . . The distance from the ground may have been 12 or 15 feet. I distinctly felt my feet touch the soft sand and grass. We collapsed to our knees, and the impenetrable darkness of black oil clouds, shot through with flames, enveloped us. We had to let go of each other's hand in order to make our way through the confusion of hot metal pieces and wires. We bent the hot metal apart with our bare hands without feeling pain.

We freed ourselves and ran through a sea of fire. It was like a dream. Our bodies had no weight. They floated like stars through space.[19]

Margaret Mather

I was thinking that it was like a scene from a medieval picture of hell. I was waiting for the crash of landing.

Suddenly I heard a loud cry! "Come out, lady!" I looked, and we were on the ground. Two or three men were peering in, beckoning and calling to us. I got up incredulous and instinctively groped with my feet for my handbag, which had been jerked from me when I fell. "Aren't you coming?" called the man, and I rushed out over little low parts of the framework which were burning on the ground.[20]

Later when the newsreel footage was timed with a stopwatch, it was found that the destruction of the *Hindenburg* took just thirty-two seconds from the appearance of the first tiny flame until the final collapse onto the ground. A hundred years of effort by uncounted numbers of airship pioneers vanished in smoke and flame at Lakehurst in slightly over half a minute.

Thirty-six people died: twenty-two crewmen, one member of the ground crew, and thirteen passengers—the first and last passengers ever to die aboard a Zeppelin. The wonder was not the number of dead, however, but rather that so many survived. Sixty-one people walked or were carried from the flames alive. One who did not survive was Ernst Lehmann. Though he walked from the wreckage, his back was a mass of burns.

Ernst Lehmann

> I intended to stay with the ship as long as I could—until we could land her if possible, but it was impossible. Everything around me was on fire. The windows were open in the central control cabin and I jumped about a hundred feet. My clothes were all ablaze.[21]

Ernst Lehmann died at six o'clock the next morning, his last words: "I don't understand it."

Capt. Hans von Schiller was flying the *Graf Zeppelin* back from Rio when he received the news by radio. On arrival at Friedrichshafen the *Graf Zeppelin* was grounded by Hugo Eckener until the cause of the crash could be determined. No Zeppelin ever made another commercial flight.

Four days after the disaster the U.S. Department of Commerce began a series of hearings to try to discover its cause. Eckener, Dr. Durr, and several other airship experts were flown by the German Air Ministry to Cherbourg where they caught the first steamer for America in order to assist in the investigation.

At the end of eighteen days of testimony from scores of witnesses, Eckener was asked to present his own personal conclusions. First he stated that Commander Rosendahl and two other airship experts standing at different parts of the field all agreed that a light or flame appeared at the top of the ship just forward of the rudder fin a few seconds before the explosion. Unfortunately, of all the photographs and newsreel footage taken of the crash, none showed this crucial moment when the tiny flame first appeared. One expert witness described it as the slowly burning flame of pure hydrogen and, Eckener concluded, at that position on the ship it could not have been anything else. The ship made a sharp turn in approaching the landing field. The strain of the turn could have snapped a bracing wire, which in turn could have torn open a gasbag in the stern. The escaping gas collected at the top of the hull just beneath the outer cover. It was ignited by static electricity when the landing ropes touched the ground in the highly charged atmosphere following the electrical storm.

This explanation offered by Eckener was built upon a number of unprovable assumptions but it was, he felt, the only logical explanation that fit the facts. With no better theory to offer, the other members of the commission adopted Eckener's conclusions as their own. He was, after all, the world's foremost airship authority. The inquiry was adjourned. Its verdict: the *Hindenburg* had died by accident of unusual, but natural, causes. A subsequent investigation conducted by the German government concurred.

Eckener's version was not accepted unanimously, however. Among the dissenters were Capt. Max Pruss, Dr. Durr, and several of the *Hindenburg*'s officers and crew. The verdict of accidental death, they contended, was directed by the Nazis, who suppressed all testimony that might lead to the conclusion that saboteurs had succeeded in destroying a creation of the Third Reich.

No air traveler either before or since has ever flown in the luxury offered to passengers aboard the *Hindenburg*. Her accommodations were surpassed only by those of the great transatlantic liners of the same era. But how many seagoing voyagers were unable to enjoy their surroundings because of seasickness, a malady unheard of aboard the *Hindenburg?* Though it may be argued that the modern-day tycoon aboard his private DC-9 enjoys equal accommodations, is he able to stroll his promenade decks and stop to gaze at the unfolding panorama a few hundred feet below his open windows? The *Hindenburg* was an ocean liner without the seasickness, a Pullman train without the rattle, a private jet but more spacious and with a much nearer view of the wonders of the world. She was and remains unique in the annals of transportation.

•

BELOW LEFT: The dining room was sixteen feet wide and forty-six feet long with space for all fifty passengers at one sitting. The port side promenade with its large slanting windows is at the left. *Luftschiffbau Zeppelin photo, courtesy Douglas Robinson.* BELOW RIGHT: The lounge is in the foreground with the reading room beyond it. The grand piano, usually in the lounge, is not shown. The starboard promenade is at the right. *Courtesy San Diego Aero-Space Museum.*

At the end of World War II when Hitler and his thousand-year Reich had crumbled to ruin, some of these crewmen came forward with information they had not given at the American investigation. In 1962 in the book *Who Destroyed the Hindenburg?* A. A. Hoehling used this material in an effort to prove that the *Hindenburg* was indeed sabotaged. He even named his suspect, a young Zeppelin Company rigger, Eric Spehl.

Two crewmen claimed actually to have seen the flame burst into being, not at the top of the ship as Eckener postulated, but halfway up the side of the number 4 gasbag just where it was pierced by the axial gangway and less than fifty feet from their landing stations in the lower fin. Both men said they heard a pop and looked up to see a circle of bright light, three feet in diameter, like a flashlight being switched on or a flashbulb igniting.

A flashbulb is, in fact, exactly what Hoehling thinks it was—a flashbulb, flashlight battery, and a photographic timer—a simple time bomb easily capable of setting off seven million cubic feet of hydrogen. But why Eric Spehl? He was one of the *Hindenburg*'s three riggers and only riggers normally used the axial gangway where the bomb was set. He was an amateur photographer familiar with timers and flashbulbs and he had some anti-Nazi friends who might have convinced him that some of Hitler's prestige rode with the *Hindenburg*.

Would anyone risk his own life and those of shipmates as part of a symbolic gesture against Hitler? Hoehling suggests that Spehl set his bomb between the gasbags when he thought the *Hindenburg* was going to land, but they were delayed by the storm and he was unable to return to stop the timer. If it had gone off just thirty minutes later, the ship would have been on the ground with most of her passengers and crew debarked.

The evidence against Spehl is certainly circumstantial. No court of law would convict him on the basis of an interest in photography and some friends who didn't like Hitler. Spehl himself cannot answer the charges. His landing station was in the bow of the *Hindenburg*. As the flames spread and the stern crashed to the ground, the ship turned for an instant into a giant chimney with the searing heat and flame roaring up toward the bow, where Spehl and eleven other crewmen were clinging to the girders. One by one they lost their grip and fell into the blazing inferno below.

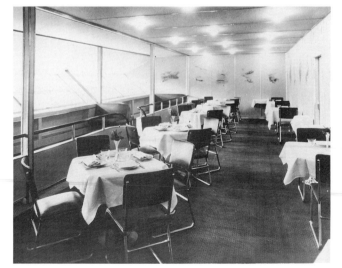

A crowd of passengers enjoys the lounge. The one thing Dr. Eckener had missed most aboard the *Graf Zeppelin* was music and singing after dinner. He had this Bluthner grand piano specially built out of aluminum. It weighed 112 pounds. *Luftschiffbau Zeppelin photo, courtesy Douglas Robinson.*

•

A typical dinner began with cream soup Hamilton, then grilled sole with parsley butter, and venison cutlets Beauval with Berny potatoes and mushrooms in cream sauce, accompanied by Rhine and Moselle wines, all topped off with a mixed cheese plate. The *Hindenburg* stocked 250 bottles of wine for each crossing. *Courtesy Zeppelin Museum, Friedrichshafen.*

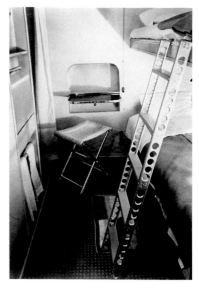

The big slanting windows on the two promenades were often open but were shielded from both wind and rain by the great bulk of the hull overhead. Even when the ship was flying at eighty miles per hour, only a slight breeze could be felt. *Courtesy Zeppelin Museum, Friedrichshafen.*

The twenty-five passenger cabins were on the upper deck between the public rooms. Each had an upper and a lower berth, a closet, a desk, and a wash basin with hot and cold water. *Courtesy San Diego Aero-Space Museum.*

10

WORLD WAR II

Now Lakehurst was dead. The ground crew had been transferred, the few remaining stood by in their barracks, idle and dejected; in hospitals round about lay the passengers and crew of the ship, Captain Lehmann had died of his burns and Captains Sammt and Pruss still hovered between life and death. Stretched out across the centre of the field lay the blackened framework of the Hindenburg, a disorderly tangle of girders, wires, and crumpled sheet metal. It appeared to me the hopeless end of a great dream, a kind of end of the world, a mournful symbol of what I, proscribed myself, expected to be the final outcome for Germany, for what went through my mind in Rosendahl's house was more than the offspring of a melancholy frame of mind caused by a pile of wreckage.[1]

Hugo Eckener

In spite of his forebodings about the future of his homeland, Eckener still had work to do. Even as the blackened wreckage of the *Hindenburg* was being shoveled into trucks and hauled away, her sister ship, the *LZ-130,* was nearing completion at Friedrichshafen. Was there still a chance to save the Zeppelin Company? Only, Eckener knew, if they could fly with helium. A year earlier he had tried to get U.S. helium for the *Hindenburg* but his request was turned down. Now the American press was pointing out that the use of helium would have prevented the catastrophe and the public was beginning to insist that the government share some of the precious gas. Perhaps there was still a chance.

Eckener went to Washington and testified before the Senate Military Affairs Committee, the first foreigner ever invited to do so. Within weeks, Congress passed a special amendment to the Helium Law allowing the export of ten million cubic feet for the specific purpose of filling and operating the Zeppelin Company's new ship.

OPPOSITE: Navy K-class blimps. The K-class blimp became the backbone of the navy's wartime airship fleet with 134 eventually being launched. The K-1, completed in 1932, was 320,000 cubic feet and ran on gaseous fuel like the *Graf Zeppelin.* The K-class ships went through a number of modifications but most were 252 feet long, with 416,000 cubic feet of helium, and a top speed of seventy-seven miles per hour. The last surviving K-ship, the *K-43,* made her final flight on March 19, 1959. *U.S. Navy photo, courtesy Roy Belotti, Garden Grove.*

Hindenburg wreckage at Lakehurst. The *Hindenburg* had flown over two hundred thousand miles in fifty-nine flights. She had crossed the ocean thirty-seven times in eight voyages to South America and eleven to North America. For more than a quarter of a century commercial Zeppelins had carried fifty thousand passengers without a fatality, for a safety record unmatched in transportation history. But all the statistics were swept away in thirty-two seconds at Lakehurst on May 6, 1937. Two years later the airplane carried its first paying passenger across the Atlantic. *Official U.S. Air Force photo.*

•

President Roosevelt signed the bill and, by the end of 1937, the first shipments began to leave the docks at Galveston bound for Germany.

Hitler's timetable, however, was not concerned with helium shipments. In March 1938 he sent his troops into Austria and all deliveries of strategic materials from America stopped. Once again Eckener sailed for New York, this time to see Interior Secretary Harold Ickes, who, as a member of the National Munitions Board, had ordered the shipments halted even though the other five members of the board, the secretaries of state, war, navy, treasury, and commerce were in favor of continuing them. Some years later Eckener recalled the conversation, one of his last in official Washington. He asked Ickes why he had stopped the scheduled deliveries.

"Because your Hitler is preparing for war."

"On this matter, Mr. Secretary, you are better informed than I am; but I hope it will not come to that."

"Hitler is going to make war."

"Very well, if that is really so, what does it have to do with withholding helium for Zeppelins?"

"With a helium-filled ship you could fly over London and drop bombs."

"No, we certainly could not."

"Why not?"

"We couldn't last a quarter-hour in the air without being shot down by enemy planes."

"But you could drop bombs on ships at sea."

"No, we couldn't possibly do that."

"Why not?"

"Even at night we couldn't possibly reach the sea without being shot down."

"But you could use the helium to inflate captive observation balloons at the Front."

"Mr. Secretary, if anybody today should really try to use captive balloons instead of using aeroplanes for observation, which would certainly be better, one would certainly not fill these captive balloons with helium, because the equipment needed is too heavy and because hydrogen would provide a greater lift."

"But you could do it."

I now became annoyed and said, "Yes, if we were German idiots, we could also try fighting with medieval swords instead of machine-guns, but you wouldn't expect us to be such fools."

To this Mr. Ickes merely repeated, "You could do it."

And I stood up, saying, "Mr. Secretary, I believe there would be no purpose in continuing the conversation," and I left.[2]

Eckener's mission was over. Without helium there was no hope of continuing to fly his Zeppelins in commercial service. Privately Eckener had to agree with Secretary Ickes when he said, "Your Hitler is going to make war."

The *LZ-130* was completed, filled with hydrogen, and test-flown in September 1938. She was christened the *Graf Zeppelin II* and, loaded with tons of electronic equipment, made two three-day flights in July and August 1939 off the coast of England analyzing British radar transmissions. But Hitler's plans did not include the use of airships, and in April 1940, both the old *Graf Zeppelin* and the new *Graf Zeppelin II* were taken apart. Their duralumin was melted down for use in fighter planes. At the same time in the United States, the dependable old *Los Angeles* was also being broken up for the same purpose.

Perhaps they met somewhere in the blazing skies over Europe—a Messerschmitt made from the *Graf Zeppelin* and a P-38 carrying a piece of the old *Los Angeles*—still part of a war they could not fight in a world that no longer needed them.

Hitler invaded Poland on September 1, 1939. Two days later, both Britain and France declared war on Germany and World War II was officially under way. But the last hope of commercial Zeppelin service had been ended nearly two years earlier, only indirectly by the threat of war. It was Germany's lack of helium that was the immediate cause of the Zeppelin's end. Yet there was one nation in the

A rare view inside one of the ship's four engine cars with a mechanic tending the thundering eleven-hundred-horsepower Daimler-Benz V-12 diesel. *Courtesy Cole Airship Collection, University of Oregon.*

•

The Zeppelin Company built a total of 119 airships. The *LZ-130* was the last. She was christened the *Graf Zeppelin II* on September 14, 1939, by Dr. Hugo Eckener. The same size as the *Hindenburg,* she was to have joined her in transatlantic service with a passenger area that had been enlarged to accommodate a hundred people. The Zeppelin Company had already begun work on another ship, the *LZ-131,* when the Nazis halted construction in mid-1939. The *Graf Zeppelin* and the new *Graf Zeppelin II* were dismantled in April 1940. *Courtesy Cole Airship Collection, University of Oregon.*

•

world that possessed both an experienced airship manufacturing and operational capacity plus abundant supplies of helium. What was happening in the United States?

After the loss of the *Macon* in 1935, the U.S. Navy's airshipmen found themselves with only five ships, the decommissioned *Los Angeles,* the tiny *ZMC-2 Metalclad,* and three blimps. With only one blimp on the West Coast, there seemed little reason to maintain the big base at Moffett Field. The navy turned it over to the Army Air Corps in exchange for three army bases. The West Coast personnel returned to Lakehurst, the navy's last remaining lighter-than-air facility.

Immediately after the crash of the *Macon,* an official committee of inquiry was appointed by President Roosevelt's Science Advisory Board to study all aspects of the U.S. lighter-than-air program. In the meantime Admiral King, the chief of the navy's Bureau of Aeronautics, requested that construction begin immediately on the three-million-cubic-foot rigid airship that had already been approved by the navy's General Board as a replacement for the obsolete *Los Angeles.* The secretary of the navy, Claude Swanson, did not share King's interest in airships and withheld action on his request until the president's committee completed its report.

The committee was headed by Dr. William F. Durand, professor emeritus of engineering at Stanford University. The other members of the blue-ribbon panel were Dr. Alfred V. De Forest, professor of metallurgy at MIT; Capt. William Hovgaard, a naval officer and the founder of the School of Marine Architecture at MIT; Dr. Stephen Timoshenko, professor of engineering at the University of Michigan; Dr. Robert A. Millikan, Nobel Prize–winning physicist at Cal Tech; Dr. Theodore von Karman, director of the Guggenheim Aeronautical Institute; Frank B. Jewett, president of Bell Telephone Laboratories; and Charles F. Kettering, president of General Motors Research Corporation.

Their investigation took nearly a year. On January 16, 1936 they handed in their report.

> [I]t is the unanimous opinion of the Committee that the best interests of the service in which airships give promise of useful and effective service, both commercial and naval, requires a continuing program of construction and use.
>
> And in pursuance of this opinion it is our recommendation that the Navy Department should continue with a positive carefully considered program of airship construction, including nonrigids and rigid ships of small or moderate size as service requirements might indicate, and extending to a ship or ships of large size, to the point, at least for the latter, of furnishing ground for definite conclusions regarding the capacity for useful naval service of constructions of this character.
>
> We further recommend most strongly that the first large airship built under such a program should, at least for a time, be considered not an adjunct to the Fleet but rather a flying laboratory or flying training ship, not only for extensive technical observations of the structure under operating conditions, but also for enlarging our knowledge regarding the best conditions of service for such vessels, and, as well, for giving opportunity for the training of officers and crew in the technique of handling airships under all conditions of weather and service.[3]

With the submission of the Durand Committee's favorable report, the Design Section of the Bureau of Aeronautics completed their plans for a new 9,500,000-cubic-foot Zeppelin capable of carrying nine Douglas SBD dive-bombers and, until

June of 1936 when he was transferred back to sea duty, Admiral King continued to insist upon the construction of the already approved replacement for the *Los Angeles.* But even after the Durand Committee's report, Secretary of the Navy Swanson persisted in rejecting King's requests.

Adm. Ernest King

[I]t seems to me that there is no necessity for any change in the wording of present existing and approved naval airship policy. The Department, through its inaction in carrying out the said approved policy, has placed itself in the unenviable position of not knowing its own mind, or else being unwilling to accept its responsibilities with regard to lighter-than-air. It should be one thing or the other.[4]

Rear Adm. Arthur B. Cook, King's successor as chief of the Bureau of Aeronautics, continued to push for construction of a rigid airship, and in 1937 the navy's General Board renewed its request for a medium-size rigid training ship to replace the *Los Angeles.* Secretary Swanson still opposed any further expenditures for rigid airships, and it soon became clear that President Roosevelt supported his secretary's position. After two more years of argument, the navy gave up.

With President Roosevelt's final rejection of new rigid construction and the dismantling of the *Los Angeles* and both *Graf Zeppelin*s at the beginning of the war, the history of the rigid airship came to an end. One hundred and sixty-five rigids had been built since Count Zeppelin's *LZ-1* and most had flown. France built one, the United States completed three, England built seventeen, while Germany launched 139. Then, in less than forty years, it was all over. The nonrigid airship, however, had a bit farther to go.

The U.S. Navy's first nonrigid had been built by the Connecticut Aircraft Company. Work began in 1915 and the blimp, designated the *A-1,* was completed two years later. She was shipped to Pensacola, Florida, and inflated, but she proved to be too heavy, even with one of her two engines removed. She made three flights and was dismantled. Her sorry performance came as no surprise to Comdr. F. R. McCrary, who had observed the *A-1*'s construction for the Navy Department. He was not overly impressed by the Connecticut Aircraft Company.

Comdr. F. R. McCrary

It could hardly be called an aircraft company. It consisted of a New Haven Railroad lawyer as financial backer; an ex-Amusement Park Concession operator as manager; an Austrian who claimed to have piloted a dirigible and two German mechanics who claimed to have been members of the crew of a Zeppelin. The "plant" was a six-by-eight office . . . and a rented boat-shed.[5]

Meanwhile, as U.S. relations with Germany deteriorated and it began to look as if we would be drawn into World War I, the secretary of the navy ordered sixteen nonrigids of a new design based largely on the British SS blimp. Nine of these new B-class ships were to be built by Goodyear, five by Goodrich, and two by the Connecticut Aircraft Company. The Curtiss Aeroplane Company was to supply the cars and engines.

Because of the urgent military situation and the experimental nature of the design, all the contractors were to exchange technical information and assistance. Goodrich brought Henri Julliot to Akron from the Lebaudy Company in Paris to act

The *DN-1,* also known as the *A-1,* was the U.S. Navy's first blimp. Ordered in June 1915 and delivered in April 1917, she was 175 feet long with 150,000 cubic feet of gas. Her envelope was built in New Haven by the Connecticut Aircraft Company, while her car was built in Boston. She was too heavy to fly, and even after one of her engines was removed she did not fly well. She was damaged on her third flight at Pensacola and was dismantled. *Courtesy San Diego Aero-Space Museum.*

The only U.S. naval airshipmen to see action during World War I were in a group headed by Comdr. Lewis H. Maxfield that took over the French naval airship station at Paimboeuf on the Bay of Biscay. They carried out patrol and reconnaissance missions in two French airships, an Astra-Torres and a Zodiac Vedette. U.S. troops were in the process of taking over three more French airship stations when the war ended. *Official U.S. Navy photo.*

•

as a consultant. With his help the first B-class ships were in the air by July 1917, five months after the contract was awarded.

When the United States entered the war, a larger airship was needed and the C-class was designed by Comdr. J. C. Hunsaker of the Bureau of Aeronautics. In 1918 contracts were placed with Goodyear and Goodrich for thirty ships, but with the war's end the order was cut to ten. The first of the series were completed in September 1918 and they were flown by both the army and the navy. They were good ships, the most famous being the navy's C-5, which almost flew across the Atlantic to Europe.

Though the army was given the postwar responsibility for nonrigid and semirigid development, the navy continued to experiment with blimps, working through the alphabet up to the J-class of ships by the middle of the 1930s.

The army abandoned their lighter-than-air program in 1937, just after the crash of the *Hindenburg*. In slightly less than twenty years they had flown forty airships. They bequeathed their last two blimps, the *TC-13* and *TC-14*, to the tiny naval airship organization at Lakehurst. With no hope of obtaining new rigids, the navy was left with only four ships, and three of these, the metal *ZMC-2*, the old *J-4*, and a recently purchased Goodyear advertising blimp, the *G-1*, were all too small for sea duty. The navy's single large blimp, the 320,000-cubic-foot *K-1*, was already five years old, and the sudden addition of the two army ships, both bigger and newer than any of the navy's, was certainly welcome.

A brand-new blimp, the four-hundred-thousand-cubic-foot *K-2*, was delivered to Lakehurst at the end of 1938 and, as Europe slipped once again into war, Congress belatedly began to augment the lighter-than-air squadron. On October 19, 1940, the navy signed a million-dollar contract with Goodyear for four more K-class ships, three of which were completed before the United States entered the war.

On December 7, 1941, the navy had ten blimps in operation, but only six of them, the two old army TC-ships and the *K-2, K-3, K-4,* and *K-5,* were large enough for antisubmarine duty. Congress quickly increased the navy's authorized blimp strength to two hundred, but it was an empty gesture. It would take many months to build new ships, and the enemy's submarine offensive against U.S. coastal shipping had already begun. The SS *Medio* was torpedoed by a Japanese sub off Eureka, California, on December 20, 1941, and three days later a sub surfaced a few miles north of Santa Barbara and shelled the highway and oil derricks with her deck gun. Along the Atlantic coast, German U-boats began to sink Allied ships within sight of the shore and crowds of spectators gathered on the beaches from Nantucket to Miami to watch their merchant ships go down.

The British had already proved the blimp's effectiveness against submarines in World War I, but now that war had come again, the navy simply did not have enough airships to do the job. In 1942, 454 merchant ships were sunk by German U-boats off the Atlantic coast. Allied ships were being sunk faster than they could be built but by the end of the year only thirteen blimps were in operation to protect them.

Early in 1942 the navy's airship organization was divided into two squadrons. One remained at Lakehurst with the four K-ships while the other was sent to Moffett Field in California with the two old TC-blimps and two small L-class training ships.

As the war progressed and more blimps were delivered, Fleet Airship Wing One headquartered at Lakehurst was expanded to four squadrons with bases at South Weymouth, Massachusetts; Lakehurst; Weeksville, North Carolina; and Glynco, Georgia. Each squadron had eight K-class blimps, giving the Airship Wing a total of thirty-two ships with which to patrol the Atlantic coastline.

Fleet Airship Wing Two was formed at Richmond, Florida, to cover the Caribbean with a total of twenty-three ships. Fifteen were stationed at wing headquarters in Richmond, four flew out of Houma, Louisiana, and four more were based at Vernam Field, Jamaica.

With the arrival of the two old TC-ships in California, Moffett Field was turned back over to the navy as the headquarters of Fleet Airship Wing Three, which eventually grew to thirty-two blimps in three squadrons stationed at Tillamook, Oregon; Moffett Field; and Santa Ana, California.

By 1943, U.S. blimps were on their way to Brazil. The *K-84* arrived at Fortaleza north of Recife on September 27, and soon the sixteen ships of Fleet Airship Wing Four were patrolling the South Atlantic from half a dozen bases along the three-thousand-mile Brazilian coastline. The only real airship base available to the wing was the one at Santa Cruz near Rio de Janeiro. It had been completed in 1936 and used that year by both the *Hindenburg* and *Graf Zeppelin,* but after the crash of the *Hindenburg* in 1937, the facility stood empty for six years until the arrival of the U.S. Navy blimps.

The last wing, Fleet Airship Wing Five, was formed to cover the southern Caribbean from Puerto Rico to French Guiana. It consisted of one squadron of eight ships stationed at Trinidad just off the coast of Venezuela.

In 1944 the six ships of blimp Squadron 14 became the first nonrigid dirigibles ever to cross the Atlantic. Four ships set out from South Weymouth, Massachusetts, on May 29, 1944, and flew to Newfoundland. From there they crossed the Atlantic to the Azores and then continued on to their new base at Port Lyautey in French Morocco on the north coast of Africa. They had covered 3,145 miles in fifty-eight hours flying time.

Eleven months after the arrival of the first group, a second flight of blimps left

In World War II, U.S. Navy blimps escorted eighty-nine thousand ships without losing any of them to enemy submarines. They flew 170,000 hours over the Pacific and 380,000 over the Atlantic. On convoy duty they saved considerable time at sea by delivering routing orders to each ship in-dividually while the convoy continued steaming under radio silence. *U.S. Navy photo, courtesy Roy Belotti, Garden Grove.*

•

Weeksville, North Carolina, headed for Morocco. With stops at Bermuda and the Azores, they successfully covered the 3,532 miles in sixty-two hours flying time. In addition to their headquarters at Port Lyautey, the airshipmen of Squadron 14 also maintained bases on the islands of Malta and Sardinia, at the *Dixmude's*, old base near Toulon, at Bizerta, Pisa, Venice, and Rome.

A second overseas squadron was preparing for the flight to England when the Germans surrendered. In the four years of war, U.S. Navy blimps made more than fifty thousand patrols over the North and South Atlantic, the Pacific, and the Mediterranean, and in all that time, only one blimp was lost to enemy action.

That loss occurred just before midnight on July 18, 1943. The *K-74*, under the command of Lt. Nelson Grills, was cruising thirty miles off the Florida Keys halfway between Florida and Cuba when she picked up a blip on her radar screen. It was a weak, intermittent contact, eight miles distant and slightly to starboard. As they bore down on the contact, the blip on the radar screen grew stronger. Lieutenant Grills ordered his men to battle stations. They were a new crew flying together for the first time and this was developing into more than they had dared hope for.

Official U.S. Navy Report

Forward lookout said "there's a sub out there" when he saw it clearly silhouetted in moonlight. Several saw sub at about same time. Others in back of car at first would hardly believe that it was a sub. There was no question in mind of anyone who saw sub as to what it was.[6]

Now that they knew what it was, the question immediately arose as to whose it was. The sub continued straight on her course apparently unaware of their presence. The Key West naval base was nearby and there was the possibility that this was an American boat. Lieutenant Grills turned the *K-74* in a tight circle to put the sub between the blimp and the full moon. The sub was nearly two miles away and all eyes strained to identify her as she glided silently through the thin path of shimmering moonlight.

Official U.S. Navy Report
> Everyone seemed agreed that there was a deck gun, long and low, aft and separated from the conning tower. They did not recall seeing any forward gun, although German 240, 517 and 740 ton subs all show a forward gun, but did believe that there was a forward gun. The 517 ton shows its after gun on a platform in the conning tower, and the 740 ton is the only German sub which shows the after gun separated from the conning tower. Several of the crew agreed that there was the typical break and railing characteristic of German subs.[7]

They were right. They had intercepted the German raider *U-134,* running on the surface to recharge her batteries. As the *K-74* made another turn the U-boat continued blissfully on her way with no sign of having seen the big blimp circling in the bright moonlight less than two miles off her port beam. Now Lieutenant Grills was faced with an important decision. His slow-moving ship was no match for a surfaced sub, and standard procedure required that he call for assistance as soon as he made contact with the enemy, but he knew that a group of Allied merchantmen had already entered the Northeast Providence Channel, headed right for the *U-134.* Rather than risk losing the sub while he waited for help, Lieutenant Grills decided to attack.

Bringing his ship down to 250 feet and up to her top speed of sixty-five miles per hour, Grills bore down on the U-boat. He had closed to within two hundred yards before the Germans saw him and opened fire. Directly over the sub, Grills ordered bombs away and his bombardier opened the releases on the ship's two depth bombs—he opened them halfway from the safety position and in the excitement, failed to turn them the rest of the way. The bombs did not release. Then the sub's guns scored a hit.

The crippled blimp rose steeply into the air as fire broke out in her starboard engine. As the sub turned sharply and crash-dived, the *K-74* settled slowly into the sea with helium hissing from dozens of holes in her envelope. She hit the water just thirteen minutes after the first radar contact. A crewman threw out the life raft but forgot to hold onto the line and the raft drifted away into the darkness. The gasbag remained afloat all through the night and the ten crewmen took turns clinging to the handrail or swimming along behind the slowly drifting ship.

At 8:30 in the morning they were spotted by a search plane and just after that, the luckless bombardier fell behind the rest of the swimmers. Then a shark fin appeared and he was gone. Half an hour later the *K-74* sank, her depth charges exploding under water as she went down. Her nine survivors were picked up by a destroyer.

Lieutenant Grills' court-martial was abandoned when his wing commander was reminded that only two weeks earlier he had ordered his men to attack enemy submarines more aggressively.

Another blimp, the training ship *L-8,* was also lost during the war, but in quite a different manner. The date was August 16, 1942, when the *L-8* returned from a mission without her crew.

The *L-8* took off at 6:00 A.M. from San Francisco's Treasure Island Naval Air Station on a routine flight. She was a small ship and carried only two men. Her pilot was twenty-seven-year-old Lt. Ernest DeWitte Cody. The copilot was thirty-eight-year-old Ens. Charles E. Adams. Both men were experienced airshipmen. Cody had graduated from Annapolis in the class of 1938 while Adams had put in twenty years of service as an enlisted man before receiving his commission. This was his first flight as an officer.

At 7:50 the Treasure Island control tower received a radio message from Lieutenant Cody. They had spotted a large oil slick five miles off the Farallon Islands and were going down to investigate. The men aboard two nearby fishing boats hurriedly pulled in their nets and withdrew to a safe distance when they saw the *L-8* descend to three hundred feet and circle the oil slick. But instead of dropping a depth charge, the blimp suddenly soared up into the cloud cover and disappeared from view. At 8:05 A.M. just fifteen minutes after Cody's message, the Treasure Island tower tried to call him again. They received no answer.

Two hours later the *L-8* drifted in from the sea near Fort Funston. Some surf fishermen tried to grab her drag lines but she was blown out of their reach. They could see that the cabin door was open and the gondola was empty.

As a sea and air search was launched for the missing men, the *L-8* continued her erratic course inland, dropped an unexploded depth bomb on the Olympic golf course, and finally came to rest on top of two cars in the middle of a residential street in Daly City, just south of San Francisco.

The first police officers to arrive on the scene peeked cautiously in the open door. The radio was still on and all the ship's equipment was in place. Only the two men and the life jackets they were required to wear when over water were missing.

The fishermen who had watched the blimp circling over the oil slick reported that they had not seen anyone fall overboard, and an intensive search off the Farallon Islands turned up nothing. Lieutenant Cody and Ensign Adams were never seen again.

With these few exceptions the navy's blimps gave remarkable service throughout the war. By the time Japan surrendered in 1945, 168 blimps had been launched. The number of naval airshipmen had grown from 430 in 1941 to 12,500 in 1945. They performed a wide variety of tasks from minesweeping in the Mediterranean to plucking downed fliers out of tiny inaccessible clearings in the Brazilian jungle. The

The army's airship program began in 1919. They flew nearly forty nonrigids and semirigids and still had four ships in service when they closed down operations on June 30, 1937. Their two newest blimps, the *TC-13* shown here and the *TC-14,* were turned over to the navy. Both were 233 feet long with 360,000 cubic feet of gas. They carried a crew of eight and were powered by two 325-horsepower Pratt & Whitney engines. The navy kept both in service until 1943. *Official U.S. Air Force photo.*

blimp's record in convoy duty first established by the British back in World War I remained intact. U.S. navy dirigibles escorted eighty-nine thousand ships without losing a single one. They spent more than half a million hours in the air and lost only one ship, the *K-74,* to enemy action.

One might imagine that the airship had finally proved her worth to the navy, but such was not the case. Many of the officers who had previously objected to the rigid airship still did not care for the blimp. Airplanes sank submarines, they pointed out, but in four years of war not a single U-boat kill could be definitely claimed by a blimp.

The problem was that all through the first year of the war, when 454 merchant ships were being sent to the bottom off the Atlantic coast, there were less than a dozen blimps in operation. By the end of 1943 when fifty-three airships had been launched, the number of ship sinkings off the coast had declined dramatically to sixty-five. At the end of 1944 there were sixty-eight blimps in the air off the coast, but the U-boats could sink only eight ships.

Though the increase in airships coincided with the decline in coastal U-boat activity, the reason for that decline was primarily due to destroyers and sub-chasers working with airplanes in hunter-killer groups. As had been the case with the German Zeppelin in World War I, the blimps were simply not ready when the war started. There weren't nearly enough of them to do the job, and by the time they were ready it was too late. The airplane, however, was even less prepared for its new role in antisubmarine warfare than the blimps. Until 1943, less than half the planes available to the Anti-Submarine Army Air Command and the navy's Gulf and Eastern Sea Frontiers were capable of flying far enough out to sea to reach the area where the U-boats were working. And, according to the navy, most army fliers were such poor navigators that they couldn't find the ships they were supposed to protect even if they had been able to fly out to where they were.

LEFT: The *L-8* came to rest in the middle of a residential street in Daly City. The door of the control car was latched open and the control car was empty. The first policemen and firemen on the scene, believing that the missing pilots must be up inside the gasbag, cut it open, thus deflating the ship. *Courtesy Judge Advocate General, United States Navy.* RIGHT: The *L-8* was photographed by a passerby as she drifted in over San Francisco from the sea. With no one aboard to adjust the air pressure in the ballonet, the contracting helium had caused the gasbag to buckle under the weight of the control car. *Courtesy Judge Advocate General, United States Navy.*

•

It is a commonly held belief that the crash of the *Hindenburg* signaled the end of the airship's useful employment. In fact, more dirigibles were in the air at the end of World War II than at any other time in history. This photograph of a flotilla of U.S. Navy L-class blimps in formation over Moffet Field was taken on December 2, 1943. These small L-class ships were modeled on Goodyear's prewar advertising blimps. They were used primarily for training and short-range patrols, usually flying with a crew of two. Of the 168 blimps launched by the U.S. Navy during the war, close to 120 were still in service at the war's end. *Official U.S. Navy photo courtesy Naval Air Station, Moffett Field, California.*

•

Naval historian Samuel Eliot Morison, in his fifteen-volume work *History of United States Naval Operations in World War II,* echoes the sentiment of many naval officers when he writes:

> An important if relatively ineffective component of the naval air arm was the lighter-than-air dirigible, the so-called blimp. Most naval officers, in view of the rapid development of planes, were very skeptical of these handsome sausage-shaped airships. But they had advocates who had been trained in their operation; the company that manufactured them was influential; and at a time when the U-boats looked like winners the Navy dared reject nothing that might contribute to eventual victory.[8]

There were, of course, dissenters from this widely held opinion and, as had been the case with rigid airships, they were usually the men who worked most closely with the dirigibles. Rear Adm. J. L. Kauffman, the commander of the Gulf Sea Frontier, noted in a letter to Admiral King that he liked the blimps because they could stay in the air for long periods of time and operate at night and in bad weather, qualities that his airplanes at that time did not possess.

Some officers complained that the big silver blimp hovering over a convoy was visible to U-boats at a great distance and could actually give the convoy's position away to a submarine that otherwise might not have seen it. This fear was not shared by the merchant seamen, however, and those who manned the freighters bringing bauxite up from the mines in Dutch and British Guiana on the northeast coast of South America threatened to mutiny until they were given blimp protection.

Under the command of Rear Adm. Charles E. Rosendahl, the U.S. Navy's blimp fleet maintained an 87 percent operational readiness throughout the war, a far better record than any other type of aircraft.

The workhorse of the blimp fleet was the K-class airship. Of the 168 blimps launched, 134 were K-ships. Most were 252 feet long with 416,000 cubic feet of gas. Two 550-horsepower Pratt & Whitney Wasp radial engines drove them at a top speed of seventy-seven miles per hour with a crew of eight to ten men aboard.

A larger M-class of blimps was also built during the war, the first being launched by Goodyear in 1942. At 293 feet in length with 640,000 cubic feet of gas, they had 50 percent more lifting power than the K-ships and were designed to escort convoys all the way across the Atlantic. Only four M-ships were built.

One might think that the reliability, all-weather capability, and safety record of the navy's wartime blimps would at last assure them a permanent place in the postwar fleet, but in fact, by June 1950 when the Korean War broke out, the navy had dismantled or sold almost all of them. They were forced to repurchase a dozen blimps that had been sold to an advertising firm.

As the cold war began to heat up, the need for larger airships was recognized, for in addition to their antisubmarine patrols, the blimps also took on the task of guarding the North American continent from surprise attack by air. Big new dirigibles were designed to carry aloft the complex machines that scanned far beyond the horizon in search of hostile jets and missiles.

The first in this new series of nonrigids was the *ZPG-1*, delivered to Lakehurst on June 17, 1952. Nearly a hundred feet longer with more than twice the gas capacity of the K-ships, the ZPG-class was 343 feet long and held nearly a million cubic feet of helium.

In addition to their early-warning radar patrols off the coast, a number of *ZPG-2* ships from Lakehurst and South Weymouth, Massachusetts, undertook a test of the blimp's all-weather flying ability. An early-warning position two hundred miles out at sea off New York City was selected, and for ten freezing days and stormy nights in January 1957, it was constantly maintained by one or more

The first ZPG-class blimp was delivered to the Navy on June 17, 1952, and seventeen ZPG-2W ships were built. They were 343 feet long, with 975,000 cubic feet of helium and a top speed of eighty miles per hour. With three onboard radar systems and a large radar dome beneath the gondola, they served as offshore electronic listening posts guarding the country from surprise nuclear attack. *Photo by the author.*

•

After World War II the navy sold a number of blimps as surplus to private individuals. This ship over Seattle, Washington, was one of four privately owned blimps on the Pacific Coast. She was purchased from the navy for thirty thousand dollars, but it cost twenty thousand dollars to fill her with helium. She carried advertising for Wonder Bread, Metro-Goldwyn-Mayer, and Mobil Oil. One advertising company eventually acquired eleven blimps on the East and West coasts. After four years, this ship was repurchased by the navy for use as a training ship during the Korean War. *Courtesy Wells McCurdy, Seattle.*

•

The first ZPG-3W, shown here beside a modified K-ship, was launched by Goodyear on June 19, 1958. With a length of 403 feet and 1,500,000 cubic feet of helium, these were the largest and the last of the navy's blimps. Each carried four radar antennas including one inside the gasbag. Four of these ships, the largest nonrigids ever built, were completed before the navy ended airship operations in 1961. Goodyear recently proposed a thirty-million-dollar government program to build a new ship of this design as the first step in restarting U.S. airship operations. *Official U.S. Navy photo.*

•

dirigibles. Partway through the test, the worst winter storm in seventy-five years struck the Northeast in all its icy fury. For three days every commercial aircraft in New England was grounded, but the navy blimps continued to maintain their station off the coast.

Another impressive airship record was also set in 1957. On March 4, the *ZPG-2* blimp *Snowbird,* piloted by navy commander Jack R. Hunt, took off with a crew of thirteen from South Weymouth and flew nonstop across the Atlantic to Portugal. Then without refueling, she turned south and flew along the coast of Africa before returning across the Atlantic to Key West, Florida. She was in the air for eleven days and covered 9,448 miles without refueling, thus breaking the old nonstop distance record of 6,980 miles set by the *Graf Zeppelin* on the Berlin-to-Tokyo leg of her round-the-world flight back in 1929. On landing in Key West, Commander Hunt received the Distinguished Flying Cross from Adm. William F. "Bull" Halsey.

In 1958 the navy ordered a series of even larger blimps. These ships, designated *ZPG-3W,* were the largest nonrigids ever built. They were 403 feet long with a 1,500,000-cubic-foot gasbag that gave them a useful lift of more than sixteen tons. Two 1,525-horsepower Wright Cyclone radial engines produced a top speed of over eighty miles per hour. Each was manned by a crew of twenty-one and carried four radar scanners. At a cost of twelve million dollars apiece, four *ZPG-3W* blimps were ordered from Goodyear by the navy. The last of them was completed in 1960, the same year one of the four crashed.

It was the afternoon of July 6, 1960. A *ZPG-3W* had been ordered out that morning from Lakehurst to join an extensive search for two sailboats that were overdue on their return from the recent Newport, Rhode Island, to Bermuda yacht race. The *ZPG-3W* was cruising fifteen miles off the New Jersey coast at an altitude of five hundred feet when, according to Petty Officer Antonio Contreras, "there was a loud burst like a blow-out, and the ship nosed down at a 45-degree angle."[9] Contreras was on the lower deck of the two-story gondola and was thrown to the floor as the ship plunged into the sea. He slid forward across the deck into the next compartment, regained his footing and climbed through an open window into the water.

Petty Officer Joseph Culligan was asleep at the time of the crash and awoke to find his compartment rapidly filling with water. "I stood up, picked up a piece of jagged metal, cut a hole in the fabric of the balloon and got out into the water."[10]

Culligan, Contreras, and two others were rescued almost immediately by a nearby fishing boat—the only survivors from the crew of twenty-one men aboard the blimp.

The *ZPG-3W* sank in one hundred feet of water eight miles southeast of Barnegat Inlet after being towed part of the way toward shore by a Coast Guard cutter. Most of the bodies of the seventeen missing men were recovered from the sunken wreck by navy divers. The two yachts for which they had been searching sailed safely into port soon afterward, unaware that they had been reported lost.

The *ZPG-3W* came to rest at the bottom of the sea less than ten miles from the *Akron's* watery grave. A subsequent investigation determined that the loss of the blimp was due to pilot error.

The wreck of the *ZPG-3W* was notable because it was the last. On July 11, 1961, the navy announced that its entire lighter-than-air program would be officially ended by November 30 of that year. There were thirteen navy blimps still in operation, twelve at Lakehurst and one stationed at South Weymouth. With their deflation, forty years of effort, both heroic and heartbreaking, on the part of thousands of naval airshipmen came finally to an end.

Now most of the airships left in the world belonged to Goodyear. The Goodyear Tire and Rubber Company had first entered aeronautics in 1911 when they purchased a British machine for coating fabric with rubber to produce balloon cloth. Two young engineers, Ralph Upson and R. A. Preston, were hired to take charge of the new department and were almost immediately confronted with the job of producing the gasbag for Melvin Vaniman's ill-fated transatlantic airship, the first *Akron.*

In 1913 Upson and Preston took one of their balloons to Europe and won the premier event in international balloon racing, the James Gordon Bennett Trophy. By the end of World War I, Goodyear's balloon room employed more than two thousand workers and had completed nearly a thousand observation balloons and a hundred blimps.

With the war's end, the demand for military balloons suddenly fell to almost nothing, and in order to keep busy, Goodyear began to build and operate their own blimp fleet. An early ship was the tiny *Pony Blimp* completed in 1919 and flown from a hangar next to the Goodyear tire factory in Los Angeles. With a ninety-five-foot-long, thirty-five-thousand-cubic-foot gasbag, the *Pony Blimp* was able to carry a pilot and two passengers. In 1920 she was put into scheduled passenger service between Los Angeles and Catalina Island, twenty-two miles off the California coast.

Goodyear's fifty-one-thousand-cubic-foot *Pilgrim* was launched in 1925 with the title of "America's first air yacht." By 1930 the company had a fleet of six blimps in the air, the largest of which, the 184-foot-long, 180,000-cubic-foot *Defender,* could carry ten passengers. Flying from collapsible, truck-mounted mooring masts, Goodyear blimps operated in every part of the country, flew across the continent and even to Cuba. By the time World War II began and the Goodyear fleet was drafted, they had carried well over three hundred thousand passengers and, like their rigid counterparts flying in commercial service in Germany, without a single passenger fatality!

At the end of the war Goodyear resumed blimp operations with the *Mayflow-*

er. The only other privately owned airship was another advertising blimp in Germany.

The Zeppelin factory at Friedrichshafen had been used during the war for the manufacture of V-2 rocket components until it was destroyed by the Eighth Air Force in 1944. The rebuilt factory now makes trucks, tractors, generators, and heavy machinery.

Hugo Eckener survived the war and in 1947 flew to the United States, where he remained for seven months assisting Goodyear in the preparation of plans for a ten-million-cubic-foot airship. She was to be 950 feet long with a seven-thousand-mile range and a top speed of ninety miles per hour. She would be able to carry 112 passengers to Europe in deluxe accommodations for a fare of $415, or she could carry 232 Pullman passengers at $200 each.

Goodyear submitted the proposal to both government and industry but no one was interested. It was widely felt that the airplane had progressed too far for the airship to catch up. When it became apparent that there was no hope of restarting the Zeppelin enterprise, Eckener left the United States for the last time and returned to Germany.

In the final year of his life, even Hugo Eckener had to admit, "The Zeppelin has given way to the airplane; a good thing has been replaced by a better!"[11] On August 14, 1954, Dr. Hugo Eckener died quietly at his home in Friedrichshafen of a heart ailment. He was eighty-six years old. He was buried not far from the Zeppelin factory—the factory that now built trucks.

Was Eckener's final judgment correct? Are all future descendants of the once mighty Zeppelin to be relegated to the lowly task of carrying advertising slogans through the sky?

The airship taught man to fly. It pioneered his commercial air routes across the world's oceans, carried him into the unknown regions of the Arctic, and brought the first terror of falling bombs to his great cities. Yet neither government nor industry could find a place for the airship. After nearly two hundred years, was it finally over?

With the end of the Zeppelin Company, Goodyear was one of the last surviving organizations with practical airship experience. Although it had been forty years since they built the *Macon* and nearly fifteen years since their last big navy blimp, the Goodyear Aerospace Corporation still maintained a lighter-than-air group of about fifty engineers and designers under the direction of Fred Nebiker. He had noted a considerable increase in the number of airship inquiries in the last few years, but Goodyear's planning was now devoted almost exclusively to nonrigid rather than rigid designs.

Fred Nebiker

Remember, rigid construction was used in the old days because that was the state of the art, the only way to go.

Rigid internal framework was necessary to give the ship its shape and streamline it as much as possible for speed, perhaps 90 to 100 knots.

The envelope over the framework was merely rubberized cotton and served only to enclose the ship and its gas cells. It was not subject to pressurization. It couldn't take strain.

But such rigidity kept airships like the Macon and the Akron from flexing under the

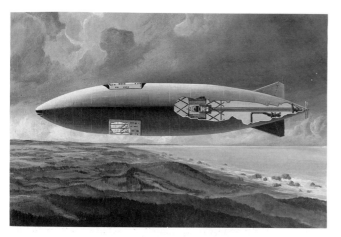

changing pressures of flight and atmosphere whereas nonrigid construction would have permitted the added safety factor of flexibility.

Things are different today. We have fibrous materials with twice the tensile strength of steel at less than one quarter of its weight.

These should permit us to eliminate rigid construction and give us safe and forgiving envelopes.[12]

Others had also been giving serious thought to the revival of the airship. A group of students at Boston University under the direction of Francis Morse, associate professor of aerospace engineering, drew up a proposal for a nuclear-powered rigid in 1964.

At 980 feet in length with a gas capacity of 12,500,000 cubic feet, the Boston University proposal was only slightly larger than the ship envisioned by Hugo Eckener and Goodyear back in 1947. Though the design closely followed the basic Zeppelin concept, the traditional construction materials were replaced by the newest developments in space age technology: high-strength aluminum alloys for the hull girders and DuPont's new synthetic fabric, Kevlar, for the outer cover and gas cells.

The ship would carry four hundred first-class passengers with more space and luxury than even those aboard the *Hindenburg* enjoyed. There would be three decks inside the hull with promenades wider than those aboard the *Queen Elizabeth,* a dining room seating two hundred, a movie theater, and, at the top of the ship, accessible by a fifteen-story elevator, would be a grand ballroom roofed over with Plexiglas, giving travelers a view of the star-filled sky at night. An eighteen-place airplane would be carried aboard to embark and disembark passengers from intermediate stops.

By far the most interesting feature of the Boston University proposal, however, was its use of a nuclear engine—one that had already been developed by the U.S. government. In 1961 the Atomic Energy Commission (AEC) abandoned the Aircraft Nuclear Propulsion program after spending more than a billion dollars in an attempt to develop an atomic airplane engine. Two nuclear power plants had actually been completed, one by Pratt & Whitney and the other by General Electric. Prototypes were designed, built, and tested, the effects of radiation on aircraft materials and instruments were examined, and the reactor-powered gas turbines were run for more than a hundred hours. Only one problem remained to be solved.

A jet airliner requires one horsepower for every eight pounds of weight. Since a *DC-8* weighs nearly 150 tons, it needs forty thousand horsepower to get itself off

Engineering students at Boston University designed a rigid airship 980 feet long and 172 feet in diameter with a gas capacity of 12,500,000 cubic feet. With a total lift of 380 tons and a disposable lift of 150 tons, it would be able to carry a 90-ton payload of passengers and cargo. A four-thousand-horsepower nuclear-powered gas turbine would drive two slow-turning, contrarotating sixty-foot propellers at the stern. Two additional one-thousand-horsepower turbofan engines could be run on either nuclear or conventional fuel in case of a reactor shutdown. With a top speed of ninety-five miles per hour, the ship would carry four hundred first-class passengers across the Atlantic in thirty-five to forty hours.

•

LEFT: Boston University Nuclear Airship, *courtesy National Oceanic and Atmospheric Administration.* RIGHT: *Boston University design courtesy Professor Francis Morse.*

•

Does the airship have a future? The navy, NASA, the World Bank, and Shell Oil all conducted studies in an attempt to answer that question. The National Oceanic and Atmospheric Administration produced this drawing depicting some potential airship applications. The helium horse is a cargo ship capable of carrying immense loads. *Courtesy J. Gordon Vaeth, National Oceanic and Atmospheric Administration.*

the ground. For an atomic engine with this much power, the amount of lead and water shielding required to protect the plane's passengers from a fatal dose of radiation would weigh 125 tons. There was no way the plane could lift its engine shielding into the air. This was the one problem the AEC's engineers could not overcome and this was what finished the Aircraft Nuclear Propulsion project.

If they had examined the airship, however, they would have found that it requires far less power than the airplane. It is lifted into the air by its helium, not by its engines, and instead of the big jet's one horsepower for every eight pounds of weight, the airship can drive 120 pounds with each single horsepower.

The student engineers at Boston University determined that their ship needed only six thousand horsepower to drive it at a top speed of 103 miles per hour, and an atomic engine of that size would weigh only sixty tons including reactor, turbines, and shielding. With a disposable lift of 150 tons, their ship could easily carry a sixty-ton engine and still have ninety tons left over for payload. When this was compared with the *Hindenburg's* twenty-ton payload, it was easy to see how Boston University's design could carry four times as many passengers as the biggest German Zeppelin.

The primary advantage of the atomic engine is that it requires almost no fuel. This would be a tremendous advantage in lighter-than-air flight. It would eliminate the immense weight of gasoline as well as the entire water recovery system that was used to compensate for the loss of the fuel's weight as it was consumed. For example, the *Hindenburg's* four Daimler-Benz diesels weighed a total of only nine tons but they required sixty-seven tons of fuel and oil to fly eighty-four hundred miles. The sixty-ton atomic engine could fly that distance and farther on only a few pounds of fuel.

In addition to the insurmountable weight problem of its nuclear airplane engine, the AEC was also unable to overcome the danger of a plane crash that would spread atomic contamination all over the crash site. This problem, too, was solved by the use of an airship, for at her lower speed, there was much less chance of a shattering crash. There was also, inside the dirigible's huge hull, plenty of room for a complete spring-loaded, shock-absorbing mounting that would keep the reactor shell intact through even the most violent crash.

This hybrid, airplane-airship design is the work of a group of aerospace engineers at Megalifter Company in Goleta, California. The first twenty feet of the fuselage is from a Lockheed C-5A cargo plane. The hull is filled with seven million cubic feet of helium, which is used to offset part of the ship's weight at takeoff. In flight, the lift will come primarily from the wings and fuselage, which is in the shape of an immense lifting body. With a length of 650 feet, the hull is only slightly shorter than the *Los Angeles*. The ship could carry a five-hundred-ton payload, take off from short runways at 70 miles per hour, and cruise at 205 miles per hour. *Courtesy John Handloser, Megalifter Company.*

•

Like the lair of some great prehistoric beast, long extinct, airship hangars still dot the landscape, now the homes of insectlike helicopters and other lesser creatures. At Lakehurst, Tustin, Akron, Toulon, Tillamook, Cardington, Karachi, Weeksville, and, as shown in this photo, at Santa Ana, California, they wait—reminders of something quite extraordinary, not so very long ago. *Photo by the author.*

In the end, however, Boston University's atomic airship met the same fate as the Eckener-Goodyear proposal. It would cost too much and perform too few tasks that could not be carried out nearly as well by airplanes.

The story of the airship has been one of time and opportunity missed. In World War I the Zeppelin was not sufficiently developed to achieve the goals set for it, and, though it was able to outperform the airplane for two full years, it could not deliver the destructive power that would have indelibly demonstrated its superiority. By the time the airship was ready, so was the airplane.

In the postwar race for commercial passenger traffic, the airship's unique transoceanic capabilities were more than offset by the difficulty in obtaining financing. The problem, as aviation writer Charles G. Grey noted, was that "airplanes breed like rabbits, airships like elephants."[13] In the twenty years between the world wars when the dirigible could have monopolized transoceanic air service, only four large commercial ships were built and the two that flew safely, the *Graf Zeppelin* and the *R.100,* could not begin to offset the disastrous image created in the public's mind by the destruction of the other two, the *R.101* and the *Hindenburg.*

In World War II the story was the same. By the time enough blimps were launched to deal with the submarine threat, that threat was over. And the navy with its greater investment in airplanes found other ways to do the airship's job.

The big jet airliner has now usurped the last of the airship's great advantages over heavier-than-air craft—its ability to fly the world's oceans carrying heavy loads.

With the official end of the U.S. Navy's blimp program on November 30, 1961, it was obvious that something both drastic and unexpected would be required if the airship was to make a comeback. And that is exactly what was about to happen.

At the mercy of the winds, the free balloon has had only limited military and commercial use. But the stationary balloon—moored to one spot by a long rope or tether—has been of considerable value over the years as an aerial observation platform. Used by both sides with varying success in the American Civil War, the tethered balloon then began to lose favor, for while there is little sense of motion in a free balloon, once it is tied to the ground it is shaken by every gust. When the wind rises to twenty miles per hour, a tethered spherical balloon becomes almost useless as an observation post. This kite balloon designed for the Prussian Airship Battalion in 1892 by Maj. August von Parseval represented a major improvement. With its elongated bag and large inflated tail fin, it did not rotate like a spherical balloon and was stable in winds of up to thirty miles per hour. The addition of horse-drawn hydrogen-generating equipment made a balloon battalion as mobile as the heavy artillery for which it scouted. The Parseval design was adopted by virtually every European army and saw action in the Balkans, in Africa, and at Port Arthur. But by 1912 the development of the airplane encouraged the French to disband their balloon forces. At the outbreak of World War I they were hurriedly reestablished with more streamlined type developed by Capt. Albert Caquot. Tethered observation balloons proved ideal for the static trench warfare that developed along the western front. With telephones aloft and motorized winches to get them quickly above the range of enemy guns, the balloons were very effective. They also made tempting targets for enemy planes. Pilots like Frank Luke specialized in balloon busting. They were not sitting ducks, however. Balloon battalions included their own antiaircraft guns and attacking airmen found heavy opposition. Each balloon pilot and observer had a parachute and was expected to bail out when attacked. By the end of the war, France had seventy-six balloon companies while the U.S. Army had seventeen balloon companies at the front, each with around 170 men. *From* Scientific American, *July 3, 1897.*

•

When Germany's Staaken and Gotha bombers began attacking London in 1917, the British devised a defensive balloon barrage. Unmanned Caquot balloons were sent up to two miles high on steel cables. Connected by cables with lighter cables dangling a thousand feet down, they presented a formidable barrier against the heavily laden bombers. By 1918 a fifty-one-mile-long barrage had been established around London. France, Italy, and Germany also began to deploy them. British development during the 1930s produced the modern shape and they were quickly reestablished at the outbreak of World War II. The Germans tried reinforcing the leading edges of their planes' wings with cable cutters but soon gave it up. The barrages were especially effective at night and against strafing attacks as they are being used here by ships heading for the Normandy invasion beaches. *U.S. Coast Guard photo in the National Archives.*

RIGHT: At the outbreak of World War II the British had more than 400 barrage balloons around London and 180 more over other cities. After the retreat from Dunkirk, 2,400 balloons were in the air ready for the Battle of Britain and most of Balloon Command's men had been replaced by women. When the Allied armies began to pour into England prior to the Normandy invasion, the British claimed that the ever-present balloons were all that kept the island afloat. The war's largest single barrage consisted of 1,750 balloons sent up to defend London against Hitler's V-1 buzz bombs. Two hundred and seventy-nine V-1s were brought down by the cables of the barrage balloons. *Courtesy Smithsonian Institution.*

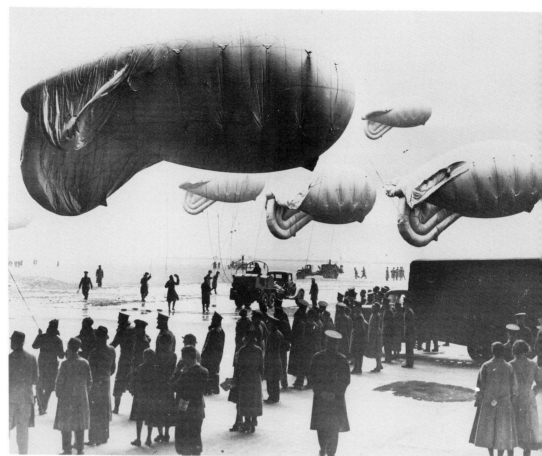

FAR AND NEAR LEFT: The great advantage of the tethered balloon is that it stays pretty much where you put it and it can be brought back to its point of origin simply by reeling it in. Westinghouse has been working with them since 1972, when it formed Tethered Communications Inc. (TCOM) and purchased the navy blimp hangars at Weeksville, North Carolina. Instead of human observers, however, Westinghouse sends their sophisticated electronics aloft. In the photo looking past the balloon's tail fins, technicians are servicing the Westinghouse TPS-63 radar system. Unmanned TCOM balloons have been used in Korea, Nigeria, and Iran as a less expensive alternative to earth-orbiting satellites for the relay of radio, TV, and telephone signals. A 350,000-cubic-foot balloon can carry an eight-thousand-pound payload up to ten thousand feet or a thirty-seven-hundred-pound load up to fifteen thousand feet. From there, its instruments can cover fifty thousand square miles. These balloons are also watching for drug smugglers along the United States' southern border. *Courtesy Westinghouse Electric Corporation.*

11
BALLOONING
· TO THE ·
· EDGE OF ·
SPACE

It is now generally recognized in scientific circles that the manned balloon capsule is the prototype of the manned space cabin. It serves not only for the study of the human factors of space flight, but for the selection and training of space pilots and as a test bed for the multitude of accessories and components which will eventually go into the construction of the sealed cabin which will carry the first man into space.

Otto C. Winzen[1]

With the perfection of the dirigible balloon, some expected the free balloon's usefulness to end. What was the point, they asked, of going wherever the wind blew, now that an airship could travel to a predetermined destination? Who would continue to be interested in ballooning?

But the balloon did not go away. More are in use today than at any time in the past. More people own and fly their own balloons than ever before. There have always been a few individuals—loosely called sportsmen—who are more interested in traveling in style than they are in actually getting anywhere. The balloon is perfect for them. Travel by balloon is nothing if not stylish. Today thousands can afford to indulge their fancy for ballooning.

A second group of people also continues to use the balloon. These are the scientists. There is one direction a balloon can go with more accuracy, assurance, and economy than any other kind of aircraft. That direction is up.

OPPOSITE: Capt. Joseph W. Kittinger moments after leaping from a balloon 102,800 feet above the earth for man's longest fall, August 16, 1960. His words as he stepped from the gondola were, "Lord, take care of me now." *Official U.S. Air Force photo.*

· 253 ·

As the first men to reach thirty thousand feet, neither Glaisher nor Coxwell nor anyone else suspected what they were getting into. At an altitude of only ten thousand feet, the brain loses 10 percent of the oxygen it needs and judgment begins to falter. At eighteen thousand feet there is a 30 percent decrease in oxygen to the brain and you can lose consciousness after thirty minutes. At thirty thousand feet you black out in less than a minute. At fifty thousand feet gases bubble out of the blood, unconsciousness is immediate, and death soon follows. In spite of his unexpected ordeal, on landing, Glaisher walked seven miles to the nearest village to borrow a cart while Coxwell guarded the balloon. Both made a number of subsequent ascents. *Courtesy Carruthers Collection, Claremont Colleges.*

•

The scientists' interest in ballooning dates from the very earliest ascents. In 1803 Etienne Robertson went aloft with an elaborate set of high-altitude experiments designed by the French Academy of Sciences. Robertson claimed to have reached 23,526 feet but he also claimed that, as the hydrogen in his balloon expanded at that height, so too did the head of his assistant, to such a size that the man's hat no longer fit!

More reliable results were obtained by James Glaisher, the head of magnetics and meteorology at Britain's Royal Observatory at Greenwich. In a ninety-thousand-cubic-foot balloon purchased by the British Association for the Advancement of Science under the direction of professional aeronaut Henry Coxwell, Glaisher made three ascents in the summer of 1862. The last of these, on September 5, took the two men into a region where no one had gone before.

One hour and fifty minutes into the flight they had risen to twenty-six thousand feet. The line to their gas release valve became tangled and Coxwell climbed up onto the load ring to free it. Glaisher took a temperature reading of five degrees below zero, then found he could no longer see his thermometer clearly. As they passed twenty-nine thousand feet he noticed even more alarming symptoms.

I laid my arm upon the table possessed of its full vigor, but on being desirous of using it I found it powerless—it must have lost its power momentarily; trying to move my other arm, I found it powerless also. Then I tried to shake myself, and succeeded, but I seemed to have no limbs. In looking at the barometer my head fell over my left shoulder; then I fell backwards, my back resting against the side of the car and my head on its edge. In this position my eyes were directed to Mr. Coxwell in the ring. When I shook my body I seemed to have full power over the muscles of my back, and considerably so over those of the neck, but none over either my arms or my legs. As in the case of the arms, so all muscular power was lost in an instant from my back and neck. I dimly saw Mr. Coxwell, and endeavoured to speak, but could not. In an instant intense darkness overcame me, so that the optic nerve lost power suddenly, but I was still conscious, with as active a brain as at the present moment whilst writing this. I thought I had been seized with asphyxia and believed I should experience nothing more, as death would come unless we speedily descended: other thoughts were entering my mind when suddenly I became unconscious as on going to sleep. I cannot tell anything of the sense of hearing, as no sound reaches the ear to break the perfect stillness and silence of the regions between six and seven miles above the earth. . . .

Whilst powerless I heard the words "temperature" and "observation," and I knew Mr. Coxwell was in the car, speaking to me and endeavouring to rouse me—therefore consciousness and hearing had returned. I then heard him speak more emphatically, but could not see, speak or move. I heard him again say, "Do try; now do." Then the instruments became dimly visible, then Mr. Coxwell, and very shortly I saw clearly. Next I arose in my seat and looked around as though waking from sleep, though not refreshed, and said to Mr. Coxwell, "I have been insensible." He said, "You have, and I too, very nearly." I then drew up my legs, and took a pencil in my hand to begin observations.[2]

Glaisher was unconscious for seven minutes. While he was busy observing his approaching death with commendable scientific detachment, Coxwell was struggling to free their valve line. When he lost the use of his arms, he caught the cord in his teeth and pulled until they began to descend.

Glaisher believed they had reached thirty-seven thousand feet but had no

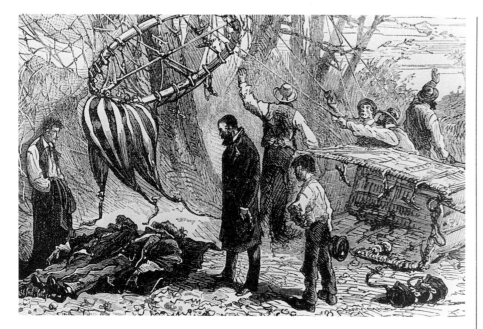

instruments for accurate measurement. They certainly surpassed thirty thousand feet, a height no one would again attempt without the aid of oxygen or a pressurized gondola.

Next to challenge the upper regions of the atmosphere were Theodore Sivel and Joseph Croce-Spinelli, accompanied by the famous aeronaut Gaston Tissandier aboard his balloon, *Zenith*. One purpose of their flight was to test a new oxygen-breathing apparatus.

Zenith arose from the Paris gasworks at La Villette on April 15, 1875. After two hours they reached equilibrium at 22,800 feet. There the oxygen tubes, when held up to the mouth, produced such a feeling of well-being they decided to release ballast and go higher.

Gaston Tissandier

Toward 8,000 meters the state of inertia in which one finds oneself is remarkable. The body and mind grow gradually and imperceptibly weaker, without one realizing it. There is no pain, rather the opposite. One feels an inner elation which is almost an effect of the shining light which surrounds one. You become indifferent; you climb and are happy to climb. . . . I want to grip hold of the oxygen tube, but I am incapable of lifting my arm. Meanwhile, my mind is very clear. I am still watching the barometer; my eyes are glued to the needle which soon reaches the figure denoting pressure −200, then passes 280. I want to shout out "We are at 8,000 meters!" But my tongue seems to be paralysed. Suddenly I close my eyes and fall senseless to the floor, losing all consciousness.[3]

Moments later Tissandier was shaken awake by Croce-Spinelli, who said the balloon was falling and they must throw out ballast. As they struggled to do so, Croce-Spinelli pitched out a piece of equipment weighing eighty pounds. The balloon shot upward and Tissandier passed out again. When he next regained consciousness, the balloon was plummeting downward and both his companions lay dead in the bottom of the basket.

In 1901 German meteorologist Arthur Berson with Reinhard Suring set a

Hawthorne C. Gray (1894–1927) was an engineering officer at Scott Field, Illinois. He enlisted in the Army Medical Corps as a private in 1915, rose to the rank of sergeant, and was commissioned a lieutenant in 1917. He entered military ballooning after the war, finishing second in the 1926 Gordon Bennett International Balloon Race. His goal was to break the twenty-six-year-old record of 35,433 feet set by Berson and Suring as well as the airplane's altitude record of 39,583 feet set in 1926 by the French aviator Callizo. Little was known of the effects of oxygen deprivation at high altitudes, and Gray thought it was the exertion of dumping a ton of sand ballast over the edge of his basket at twenty-seven thousand feet that caused him to pass out on his first ascent. On his fatal flight of November 4, 1927, he carried only three cylinders of oxygen, judged sufficient for ninety minutes of continuous breathing. His body was found the next day near Sparta, Tennessee, still in his basket. *Official U.S. Air Force photo.*

manned record that would stand for decades. In the three-hundred-thousand-cubic foot balloon *Preussen (Prussia)* they rose to 35,433 feet. They carried oxygen in cylinders but still lost consciousness when the effort to lift the mouthpiece proved too great.

A year later French meteorologist Teisserenc de Bort announced that his unmanned balloons had found a layer in the atmosphere beginning up around seven miles where the air temperature stopped falling. It was the stratosphere, the region above most of the Earth's clouds where temperatures begin at around seventy degrees below zero Fahrenheit then rise to thirty degrees above zero at thirty miles before dropping again to ninety degrees below zero at fifty miles.

It seemed a terrible place, with little to attract visitors until, in August 1912, Austrian physicist Victor Hess took three electroscopes up to sixteen thousand feet in a balloon and, to his surprise, discovered cosmic rays.

The upper atmosphere was being bombarded by mysterious, high-energy particles that did not reach the Earth's surface. The problem was how to get up there to study them. By the early 1920s test planes were beginning to approach forty thousand feet, but these tiny supercharged biplanes had no room for scientists and their bulky equipment. The best solution still seemed the manned balloon but this time, with oxygen masks fitted to the aeronaut's face to supply a constant source of breathable air.

Capt. Hawthorne C. Gray was an experienced army balloonist. Berson and Suring's world altitude record had stood for more than a quarter of a century. Gray meant to break it and, incidentally, to open the way to the stratosphere.

On May 4, 1927, he took off from Scott Field, Illinois, beneath an eighty-thousand-cubic-foot balloon. By the time he reached forty thousand feet in his open basket, frost was so thick on his goggles it obscured his view of his instruments. At that altitude all his ballast was expended and his balloon had come into equilibrium. He changed to a fresh cylinder of oxygen and dropped the empty one overboard. This brought him slowly up to 42,240 feet and a new world record.

He then valved gas to begin his descent, which quickly reached the uncomfortable speed of nine hundred feet per minute. His balloon had been designed to billow up into the shape of a giant parachute as its gas began to contract, but at twenty thousand feet when the ice cleared from his goggles, Gray saw that this had not happened. He threw out a small parachute with a message attached and watched in alarm as the parachute appeared to drift upward. He was falling faster than it was.

At eight thousand feet the only ballast left was Gray himself. He attached his parachute and bailed out. This disqualified his record as a manned ascent because the International Aeronautical Federation (FAI) insisted that it wasn't a manned flight if you jumped out partway down. Six months later, in another attempt on the record, Hawthorne Gray ran out of oxygen while making a much slower descent and died.

His death showed that the hostile regions above most of the Earth's air would not give up their secrets easily. Lack of oxygen impaired the brain's judgment far more than anyone had suspected. There was also the problem of the balloon's lifting gas. It expanded against the thin atmosphere and blew away to such a degree that, without somehow saving tons of ballast with which to arrest the final fatal plunge, there was no way to return the basket and its precious cargo of scientific data safely to the ground.

A new kind of ballooning had to be invented. The man who did it was a professor of physics at the University of Brussels. His name was Auguste Piccard. As one of Europe's leading specialists in cosmic rays, he had to get up to where they were. As an experienced balloonist, he thought he knew the way.

Hawthorne Gray showed that it was simply too dangerous to fly above forty thousand feet in an open gondola. Piccard would not even attempt it. He would take his air pressure up with him. He would survive inside a sealed aluminum gondola where he could generate his own air and maintain it at near-sea-level densities. The technology was already in place. The oxygen regenerator had been developed for Germany's World War I U-boats and the aluminum brewing vat had recently been perfected by Europe's beer industry.

As for the expansion and loss of his balloon's lifting gas in the stratosphere, Piccard thought he had solved that problem too. He would simply use an envelope five times larger than necessary to get off the ground. His calculations showed he would need the lift of one hundred thousand cubic feet of hydrogen. He would put it inside a five-hundred-thousand-cubic-foot gasbag. At the altitude he hoped to reach, it would expand to fill the balloon completely but none would be lost. Thus, all hundred thousand cubic feet of lift would still be there when he needed it to bring him safely back to Earth.

By September 1931, everything was ready. But the launch of the immense balloon and its delicate aluminum sphere required a dead calm. They almost got off on September 13 but the wind rose before inflation was completed and the flight had to be canceled. Piccard instantly became an object of ridicule in the world's press. Tall, gaunt, and properly professorial, he had been a popular subject for interviews. Now the newspapers asserted that, as a typical absent-minded professor, Piccard had misplaced a decimal point and ascended to an altitude of ten feet rather than ten miles.

Piccard stood his ground. Wind conditions would not be right again for nearly a year. He waited. On May 27, 1931, he was ready.

Launch procedures were a little ragged. The crew neglected to notify the two men inside the sealed capsule that they were off. The first they knew of it was when Paul Kipfer, Piccard's assistant, noticed the top of a passing smokestack through the porthole. They had received a severe bump on liftoff that bent a through-hull fitting into which a sensor was to be screwed. That left an inch-wide hole through which their precious air was escaping. Piccard hastened to stuff it with caulking and Vaseline brought along for just such an emergency but they passed forty thousand feet before they were fully airtight.

Half the gondola had been painted black. Piccard intended to regulate its temperature by turning either the black side to the sun to absorb its rays, or the shiny aluminum side to reflect them. But the turning mechanism refused to work. The black side faced the sun and in spite of its being seventy degrees below zero outside their thin metal hull, the two scientists were soon sweating in a 104-degree temperature inside. They had only one small water bottle between them. Fortunately, ice began to form on the shaded side of their sphere, which they were able to lick off to keep thirst to a minimum.

There was also a problem with the valve line. Through a launch oversight, it didn't work. The men couldn't valve gas and descend. They had to wait for nightfall when their hydrogen would begin to cool. This was where Hawthorne Gray ran out

Professor Auguste Piccard (right) poses with his assistant, Paul Kipfer, and Kipfer's family in front of their black and white gondola. The aeronauts' curious headgear was Piccard's idea. They used the two pillows to sit on during the flight and kept some of their delicate instruments in the baskets. Just before landing it was a simple matter to combine the two into perfectly serviceable protective headgear. It was functional, efficient, logical, and silly looking. The newspapers loved it. Their takeoff was so disorganized that their valve line got fouled, and they were unable to descend until the sun set and their gas cooled. Yet Piccard never seemed to lose faith in his ability to find a scientific solution to any problem. Kipfer, on the other hand, declined to make the second flight. Perhaps that was at the insistence of his wife who appears to be having second thoughts—even on the ground. *Courtesy Wide World Photos.*

•

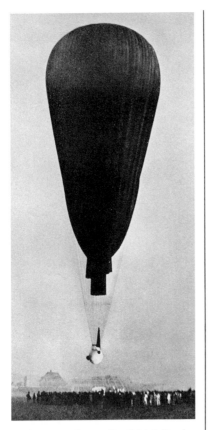

In Auguste Piccard's *F.N.R.S.* the world got its first look at the now standard teardrop shape of the large stratospheric balloon that is only partially filled with gas. The hundred thousand cubic feet of hydrogen will expand in the thin air of the stratosphere to fill the five-hundred-thousand-cubic-foot gasbag completely. Only up there will the balloon take on its traditional round shape. The name *F.N.R.S.* stands for the Fonds National de Recherche Scientifique, the Belgian scientific support organization that put up the fourteen thousand dollars to fund the project. Built and launched from the Riedinger balloon factory at Augsburg, Germany, the bag weighed 1,600 pounds, the empty gondola only 300, which went up to 850 when Piccard, Kipfer, and their equipment were aboard. *Courtesy Carruthers Collection, Claremont Colleges.*

of oxygen and died. But Piccard and Kipfer were regenerating their own air. By 8:50 that night, they were down to twelve thousand feet and could open the hatch. With a great deal of luck they landed safely on the Gurgl glacier, not far from Innsbruck, Austria.

A year later with the same balloon but a new gondola—not painted partly black—and a new assistant, Piccard went up again. This second ascent, he later declared, was "almost commonplace, lacking adventure." He meant that hardly anything went wrong and he was able to concentrate on his scientific measurements.

Piccard's first flight reached a record altitude of 51,775 feet. The second got up to 53,152 feet or 10.07 miles. A month later, on September 16, 1932, Capt. Cyril Uwins set an altitude record for airplanes of 8.3 miles.

Piccard, now universally hailed as the conqueror of the stratosphere, was invited to make a flight from the Chicago World's Fair. Auguste was too busy but he suggested that his twin brother, Jean, be allowed to do it. Jean was already in the United States as head of research at the Hercules Powder Company in Wilmington, Delaware.

Both brothers supervised the construction of the six-hundred-thousand-cubic-foot *A Century of Progress* balloon at Goodyear-Zeppelin in Akron. Jean's wife, Jeannette Piccard, qualified for her balloon pilot's license in preparation for the flight but the fair's sponsors refused to risk their expensive new balloon in the hands of a mere woman. It was finally decided that Lt. Tex Settle, one of the navy's top balloon racers, would make the flight alone. On August 4, 1933, he rose from Soldier's Field in Chicago before a large crowd and immediately fell into the Burlington railroad yard at Fourteenth and Canal streets.

Six weeks later an immense 859,688-cubic-foot Russian balloon, the *CCCP (USSR)*, with three men aboard ascended to 60,695 feet and a new record.

Two months after that, Lieutenant Settle and Marine Corps Major Chester Fordney set out again aboard *A Century of Progress,* this time from Akron. They snatched the world altitude record back from the Russians with an ascent to 61,237 feet.

Two months later on January 30, 1934, the Soviet balloon *Syrius* recaptured the record by rising to 72,178 feet—a stunning two miles higher. But as it started to descend, something went wrong. At fifty-seven thousand feet the gondola broke loose from the balloon. The three aeronauts, Paul Fedoseyenko, Andrey Vasenko, and Ilya Ousyskin, had parachutes but there was only a single hatch. That hatch was secured by twenty-four bolts. In the wreckage it was found that they had only time to remove seven of the twenty-four hatch nuts. All three men were killed in the crash. They were buried in the Kremlin wall after a state funeral attended by Stalin and Molotov.

National prestige had suddenly become a factor in the exploration of the stratosphere. The stratosphere had become the military "high ground." It was a race. There was even an argument between proponents of manned and unmanned flights to secure this new high ground. If it all sounds familiar, it may be because it still echoes half a century later, in today's conquest of space. The difference is that the high ground has now moved a good deal higher.

Auguste Piccard led the way in applying modern technology to the problem of the high-altitude balloon. Capt. Albert Stevens of the Army Air Corps proposed to go a step further. In 1933 he turned the question around and took it to Dr. Karl

Arnstein at Goodyear-Zeppelin for an answer. The problem as Captain Stevens saw it was not to build a balloon and then see how high it would go. He asked instead how big a balloon it would take to reach eighty thousand feet and return safely to Earth.

The answer from the engineers at Goodyear-Zeppelin was a bit of a shock. To carry a one-ton payload to eighty thousand feet and still retain enough ballast to land safely would require a balloon of three million cubic feet. That would be more than three times the size of the largest balloon yet built, or nearly half the size of the *Macon,* which had just joined the Pacific Fleet. But the *Macon* was built to carry a crew of eighty plus four airplanes. This immense balloon would carry only three.

Captain Stevens now needed someone willing to finance his project. But what might have seemed an impossible scheme only a few months earlier had begun to take on a life of its own. The world altitude was now unofficially the property of the Soviet Union. Mere science was no longer the deciding factor. National prestige had entered the picture.

Captain Stevens found his sponsor in the National Geographic Society. They would pay for the balloon if the Army Air Corps would supply the rest of the equipment and the personnel. Christened *Explorer,* the new balloon would be 179 feet in diameter and 307 feet high.

Now the only problem was to find a place where a thirty-story-high balloon could safely be inflated and launched. The search fell to Maj. William Kepner and Capt. Orville Anderson. They found what they were looking for eleven miles south of Rapid City, South Dakota. It was a grassy meadow set in a natural amphitheater with high rock walls that would shield the fragile balloon from the wind while it was being inflated. In addition the site featured road and rail access and, what pleased Major Kepner most, a nearby trout stream. Soon dubbed the Stratobowl, it would become the Cape Kennedy of its day.

Major Kepner, an experienced balloonist, was selected as command pilot with Anderson as copilot and Stevens as scientific observer. They took off at 5:00 A.M. on July 28, 1934. As they approached sixty thousand feet the three men heard a clattering noise on the roof of their pressurized gondola. Looking up through the porthole they saw that a rope had fallen. Looking further up to see where the rope had come from they saw to their horror that there was a large rip in the lower part of the balloon. Fortunately their lifting gas had not yet expanded down into that part of the envelope so they weren't losing hydrogen. They pulled the valve cord and began to descend.

At twenty thousand feet they opened the hatches and climbed out on top of the gondola. Then the entire bottom half of the balloon tore away. The top half, still full of hydrogen, formed a giant parachute. At three thousand feet above the ground the hydrogen exploded from a static spark and the three men had to jump for their lives. As their parachutes opened they watched the *Explorer* crash into the middle of a Nebraska cornfield.

The National Geographic Society had the foresight to insure the balloon with Lloyds of London, so the loss was minimal and work on *Explorer II* was soon begun. As a result of the hydrogen explosion, all subsequent American balloons would fly with helium. The new envelope was therefore expanded to 3,700,000 cubic feet to compensate for the nonflammable gas's lower lift. The gondola was also built with a larger hatch, the result of Captain Stevens getting stuck halfway through the old one.

A Century of Progress, being inflated at Soldier's Field in Chicago with 125,000 cubic feet of hydrogen, was slightly larger than Auguste Piccard's *F.N.R.S.* but built to his same design. Because the bag's fabric was so loose at takeoff, he was afraid it might tear as the gas expanded with altitude if it were enclosed in the rope netting used on traditional balloons. He abandoned the netting in favor of an upper and lower catenary band sewed directly into the fabric. Here the upper band is restraining the partly inflated balloon. The ropes pass through eyes in the band and will be pulled free before takeoff. The ropes attached to the lower catenary band hold the gondola, which is now white on top to reflect the sun's rays but black on the bottom to absorb heat from the ground. Navy lieutenant Tex Settle piloted *A Century of Progress* up to five thousand feet, where the gas valve stuck open. He was forced to land in a railroadyard less than two miles away. *Official U.S. Navy photos.*

Swiss-born twin brothers Jean (left) and Auguste Piccard check their *A Century of Progress* gondola. Auguste's interest in cosmic rays led him to devise the pressurized gondola and the stratospheric balloon. He used the same principles in the development of his deep-diving bathyscaphe, which opened up the depths of the sea. Jean, on the other hand, as a teacher at the University of Minnesota, influenced an entire generation of students who turned Minneapolis into the center of stratospheric research and eventually led to America's man in space program. Rarely is the connection between scientific research and its practical application so clearly seen. *Courtesy Piccard Collection, Wilson Library, University of Minnesota.*

•

A further safety measure was the addition of an eighty-foot-diameter parachute attached directly to the gondola.

On November 11, 1935, *Explorer II* with Stevens and Anderson aboard, rose to 72,395 feet. They became the first two men to actually see the curvature of the Earth.

The world's manned-balloon record was now back in American hands and would stand for twenty-two years. It had been an ambitious, exciting, and expensive series of ascents. But in the worldwide depression of the 1930s, unmanned balloons were to prove far less expensive and thus more practical. Three months later the Russians claimed to have reached 132,840 feet with one.

While the balloon was hard at work exploring the stratosphere, it was also at play in one of the most extraordinary sporting events since the days of the Roman Colosseum.

The year was 1906 and James Gordon Bennett was one of the world's leading sportsmen. The millionaire owner of the *New York Herald,* Bennett was also an accomplished sailor and horseman who introduced the game of polo to the United States. He had already established an auto racing trophy for teams from the various national automobile clubs. This proved so popular with the fledgling auto industry, not to mention Bennett's newspaper readers, that he decided to do the same for aviation.

The Gordon Bennett International Balloon Race was to feature a trophy and an annual prize of twenty-five hundred dollars for a competition between national aero clubs. Each nation would select its top aeronauts who would then compete for the international prize. The first event was to be held in Paris, with each subsequent race being held in the country of the previous year's winner. Bennett turned the running of his race over to the newly formed International Aeronautical Federation (FAI) with the recommendation that the competition be open to "all kinds of apparatus for aerial locomotion, and especially on its first offering, to motor aerostats." His thinking was doubtless that in 1906 the dirigible held little advantage over the balloon in speed and none in endurance. The FAI ignored his suggestion and limited the competition to free balloons.

A balloon race is unique in that it has little to do with swiftness. Every balloon, no matter what its size or shape, will travel at the same speed in the same wind. And

Rising like a giant floodlit flower into the night, *Explorer* is inflated on the floor of the Stratobowl in this photo taken from the rim. The three million cubic feet of hydrogen inside the gasbag have a total lift of just under seven tons. Mooring ropes are passed through eyelets on the upper catenary band and are doubled. When one end of the rope is let go, it can be pulled through the eye and dropped so the envelope is free of the rope's weight when it ascends. Heavier cold air trapped down inside the Stratobowl tends to protect the balloon even when light winds are blowing across the rim. A further advantage of the site is the fact that it is about as far from any major body of water as it is possible to get. Balloons launched from the Stratobowl have a good chance of coming down on dry land. *Official U.S. Air Force photo in the Air Force Museum, Dayton.*

•

while a balloonist may change altitude in search of a stronger wind, if he finds it he not only goes faster, he also is likely to go off in an entirely new direction. A balloon race must therefore be one of distance rather than speed. The prize goes to the aeronaut who flies farthest from the starting line in whichever direction the winds decide.

Therein lay the fascination of the Gordon Bennett Race. Six years earlier, also from Paris, Count Henri de La Vaulx set the world's record long-distance balloon flight of 1,195 miles in thirty-six hours to Korosticheff near Kiev in Russia. Now the count was ready to try again as the pilot of one of the French entries. Distances like his meant that everywhere from Africa to the Arctic was a potential landing site, including a good deal of water. Aside from the strong possibility of being fatal, a landing at sea was against the rules of the competition.

Here was a race that scorned anything as mundane as a predetermined course, one where risk and skill were present in equal measure and the finish line could be anywhere within twenty-five nations and a million square miles. Two hundred thousand Parisians turned out to see the start.

Britain, Spain, France, and Germany each entered three balloons. The United States had two—one piloted by Alberto Santos-Dumont, the other by Lt. Frank P. Lahm. Belgium and Italy each fielded a single entrant, for a grand total of sixteen balloons from seven countries. On October 27, 1906, they rose at five-minute intervals from the Tuileries Gardens. The wind was toward the north. Nightfall found the aeronauts faced with the choice of landing on the beaches of Normandy or of crossing the English Channel in the dark.

The crippled *Explorer* falls toward the ground near Loomis, Nebraska. The three aeronauts opened the hatch at twenty thousand feet, climbed out on top of the gondola, and watched as more and more of the envelope ripped away. At seven thousand feet when this photo was taken, *Explorer* was falling at seven hundred feet per minute. Nearly all the fabric below the lower catenary band has torn away and the gasbag has transformed itself into a giant parachute. The hydrogen is still intact in the upper half of the envelope but is mixing with the air. A few moments later a static spark created by the tearing fabric set off an explosion that blew the rest of the bag away and the men had to jump for their lives. The fault was later found to be in the way the balloon was packed into its box rather than with the fabric or design and, since its sixty-thousand-dollar cost was insured while in flight by Lloyds of London, work soon began on *Explorer II. Official U.S. Air Force photo in the Air Force Museum, Dayton.*

Stevens, Kepner, and Anderson (left to right) were all veterans of World War I. Major William E. Kepner enlisted in the marines at sixteen, served four years, then was commissioned as an army lieutenant in 1917. He was wounded three times by bullet and bayonet. In 1920 he attended the army's LTA school at Langley Field and the navy's LTA program at Lakehurst. He served as assistant navigator on the navy's *Los Angeles,* commanded the Army's *RS-1* on a storm-tossed thousand-mile flight from San Antonio to Illinois, won the 1928 Gordon Bennett International Balloon Race, was chief test pilot for the navy's all-metal *ZMC-2,* then became command pilot for the army's *Explorer.* He retired from the air force with the rank of general after World War II. Capt. Orville Anderson enlisted in 1917, instructed balloon observers, commanded the Sixty-first Airship Company, and flew airplanes in the Philippines. Capt. Albert Stevens had a doctorate from the University of Maine, specialized in aerial reconnaissance for the Signal Corps, mapped the Amazon for the *National Geographic* on his holidays, and was first to photograph the moon's shadow on the earth during an eclipse. *Official U.S. Air Force photo in the Air Force Museum, Dayton.*

•

That decision had already been made for Alberto Santos-Dumont. His was the only motorized balloon. A six-horsepower engine drove two horizontal propellers designed to keep the balloon from rising too high, thus conserving both gas and ballast. Shortly after takeoff he caught his arm in the gears and was forced to land.

Lt. Frank P. Lahm in the second American balloon was one of seven who chose to attempt the Channel. He and his copilot, Maj. Henry B. Hersey, drifted across the south and east of England before landing near Whitby on the edge of the North Sea. Their winning flight covered 395 miles in twenty-two hours, twenty-eight minutes.

America's win brought the 1907 Gordon Bennett Race to St. Louis, where it was won by a German, Oscar Erbsloeh, thus sending the 1908 race to Berlin. Erbsloeh's voyage of 872 miles to Asbury Park, New Jersey, broke John Wise's U.S. record of 809 miles also from St. Louis to Henderson, New York, set in 1895.

The Gordon Bennett International Balloon Race was held in twenty-six of the next thirty-three years, canceled only from 1914 to 1919 because of World War I and in the depression year of 1931 when most European balloonists couldn't afford to make the trip to the United States, where it was scheduled to be held.

In 1913, on the eve of war, the race had returned again to Paris. Ralph Upson and R.A.D. Preston won the preliminary U.S. National Balloon Race from Kansas City. That gave them the right to represent the United States in Paris. Upson was a trained engineer and head of the Balloon and Airship Department at Goodyear. His balloon, *Goodyear,* was of his own design. He came to Paris specifically to demonstrate a new theory of balloon flying he called "scientific management."

Most pilots, he felt, were content to drift along, conserving ballast as best they could, without any "systematically coordinated data on which to base judgment or satisfactory means for recording it."[4] Upson and Preston meant to control their flight according to developing weather patterns rather than merely the seat-of-the-pants weather sense most balloonists used. To that end, their basket resembled an airborne weather station more than it did a racing vehicle.

Second to last of the eighteen balloons to start, they began by drifting south, which Upson had already determined was opposite to the direction the wind would eventually blow. He therefore remained low over Paris where the wind was weaker, rather than following the other balloons to higher altitudes where the winds were stronger but, he firmly believed, in the wrong direction.

After a few hours the wind began to veer around to the west and they decided it would probably continue around in a clockwise direction. They made every effort to find altitudes where the wind was strongest to the west so that when it finally turned to the north, they would be aimed at the center of England rather than at the North Sea. They crossed the Channel that night and reached England shortly after sunrise on their second day aloft.

Ralph Upson

The upper currents were now plainly towards the northeast, and our direction readings showed us that only by holding within a few hundred feet of the ground could we hope to make our distance through England. We were willing to try it, however, and I decided that if we could hold the balloon low enough, and our direction did not become worse for a couple of hours, we could safely expect to reach the destination. At first we skimmed the ground simply by the aid of gas and ballast. But this became increasingly difficult as the air became more unstable, until finally even our large supply of ballast

Lt. Frank P. Lahm and Maj. Henry B. Hersey prepare to take off in the first Gordon Bennett International Balloon Race. Lieutenant Lahm was a cavalry officer, an instructor at West Point, and an experienced balloonist who was in Paris on other business when he was asked to take his father's place in the race. Major Hersey, his copilot, was a meteorologist and a former member of Walter Wellman's polar expedition. Hersey piloted his own balloon to second place the following year in the second Gordon Bennett Race from St. Louis. In its long history, the race was never without incident. Balloonists have been imprisoned as spies in Russia and forced to walk for eight days back to civilization out of the wilds of northern Canada. In 1925, American balloonist Ward Van Orman landed on the deck of a passing freighter in the dead of night sixty miles off the coast of France and was disqualified for landing at sea, though the winner came down in the surf off northern Spain. The 1923 race from Brussels was launched into a storm and the Swiss, Spanish, and American balloons were all struck by lightning, killing five. Ballooning has never been a sport for the timid. *Courtesy Carruthers Collection, Claremont Colleges.*

•

seemed in danger of premature exhaustion. It was then that we let down the drag-rope for the first time. This did not allow us to descend quite so low, also made it rather rough going, and at times it was hard on fences and wires; but it saved us ballast and that was the main consideration of the moment.

As expected, our direction gradually worked around to the east, but not enough to be alarming, and when we finally passed over the Humber River just below Hull we felt our object won. We wanted to go the limit, however; so kept on up through Yorkshire. It was here that we came under the influence of a slight sea breeze which swung us around a little and for a brief time gave us the hope of being able to get into Scotland. We were gradually brought around parallel to the coast and finally when near Bridlington actually moved away from it.

We took careful direction readings and found to our great satisfaction that we were going thirty degrees west of north. But our joy was shortlived. Two minutes later a squall was encountered that carried us directly toward the cliffs above Flamborough Head at about forty miles an hour. We had no time for such things as packing instruments. Preston, who was on the lookout, gave the warning and I hung onto the valve until we dropped like a shot. While still fifty feet in the air, we dumped three bags of ballast and pulled out the rip panel. We dragged for about a hundred yards, stopping two hundred and fifty yards from the cliff.

We were fairly sure of having won, because anyone coming across the Channel later would have been carried to the shore of the North Sea at a point further south, but we were indeed surprised to learn later that no one else had gone out of France.[5]

The 1938 Gordon Bennett Race was won by Antoni Yanusz of Poland. That meant the 1939 race was to start from Warsaw on September 3. Hitler invaded Poland on September 1 and the original series came to an end.

In the war that followed, manned balloons had little place. In World War I they had been used extensively by both sides as tethered observation platforms high above the trenches where they spied on troop movements and directed artillery fire. Tethered but unmanned balloons were also used over London as a defense against the low-flying Staaken and Gotha bombers when they began to attack the city in 1917.

The highly mobile armies of World War II had no use for balloon-borne

By the end of December 1944, the sand in the balloons' ballast bags had been analyzed and found to have originated on five beaches in Japan. These sites were photographed by aerial reconnaissance and several pearl-gray spheres were found at one—balloons being readied for their voyage to America. Of the 9,300 that were released, the remains of 285 were found from Alaska all the way down into Mexico. The six people in Oregon are the only known victims of the attacks, which ended in April 1945. Had they continued into the summer, incendiary bombs in the dry western forests could have had serious consequences. Each balloon was thirty-three feet in diameter, made of paper or silk. The ingenious mechanism, shown here on the cover of the intelligence report, automatically released hydrogen when the balloon rose above thirty-five thousand feet and ballast when it sank to thirty thousand feet. The ballast was in thirty six-pound bags of sand attached to the horizontal wheel by an explosive fuse and was dropped in sequence when the fuse was fired electrically by current through a barometer. It was then designed to start dropping its four or five bombs, the theory being that it would be over land by then. *Official U.S. Air Force photo in the Air Force Museum, Dayton.*

observers but, to the surprise of some, the balloon itself continued to prove as useful as the dirigible. Balloon barrages were in use throughout the war against both airplanes and V-1 flying bombs. The war's largest single balloon barrage consisted of 1,750 balloons sent up to defend London against Hitler's buzz bombs. The Germans launched an average of a hundred V-1s every day for eighty days. Twenty-nine percent of them got through Britain's antiaircraft, fighter, and balloon defenses. Of those that didn't, 279 were brought down by the steel cables of the barrage balloons.

The war in the Pacific saw its own unusual use of balloons. To retaliate against the United States for General Doolittle's raid on Tokyo on April 18, 1942, the Japanese set a research program in motion that eventually resulted in a series of Fu-Go balloons designed to rise to nearly thirty-five thousand feet where the prevailing winds swept them at up to two hundred miles per hour toward the United States.

Armed with fragmentation and incendiary bombs and an ingenious system to maintain their altitude for the four days it took to cross the Pacific, they landed from Alaska to Mexico and as far inland as Wyoming. A news blackout kept the Japanese from learning of the success of their scheme. It also kept the American public unaware of it. The only victims of the ninety-three hundred balloon attacks were a woman and five children who were killed on May 5, 1945, near Lakeview, Oregon, when they tried to pull one of the balloons out from beneath some trees.

The end of the war was only the beginning for the technology that had enabled the unmanned Fu-Gos to cross the Pacific. Employing new thin-film stratospheric balloons launched into weather patterns that would carry them over the Soviet Union, the air force began a long-term program to photograph Russia and China and to monitor those nations' atomic tests. Rather like Germany's Zeppelins early in World War I, these new cold war spy balloons drifted at leisure high above enemy territory, automatically snapping photos and collecting data until they were brought to a lower altitude by radio command where they could be scooped up by C-119 retrieval planes. By 1958 when Soviet protests finally ended the project, the air force "weather balloons" had photographed 8 percent of the Soviet Union and China. By then the U-2 had already taken over the balloon's spy flights.

The first thin-film balloons had been launched by Jean Piccard at the University of Minnesota before the war. Both the *Explorer* high-altitude balloons of 1934 and 1935 had been made of rubberized cotton. Piccard was searching for a less expensive material that would retain gas and be strong enough to survive at high altitudes. All he could find was cellophane. Though it tended to crack in cold weather, he used it in several successful unmanned ascents.

World War II saw the development of polyethylene. With it, Jean Piccard's first *Skyhook* balloon launched on September 25, 1947, reached an altitude of one hundred thousand feet in spite of the presence of millions of tiny pinholes in the delicate plastic. It was the beginning of an entirely new chapter in the science of ballooning.

Piccard's plan was to go aloft beneath a cluster of thin-film balloons. With the aid of Otto Winzen he got the General Mills company to build a pressurized gondola. Financing was obtained from the Office of Naval Research (ONR) which, after the war, financed a number of unusual projects. When Piccard couldn't find anyone else to build his polyethylene gasbags, General Mills undertook that part of the project as well. Though the cluster balloon never got off the ground, it brought together all the elements necessary for a new and far-reaching industry. Besides Wheaties and Betty Crocker cake mixes, General Mills had also manufactured bombsights during the war. Now their Aeronautical Research Laboratories would launch Minnesota into world leadership in thin-film balloon research and manufacture. Funded by the ONR and staffed by eager University of Minnesota students influenced by teachers Jean Piccard and Ralph Upson, their efforts would lead to the very edge of space.

Within a few years the stratosphere was filled with huge unmanned thin-film balloons. Those that weren't looking down on Russia and China were gazing up at the sun and planets where, above 99 percent of the Earth's atmosphere, telescopes were able to record detail never before seen by planet-bound observers.

An early manned ascent beneath a thin-film balloon took place on August 10, 1956. Navy Lt. Comdrs. Malcolm Ross and Morton Lewis ascended in an open gondola to forty thousand feet. This was the first in the navy's Strato-lab series of balloon flights. Together with the air force's Manhigh and Excelsior programs, it was the beginning of an extraordinary era of stratospheric exploration.

Three months later on November 8, 1956, Ross and Lewis in *Strato-lab II* ascended again, this time from the Stratobowl in a pressurized gondola to seventy-six thousand feet. This bettered *Explorer II*'s record set twenty-one years earlier by nearly three-quarters of a mile.

The air force's balloon program was dubbed Manhigh. When it originated in 1955, its sole purpose was to study cosmic rays. But in the two years it took to prepare for the first flight, Manhigh evolved into a forerunner of the man in space program. Capt. Joseph W. Kittinger, Jr., a thirty-year-old test pilot was selected for the first ascent. He would go alone.

It was one thing to sit in a cramped capsule in a test chamber knowing that, should anything go wrong, help was just outside the door. It was quite another matter to sit in that same capsule fifteen miles above the Earth. No matter how clever the simulation, the test chamber subject always knew he was really on the ground and help was near. How would his reactions change when he was all alone at the edge of space?

That was why Glaisher, Tissandier, Auguste Piccard, the Russians, the two *Explorers,* even the *Strato-labs* had opted for the crucial psychological safety factor of two or three men together against the stratosphere. Only Hawthorne Gray had dared to ascend alone and his death might have been prevented had someone been up there with him.

The question was no longer academic. America's most powerful rocket was barely big enough to lift a one-man capsule. Our first man into space would go alone.

On June 2, 1957, Joe Kittinger took off from Fleming Field, Minnesota, aboard *Manhigh I.* In seventy-five minutes he was up to a record ninety-six thousand feet. Then he noticed that his oxygen was half gone. The flight was scheduled to last twelve hours but Kittinger was ordered to begin his descent immediately. In a high-altitude balloon, coming down is far more hazardous and time-consuming than going up. It took Kittinger four hours. By the time he landed, he was nearly out of oxygen. Someone had put a sensor in backward. Instead of pumping oxygen into the capsule, it was all going outside.

By 1946 a program of high-altitude research had begun using German V-2 and American-built rockets. Except for a few shipboard launches, all had to be fired from the military launch facilities at White Sands, New Mexico. Aside from the limited data available from a single launch site, an Aerobee rocket cost $25,000, while a Viking cost $450,000. By June 1952, James Van Allen and Melvin Gottlieb of the University of Iowa had developed the first of their Rockoons, a rocket-balloon combination that could be set off anywhere in the world and cost only $1,800. They used a nine-foot-long Deacon rocket, which when launched from the ground could reach less than 100,000 feet but when carried up to, in one instance, 57,000 feet by a General Mills balloon and ignited, attained an altitude of 295,000 feet. The photo shows a Rockoon ascending from the Coast Guard cutter *Eastwind* off Greenland in 1952. Rockoons enabled Dr. Van Allen to make the first direct observations of the energetic particles that cause the aurora borealis (northern lights). *Courtesy Dr. James Van Allen, University of Iowa.*

The Manhigh capsule was built by Winzen Research, Inc. It was three feet in diameter, eight feet high, and crammed with life-support systems. Animals were sent in it five times to one hundred thousand feet. Then it was Capt. Joe Kittinger's turn. He called it his "scientific shoebox" and is here awaiting the launch of *Manhigh I.* Stuffed in with his parachute, environmental systems, and high-altitude experiments, he had barely enough room to move his arms and legs, none at all in which to stand or stretch. Indeed, part of the experiment was to find out whether claustrophobia would become a problem in space. Within minutes after takeoff his VHF radio failed and he was forced to switch to the backup system—a Morse code key! At forty-five thousand feet he encountered the tropopause, the boundary between the troposphere and the stratosphere. Fully half of all high-altitude balloon flight failures occur in this often violent layer and Kittinger watched through the porthole in horror as his gasbag bowed into a grotesque concave shape as it met a one-hundred-mile-per-hour jet stream. Once safely into the relative calm of the stratosphere he found that half his oxygen was gone. *Official U.S. Air Force photo.*

The Manhigh project now held the world altitude record. It was also out of money. Otto Winzen's firm made food wrap bags and stratospheric balloons. The former accounted for most of his profits, the latter took up nearly all his time. His Winzen Research, Inc., offered to underwrite the second Manhigh flight. It would be made by Maj. David G. Simons, a physician and head of the Space Biology Branch at Holloman Air Force Base. Strapped into the same tiny capsule but with a larger balloon, Simons was launched from a 425-foot-deep open-pit iron mine near Crosby, Minnesota, on the morning of August 19, 1957. He reached a record altitude of 101,516 feet—better than nineteen miles above the Earth. The United States seemed once again firmly in command of the high ground. Less than two months later the Soviet Union launched *Sputnik I.*

The world was stunned by the Soviet achievement. The high ground had suddenly been moved much farther up, the United States was no longer in the lead, and last but not least, Otto Winzen would no longer have to fund America's subspace research program.

The country's leisurely underfinanced balloon programs were now asked to supply quick answers to the Russian challenge. It was time to begin a systematic pilot selection and training program that could also be used to pick America's first men in space. Six candidates were put through a prototype of the Mercury astronaut selection process. From this, Lt. Clifton McClure was chosen to fly *Manhigh III.*

He was sealed into his capsule at 1:00 on the morning of October 6, 1958, at Holloman Air Force Base, New Mexico. Fifteen minutes after that, Lieutenant McClure accidentally opened his parachute. A hundred yards of silk poured out around his feet. It was the only high-altitude parachute on the base. If he reported it, the flight would be scrubbed. McClure decided to keep quiet and repack the chute himself. It took nearly four hours. At 7:00 A.M. inflation was completed and he lifted off. By the time the balloon leveled off at 99,700 feet, McClure's responses to ground control had become sluggish and his rectal thermometer showed that he had a temperature of 101.4 degrees. He was ordered to descend but by then the helium in his balloon was absorbing heat and lift from the morning sun. The descent was painfully slow and McClure's temperature rose to 104 degrees. Even in his distracted condition, it was McClure himself who realized that his sweat from repacking the chute had overburdened the chemical in his air regeneration system causing it to emit heat that had spread throughout the tiny capsule.

By 5:00 that evening he was down to sixty thousand feet but his temperature was up to 106.6 degrees. He still had two hours to go. McClure finally landed safely and insisted on walking to the waiting helicopter. His temperature was 108.5 degrees. By the next day his recovery was nearly complete.

His was the last Manhigh ascent. Further tests for the space program were taken over by the navy's Strato-lab project. The air force had a problem of its own to solve. Now that its pilots were routinely flying at altitudes well in excess of twenty thousand feet, there was no way for them to bail out safely.

If the pilot opened his parachute immediately, he could die from sudden decompression, lack of oxygen, intense cold, or any combination of the three. If he elected to go into free-fall in order to reach the more hospitable lower altitudes as quickly as possible, he was almost certain to go into a fatal spin.

The laws of physics state that any aerodynamically unstable object—like a human body—will begin to spin at up to two hundred revolutions per minute as it falls. Tests showed that a man spinning at 140 revolutions per minute could die. The air force thought it had a solution in a small stabilizing chute developed by Francis Beaupre. The test program was christened Excelsior. Capt. Joe Kittinger from *Manhigh I* would fly it.

His first jump was in October 1959 from a C-130 at twenty-eight thousand feet. Everything worked perfectly. A month later in an open gondola beneath the *Excelsior I* balloon, nothing went right.

Joe Kittinger

Before I jumped from the gondola at 76,400 feet, the timer lanyard of the stabilization unit was pulled prematurely and the 6-foot canopy and shrouds popped out after only two seconds of free fall, instead of 16, promptly fouling around me.

At first I thought I might retard the free spin that began to envelop me, but despite my efforts I whirled faster and faster. Soon I knew there was nothing I could do. I thought this was the end. I began to pray, and then I lost consciousness.

I owe my life to my emergency parachute, set to open automatically at 10,000 feet. When I came to, I was floating lazily down beneath the beautiful canopy of the emergency chute. I want to tell you I had a long thank-you session with the good Lord right then and there.[6]

Kittinger had reached a falling velocity of 422 miles per hour. His main parachute had opened automatically at eleven thousand feet, had promptly tangled with the Beaupre chute, and both had been torn away. Then his emergency chute opened and carried him safely to the ground.

Less than a month later he was aloft again. In *Excelsior II* he bailed out at 74,700 feet and everything worked perfectly. With faith in the equipment restored, *Excelsior III* was to be the ultimate test. Kittinger would ascend to a world record altitude, then jump.

For the previous week his diet consisted mainly of meat and potatoes. Gas-producing foods could expand to such an extent in the open gondola that the pain might force a premature jump. Air force weathermen selected a launch site eighteen miles north of Holloman. Kittinger was put on pure oxygen two and a half hours before launch to purge his system of the nitrogen that could cause bubbles in his blood.

At 5:29 on the morning of August 16, 1960, explosive charges were fired to cut the lines that restrained the balloon. At forty-three thousand feet Kittinger discovered that the right-hand glove of his pressure suit was not working properly. From previous experience he knew that his hand would swell and lose most of its circulation. He also knew that he could work everything in the gondola with his other hand. He decided to continue. At fifty thousand feet the temperature had dropped to ninety-four below zero. Then it started to rise. He had entered the stratosphere. At sixty thousand feet his balloon was climbing at thirteen hundred feet per minute, almost faster than the delicate plastic of the envelope could stand. Flight control at Holloman asked him to valve enough helium to slow his ascent to 950 feet per minute. A solid cloud cover had formed far below him. Only radar could still track the balloon. An hour and thirty-one minutes after launch, Kittinger was at 102,800 feet.

An automatic camera put aboard his open gondola by National Geographic photographer Volkmar Wentzel recorded the instant when Kittinger stepped out into space. Kittinger recalled rolling onto his back as he dropped and being stunned by the brightness of his white balloon, 200 feet in diameter, shining against the black sky like an immense light. It seemed to shoot away from him with explosive speed, though of course it was he who was in motion, falling at hundreds of miles per hour while the balloon floated serenely at the edge of space. Kittinger's historic leap was the culmination of 140 test drops conducted by the Air Force over the previous two years. *Official U.S. Air Force photo.*

•

Joe Kittinger

A mixed feeling of awe and remoteness has been building up all through the ascent, and now it almost overcomes me. I feel awe at the thought of floating easily at a height that man has never achieved before without the protection of a sealed cabin. I feel remoteness because I am beyond reach of help and friends if anything should go wrong.

I want to describe my impressions of this high, alien world. Striving for the right words, I send a message to ground control:

"There is a hostile sky above me. Man will never conquer space. He may live in it, but he will never conquer it. The sky above is void and very black and very hostile."

I am grateful that the balloon revolves slowly, because I have a chance to sweep the horizon through the gondola's open door.

I note the change in the sky's hue: normal blue to about 15 degrees above the horizon, then increasingly dark until it attains the inky depth of night around the balloon. Such a dark sky without stars seems strange, but I stare in vain to find just one. . . .

Burdened by heavy clothes and gear, I begin to pay the physical toll for my altitude. Every move demands a high cost in energy. My eyes smart from the fierce glare of the sun. When it beams in the gondola door on my left side, I feel the effect of strong radiation and begin to sweat. On my right side, mostly in shadow, heat escaping from my garments makes a vapor like steam. Circulation has almost stopped in my unpressurized right hand, which feels still and painful.

After nine minutes at peak altitude, Kittinger was ready to leave. He called ground control and they began a three-minute countdown to jump.

At zero count I step into space. No wind whistles or billows my clothing. I accelerate with the speed of an object falling in a vacuum. Every second I drop 22 miles an hour faster but have no sensation of velocity. In eerie silence, earth, sky and departing balloon revolve around me as if I were the center of the universe. I feel like a man in suspended animation.

I drop facing the clouds. Then I roll over on my back and find an eerie sight. The white balloon contrasts starkly with a sky as black as night, though it is 7:12 in the morning and I am bathed in sunshine. Again I look for stars, but see none.[7]

The Beaupre stabilization chute popped out precisely on schedule at ninety-six thousand feet and Kittinger found himself perfectly anchored against flat spin. He could change his position simply by moving an arm or leg. The tops of the clouds now began to rush up at him and he had to remind himself that they were not as solid as they appeared. He met them at twenty-one thousand feet. Then thirty-five hundred feet further down, after a record free-fall of four minutes, thirty-eight seconds, his main chute opened. He had reached a peak speed of 614 miles per hour, nine-tenths the speed of sound—certainly the fastest any man has ever gone without a vehicle of any kind.

Thirteen minutes, forty-five seconds after bailing out, Kittinger made "a landing as hard as any I have ever made in my life" but he was down in one piece. After three hours on the ground the swelling in his hand disappeared.

His altitude record was not an official one. Like Hawthorne Gray, he didn't ride his craft back to the ground. Less than nine months later it all became academic anyway. On May 4, 1961, the U.S. Navy's *Strato-lab V*—at ten million cubic feet, the largest manned balloon ever—was launched from the deck of the aircraft carrier *Antietam*. Comdr. Malcolm Ross and Lt. Comdr. Victor Prather rose to 113,740

If you happen to have one available, an aircraft carrier makes a perfect launch vehicle for a very large balloon. It can match winds of thirty miles per hour or more and, as long as the wind blows steadily, can reduce its relative force across the flight deck to the equivalent of a dead calm. As part of the U.S. Navy's Skyhook program, a series of three ten-million-cubic-foot Winzen balloons were launched from the deck of the *Valley Forge* in the Caribbean, beginning with this one on January 26, 1960. Each five-hundred-foot-high balloon carried a one-ton payload of cosmic ray equipment for the National Science Foundation to well above one hundred thousand feet. Note that the carrier is steaming along at a considerable speed as seen from its wake, and although the wind is strong enough to form whitecaps on the sea, the balloon rises straight up. *Official U.S. Navy photos.*

•

feet, bettering Maj. David Simons's record by more than two miles. After landing at sea in the Gulf of Mexico, Prather drowned when his space suit, being tested for the Mercury astronaut program, filled with water and sank.

Three weeks before the flight of *Strato-lab V,* Yuri Gagarin became the first man in space. One day after *Strato-lab V,* Alan Shepard was launched on America's first suborbital flight. The manned balloon had led the way. Now its task was nearly complete. Ross and Prather's altitude record is the one that stands today.

Theirs was not, however, the last attempt. That was made on February 2, 1966, when Nick Piantanida bettered their mark by nearly two miles. He ascended to 123,800 feet. From there, more than twenty-three miles straight up, Piantanida intended to break Kittinger's free-fall parachute record. But when he attempted to

The success of the three unmanned Skyhook launches from the deck of the *Valley Forge* encouraged the navy to attempt a similar one in the manned Strato-lab series. On May 4, 1961, beneath another ten-million-cubic-foot Winzen balloon from the deck of the carrier, *Antietam*, Comdr. Malcolm Ross and Lt. Comdr. Victor Prather rose to a new world altitude record of 113,740 feet. Notice the blinds that will shield the two aeronauts from the sun in their open gondola. During the landing at sea, Lieutenant Commander Prather's space suit filled with water and he drowned. Theirs is the manned altitude record that stands today. *Official U.S. Navy photo.*

•

switch from his gondola's oxygen supply to that in his backpack, he found the coupling had frozen. Instead of bailing out, he was forced to ride the gondola as it parachuted back to Earth. Since he and the gondola returned without the balloon, the record was not accepted by the FAI. Three months later, at fifty-seven thousand feet, a seal on his pressure suit failed. He was without oxygen for three minutes before he could land. Nick Piantanida went into a coma and died four months later.

With the opening of the space age, the need for men to risk their lives aboard balloons in the stratosphere came to an end. The arena had changed.

Unmanned balloons, including the brand-new superpressure balloons, continue to be launched into the upper air by the hundreds to this very day. High technology had transformed the gas balloon from a sideshow attraction into an invaluable vehicle on the cutting edge of scientific research. The hot-air balloon, on the other hand, had virtually ceased to exist. Was this to be the ultimate triumph of the Charlière over the Montgolfière?

In Europe both before and after World War II a handful of enthusiasts had built and briefly flown their own hot-air balloons. A variety of burners or "petrol ovens" were tried but all were too heavy for the amount of heat they produced. Experienced gas balloonists found the roar of these burners disconcerting after the absolute silence of their hydrogen-powered machines, though a few felt that being able to enjoy a cigarette while aloft was a fair exchange for the added noise.

Smoke balloons were still sometimes flown but they were charged with hot air from a fire or other heat source that remained on the ground. Their flights were thus limited by the length of time the air inside the bag retained the heat of its first charge. A true hot-air balloon would have to take its heat source aloft with it just as the Montgolfier brothers had.

That heat source turned out to be a plumber's blowtorch. In 1953 Ed Yost was working for General Mills in Minneapolis. He was building balloons to be launched from West Germany by Radio Free Europe to carry propaganda leaflets behind the Iron Curtain. Each polyethylene balloon carried four pounds of leaflets and used a chunk of dry ice as automatic ballast. In an attempt to increase the payload, Yost attached a plumber's blowtorch to the balloon. When this proved successful he put three blowtorches together and got a forty-pound payload into the air.

In 1956 Yost and some others left General Mills to start their own company, Raven Industries, in Sioux Falls, South Dakota. With support from the Office of Naval Research, they continued to develop the hot-air balloon as a potential low-cost trainer for navy blimp pilots. After four years' work they had a thirty-thousand-cubic-foot polyurethane-coated nylon gasbag powered by a rebuilt propane weed burner.

Yost made the first flight at Bruning, Nebraska, on October 10, 1960. A month later he rose to ninety-three hundred feet from the Stratobowl. Joined by Don Piccard, son of Jean and Jeanette Piccard, he made a flight across the English Channel in March, 1963, and sponsored one of the first hot-air balloon races, from Catalina Island, twenty-six miles off the southern California coast in January, 1964.

Today the hot-air balloon, as manufactured by a dozen firms around the world, is one of the most popular sportsman's aircraft ever created.

Modern technology had transformed both the Montgolfière and the Charlière. Was it now time to apply it to ballooning's last great challenge? Was man ready once again to attempt an Atlantic crossing by balloon?

The world's first transatlantic flight had been reported on the front page of the *New York Sun* on April 17, 1844. Unfortunately for the *Sun,* it had occurred only in the fertile imagination of Edgar Allan Poe who, desperate for money, sold it to the newspaper as fact. Poe's balloonists flew from England to South Carolina—in spite of the fact that the prevailing winds blow in the opposite direction.

John Wise, America's most famous balloonist, had already realized that there was a great "atmospherical current that always blows from west to east in the higher regions of the air."[8] Wise was, however, much too experienced a balloonist and sensible a businessman to attempt the Atlantic on his own. In 1843 he asked Congress to finance the crossing. Senator Stephen A. Douglas of Illinois presented his petition four times and four times it was rejected.

Thaddeus Lowe also dreamed of the Atlantic crossing. On September 8, 1860, he was within half an hour of departure when a sudden squall burst his 725,000-cubic-foot *Great Western.* Then in 1871 Wise and Washington H. Donaldson, a balloonist and trapeze artist, formed a partnership to make the attempt. They secured backing from the *New York Daily Graphic* and work on the *Daily Graphic* began at the end of June 1873. Inflation was already underway when Wise expressed misgivings about the balloon's being made of cotton rather than silk and withdrew. As if in reply, the bag split open and all 325,000 cubic feet of hydrogen escaped.

Donaldson made repairs and began again. His crew would be George Lunt and a *Graphic* reporter, Alfred Ford. Inflation was completed at 9:00 A.M. on October 6, 1873. The ropes were cut and the *Daily Graphic* rose from Brooklyn with "amazing velocity" bound for Europe. By noon the three men were back on the ground not far from New Canaan, Connecticut, staring at the wreckage of their overweight balloon after a flight of forty-eight miles.

Eighty-five years later someone decided to try again. Arnold Eiloart, his son Tim, Colin Mudie, and his wife Rosemary were all experienced small-boat sailors. It was deep in the English winter of 1957 when they met to reminisce about the warm South Atlantic and recall dreams of drifting with the clouds on tropical northeast trade winds. That led to talk of balloons and a decision. They would fly the Atlantic by balloon—not from west to east high up in John Wise's jet stream but rather east to west, low to the water on the trade winds.

Colin Mudie was a yacht designer. He built their gondola in the shape of a boat, one that could survive a fall from a height. He tested it by dropping models from bridges into the Thames. Arnold Eiloart was to pilot the balloon. But he had never been in one and without a single licensed balloonist in all of England to learn from, he had to go to Holland and Jean Boesman at the Hague Balloon Club to learn to fly.

They christened their balloon the *Small World.* Several major British corporations supported the project, one with the loan of a banana boat to transport their forty-five tons of equipment, including 690 hydrogen cylinders, to Tenerife in the Canary Islands. They set out on December 12, 1958. After four days and twelve hundred miles, they ran out of ballast and were forced into the sea. They sailed the last 1,450 miles in their gondola, arriving at Barbados on January 5.

Theirs was the only attempt to fly from east to west but others now turned their thoughts to the crossing. Some would not be as lucky as *Small World.* Malcolm Brighton and Rodney and Pamela Anderson set out aboard a combination hot-air

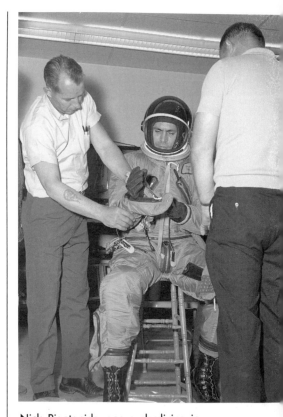

Nick Piantanida was a skydiving instructor from Brick Town, New Jersey. He planned to jump from a world record altitude above 120,000 feet, then free-fall to 7,000 feet. On February 2, 1966, he ascended to a record 123,800 feet from Sioux Falls, South Dakota, but was unable to change over to the oxygen supply in his backpack when the valve froze. He was forced to cut his gondola loose from the balloon and ride it as it parachuted back to the ground. Piantanida made a second attempt on May 1, 1966, but a seal on his pressure suit gave way at fifty-seven thousand feet. He was without oxygen for three minutes, went into a coma, and died four months later. *Photo by Jim Winker, courtesy Raven Industries.*

The hot-air airship is a hot-air balloon shaped like an airship—with an engine. Don Cameron built and flew the first successful one in England on January 4, 1972. This one was built by George Stokes in Costa Mesa, California. The *Busch* ship is one of two Stokes ships built for Budweiser in 1980. It is 175 feet long, has a top speed of twenty miles per hour, and can carry four people beneath its 225,000-cubic-foot hull. At two hundred thousand dollars, it is less than one-tenth the cost of a blimp and, like a balloon, is folded up and stored away when not in use. This saves the cost of hangar, mooring mast, and a twenty-four-hour crew. But also like a hot-air balloon, the envelope has a shorter life span than a blimp's and must be three and a half times larger to lift the same load. *Courtesy George Stokes Airship & Balloon Design Inc., Costa Mesa, California.*

•

and helium balloon named *Free Life* on September 20, 1970. They met a storm fourteen hundred miles off Newfoundland and were never seen again. Thomas Gatch took off from Harrisburg, Pennsylvania, on February 18, 1974, in a pressurized gondola beneath a cluster of ten superpressure balloons he named *Light Heart*. His plan was to cross the Atlantic in the jet stream at thirty-nine thousand feet. He was last seen four days later by a freighter 960 miles off the west coast of Africa. On August 6, 1974, Robert Berger took off from Lakehurst in a closed gondola hoping to cross the Atlantic at thirty-six thousand feet. He had never flown in a balloon before. His homemade Mylar *Spirit of Man* burst at seven thousand feet and he was killed by the fall into Barnegat Bay.

By 1976 ten attempts had been made to fly the Atlantic by balloon. All failed and five people had died. Now it was Ed Yost's turn. "A bunch of us kept watching the amateurs trying it year after year and failing, and we decided we'd go out and do it."[9]

His sixty-thousand-cubic-foot balloon was built by Dakota Industries, the company Yost founded when he left Raven in 1968. The open gondola was designed to function as a boat. His support crew included Joe Kittinger and a number of experienced balloonists. Christened *Silver Fox,* the entire vehicle weighed less than two tons and a ton of that was ballast. Yost's plan was to stay aloft as long as possible and trust to the prevailing easterlies to get him to Europe. He set out from Milbridge, Maine, on October 5, 1976. Five days later he had broken both the world distance and duration records but was still seven hundred miles short of Europe with little hope of favorable winds.

Ed Yost

I could have stayed up another thousand miles but by then I would have been out of the path of commercial shipping. The place where I put down, there were three ships within 25 miles. My mother didn't raise no foolish children. If I ever cross the Atlantic, I won't do it the way I did it the last time. I'll go up to 30,000 feet and ride the jet stream and be there in two days.[10]

That was exactly how two self-made millionaires from Albuquerque, New Mexico, decided to do it. Both were experienced hot-air balloonists who had never considered the Atlantic crossing until they read Yost's account of his attempt in the *National Geographic*.

Ben Abruzzo made his fortune as a real estate developer in Albuquerque. Maxie Anderson owned uranium mines. Both flew their own hot-air balloons. But gas ballooning is a bit different. A gas balloon's lift is determined by the amount of gas in its envelope while the length of its flight depends on the amount of ballast it carries. Hot-air balloons generally carry no ballast and can lift only enough fuel in propane containers for a few hours of flight. Anderson and Abruzzo would have to learn a different kind of flying. They would also have to buy a new balloon. They went to Ed Yost for both.

Their new balloon was named *Double Eagle* in honor of the Lone Eagle, their hero, Charles Lindbergh. They would land, they vowed, as he had, in Paris. Ed Yost built the balloon and taught them to fly it. Their boat-shaped gondola resembled his. They also hired Yost's weather advisor, meteorologist Bob Rice, a leading authority on weather patterns over the North Atlantic.

On January 6, 1975, balloonist and magazine publisher Malcolm Forbes and Dr. Thomas Heinsheimer attempted an Atlantic crossing beneath a cluster of high-altitude superpressure balloons. Their plan was to launch the *Windborne* from the navy's blimp hangars at Tustin, California, fly across the continent at forty thousand feet, and, when they were sure all systems were functioning properly, continue across the Atlantic. On route they would conduct atmospheric experiments designed by NASA, UCLA, and the French National Center for Scientific Research. Onboard systems included VHF, VOR, LORAN, and the Synchronous Meteorological Satellite. But after the first cluster of balloons at the left was released, their lift added to that of the second cluster proved too much for the ground-handling equipment. The third and fourth clusters broke free and pitched the pressurized gondola over on its side before they were cut loose and escaped. The next day Forbes declared that it had been "the most expensive twenty-foot trip in history." *Photo by the author.*

•

Rice had a flight plan already in mind. Anderson and Abruzzo accepted it. They would rise to eighteen thousand feet just as a high-pressure ridge swept down out of the Arctic. They would, in effect, ride the pressure ridge like a surfer rides a wave—an invisible eighteen-thousand-foot-high wave that would blow them all the way to Europe.

A launch site was selected at Marshfield, Massachusetts. They were still unpacking when favorable weather conditions began to develop. It was September 9, 1977. They would have to be in the air by 5:00 that evening. As the bustle of last-minute preparations surged around him, Ben Abruzzo experienced the curious sense of detached calm often noted by adventurers before stepping off into the unknown.

Ben Abruzzo

I knew I had thought it all out—all the things that can happen to you, and I knew I could survive all those kinds of experiences. By doing that, you condition your mind to the point that when it's time to take off, you have no problem at all—none; no anxiety, no stress, no fear, no nothing. You've already made your mind live through that before you fly. The last two weeks you have a very serene feeling, a very nice feeling of no anxiety at all.[11]

Things had already gone wrong, however. They were supposed to be in the air by 5:00 p.m. to meet the front. They didn't get off until 8:16. They were to ride the front like a surfer—but in surfing, a late takeoff can be dangerous.

They had also assumed that in case of rain, their gasbag would act as a huge umbrella. Instead it turned out to be more like an immense funnel pouring gallons of freezing water directly into their gondola. Ben Abruzzo's ski jacket was not waterproof. After sixty-five hours of freezing cold and rain they were forced to ditch in twenty-five-foot seas three miles off the coast of Iceland. They had come 2,440 miles in sixty-five hours but were far to the north of the course to Europe. A U.S. Air Force helicopter plucked them from the icy sea while an Icelandic Coast Guard cutter retrieved their gondola.

Double Eagle II is being prepared for her 8:42 P.M. launch from Presque Isle, Maine. The top of the balloon is silver to reflect heat from the sun while the bottom is black to absorb heat from the earth. If left to itself, a balloon rises into thinner air throughout the day as its gas absorbs the sun's heat. At nightfall the gas begins to cool and the balloon falls. As it does so, the increasing air pressure adds to the gas's contraction. Without enough ballast to stop this descent, the balloonist could fall out of the sky. This is why the amount of ballast he carries determines the length of a gas balloonist's flight. It is also why distance flights such as this start after sunset. *Double Eagle II* will be twelve hours on her way before the first sunrise starts to expand her helium. *Photo by Dick Kent, Courtesy Anderson-Abruzzo International Balloon Museum, Albuquerque.*

•

But safely back in Albuquerque, the dream would not let Maxie Anderson go.

Maxie Anderson

I was driven to do it, compelled to complete the task, almost beyond my will. It was as if I didn't really have a choice, that my mind would not let me contemplate quitting. I was convinced that flying that ocean in a balloon could and should be done. It became almost an obsession, a driving force, a fixation.[12]

Ben Abruzzo was less enthusiastic. He had nearly frozen to death on their first attempt. He had a seriously frostbitten foot. Though he had lost no toes, it made walking difficult and was very painful. He asked Anderson why he felt compelled to try it again. "To me," Anderson replied, "it's a way of entering history."[13]

In the end, Ben Abruzzo agreed to try again. He didn't like failure any more than Anderson did.

The first attempt had cost them $100,000. The second would cost $150,000. They returned to Sioux Falls and Ed Yost. *Double Eagle II* was sixty-five feet in diameter and ninety-seven feet high, with 160,000 cubic feet of helium. Its payload at takeoff would be 10,500 pounds—including a third aeronaut. Larry Newman, a

Maxie Anderson, Ben Abruzzo, and Larry Newman (left to right) triumphant in a barley field sixty-seven miles from Paris after five and a half days in the air. Anderson and Abruzzo went on to win the first of the revived Gordon Bennett races in 1979 but a fistfight aboard that balloon convinced them that no aircraft can fly with two pilots. They decided to continue their flying careers as they had begun—as friendly rivals rather than copilots. Maxie Anderson died on June 27, 1983, while trying to land his balloon near Fulda, Germany, after taking off from Paris in the 1983 Gordon Bennett Race. Ben Abruzzo was killed on February 12, 1985, when the twin-engine Cessna he was piloting crashed shortly after takeoff from Albuquerque. *Photo by Marc Bulka, Sipa Press.*

•

commercial pilot and hang-glider manufacturer from Albuquerque, was added to the crew.

Launch was set this time from Presque Isle, Maine. They needed another high-pressure ridge moving slowly toward the Atlantic from the Great Lakes region plus a low-pressure system out over the mid-Atlantic. That would provide them with a more southerly flow of air at the end of their flight.

And that's what they got. Almost immediately after their arrival in Maine, the approach of nearly perfect conditions set them once again into a frenzy of preparation. When only 135,000 cubic feet of helium arrived to fill the 160,000-cubic-foot balloon, they took off anyway.

It was 8:42 P.M., August 11, 1978. They crossed the coast of Ireland at 10:00 P.M. five days later. They continued on across Ireland and England heading in the general direction of Paris but were forced to land as darkness fell on their sixth day aloft. Their 6,240 pounds of ballast was down to just 250 pounds, not enough for another night in the air. They came to rest in a field of barley near the village of Miserey, sixty-seven miles northwest of Paris. They had covered 3,120 miles in 137 hours, six minutes, and entered the history books forever. They were greeted by cheering crowds and took turns over the next few nights sleeping in the same bed at the American Embassy that Charles Lindbergh slept in after his arrival in Paris.

A year later, *Double Eagle III* carried Anderson and Abruzzo to first place in the revival of an old event. They won the 1979 Gordon Bennett International Balloon Race with a 617-mile flight from Long Beach, California, to Dove Creek, Colorado. Ben Abruzzo and Larry Newman entered the 1980 Gordon Bennett Race in *Double Eagle IV*. They set a new endurance record for the race but didn't win.

Double Eagle V crossed the Pacific. On November 9, 1981, with Ben Abruzzo, Larry Newman, Rocky Aoki, and Ron Clark aboard, they set out from Nagashima and landed four days later on a mountainside near Covelo, California. Their 5,768 mile flight was a new manned-balloon record.

In 1984, a familiar figure, Joe Kittinger, flew his *Rosie O'Grady's Balloon of Peace* from Caribou, Maine, to Savona, Italy, a distance of 3,500 miles and a new

ABOVE: One of the newest events in the balloon's return to popularity is, appropriately, the revival of the Gordon Bennett Race. Organized by Dr. Thomas Heinsheimer, the first in the new series lifted off from Long Beach, California, on May 26, 1979, after a lapse of forty-one years. It featured seventeen balloons with entrants from ten nations. Concerns of air traffic control at Los Angeles Airport caused the event to move to Fountain Valley, California, where this photo of the 1981 race was made. It was won by Ben Abruzzo and Rocky Aoki in *Benihana* with a 1,348-mile flight to Millarton, North Dakota. Joe Kittinger won the race in 1982 with a flight to Cody, Wyoming. He won again in 1984 with a flight to Hobart, Oklahoma, in 1985 to Gunderson, Nevada, and in 1988 to a desert island off the coast of Mexico. *Photo by Gary Ambrose.* RIGHT: The world's most popular ballooning event is the Albuquerque Balloon Fiesta held annually since 1972. Wind conditions unique to the area allow the aeronauts to fly off across the high desert, find a contrary wind at a different altitude, and return often very nearly to their starting point. Today, two hundred balloons can be laid out for launch at the same time and once they are off, two hundred more often follow. *Photo by the author.*

record for a lone balloonist. Then in 1987, Per Lindstrand and Richard Branson became the first to fly the Atlantic in a hot-air balloon. To prove that was no fluke, Branson and Lindstrand flew the Pacific in January, 1991, also in a hot-air balloon. Carrying nearly five tons of propane tanks, they flew from Miyakonojo, Japan, to a spot 150 miles west of Yellowknife in Canada's Northwest Territory, a record voyage of 6,700 miles in 46 hours.

It has been a busy decade in the history of ballooning and there is more to come. One flight remains. One goal is yet to be achieved. It is the circumnavigation of the earth.

Maxie Anderson and Don Ida attempted a world flight in 1981. Rising from Luxor, Egypt, beneath a 200,000-cubic-foot helium balloon, they hoped to stay above 25,000 feet, but after a 3,000-mile flight were forced to land at Murchpur, India, when a slow leak prevented them from clearing the Himalayas.

Larry Newman will attempt a world flight late in 1991 in a unique double balloon system he calls *Earthwinds*. With him will be Richard Branson and Soviet Cosmonaut Vladimir Dzhanibekov.

What will remain for ballooning when all the world's great voyages have been achieved? That next flight has already been planned. In 1994, if all goes according to schedule, a Soviet spacecraft will deploy a French balloon on the surface of Mars. After two hundred years, the challenges to ballooning seem only to have begun.

The challenge of crossing the Atlantic in a hot-air balloon was accepted by Per Lindstrand, a founder of Thunder & Colt Ltd., Britain's leading balloon builder. Financed by Richard Branson, owner of Virgin Atlantic Airways and Virgin Records, Lindstrand created the world's largest hot-air balloon. Its 2.3-million-cubic-foot, 3-ply metallized fabric proved so efficient it could remain aloft during the day almost entirely on the sun's heat, reserving its propane burners for lift at night. Those burners were specially rebuilt to operate above nine thousand feet and were fired by igniters taken from a Rolls-Royce jet engine. Lindstrand and Branson flew the Atlantic in July 1987, landing in Ireland after a 3,075-mile voyage. Then, in an even larger 2.6-million-cubic-foot balloon with five tons of propane tanks aboard, they took on the Pacific. On January 16, 1991, they set out on a world-record 6,761-mile flight from Miyakonojo, Japan, landing on a frozen lake 150 miles west of Yellowknife in Canada's Northwest Territory. In this photo, Branson, in the center, and Lindstrand, on the right, stand before their pressurized capsule, which is lying on its side prior to launch. The burners are at the left. *Courtesy Virgin Atlantic Airways.*

Larry Newman believes that a manned balloon can circle the earth in twelve to twenty-one days, and he has initiated the Earthwinds project to prove it. However, a gas balloon cannot carry enough ballast to remain aloft that long, and a hot-air balloon cannot lift enough propane tanks. Newman has already test-flown an ingenious two-balloon solution to the problem. Lift is supplied by a 1.4-million-cubic-foot helium balloon. But a second hundred-foot-diameter anchor balloon beneath the gondola will be pumped full of air under pressure. This denser air will have considerable weight in the thin upper atmosphere and this weight can be released at will and retrieved simply by starting up a pump. The disposable weight of air in this anchor balloon will take the place of ballast and enable the balloonists to retain their helium long enough to circle the globe. The balloonists will be Newman, Richard Branson, a sponsor of the project, plus Soviet cosmonaut Vladimir Dzhanibekov, the major general in charge of all cosmonaut training, who himself has 146 days in space. If all goes as planned, *Earthwinds* will set out on a globe circling flight in late 1991 or early 1992. *Drawing courtesy Virgin Atlantic Airways.*

Mylar is a polyester that is ten times stronger than polyethylene. The development of Mylar led to a balloon that can remain aloft at a predetermined altitude for months at a time—even for years! When it becomes fully inflated at altitude as in this air inflation test at Raven Industries, there is no valve through which the expanding gas can escape. An ordinary balloon would burst, but the Mylar is too strong. It is the gas that must give way. Rather than continue to expand, it must start to contract, which reduces its lift and brings the balloon into equilibrium at the altitude predetermined by its size, payload, and helium charge. Superpressure Mylar balloons such as these have been launched into weather patterns all over the world. The length of time they can remain aloft—called float duration—is limited only by the deterioration of their plastic caused by solar radiation. Some have circled the globe twice in thirty-six days while others have remained aloft for more than two years. Their instruments have recorded wind and weather patterns, collected micrometeorites, monitored atmospheric pollution, and studied the magnetosphere, solar wind, radiation belts, and plasma wave particles. *Courtesy Raven Industries.*

12

· T H E ·
AIRSHIP
· A N D   T H E ·
FUTURE

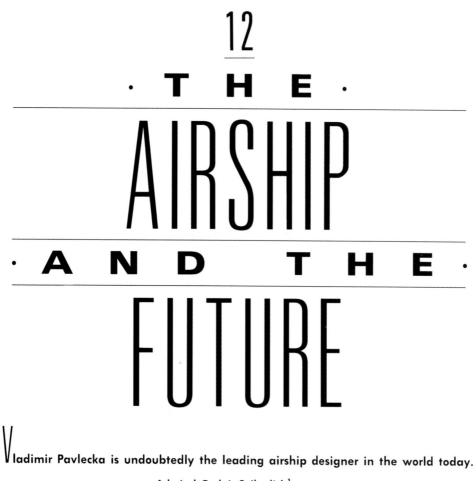

Vladimir Pavlecka is undoubtedly the leading airship designer in the world today.

Admiral Carl J. Seiberlich[1]

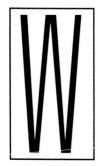

hen the last U.S. Navy blimp was dismantled in September 1962 it seemed like the closing of a chapter in the history of aviation. The airship had been born, had ruled the skies and then had died, all in less than two hundred years. It was a tale that had run its course and all that remained of the world's once mighty dirigible fleets were two little blimps—Goodyear's *Mayflower* in the United States and another advertising blimp in Germany. At no other time in this century had the airship's numbers or its fortunes fallen so low.

What went wrong? The airplane had finally caught up. But it was not, as many still believe, the fiery crash of the *Hindenburg* in 1937 that put an end to the airship's monopoly on transoceanic air service. That could occur only when an economically viable alternative form of air transport appeared on the scene. That had to wait until 1952 and the first flights of Britain's Comet jetliner. By then it was no longer a question of the airplane's ability to fly the Atlantic. Hundreds of World War II bombers had done that. But it was still a question of the airplane's being able to do it at a profit. The invention of the jet engine allowed the commercial airliner to operate in the thin air above thirty thousand feet where very low air temperatures produce high thermal efficiency. This enables the airplane to fly economically at high speeds over very long distances.

Britain's introduction of the jet airliner in the early 1950s finally allowed the airplane to equal the airship's great range and low operating cost. The jetliner's additional advantage of high speed—five times that of the airship—tipped the scale in its favor. The airship could no longer compete.

But if the end of the dirigible's use in commercial air transportation can be explained, the end of its military usefulness is less clear. Its endurance, range, load capacity, and all-weather capability remain, to this day, beyond that of any other aircraft. Why, then, could no use be found for it back in 1962?

Jack R. Hunt was often asked that question. He was operations officer of the Naval Air Development Unit, South Weymouth, Massachusetts, from 1955 to 1958 during the offshore station-keeping experiments in the worst winter weather in seventy-five years. He was also command pilot of ZPG-2 *Snowbird* on her epic eleven-day, unrefueled, nonstop flight from the United States to Africa and back again. Then in civilian life Jack Hunt became president of Embry-Riddle Aeronautical University and traveled widely as he struggled to establish that now flourishing institution. He sought support from everyone connected with aviation. The question was often asked of him by former naval airshipmen who loved their blimps and knew what they could do. Why was there no longer a place in military aviation for the airship?

In reply, Hunt would ask his questioner to name as many airplane manufacturers as he could. Boeing, Douglas, Lockheed, Northrop, North American, McDonnell, Martin, Grumman, Convair, Bell, Hughes. It was an impressive list. Then Hunt would ask how many companies built airships. Goodyear. His questioner began to see Hunt's point. But he could make it even clearer. How many congressmen are directly responsible to voters who make their living building airplanes or parts of airplanes? Even if the airship is better than the airplane in several important areas, given enough time and enough of the taxpayers' money, it is always possible to find some way for an airplane to perform the airship's missions almost as well as the airship can. The airplane simply had too many friends and the airship found itself out of a job.

Yet even the influence of friends in high places cannot prevail forever against the laws of economics. The jet airplane's single greatest advantage over the airship is its speed. But that speed has a price. The price is high fuel consumption—70 percent greater than that of an airship carrying the same load. When the jet offered its higher speed at an equal cost, there was no question of its advantage over the dirigible. But in the 1970s, OPEC changed the equation. Jet fuel that sold for a dime a gallon in 1973 rose to a dollar a gallon by the end of the decade. Lines formed at the gas pumps, Detroit found itself building the wrong kinds of cars, everyone became interested in alternative energy sources, and a number of people suddenly realized that an airship is a very fuel-efficient vehicle.

In the stress of worldwide economic disruption, the seeds of the airship's rebirth had already begun to stir. As oil prices skyrocketed, so did the airship's perceived potential. Interest crystallized in 1974 when the navy, NASA, the FAA, and the

Launched in February 1979, at Card-ington, England, the *Skyship 500* is 164 feet long and 46 feet in diameter. When filled with 181,200 cubic feet of helium, she can carry up to eight passengers and a crew of two. Powered by two Porsche 930 engines, she has a top speed of nearly seventy miles per hour. The ship's propellers are mounted inside ducts for improved efficiency. They are also vectorable, that is, they can be turned downward as shown in the photo for added thrust during takeoffs and landings. *Courtesy Airship Industries Ltd.*

•

Department of Transportation sponsored a workshop on lighter-than-air vehicles at Monterey, California. To everyone's surprise, seventy-nine scientists and engineers from seven different countries asked to present papers.

The gates were open. If the first four decades of this century can be called the "age of the airship," then the decade of the 1970s was surely the "age of the airship study." Both the U.S. Forest Service and its Canadian counterpart studied the airship's potential in logging operations. The Shell Oil Company investigated the possibility of transporting natural gas from North Africa to Europe by dirigible. The World Bank and the Canadian Province of Alberta considered the use of airships as a means of servicing underdeveloped areas that have few roads, railways, or airports. The Japan Industrial Technology Association concluded that dirigibles would be valuable in providing air service to the many small Japanese islands that have no room for airfields. A member of the Hawaiian State Legislature similarly suggested that the airship would be an ideal vehicle for inter-island freight and passenger service.

The U.S. Navy and the Coast Guard found that the airship really might, as its adherents claimed, combine the versatility of a helicopter with the range of an airplane while adding a flight endurance far beyond the capability of either—all valuable qualities in the management of the United States' new two-hundred-mile-wide ocean frontiers.

The studies were unanimous in concluding that there were a number of jobs the modern airship could do. But there remained considerable disagreement as to how profitable the airship would be and how many were needed. A Booz-Allen-Hamilton study for NASA's Ames Research Center projected a worldwide market for 1,270 dirigibles of all sizes.

Each passing year brought new studies. Aerospace companies such as Bell, Goodyear, Boeing-Vertol, and Lockheed became involved. Paper proliferated. Dirigibles did not. It eventually became clear that it was time to stop studying the problem and start building ships. By the end of the decade every assumption had been assessed, every econometric parameter had been extrapolated, and, most important, the people who were really serious about airships had begun to build them.

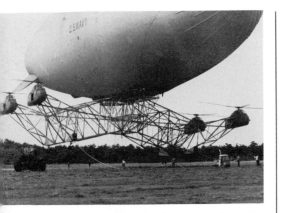

Frank Piasecki demonstrated his first helicopter in 1942. By the 1950s Piasecki had built his company into one of the largest helicopter manufacturers in the world. After selling it to Boeing in 1955 he concentrated on new vertical-lift concepts including the Heli-Stat. Originally funded at $10.7 million by the U.S. Forest Service, this first tethered flight took place at Lakehurst on October 22, 1985. By using the old ZPG-2 blimp bag and surplus army H-34 helicopters, Piasecki hoped to cut costs and speed development. Only the intricate connecting structure was newly designed for the aircraft. It was flown by a pilot in the left rear helicopter. Each of the other three are manned by a mechanic. Thrust from the four 1,525-horsepower rotors was expected to lift a twenty-five-ton payload, nearly twice that of the largest helicopters currently used in logging. *Courtesy Piasecki Aircraft Corporation.*

•

Goodyear had a head start. *Columbia* and *America* joined *Mayflower* in 1969 and *Europa* was erected at Cardington, England, in 1972.

John Wood and Roger Munk were also in England. They had originally been hired by Shell to assess the feasibility of transporting natural gas by airship. When that project was dropped, the two men decided to build a small dirigible of their own. With financial backing obtained in Venezuela, their ship was assembled in the *R.101*'s old hangar at Cardington and launched on February 3, 1979. A little more than a month later she was caught at the mast by a storm and had to be deflated. She was rebuilt and a number of sister ships have followed. Wood's and Munk's company is called Airship Industries and their ship is the Skyship 500.

Though similar in size and design to Goodyear's advertising blimps, the Skyship 500s were unique in that they were built with the latest in space-age materials. They featured a Kevlar-reinforced bow on a French-built titanium dioxide and polyurethane-coated polyester gasbag. They were powered by two Porsche engines with vectored-thrust propellers.

A year after the Skyship 500 was launched in England, work began in the United States on a completely different type of airship, the Heli-Stat. This was the creation of Frank Piasecki, a pioneer in modern helicopter technology. With $10.7 million from the U.S. Forest Service and the use of one of the navy's big airship hangars at Lakehurst, he set out to build a hybrid aircraft, one that joined four surplus army H-34 helicopters together with a twenty-year-old navy ZPG-2 blimp bag. Piasecki's idea was that the million cubic feet of helium inside the blimp bag would lift the entire weight of the ship. The thrust from the four helicopter rotors would then be available to lift a cargo of up to twenty-four tons.

Unfortunately the extensive framework required to connect the helicopters and the blimp bag turned out to be heavier than expected. Instead of achieving neutral buoyancy with all the ship's weight offset by the lift of its helium, the Heli-Stat weighed six tons. It therefore required the thrust from its helicopters to take off and remain in the air. And all four helicopters had to act in concert or the craft would become seriously unbalanced.

On July 1, 1986, after a four-minute hovering test, the Heli-Stat landed, turned eighty degrees and took off again. Seconds after the wheels left the runway the right rear helicopter lost power and appeared to break loose from the connecting framework. With that, the entire craft began to disintegrate. Fragments of the rotor blades sliced through the gasbag, which folded up and settled to the ground. Fuel tanks ruptured and ignited but were extinguished by navy firefighters. Four of the ship's five crewmen suffered minor injuries. The fifth, aboard the helicopter that first lost power and broke off, was killed.

While the Heli-Stat was using secondhand components in an attempt to keep costs down, an entirely new but equally unconventional aircraft was under construction in the former navy blimp hangar at Tillamook, Oregon. Called the Cyclo-Crane, its development was sponsored by FERIC, the Forest Engineering Research Institute of Canada, as a joint venture with four of the largest lumber companies in British Columbia.

Developed by Don Doolittle and Arthur Crimmins, much of the Cyclo-Crane's engineering and computer simulation was done by Dr. H. C. Curtiss of Princeton University. He predicted that the Cyclo-Crane would have the controllability of a helicopter, something no airship had yet achieved.

FERIC is the Canadian counterpart of the U.S. Forest Service. Their studies show that helicopters are currently being used in only 1 percent of Canadian logging operations. But airships, with their lower operating costs and greater load capacity, could profitably assist in 20 percent of the timber harvest.

The $4.5 million Cyclo-Crane was first brought out of her hangar on August 5, 1982. A month later the U.S. Forest Service joined the project by awarding the company, Aero Lift Inc., $850,000 toward the ship's test program. Two months after that, the Cyclo-Crane broke loose from her mooring mast and crashed in a nearby field.

Of the first three new airship designs, not one survived its test program. But while Piasecki's Heli-Stat was a total loss, both the Skyship 500 and the Cyclo-Crane were rebuilt and flew again.

A second Canadian-financed project was underway in Ottawa. There a $2.5 million, one-tenth-scale prototype had been designed and built by Frederick Ferguson. His design was based on principles discovered by nineteenth-century German physicist Heinrich Magnus. Magnus found that a rapidly spinning ball would fly farther than one that does not spin. The effect became even more pronounced when the surface of the ball was rough rather than smooth. This was proved by the British in the 1870s when they found that they could hit a worn cricket ball farther than they could a new one. This, in turn, led to the dimpled surface on modern golf balls.

Ferguson applied the principle to an airship. Wind tunnel tests at the University of Toronto showed that by spinning the round hull of his Magnus-effect ship on its horizontal axis, additional lift was produced while drag was reduced. Ferguson's Van Dusen Development Corporation announced plans for a $4.5 million full-scale ship.

Aside from logging, which most studies pinpoint as the industry where airships would prove most useful, similar potential may exist in heavy-lift support of construction projects in remote regions where rail and road networks are lacking. Pipelines and refineries in Alaska and the Canadian north are mentioned as the areas where heavy-lift dirigibles would seem to be the most cost-effective.

But there is a third part of the world that appears to have been specifically designed for modern airships. It is the only nation aside from the United States that has commercial quantities of helium, the nonflammable lifting gas. It is the Soviet Union.

The Russians have long been interested in airships and have studied the potential of their use in Siberia. There, new dams in the far north are being planned to supply hydroelectric power to the cities of the south. The electricity will have to be transmitted over hundreds of miles of power lines. The job of setting in place the huge steel towers that carry these transmission lines has been identified in a number of studies as one of the tasks best performed by heavy-lift airships, especially when these lines must cross inaccessible terrain where roads do not exist.

A long power line is supported by thousands of these huge towers, each of which is too heavy for even the largest helicopter. In the past the towers have been assembled in place along the route. Girders and assembly crews are trucked or airlifted to each site and with three or four towers per mile, a thousand-mile transmission line is a massive undertaking. Considerable savings in time and labor would be possible if the towers could be assembled at a central location and lifted by airship to their sites.

Described as resembling a manta ray hugging a beach ball, this is a one-tenth-scale prototype of a Magnus-effect, heavy-lift dirigible. Designed by Frederick Ferguson and built by his Van Dusen Development Company in Ottawa, Canada, this $2.5 million test vehicle features a twenty-foot, helium-filled sphere that rotates around a horizontal axis from which is suspended an aerodynamically designed gondola. The ship is powered by engines mounted at each end of the horizontal axis. The sphere on a full-scale dirigible would be 160 feet in diameter and hold 2,100,000 cubic feet of helium. This would provide seventy tons of lift. *Courtesy Van Dusen Development Company.*

McBlimp was the second ship built by Theodor Wullenkemper in West Germany. His first blimp was launched by his Westdeutsche Luftwerbung in August 1972 and flew in Germany for several years before being sold to Japan. This was his first ship to reach the United States. *McBlimp* was 193 feet long and 54 feet in diameter, with 211,888 cubic feet of helium. She could carry up to eight people and featured a large computer-controlled night advertising sign similar to the ones on Goodyear blimps. McDonald's cancelled their lease after a number of franchises complained about paying for a blimp that was unlikely to ever visit more than a handful of the chain's restaurants. Since then, the ship has flown for Sea World and for Metropolitan Life. *Courtesy McDonald's Corporation.*

•

Reports in the Soviet press suggest that their projected heavy-lift airships might be driven by electric engines that can be charged from the same power lines that the ships are helping to lay. This would eliminate the airship's traditional problems with the change in equilibrium as the weight of fuel is consumed.

If any of these plans can be turned into reality, it would represent a significant advance in airship technology. Engineers at the Bechtel Corporation in San Francisco have determined that the use of heavy-lift airships could save 20 percent of the cost of their Arctic and sub-Arctic construction projects. Soviet engineers may well have reached the same conclusions.

It is interesting to note that most of the airship projects now underway are privately financed. The military, which in the past played a major role in funding airship development, has come late to its rebirth. That does not mean, however, that there has been a shortage of studies of modern military airship applications.

Maj. Reed M. Anderson, USAF, 1977 Air University Report
Any vehicle that has the potential to move large quantities of outsized cargo to Europe in three days can significantly enhance the military strategic airlift capability.[2]

Maj. Jimmy L. Badger and Maj. Ronald M. Lebert, USAF, 1977 Air University Report
The authors feel that there are a number of vital roles that the airship could fulfill as well as, if not better than, any other aircraft now in the inventory or planned for the future.[3]

These authors all caution that important questions concerning the military potential of the modern dirigible remain to be answered. The U.S. Navy hoped to find many of these answers by observing the Coast Guard's Maritime Patrol Airship in action. Working through the Naval Air Development Center (NADC) at Warminster, Pennsylvania, the Coast Guard drew up ten mission profiles for tasks ranging from search and rescue to antisubmarine warfare to buoy tending.

The Coast Guard needed a vehicle that was faster than a patrol boat, with greater range and load-carrying capacity than a helicopter, yet one that could remain on station for days at a time in every kind of weather, deliver emergency equipment, and remove injured personnel from ships at sea—all while burning significantly less fuel than their present ships, helicopters, and airplanes.

It was obvious that the vehicle the Coast Guard needed was an airship. During World War II these missions were repeatedly performed by navy blimps. A preliminary contract statement was prepared by NADC and issued on January 21, 1981.

The Coast Guard was not, however, looking for a recycled 1950s blimp. By setting their mission specifications beyond the performance of those last navy airships, NADC and the Coast Guard planned to lead the way toward a new generation of lighter-than-air vehicle. The Maritime Patrol Airship was to have a top speed of ninety knots (103.5 miles per hour), be able to hover within a ten-foot-diameter circle, and land with a ground crew of less than eight people. Each of these requirements is beyond the capabilities of any airship that has ever flown before.

The bidders' conference on the Coast Guard contract was held at Warminster on September 23, 1981. Representatives from a number of interested companies including Westinghouse, Northrop, Grumman, and Goodyear were present. A week later a telegram from NADC to all prospective bidders canceled the project "due to severe curtailment of funding allocations previously designated." The Reagan administration had scuttled the Coast Guard's airship.

In spite of funding constraints, the navy's interest in airships continued. They had already invited Goodyear to give a live demonstration of airship capabilities to the Coast Guard and the Customs Service. Preliminary flights were made by the Goodyear blimp *Enterprise* in August, 1981. More extensive tests were conducted in November, immediately after the NADC contract cancellation.

The mission was to interdict drugs being smuggled into South Florida from the Bahamas as well as those that were brought north aboard large ships and transferred to speedboats off the coast. Goodyear's *Enterprise,* based at Pompano Beach, was in an ideal location but with a volume of only 202,700 cubic feet was a bit small for the mission. The Coast Guard's proposal had called for a demonstration ship of around 240,000 cubic feet to be followed by a fleet of eight-hundred-thousand-cubic foot ships.

Still, the results with *Enterprise* proved interesting. On one of her first flights she encountered a heavily laden cruiser moving out at high speed from Bimini toward the Florida coast. As soon as the blimp was spotted, the boat turned tail and ran back to the island.

It wasn't until the last phase of the program in December 1981 that effective surveillance equipment finally arrived. When this airborne radar from Litton Systems Canada was installed, several night flights were undertaken. Night vision equipment was also used.

By the end of the experiment in January 1982, the Coast Guard had arrived at four official conclusions:

1. The airship is a stable observation platform.
2. It is adapted to the use of radar systems.
3. Only the airship can provide long aerial endurance.
4. Personnel fatigue is low on an airship.

None of these conclusions would come as startling news to the hundreds of naval officers and men who routinely flew thousands of airship hours during and after World War II, but perhaps they had to be proven once again to a new generation of bureaucrats.

At the operations level the experiment had gone smoothly. Further up the chain of command at both NADC and Goodyear, there were problems. Goodyear was accused of arrogance—as if theirs were the only blimps in town—which, in fact, they were. Some were annoyed that, with the tests conducted during football season, Goodyear chose to honor *Enterprise*'s previous commitments to the television networks. This meant the blimp was available only from Tuesday through Thursday and that the surveillance equipment had to be removed every Thursday and reinstalled every Tuesday.

For their part, some people at Goodyear were annoyed by reports that the military was annoyed, especially in light of the fact that they were getting it all for free. At the end of the test program in February 1982, Goodyear offered to lease the retired *America* to the Coast Guard at what a company spokesman described as "a very attractive rate." The Coast Guard was then forced to concede that they had no money in their budget for an airship and were even being forced to lay up some of their cutters because they couldn't afford the fuel to run them.

LEFT: The modern airship has a number of potential military applications. Coastal surveillance and protection is one of the most obvious. In the United States this is the job that falls traditionally to the Coast Guard. The Coast Guard's missions include fisheries regulation, drug smuggling interdiction, oil spill detection and cleanup, international ice patrol, airborne radiation monitoring, NOAA data buoy support, escort of vessels carrying hazardous cargo, port traffic control and fire fighting, search and rescue, buoy maintenance, and, in wartime, antisubmarine warfare, convoy escort, minelaying, and minesweeping. Airships would seem to be the most appropriate vehicle for all these tasks, but so far the money has not been allocated. *Painting by John Mellberg, courtesy Airships International Inc.* RIGHT: The Falkland Islands War demonstrated an area where airships could be of service. Fleet protection on station and in convoy, even when aircraft carriers are present, would allow more of the carrier's planes to be used for attack rather than defense. Other potential military applications include servicing unmanned Arctic early-warning stations, tracking Soviet submarines under the Arctic icecap, as cruise missile launchers, for beam weaponry and for air mobility with the Rapid Deployment Force. *Painting by John Mellberg, courtesy Airships International Inc.*

•

Two months later on April 2, 1982, Argentina invaded the Falkland Islands. The entire world was about to receive a demonstration of the potential value of the airship.

As the British fleet steamed south they had time to reconsider the wisdom of selling their last aircraft carrier. Operating thousands of miles from a friendly airfield, they were forced to rely on Nimrod radar planes for long-range detection of incoming Argentine planes and missiles. But each Nimrod required air-to-air refueling sixteen times on the flight to the Falklands and back. And after all that, it was able to spend only two hours on station over the fleet. The British had to use refueling planes to refuel their refueling planes and they still lost ships and men when the Nimrods were not on station.

A ZPG-2 blimp, on the other hand, could have flown to the Falklands, refueled from a ship of the fleet, and remained on station with its early-warning radar for weeks at a time. And the ZPG-2 is a thirty-year-old design. What might a modern airship be able to do?

The Falkland Islands War gave the U.S. Navy a number of things to think about. The most disquieting conclusion to emerge from their analysis was the vulnerability of surface ships with no early-warning air cover. The best defensive systems had proven less than effective against only moderately sophisticated air-launched Exocet missiles.

The U.S. Navy had plans for four task groups to be formed around recommissioned battleships. These task groups would have no carriers.

As a result of these deliberations, NADC announced immediate plans to bring a Skyship 500 to the U.S. for tests. The contract was signed in January 1983, and two months later, Skyship *500-03* was shipped from England by air to Toronto, where she was inflated. The navy and Coast Guard each paid $350,000 toward the lease while NASA added one hundred thousand dollars more. The demonstrations were flown out of the Naval Air Test Center at Patuxent River, Maryland, and the Coast Guard station at Elizabeth City, North Carolina, during the summer of 1983.

All those who professed disappointment at the performance of Goodyear's *Enterprise* in the winter of 1982 declared themselves delighted with the Skyship 500 in the summer of 1983. Though smaller than the *Enterprise,* the new ship was not weighed down with a night advertising sign. This gave her 2,270 pounds more disposable lift: 5,090 pounds versus *Enterprise*'s 2,820. The Skyship 500 was also fifteen miles per hour faster and, thanks to her vectored-thrust propellers, noticeably easier to maneuver.

The turnaround seems surprising. Before the Falkland Islands War the Coast Guard was alone in its desire for airships. The *Enterprise* trials were paid for by Goodyear. Then eight hundred thousand dollars was found to lease a Skyship 500 and everyone was excited by the results.

The navy spent all of 1984 trying to find some other solution to their problem. There was none. The airship appeared to be the only airborne platform capable of early detection and tracking of low-flying Soviet cruise missiles either at sea, the navy's prime concern, or in the Arctic, where the air force has jurisdiction. The air force hopes to automate its radar stations in northern Canada and in Alaska. The stations are beyond the range of helicopters, there are no roads and, without anyone to shovel the snow off the runways, planes cannot land. There, too, airships seem the only answer.

Meanwhile, 1984 proved to be a banner year for Airship Industries. They sold a Skyship 500 to Japan Air Lines and leased another to Fuji Film for use at the Los Angeles Olympics. Australian businessman Alan Bond bought 31 percent of the still struggling company and, most important, their new Skyship 600 made her first flight. An expanded version of the 500, she was larger than the Goodyear blimps, designed to carry twenty passengers. The newest company in the airship business was now flying the biggest ship in the sky. Goodyear's response would not be airborne until August 1987.

In February 1985, after a year of deliberation, NADC issued a request for proposals for a Battle Surveillance Airship. It was to perform both AEW (airborne early warning) and ASW (antisubmarine warfare) missions with a naval task group that would not include an aircraft carrier. The airship was to be deployed as a regular naval unit accompanying the group. It would be resupplied by other ships in the group. It would be expected to demonstrate low-speed controllability and the ability to take on supplies while the group was underway. NADC announced that it had two hundred million dollars to spend.

To anyone unfamiliar with government procurement procedures, the system needs a bit of explaining. In the first stage, the navy decided that it really wanted an airship and was willing to pay for it. This took up all of 1984. NADC then drew up a detailed list of mission requirements, things the proposed airship would be expected to do. Then it issued the RFP, the request for proposals. Anyone who wanted to build the navy's airship was entitled to ask for the specifications and submit a bid. The catch was that if NADC decided from your bid that you didn't know much about airships, they were allowed to throw it out.

LEFT: Airship Industries' largest ship was the Skyship 600, a stretched version of their 500 series. Her first flight was made at Cardington on March 6, 1984. With a gas capacity of 235,400 cubic feet and a length of 194 feet, she was 30 feet longer than the 500 and could carry up to twenty passengers. *Courtesy Airship Industries Ltd.* RIGHT: Of the three hundred airships built by Goodyear since Melvin Vaniman's *Akron* in 1912, fifty-five were retained by the company and flown as part of their own blimp fleet. This newest blimp, *Spirit of Akron*, was christened on August 4, 1987. Built partly as a response to Airship Industries' Skyship 600, the *Spirit of Akron* is the largest airship now flying. She is 205.5 feet long, 47 feet in diameter, and holds 247,800 cubic feet of helium. Ships of this new GZ-22 design were to replace all four of Goodyear's GZ-20 blimps. The GZ-20s are 192 feet long with a volume of 202,700 cubic feet and a top speed of fifty miles per hour. The new ship is fifteen miles per hour faster with vectored thrust propellers. She carries ten people rather than the GZ-20's seven, plus a more elaborate night advertising sign. But since the sale of Goodyear's aerospace division to Loral, it is unclear whether any more GZ-22s will be built. *Courtesy Goodyear Tire and Rubber Company.*

Jack R. Hunt always insisted that the return of the airship must begin with many small ships rather than a few very large ones. The old skills would have to be relearned in the shop, on the ground, and in the air with smaller ships before they could be transferred again to the big ones. On the civilian side this process is already underway as can be seen in the Great Blimp Race over New York harbor on July 5, 1986, during the birthday celebration for the Statue of Liberty. The five blimps in the race were (back to front) Westdeutsch Luftwerbung's *McDonald's,* Fuji's *Skyship 500-06,* Resorts International's *SK 600-03,* Citibank's *SK 500-03,* and the sponsoring *Daily News*'s *SK 600-04.* The Fuji blimp won. *Courtesy Airship Industries Ltd.*

•

After reading all the bids, some of which ran to hundreds of pages, NADC selected the finalists. These were companies or teams of companies that submitted serious proposals for ships that looked like they could perform the navy's missions.

Now NADC had to come up with enough money to allow each finalist to prepare a much more detailed design of the ship they wanted to build. This money was allocated so as not to penalize a small company that might have a good idea but could not afford the extensive engineering work required to make sure their idea would really fly. The government paid the finalists to prepare their proposals.

In May 1985, NADC awarded three $650,000 study contracts to Goodyear teamed with Sperry and Litton, to Westinghouse teamed with Airship Industries, and to Boeing teamed with Wren Skyships. Three additional contracts of three hundred thousand dollars apiece were awarded to Hughes, Westinghouse, and RCA for the ship's electronics.

Boeing put in eighteen months' work on a 4.2-million-cubic-foot, semimonocoque design before dropping out of the competition. Then Goodyear unexpectedly found itself under attack by a corporate raider, Sir James Goldsmith. He had acquired twelve million shares of Goodyear stock and declared his intention of taking over the company. Goodyear management fought back. They announced a tender offer for fifty million of their own shares. But in order to finance the massive debt this move required, they were forced to sell several subsidiaries—including Goodyear Aerospace.

Goodyear is the largest tire manufacturer in the world. Airships have always been a highly visible but generally unprofitable sideline. The deal was made. The management of the Goodyear Tire & Rubber Company retained control of the core of their organization. Sir James Goldsmith reportedly took home a profit of ninety-three million dollars by selling his stock back to the company. He had to promise not to do it again for five years.

Everyone was pleased with the arrangement—with the possible exception of the entire lighter-than-air organization.

In March 1987, Goodyear Aerospace was sold to the Loral Corporation, a New York–based defense electronics contractor, for $588 million. Three months after that, on June 5, 1987, the U.S. Navy awarded a $168,900,000 contract for a single prototype Radar Surveillance Airship to Westinghouse and Airship Industries.

Goodyear lost the competition by proposing an updated version of the 1,500,000-cubic-foot ZPG-3W. They had even retrieved a discarded ZPG-3W control car from Lakehurst where it had been sitting for nearly thirty years and hauled it back to Akron to see if it could be reused. Loral later raised the size of Goodyear's proposal to 1,933,000 cubic feet but it was too late.

Airship Industries won with a design they called their *Sentinel 5000.* It would be 423 feet long and 105 feet in diameter, with a volume of 2,350,000 cubic feet—more gas than the *Shenandoah!* It would carry a crew of ten and be powered by two Italian-built 1,625-horsepower diesel engines driving two vectored-thrust propellers. It would also have a 1,750-horsepower turboprop engine in the rear of the control car driving its own pusher propeller. This engine would be for short, high-speed runs while the two more fuel-efficient diesels would be used for extended cruising at lower speeds. The control car would be eighty-one feet long and three decks high. The ship would carry a Westinghouse phased-array radar antenna with a two-hundred-mile range and be armed with air-to-air missiles and ASW

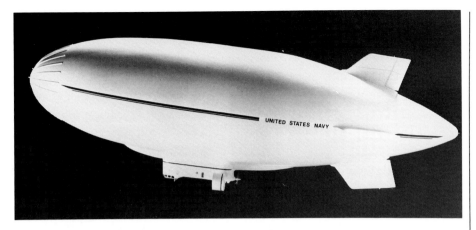

weapons. It would be ready for navy service by June 1992.

As Adm. Robert Leuschner, director of Anti-Submarine and Assault Programs, Naval Air Systems Command, freely admitted, the proposed Battle Surveillance Airship would be called upon to revive technology that has been absent from the navy for over a quarter of a century. And it would have to do it with a single vehicle, one 50 percent larger than any nonrigid airship ever built before, which would be maintained and flown by an inexperienced crew.

Whether this unusual approach will lead to success may never be known. Most of the funds for the new airship were cut from the Pentagon's 1989 budget and its completion date was extended by several years.

Does this mean the navy's search for an alternative to the airship has been successful? Not according to Adm. Robert F. Dunn, deputy chief of naval operations for air warfare. In the *Proceedings of the U.S. Naval Institute,* he said that the budget cut reflects the need to save money, not the merit of the concept, which is as valid as ever.

The fate of both the Coast Guard's Maritime Patrol Airship and the navy's Battle Surveillance Airship offers further proof of Jack R. Hunt's contention. The airship still lacks friends in high places—influential congressmen who can shepherd appropriations safely through the budgetary gauntlet. These episodes also underline two drawbacks to dealing with the U.S. government. The first is that its word is not necessarily its bond. The second is less obvious. Airship Industries' design for the *Sentinel 5000* now belongs to the U.S. Navy. So does Goodyear's plan for an updated ZPG-3W and Boeing's for their semimonocoque ship. The navy paid $650,000 apiece for them. By entering the design competition, the companies lost exclusive control over their own work.

One man who hoped to avoid these pitfalls was Vladimir Pavlecka. After a lifetime spent working on government-sponsored research projects, he vowed he would build his airship with private funds. Had he been successful, his innovative design would now be in the air and available for purchase at far less than the navy's projected cost. Unfortunately, Pavlecka found that private industry in the United States—once bold and innovative—has grown timorous and obsessed by short-term profit. His ship remains on the drawing board.

Why should Pavlecka's design be of more interest than any of a thousand others—all unbuilt? How did he elicit comments like those of Admiral Seiberlich's at the beginning of this chapter?

Working with America's leading dirigible designer, Pavlecka helped build the

If completed, the *Sentinel 5000* will be 423 feet long and hold 2,350,000 cubic feet of helium, the largest non-rigid ever built. Her hull will be a single ply of Dacron laminated to films of Mylar for strength and Tedlar for impermeability to helium. Though the concept was originally designated the Battle Surveillance Airship, it was later called the ODM or Operational Development Model. It is not the same as the NAP or Naval Airship Program, which is to follow, assuming that the ODM proves successful. The navy has already decided that follow-on airships will have to be larger than the ODM. This ship will therefore be a one-of-a-kind dirigible whose main function is to provide data to support the studies that show the airship can perform the navy's missions. *Courtesy Westinghouse-Airship Industries Inc.*

•

In 1936 the only way to fly from Europe to the Midwest was to cross the Atlantic aboard the Hindenburg, then make the connection at Lakehurst by DC-3 to Chicago. These two machines stood together as the most advanced aircraft in their respective fields of aviation. In the half-century since this photograph was taken, the DC-3 has evolved into the Concorde, the Stealth bomber, and the Space Shuttle. What kind of dirigibles would be flying today if lighter-than-air technology had come as far? *U.S. Navy photo in the National Archives.*

•

most advanced airship of its day. That was sixty years ago. Since then he has played a major role in the creation of the modern aerospace industry. The past and the future were uniquely combined in this singular individual whose vision of the airship of tomorrow deserves a closer look.

Vladimir Pavlecka was born in 1901 in Bohemia, then part of the Austro-Hungarian Empire, now Czechoslovakia. The first aircraft he ever saw were German Zeppelins that flew over his village on their way to the eastern front.

Vladimir Pavlecka

Sometimes at school we would hear the sound of their engines but by the time we ran to the windows they would be far off on the horizon. Then one day, one came over flying against a strong headwind that slowed him down quite a bit. He was not over six hundred or seven hundred feet high. I ran along beneath it and could easily keep up with it. I could see the crewmen looking down at me and smiling as I ran along. I ran with it for miles and miles, fascinated by the huge ship floating in the air over my head, until finally it flew away and I found myself far from home. But I didn't mind the long walk back.[4]

Pavlecka's father was an engineer and young Vladimir graduated from the technical school at Praha where he studied turbine engineering with Professor Zvonicek, one of the men who developed the modern turbine. He also learned thermodynamics at a time when that science wasn't yet being taught in the United States.

He left Praha in 1923 to study electrical engineering at Union College in Schenectady, New York. After graduation he moved to Detroit where his brother got him a job at General Motors Research Laboratories. There he worked on the layouts for the first Buick straight-eight engine. He also met two young men in the same building who were designing an all-metal dirigible. At the end of 1925 Pavlecka left General Motors to join their company, the Aircraft Development Corporation.

One of Pavlecka's new employers was Carl Fritsche, a lawyer and Republican Party fund-raiser. The other was Ralph Upson, the former head of Goodyear's Aeronautics Department and a leading balloonist. He won the Gordon Bennett International Balloon Race in 1913 and the National Balloon Race in 1919 and again in 1921. In 1920 when he left Goodyear to start the Aircraft Development Corporation, he was the leading dirigible designer in the United States.

Vladimir Pavlecka

The story of the founding of the company is so unusual that it invites doubt. But Carl Fritsche told this to me personally as we were driving in a car together, just the two of us, and I have absolutely no doubt that he was telling the truth. He said he was sailing on a Great Lakes steamer from Detroit to Cleveland on Lake Erie. This was in the days when passenger ships made overnight trips between cities on the Great Lakes. It was August and there was a beautiful full moon. Rather than go down to his cabin, Fritsche decided to spend the night on deck. He was sitting there in the moonlight when an old man came up to him and they fell into conversation. The old man was talking about metal airships and his enthusiasm soon infected Fritsche. They discussed the subject for hours and when Fritsche finally excused himself and went below to his cabin, he realized that he had forgotten to ask the old man his name. The steamer was docking in Cleveland early the next morning and Fritsche went up before they put the gangway over so he would be sure to see the old man when he got off. But the old man did not appear and Fritsche never saw him again. But his enthusiasm for metal airships remained and at the first opportunity Fritsche went to Goodyear in Akron, the only company in the United States that was then producing airships. There he was introduced to Ralph Upson and when Fritsche explained his newfound enthusiasm for metal airships to Upson, Ralph said that he had been considering the design problems of the metal airship for some time. They formed a partnership and Fritsche went out to raise the money. He had been doing this for years for the Republican Party. He went to his friends in the Detroit automobile industry. Ford was already involved in the Stout trimotor airplane. This seemed like an opportunity to make Detroit the aviation as well as the automotive capital of the world. Fritsche got backing from Edsel Ford, Charles Mott who was the biggest stockholder in General Motors, Charles F. Kettering, and a number of others. When the development work was completed and they were ready to build their ship, Fritsche went to his friend, Arthur Vandenberg, the Republican leader of the Senate. Once Fritsche convinced him of the value of the metal airship Vandenberg added an appropriation for a metal ship to the navy's budget request for that year. When the budget was approved, the navy found itself with money it had never asked for to build a ship it didn't want and the only company capable of building it was, of course, the Aircraft Development Corporation of Detroit.[5]

Construction began in 1926. The next year, the company moved into its own hangar at the southern end of Grosse Ile, a wooded island in the Detroit River not far from downtown Detroit. As Pavlecka recalled, "The hangar was right in the woods. I would open the window of my laboratory and a tree branch would come in."

Fritsche convinced Alcoa, the Aluminum Company of America, to join the venture. They supplied quantities of 17-ST alloy aluminum sheet that arrived packed in fish oil against corrosion. "The whole place smelled of it," Pavlecka said. The largest sheets Alcoa could produce were ten feet long but only eighteen inches wide.

Ralph Hazlett Upson (1888–1968). A graduate in mechanical engineering from Stevens Institute of Technology, Upson joined Goodyear in 1910. He was construction supervisor on the gasbag of Melvin Vaniman's *Akron* in 1912 and helped develop all the navy's early blimps after the *DN-1*. He also designed a number of army blimps including the first TC ships. During World War II he worked on gliders for the Heinz Company in Pittsburgh and ended his career in Seattle on the X-20 Dyna-Soar project. He died at the age of eighty while on a mountain-climbing expedition. Vladimir Pavlecka said of Upson, "He was an intellectual of the first magnitude. He seemed to see things much bigger than the rest of us saw them." *Courtesy Vladimir Pavlecka.*

•

Vladimir Pavlecka at the age of twenty-eight at one of the *ZMC-2*'s hull access ports.

In 1919, just as my brother and I entered the technical school of higher learning in Praha, there descended on all the schools a great number of young men, former soldiers, whose education had been delayed by the war. Now they were all coming at once to make up for this postponement and it was apparent that they, who were several years older than the rest of us, would receive preference in finding jobs upon graduation. So the future for those of us who were too young to be in the war but who would be graduating at the same time, did not look good. My brother and I studied English then and upon graduation in 1923, we came to the United States. This I have never regretted.

Vladimir Pavlecka

Photo courtesy John Roda.

The completed stern section hanging from the top of the construction shed shows the ripples in the unpressurized metal skin. Though the aluminum-coated duralumin was rolled to a thickness of only .0095 of an inch, about the same as that of a match-book cover, it had considerable strength, which was increased even further when the hull was filled with helium under pressure. "Then," Pav-lecka said, "all the wrinkles which were present simply disappeared as if it were alive." When the two halves of the metal hull, the bow and stern sections, were lowered to the horizontal and joined together, they fit per-fectly. No adjustments were neces-sary and the final seam was riveted from the inside by hand. *Courtesy John Roda.*

•

A riveting machine had to be designed to stitch the many pieces together auto-matically with a gastight seam. As work progressed on the stern section it was found that the first sheets had already begun to corrode. Upson pleaded with Alcoa to find a better alloy. This was eventually discovered in an expired French patent. Made of duralumin rolled in pure aluminum, it was christened Alclad and is still in use in airplanes today.

While they were waiting for the first shipment of the new alloy, the original stern section was set in concrete and filled with water until it began to pull away from its base. Then the water was pumped out until the vacuum caused the section to collapse. Finally it was refilled with water until it popped back into shape. Close examination revealed no signs of failure. It was then that Upson knew his concept would work.

By this time Pavlecka had been promoted to chief of hull design. The *ZMC-2* was launched on August 19, 1929. She remained in navy service until early in 1941 when, still airworthy but too small for long patrols, she was dismantled. She was the world's first and only successful all-metal airship. Fritsche and Upson tried to interest the government in larger metalclad designs but without success.

After the completion of the *ZMC-2* the company changed its name to the Metalclad Airship Corporation and, as the depression worsened, purchased a number of failing airplane manufacturers including Ryan, Lockheed, Blackburn of England, the Eastman Flying Boat Company, and even Parks Air College. Detroit was truly going to be the aviation capital of the world. But in 1931 the depression caught up with the Metalclad Airship Corporation and it, too, went bankrupt. The Lockheed and Ryan engineers who had been brought to Detroit returned to Califor-nia and, two years later, Pavlecka and his friend and co-worker, John Roda, went west to join them.

The Douglas Aircraft Company at that time had a problem. They had just completed what was to become the most successful airliner of its day, the DC-2. Its prototype, the DC-1, carried twelve passengers. The DC-2 had been lengthened by two feet so it could carry fourteen. The airlines wanted still more but the DC-2 was already the largest twin-engine landplane ever built in the U.S. How was Douglas to put more people inside without making the outside too big to fly?

The obvious answer was to make the plane lighter. Less metal meant more lift for more passengers. Douglas needed an expert on light-metal aircraft structures, someone, for instance, who had just built a metal balloon.

Vladimir Pavlecka

I got three job offers that day, one at Lockheed, one at Douglas, and one at Vultee. I took the one at Douglas. I was hired by Lee Atwood, who was the head of the proposals department. He later became president of North American Aviation. Douglas had around 150 engineers, which was a big operation in those days. I got the job because I knew light metals. There was no history of light-metal aircraft structures in the U.S. Germany was ahead of us. There the experience had come from airships where every extra pound has to be eliminated. In Germany it started with two men, Claude Dornier and Adolph Rohrbach, and both of them got their start with Count Zeppelin. He set both of them up in the metal airplane business. Rohrbach built some very advanced metal flying boats after World War I and licensed them in England, France, Czechoslovakia, and to Heinkel in Germany. His principle was of a series of metal boxes united one to another, each gaining strength from the others. That way, each box could be of a lighter

gauge than if it had to stand alone. This was the principle that came from Zeppelin construction through Rohrbach to airplane construction. It was a technique that was introduced in this country by John Northrop. He built some very beautiful single-engine airplanes with it. And this principle was continued in the DC-2 but it was still too heavy. To accept light gauges still made people very uneasy. The pieces did not look strong enough and individually they weren't but collectively they were. From the outside, the DC-3 looked like the DC-2. It was only twenty-six inches wider and had 5 percent more wing surface. But inside, it was a very different airplane.[6]

The DC-3 could carry a 50 percent greater payload than its predecessor: twenty-one passengers instead of fourteen. For the first time the airlines had a plane that could make a profit on passengers alone. They no longer needed a government mail contract. "The pilots were scared to death of the first DC-3s," Pavlecka recalled, "because the wings flexed. They had never seen that before. I gave seminars for the airlines explaining the principles involved but the pilots didn't believe me. Only experience allayed their fears."[7]

For his work on the DC-3, Douglas promoted Pavlecka to head of structural research. He was given his own shop and a staff of twenty-two engineers. They invented the hexagonal stop nut, hydraulic wing folding for naval aircraft, and flush riveting. They developed the first tricycle landing gear ever used on a large airplane, the B-19, as well as its mechanically self-sealing fuel tanks. They designed Douglas's first pressurized fuselage for the DC-4, developed the modern method of hydropressing with rubber dies, and changed Douglas from extruded to rolled sheet metal sections, the aerospace industry standard today. "It's one of the few improvements Boeing ever had to learn from Douglas," Pavlecka proudly recalled.

Pavlecka's early schooling in turbine technology was still with him. In Detroit he had designed a steam turbine for a large metalclad that was never built.

Vladimir Pavlecka

When we began to design very large airships we encountered a problem. There were no suitable engines for them. We ended up proposing to use the Curtiss V-12 pursuit plane engine, which was totally unacceptable but there was nothing else. So I began thinking about steam turbines and I did quite a bit of work on it. I determined that it was feasible but nothing ever came of it. Then later at Douglas we had the same problem. In 1935 we

LEFT: The *ZMC-2* is shown as she neared completion inside the construction shed on Grosse Ile in the Detroit River. Hundreds of helium containers are stacked on the hangar floor. The first attempt to build the hull had to be halted when the aluminum began to corrode. Alcoa was then encouraged to develop Alclad, an alloy originally used on the *ZMC-2* and still in wide use today. Sections of the *ZMC-2* hull that still survive at Northrop University and in the National Air and Space Museum remain as supple and corrosion-free as when they were first rolled, more than half a century ago. *Courtesy Northrop University.* RIGHT: Launched on August 19, 1929, the *ZMC-2* remained in navy service until 1941 when she was dismantled and her hull melted down for the aluminum. She logged a total of twenty-three hundred hours of flying time during her twelve-year career. The inscription on this photograph to John Roda, one of the crew members on the first test flight, is from the ship's official army test pilot, Maj. William Kepner. It says, "To John W. Roda a crew member of the *ZMC-2*. It was, in my opinion, the strongest airship ever built. It exceeded all requirements of the U.S. Navy acceptance tests. It could have provided many answers to airship 'Air Transportation.'" Kepner, an experienced balloon and airship pilot, retired with the rank of major general after World War II. *Courtesy John Roda.*

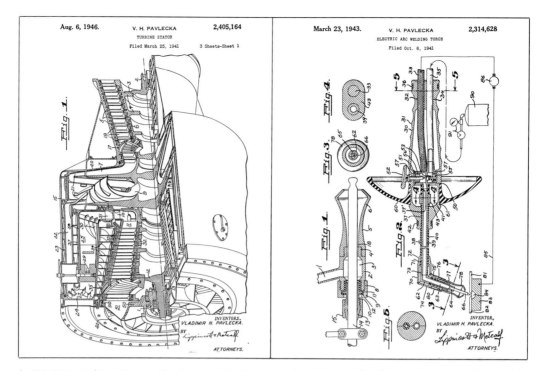

LEFT: Patent 2,405,164, Turbine Stator. This is the original stator patent that was finally issued to Pavlecka in 1946 after eleven years of delay and disinterest in the jet engine on the part of both government and industry. In those same years the jet engine was developed independently in England and Germany. Frank Whittle's engine was financed by private investors in England while Hans von Ohain's was built by Ernst Heinkel in Germany. Both flew before the end of World War II and only Hitler's meddling prevented the German jet fighter from playing a significant role in the war. The first jet plane to fly in the United States, the P-59, was powered by a U.S. copy of Whittle's British engine. RIGHT: Patent 2,314,628, Electric Arc Welding Torch.

In the oxyacetylene welding process, impurities are picked up from the air and show up in the weld. The idea of shielding the welding arc with an inert gas like helium or argon was related to my familiarity with the use of helium in airships. I remember being called into Jack Northrop's office one day. The chairman of the board was even there so I knew it was something important. They said I was spending too much money trying to develop this welding thing. I asked how much I had spent. They said it was already up to $3,400. I looked at the figures and I showed them where the welding department had been charging their expenses to my research department. I had, in fact, spent only three hundred dollars on it. They let me continue with the project but only if I was able to finish it up in one more month. Well, we did finish it, and a few years ago *Fortune* magazine said that Heliarc welding is now a six-billion-dollar industry. That's not bad for a three-hundred-dollar investment.

Vladimir Pavlecka

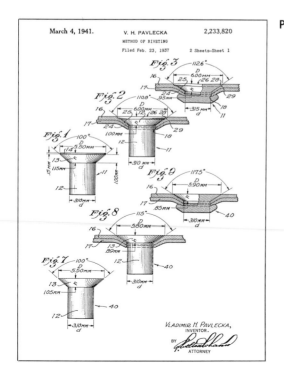

Patent 2,233,820, Method of Riveting.

The standard rivet was then eighty-six degrees. It didn't produce a good flush rivet because it had too much metal in the head so we had considerable redesigning to do to get the particular form of the one-hundred-degree rivet that is the standard in the industry today. When the patent for the riveting tool was applied for, I put the names of myself and five of my staff on the application. The patent examiner responded by saying that six people could not invent anything. I asked him how many people could and he said that three is the largest number of people who can invent something. So the patent has only three of us on it. There is a story that Howard Hughes heard about our rivet just as his newest speed plane was nearing completion. He ordered all the old rivets removed and our new flush rivets installed. There were thousands of them but he gained a significant increase in speed because of the smoother surfaces.

Vladimir Pavlecka

designed the B-19, the largest plane ever built and it was driven by engines that were much too small for it because there was nothing else. And I began to think again of turbines. Not steam turbines because they would be too heavy in an airplane, but gas turbines. The gas turbine had a bad reputation among engineers then. One had been built in France in 1906. It worked but had an efficiency of only 3 percent. Yet the company made a fortune on it. All the torpedoes in those days were powered by steam turbines. This company replaced them all with gas turbines. It is an interesting fact that no company has ever lost money building turbines. I collected all the information I could find on gas turbines and determined that, despite its bad reputation, it could be used as an efficient aircraft powerplant.[8]

Conceived in 1935, begun in 1940, changed from a jet to a turboprop by the navy early in 1941, and not completed until 1945, Northrop's Turbodyne engine never flew. John Northrop may have intended to use the engine to power his Flying Wing, another farsighted project that was delayed and eventually killed by government interference. Pavlecka was forced to leave Northrop after a series of disagreements with Theodore von Karman, a Northrop consultant. Pavlecka was forced out at the end of 1942. "To leave that engine was the hardest thing I ever had to do," he said. "It was like leaving a child to be raised by others." *Courtesy Northrop Corporation.*

•

In 1935 Pavlecka took his preliminary designs to Douglas management. Douglas gave them to Pratt & Whitney who sent them to their consultants at the Massachusetts Institute of Technology. Three months later an answer came back from Pratt & Whitney. They agreed with their experts at MIT. The jet engine could not work and even if it did, there would be nothing useful for it to do.

It took four years before Pavlecka found someone to back his jet engine. In 1939 John Northrop asked him to join his new company as its first chief of research. Pavlecka agreed but only if Northrop would seriously consider his jet engine. "What's a jet engine?" Northrop asked. Pavlecka explained and Northrop agreed. Northrop Aircraft was formed late in 1939. Work began on America's first jet engine early in 1940.

Northrop financed the initial work with company funds. When they took their plans to the Army Air Corps, no one understood what they were talking about. The navy was afraid the flame from the jet exhaust would set the wooden decks of their aircraft carriers on fire and ordered the design changed to a turboprop. It became Northrop's Turbodyne project and was not completed until 1945.

Meanwhile in England, Gen. Hap Arnold was invited out into the countryside to witness a test flight of a new airplane, the Gloster E 28/39. Arnold approached the plane with curiosity. "Where is the propeller?" he asked.

"There is none," his British hosts replied. "It's a jet."

"What's a jet?" Arnold asked.

The man at Arnold's side, Maj. Donald Keirn, knew what a jet was. Nine months earlier it had all been carefully explained to him by Vladimir Pavlecka. Keirn hadn't believed it then. He began to believe it now.

The E 28/39 made two brief flights that day. Arnold was astonished. He sent for a B-17 to fly two of the new British engines back to the U.S. They were delivered

Vladimir Pavlecka (left) and John Roda in front of a DC-3 on display at the National Air and Space Museum in Washington, D.C. Both men began their careers working on the *ZMC-2,* then came to Douglas. Pavlecka became head of structural research while John Roda served for twenty-seven years as general factory superintendent at Douglas's El Segundo plant, where he originated the multi-model, variable-speed production line. He also lectured on prototype and production aircraft manufacturing techniques at Caltech. Without the production procedures pioneered by these two men, especially the use of sheet metal rather than extruded sections, the American aircraft industry would have been even harder pressed to meet the challenges forced upon it at the beginning of World War II. *Photo by the author.*

•

to General Electric. The reasoning was that since GE already made turbines for hydroelectric power plants, they should also be able to quickly produce turbines for airplanes. The reasoning was wrong. The only jets to fly in combat in World War II were German.

Back at Northrop, Pavlecka invented the Heliarc welding process and then returned to Douglas where, in nine days, he and Fred Dallenbach designed the world's first production turboprop engine, the Allison T-38, which was later used to power the Lockheed Electra. After that he worked on the Apollo moon rocket and completed development of the centripetal compressor and the contra-rotating gas turbine.

In a history such as this, with events taking place in a dozen nations and from the North Pole to the jungles of Brazil, it is easy to lose track of the fact that all this has happened within a very short time span. But here we have a single individual, Vladimir Pavlecka, who watched in awe as German Zeppelins flew over his village schoolhouse on their way to the eastern front, and who also worked on the rocket engines that lifted the *Lunar Lander* from the surface of the moon.

It has been a period of incredible technological progress. Even more surprising is the fact that so much of it has been touched by the efforts of this same individual. Take the Boeing 747 as an example. Its Alclad sheet metal sections formed by hydropressing, its tricycle landing gear, its jet engines, and pressurized fuselage—Vladimir Pavlecka had a hand in all of them. The 747's stop nuts, its flush rivets, and its Heliarc welds—all these patents have his name on them. Yet even after fifty years at the very center of the modern aerospace industry, he never forgot his first love, the metal airship.

Vladimir Pavlecka

I have always regarded airships as an important form of transportation. I was dismayed that they were not taken more seriously by others in the aerospace industry. Even after the very successful performance of the navy blimps in World War II, I was amazed at the depth of negative feeling about them. I even hesitated to talk about them for fear that I would be considered odd. But that did not stop me from continuing to work on their development. And I am convinced now more than ever that Ralph Upson's metalclad principle is the key to the future. At first he tried to convert a fabric ship into metal. He was very familiar with fabric ships but their shape is deformed by the pressure of their lifting gas. They are not circular in cross section and they are generally working with different principles than metalclad ships are. Upson's was a completely original concept in shell structures. We knew very little about shell structures at that time. Since then a great deal of work has been done on them in the United States, in Europe, and in Russia. But Upson's contribution, his insight, was a very fundamental one, yet one that was completely original with him. We proved it first in the water model and then in the *ZMC-2.* There is no doubt in my mind that it will be the basis of the airship of the future and I have continued to work toward its perfection over all these years.[9]

His continuing interest in airships combined with his pioneering work in the aerospace industry placed Pavlecka in a unique position with regard to the airship's revival. In the past the key to success in lighter-than-air design has been the experience of the people involved: hard-won experience gained over years of work building and flying airships. Today that experience is almost gone. Yet even if the men who built the great rigid airships were still active, their knowledge would be half a century out of date. The *Hindenburg* and her sister ship, the *LZ-130,*

The *MC-7* is Vladimir Pavlecka's vision of the airship of the future, the next logical step beyond the modern blimp. Its design specifically addresses the blimp's two primary shortcomings of low speed and the necessity for a large ground crew. A metalclad, the MC-7 hull varies in thickness from .006 to .008 of an inch. Its computer-controlled thrusters at the bow and stern are activated by electronic sensors for precise hovering and ground control. With no tail fins to add to drag and with hull slots for boundary layer removal, the ship's two internal five-hundred-horsepower turbine engines will be able to drive it at speeds in excess of a hundred miles per hour. *Painting by John Mellberg, Courtesy Airships International Inc.*

•

represented the highest achievements in rigid Zeppelin design but they are no more modern dirigibles than their contemporary, the DC-3, is a modern airplane.

Technology has come a long way in the last fifty years and few people combine both the hard-won airship experience of the past with a knowledge of the very latest in aerospace materials and techniques. One who did was Vladimir Pavlecka.

Several years ago, after completing contract studies on the subject for NASA and the navy, Pavlecka became convinced that the time would soon be right for the return of the airship. He and John Roda, with financial backing from Dr. Earl Kiernan, a former Strategic Air Command flight surgeon, formed Airships International in Tustin, California. Joined by several leading specialists in the aerospace industry, friends of long standing who added their expertise to his, Pavlecka set to work. His goal was the creation of a truly modern all-metal airship.

Vladimir Pavlecka

The *ZMC-2* gave us Alclad and the development of light-metal structures that led through the DC-3 to modern aviation. Now the aerospace industry can return the favor. There are things we wanted to do on the *ZMC-2* that simply couldn't be done. The technology was not yet in place. Today it is. Today, with metal bonding, epoxy laminates, aluminum-magnesium-lithium alloys, carbon and boron fibers, gaseous fuel turbines, computer-activated thruster control, and boundary layer removal, we can create a new generation of metal ships as far ahead of the *ZMC-2* as today's jumbo jets are beyond the plywood airliners of the 1920s.[10]

A number of the developments that Pavlecka envisioned for use in his new metalclads are still on the drawing boards. Pavlecka was always ahead of his time but, as a practical engineer, he designed his first modern dirigible around systems and materials already available.

This first design doesn't look quite like other airships. It has no tail fins. These have always been a problem in airships. They add considerable weight to the tail where the least amount of lifting gas is available to carry that weight. Pavlecka calculated that tail fins with their control surfaces, the rudders and elevators, add an average of 20 percent to hull weight and 14 percent to drag. In addition, they are useless when the ship is flying slowly or is stopped in the air. With no airflow over its

The *Omnia Dir* was a semirigid, 170 feet long, forty feet in diameter, with a gas capacity of 140,000 cubic feet. She was completed in 1931 after the death of her designer, Enrico Forlanini. She was described as an experimental prototype built only to test the new maneuvering system. She was powered by an old 150-horsepower Isotta-Frascheni engine that also turned two centrifugal fans, which blew into cloth tubes sending compressed air to the bow and stern where it could be directed in any of five directions through the valves. *Courtesy Stato Maggiore Aeronautica, Rome.*

•

control surfaces, the dirigible becomes little more than a free balloon and requires a large ground crew to assist in landing it.

This is, in fact, one of the major shortcomings of the airship that the Coast Guard hoped to eliminate in its Maritime Patrol Airship by requiring the ability to maneuver within a ten-foot-diameter circle and land with a ground crew of less than eight people.

Pavlecka felt he had solved the problem by replacing the traditional tail fins with cold-air thrusters at his ship's bow and stern. The idea of thrusters was originated back in 1930 by Italian dirigible designer Enrico Forlanini. His ship, the *Omnia Dir,* was completed after his death and on June 11, 1931, was flown directly out of her hangar at La Valle airport near Baggio without the aid of any ground crew at all.

Città Del Popola, June 12, 1931

Angioletta Forlanini, age five, the granddaughter of the inventor and godmother of the new ship, pulled the string that made the traditional champagne bottle break against the propeller hub. The *Omnia Dir* received in this way her baptism. It was then that the dirigible moved out of the hangar on its own means, the airmen on the field restricting themselves to crowd control duties. After a few minutes, the *Omnia Dir* lifted off and, with propeller turning, set off to Milan. After circling for some time, the dirigible came back to the airport and with surprising nimbleness repeated the maneuver, landing without throwing out the ballast rope. Just as easily, it moved rapidly into the hangar. The Duke of Bergamo, the only passenger on this first flight, jumped out of the cabin, and expressed his best congratulations to the relatives of Forlanini and to the workmen.[11]

Since their introduction by Forlanini, thrusters have been used on the *Lunar Lander* and are built into most modern merchant ships. Ships have the same maneuvering problems as dirigibles. In port at slow speed, a large ship has no flow of water past its rudder and requires the assistance of tugboats to get it to the dock. An airship must use people hauling on landing lines for the same purpose.

Pavlecka believed that computer-controlled thrusters mounted firmly on his airship's rigid metal hull would give it the same maneuverability as a helicopter. When this is added to the dirigible's great range, load-carrying ability, and fuel efficiency, it will result in a vehicle of unequaled versatility.

The second of the airship's traditional shortcomings that Pavlecka addressed was speed. This is the problem that concerned the Coast Guard when they required a top speed for their Maritime Patrol Airship of ninety knots (103.5 mph). The U.S. Navy's ZPG-3W blimps were the fastest airships ever built but their top speed was less than ninety miles per hour.

A blimp's speed is limited by a phenomenon called bow dimpling—an innocuous way of describing the collapse of the ship's bow by the pressure of the air pushing against it at high speeds. The lines that can be seen radiating from the bows of most blimps are battens, strips of reinforcing material attached to the envelope to give the bow more support.

But a metal-hulled ship with a pressurized interior would be far more resistant to bow dimpling and the resulting increase in drag. In addition, Pavlecka proposed to insert boundary layer removal slots near the stern of his ship to siphon away the turbulent air that attaches itself to all aircraft hulls at high speeds and results in additional drag. In this way he believed that the 10 percent increase in speed required by the Coast Guard could easily be attained and surpassed.

Pavlecka's design was well advanced at his death. He called it the MC-7. (The MC stands for metalclad.) One of the errors he had noted in the schemes of airship promoters over the years was their fondness for immense ships.

Vladimir Pavlecka

Even Count Zeppelin didn't start with the *Hindenburg*. We have to start back at the beginning with small ships both to prove the design concepts and to train the people who are going to build and fly them. Yet by the same token, we made a mistake with the *ZMC-2* by building it too small to perform a useful mission. What we need to design is the smallest airship that can still accomplish an economically useful function.[12]

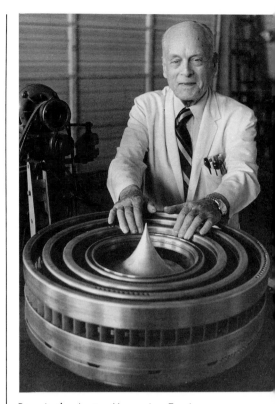

Born in the Austro-Hungarian Empire before the Wright brothers flew at Kitty Hawk, Vladimir Pavlecka helped build the engines that lifted men from the moon. His work goes on, continued by Dr. Earl R. Kiernan and by his friends from the aerospace industry through Airships International, the company he and Kiernan founded in Tustin, California. Here he is shown with his contrarotating centripetal compressor. At 92.5 percent, it is the world's most efficient. Work continues on his shrouded wind and water turbines, his turbo-supercharger and on his metal airship. *Photo by the author.*

Pavlecka's *MC-7* was to be 277 feet long and seventy feet in diameter, with a gas capacity of seven hundred thousand cubic feet. This would give it a useful lift of ten tons. Two five-hundred-horsepower turbine engines would drive it at a top speed of one hundred miles per hour. It would have a maximum range of forty-three hundred miles.

On June 28, 1980, while shopping for a new suitcase to replace one lost by the airlines, Vladimir Pavlecka suffered a heart attack and died. The modern airship, like so many of his dreams for man's future, was still a vision on his drawing board. What was it that drove him to this last task when most men his age were already into their second decade of retirement?

Vladimir Pavlecka

I am the last surviving member of the *ZMC-2* design team. If I don't do this, it may not get done. All the plans to revive the airship must deal with the fact that the men who built them, the engineers with a lifetime's experience, the skilled workmen, and technicians, have all grown old and retired and many of the best have died. Anyone else would have to start back at the very beginning. I can do it but it has to be now. I feel a great responsibility to pass my knowledge on. I owe it to Upson and Fritsche and to all those people who believed in the airship. And I owe it to my country. I owe it to the United States.[13]

Vladimir Pavlecka died before his work was completed. Yet his dream of the return of the airship may still come true. New ships have already been launched in the U.S., Canada, England, Germany, and the Soviet Union. Government funding continues for the *Sentinel 5000* but at a lower rate than originally planned.

Modern materials and technology, when applied to the balloon, led to vehicles that can remain aloft for years at the very edge of space. What will be the result when truly modern technology is finally applied to the airship?

· E P I L O G U E ·

At a distance of fifty years and more, the event stands out in memory without prologue or epilogue—a day in the life of a ten year old boy, vanished and irretrievable, except for a few seconds when a great silver ship thundered by.

I do not recall that there was any expectation that the *Akron* would appear. The first indication was a shout from someone outside the house, together with the sound of engines, engines such as were not commonly heard in 1932. I rushed out the back door and there it was, immense and gleaming in the morning sun, not very high, closely framed by the trees and houses which hemmed in the small backyard. In a few seconds the airship had moved swiftly behind the trees and was gone. The engines were not thrumming with quiet power and the airship was not moving with the measured majesty that the *Hindenburg* presented when I saw it at a much greater distance in the early fall of 1936. The *Akron* was barreling along, its engines roaring with purposeful urgency. Can this be correct? In my mind it is; the mind in this case, curiously, of a ten year old, yet at the same time the mind of a sixty year old considering a memory that stands out against the far horizon of the remembered past. It is often said that no one who ever saw a rigid airship ever forgot it. Considering the vivid quality of this close encounter, as strange in its way as any we hear about in these later days, that is hardly to be wondered at.

I think I may have read somewhere of a flight by the *Akron* up to Boston about this time but I cannot find it now. Probably the exact date of this marvelous apparition could be discovered. Its like will not be seen again, and we, now old, were fortunate to see it when young, sometimes in a most dramatic way.

> R ALPH M. H OLMES **of Costa Mesa, California,**
> **recalling a memory from his boyhood in Stoughton, Massachusetts.**
> **Quoted in *Buoyant Flight*, May–June 1983.**

· N O T E S ·

1. The Balloon

1. Walter Wellman, *The Aerial Age*. New York: A. R. Keller & Co., 1911.
2. Joseph Montgolfier quoted by Francis Trevelyan Miller, *The World in the Air*, Vol. 1. New York: G. P. Putnam's Sons, 1930.
3. Etienne Montgolfier quoted by Fulgence Marion, *Wonderful Balloon Ascents*. New York: Charles Scribner & Sons, 1871.
4. French Government Proclamation quoted by Hatton Turnor, *Astra Castra, Experiments and Adventures in the Atmosphere*. London: Chapman & Hall, 1865.
5. Pilatre de Rozier quoted in *Harper's New Monthly Magazine* (March 1854).
6. Marquis d'Arlandes quoted by Hatton Turnor, *Astra Castra*.
7. Benjamin Franklin quoted by A. H. Smyth, *The Writings of Benjamin Franklin*. Vol. 9. New York: 1906.
8. J. A. C. Charles quoted by Lt. Col. C. V. Glines, *Lighter-Than-Air Flight*. New York: Franklin Watts Inc., 1965.
9. *The Gentleman's Magazine* quoted by Neville Duke and Edward Lanchbery, *The Saga of Flight*. New York: The John Day Co., 1961.
10. *The Federal Gazette and Philadelphia Daily Advertiser* (January 10, 1793).
11. Jean-Pierre Blanchard quoted in *The American Heritage History of Flight*. New York: American Heritage Publishing Co., 1962.
12. Jean-Pierre Blanchard quoted in *The American Heritage History of Flight*.
13. Henry Mayhew in the *Illustrated London News* quoted by L. T. C. Rolt, *The Aeronauts*. New York: Walker & Co., 1966.
14. Capt. Jean Marie-Joseph Coutelle quoted by Hatton Turnor, *Astra Castra*.
15. Capt. Jean Marie-Joseph Coutelle quoted by Lt. Col. C. V. Glines, *Lighter-Than-Air Flight*.
16. Gen. James Longstreet quoted in *The American Review of Reviews* (February 1911).
17. Lt. C. de W. Willcox, "Modern Engines of War," *Munsey's Magazine* (May 1900).
18. Wilfrid de Fonvielle quoted in *The American Heritage History of Flight*.
19. An unidentified French aeronaut of 1870 quoted by Archibald Williams, *Conquering the Air*. New York: Thos. Nelson & Sons, 1926.
20. Salomon Andrée quoted by Edward Adams-Ray, *Andrée's Story*. New York: The Viking Press, 1960.
21. Salomon Andrée quoted by Edward Adams-Ray, *Andrée's Story*.
22. Salomon Andrée quoted by Edward Adams-Ray, *Andrée's Story*.
23. Andrée, Strindberg, and Fraenkel quoted in the *Century Magazine* (November 1897).
24. Andrée, Strindberg, and Fraenkel quoted by Edward Adams-Ray, *Andrée's Story*.
25. Salomon Andrée quoted by Edward Adams-Ray, *Andrée's Story*.

2. The Search for Dirigibility

1. The *Berlin Tageblatt* reprinted in the *Scientific American* (July 24, 1897).
2. Alberto Santos-Dumont, *My Air-Ships*. New York: The Century Co., 1904.
3. Alberto Santos-Dumont, *My Air-Ships*.
4. Alberto Santos-Dumont, *My Air-Ships*.
5. Alberto Santos-Dumont, *My Air-Ships*.
6. Alberto Santos-Dumont, *My Air-Ships*.
7. Alberto Santos-Dumont, *My Air-Ships*.
8. William Edward Ward, *Scientific American* (October 18, 1902).
9. *Scientific American* (November 8, 1902).
10. A. Roy Knabenshue quoted in the *Los Angeles Times* (March 7, 1960).
11. George H. Guy, "Real Navigation of the Air," *The American Review of Reviews* (September 1908).
12. *Scientific American* (June 13, 1908).
13. Walter Wellman, *The Aerial Age*. New York: A. R. Keller & Co., 1911.
14. Walter Wellman, *The Aerial Age*.
15. Walter Wellman, *The Aerial Age*.
16. Walter Wellman, *The Aerial Age*.
17. Captain Sawyer quoted by Walter Wellman, *The Aerial Age*.
18. Walter Wellman, *The Aerial Age*.
19. Murray Simon quoted by Walter Wellman, *The Aerial Age*.
20. The *Chicago Tribune* quoted by Edward Mabley, *The Motor Balloon "America."* Brattleboro, Vermont: The Stephen Greene Press, 1969.
21. Alberto Santos-Dumont, *My Air-Ships*.

3. Zeppelin—The Man and His Airships

1. Count Zeppelin quoted by Hugo Eckener, *Count Zeppelin: The Man and His Work*. Translated by Leigh Farnell. London: Massie Publishing Co., Ltd., 1938.
2. Count Friedrich von Zeppelin quoted by Hugo Eckener, *Count Zeppelin: The Man and His Work*.
3. A French naval officer writing in *Paris Temps* quoted by Margaret Goldsmith, *Zeppelin: A Biography*. New York: William Morrow & Co., 1931.
4. Count Zeppelin quoted by Hugo Eckener, *Count Zeppelin: The Man and His Work*.
5. Count Zeppelin quoted by Hugo Eckener, *Count Zeppelin: The Man and His Work*.
6. Count Zeppelin quoted by Hugo Eckener, *Count Zeppelin: The Man and His Work*.
7. Count Zeppelin quoted by Hugo Eckener, *Count Zeppelin: The Man and His Work*.
8. Count Zeppelin quoted by Hugo Eckener, *Count Zeppelin: The Man and His Work*.
9. Count Zeppelin quoted by Hugo Eckener, *Count Zeppelin: The Man and His Work*.
10. Ernst Lehmann and Leonhard Adelt, *Zeppelin*. New York: Longmans, Green & Co., 1937.
11. Count Zeppelin quoted by Hugo Eckener, *Count Zeppelin: The Man and His Work*.

12. Hugo Eckener in the *Frankfurter Zeitung* quoted by Thor Nielsen, *The Zeppelin Story.* London: Allan Wingate Ltd., 1955.

13. Count Zeppelin quoted by Margaret Goldsmith, *Zeppelin: A Biography.*

14. David Lloyd George, *War Memories of David Lloyd George 1914–1915.* Boston: 1933.

15. *The American Review of Reviews* (July 1909).

16. Associated Press Night Report reproduced in Houston Peterson's scrapbook, *See Them Flying.* New York: Richard W. Baron Co., 1969.

17. Associated Press Night Report reproduced in Houston Peterson's scrapbook, *See Them Flying.*

18. Edouard Surcouf quoted by Hugo Eckener, *Count Zeppelin: The Man and His Work.*

19. Hugo Eckener, *Count Zeppelin: The Man and His Work.*

20. "An Air Line over Germany," *The World's Work* (November 1912).

21. The Paris correspondent of the *London Daily Mail* quoted in *The Literary Digest* (April 26, 1913).

22. The *Berlin Post* quoted in *The Literary Digest* (April 26, 1913).

4. The Airship at War

1. Winston Churchill, *The World Crisis, 1911–1914.* London: Thornton Butterworth Ltd., 1923.

2. Winston Churchill, *The World Crisis, 1911–1914.*

3. Winston Churchill in a letter to Sir Edward Grey quoted by Martin Gilbert, *Winston S. Churchill, Vol. 3, The Challenge of War 1914–1916.* Boston: Houghton Mifflin Co., 1971.

4. The *London Star, London Times,* and *London Daily Telegraph* quoted in *The Literary Digest* (February 6, 1915).

5. The unidentified gunner's report quoted by Ernst Lehmann and Leonhard Adelt, *Zeppelin.* New York: Longmans, Green & Co., 1937.

6. Heinrich Mathy interviewed by Karl von Wiegand for the *New York World,* reprinted in *The Literary Digest* (October 9, 1915).

7. Heinrich Mathy interviewed by Karl von Wiegand for the *New York World,* reprinted in *The Literary Digest.*

8. Oberleutnant Lampel quoted by Kenneth Poolman, *Zeppelins Against London.* New York: The John Day Co., 1961.

9. Reginald A. J. Warneford quoted by Kenneth Poolman, *Zeppelins Against London.*

10. Alfred Muhler quoted by Ernst Lehmann and Leonhard Adelt, *Zeppelin.*

11. Ernst Lehmann and Leonhard Adelt, *Zeppelin.*

12. Ernst Lehmann and Leonhard Adelt, *Zeppelin.*

13. Sir Philip Gibbs quoted by Ernest Dudley, *Monsters of the Purple Twilight.* London: George G. Harrap & Co. Ltd., 1960.

14. Lt. William Leefe Robinson's official report in the Imperial War Museum quoted by Arch Whitehouse, *The Zeppelin Fighters.* Garden City, New York: Doubleday & Co., 1966.

15. Lt. William Leefe Robinson's official report in the Imperial War Museum quoted by Arch Whitehouse, *The Zeppelin Fighters.*

16. Lt. William Leefe Robinson's official report in the Imperial War Museum quoted by Arch Whitehouse, *The Zeppelin Fighters.*

17. Ernst Lehmann and Leonhard Adelt, *Zeppelin.*

18. Lt. William Leefe Robinson's official report in the Imperial War Museum quoted by Arch Whitehouse, *The Zeppelin Fighters.*

19. Ernst Lehmann and Leonhard Adelt, *Zeppelin.*

20. Ernst Lehmann and Leonhard Adelt, *Zeppelin.*

21. Heinrich Mathy quoted by Ernst Lehmann and Leonhard Adelt, *Zeppelin.*

22. Heinrich Mathy quoted by Ernst Lehmann and Leonhard Adelt, *Zeppelin.*

23. Lt. Wulston Joseph Tempest in a letter quoted by Arch Whitehouse, *The Zeppelin Fighters.*

24. Heinrich Mathy interviewed by Karl von Wiegand for the *New York World,* reprinted in *The Literary Digest.*

25. Sir Egbert Cadbury in a radio broadcast marking the fortieth anniversary of the RAF, quoted by Basil Clarke, *The History of the Airships.* London: Herbert Jenkins Ltd., 1961.

26. Maj. Egbert Cadbury in a letter to his father quoted by C. F. Snowden Gamble, *The Story of a North Sea Air Station.* London: Oxford University Press, 1928.

27. Freiherr Treusch von Buttlar-Brandenfels, *Zeppelins over England.* Translated by Huntley Paterson. New York: Harcourt, Brace & Co., 1932.

28. "The Zeppelin Raid into England," *The Literary Digest* (March 24, 1917).

29. Admiral Scheer, *Germany's High Seas Fleet in the World War.* London: Cassell & Co. Ltd., 1920.

30. Admiral Jellicoe, *The Grand Fleet 1914–1916, Its Creation, Development and Work.* London: Cassell & Co. Ltd., 1919.

31. Admiral Scheer, *Germany's High Seas Fleet in the World War.*

5. Postwar Airship Enthusiasm

1. E. M. Maitland, *The Log of H.M.A. R.34.* London: Hodder & Stoughton, 1920.

2. James Gleason O'Brien, "An Aristocrat of the Sky" in the *New York Tribune Magazine* section quoted in *The Literary Digest* (August 27, 1921).

3. "America's Super Zeppelin," *The Literary Digest* (August 27, 1921).

4. Richard E. Byrd, *Skyward.* New York: Blue Ribbon Books, 1928.

5. Norman Walker, *London Times* (August 26, 1921).

6. Maxime Baze, *The Literary Digest* (January 12, 1924).

7. Lt. Clifford Smythe, *New York Herald* (February 23, 1922).

8. Sgt. J. M. Beall from the *New York World* quoted in *The Literary Digest* (March 4, 1922).

9. The Washington correspondent of the *New York World* quoted in *The Literary Digest* (March 11, 1922).

10. The *New York Globe* quoted in *The Literary Digest* (March 11, 1922).

11. The *New York Herald* quoted in *The Literary Digest* (March 11, 1922).

12. Junius B. Wood, "Seeing America from the Shenandoah," *National Geographic* (January 1925).

13. Charles Rosendahl, "The Loss of the Shenandoah," *Journal of the American Society of Engineers* (August 1926).

14. Charles Rosendahl, *Up Ship.* New York: Dodd, Mead & Co., 1931.

15. Charles Rosendahl, *Up Ship.*

16. Charles Rosendahl, *Up Ship.*

17. Ralph Jones, *The Literary Digest* (September 26, 1925).

18. Ernest Nichols from the *New York Evening World* quoted in *The Literary Digest* (September 26, 1925).

19. Col. William Mitchell quoted by Roger Burlingame, *General Billy Mitchell.* New York: McGraw-Hill, 1952.

20. Capt. Anton Heinen, *New York Times* (September 6, 1925).

6. To the Arctic

1. Roald Amundsen quoted by Lincoln Ellsworth, *Beyond Horizons.* New York: Doubleday, Doran & Co., 1937.

2. Roald Amundsen, *My Life as an Explorer,* New York: Doubleday, Doran & Co., 1928.

3. Roald Amundsen, *My Life as an Explorer.*

4. Umberto Nobile, *My Polar Flights.* New York: G. P. Putnam's Sons, 1961.

5. Roald Amundsen, *My Life as an Explorer.*

6. Lincoln Ellsworth, *Beyond Horizons.*

7. Umberto Nobile, *My Polar Flights.*

8. Lincoln Ellsworth, *Search.* New York: Brewer, Warren & Putnam, 1932.

9. Roald Amundsen, *My Life as an Explorer.*

10. Umberto Nobile, *My Polar Flights.*

11. *New York Herald Tribune* quoted in *The Literary Digest* (May 22, 1926).

12. Lincoln Ellsworth, *Search.*

13. Lincoln Ellsworth, *Search.*

14. Roald Amundsen, *My Life as an Explorer.*

15. Gen. Umberto Nobile, "Navigating the Norge from Rome to the North Pole and Beyond," *National Geographic* (August 1927).

16. Roald Amundsen, "The Rows Aboard the Norge," *The World's Work* (August 1927).

17. Gen. Umberto Nobile, "More Rows Aboard the Norge," *The World's Work* (January 1928).

18. Umberto Nobile, *My Polar Flights.*

19. Umberto Nobile, *My Polar Flights.*

20. Umberto Nobile, *My Polar Flights.*

21. Umberto Nobile, *My Polar Flights.*

22. Lt. Einar-Paal Lundborg, North American Newspaper Alliance quoted in *The Literary Digest* (September 8, 1928).

23. Umberto Nobile, *My Polar Flights.*

24. *Current History Magazine* of the *New York Times* (September 1928).

25. *New York World* quoted in *The Literary Digest* (September 8, 1928).

26. *The World's Work* quoted in *The Literary Digest* (September 8, 1928).

27. *Schenectady Union-Star* quoted in *The Literary Digest* (September 8, 1928).

28. Roald Amundsen, *My Life as an Explorer.*

29. Odd Arnesen, *Roald Amundsen som han var.* Oslo: Oppendal Norsk Vorlag, 1929.

7. Hugo Eckener and the *Graf Zeppelin*

1. Hugo Eckener in the *Frankfurter Zeitung* quoted by Thor Nielsen, *The Zeppelin Story.*

2. Hugo Eckener, *My Zeppelins.*

3. Hugo Eckener, *My Zeppelins.*

4. Hugo Eckener, *My Zeppelins.*

5. Hugo Eckener, *My Zeppelins.*

6. The French Air Ministry quoted by J. Gordon Vaeth, *Graf Zeppelin.* New York: Harper & Bros., 1958.

7. Hugo Eckener, *My Zeppelins.*

8. Hugo Eckener, "The First Airship Flight Around the World," *National Geographic* (June 1930).

9. Hugo Eckener, "The First Airship Flight Around the World," *National Geographic* (June 1930).

10. *New York Times* (August 26, 1929).

11. Hugo Eckener, *My Zeppelins.*

12. Hugo Eckener, *My Zeppelins.*

13. William Randolph Hearst's contract quoted by Hugo Eckener, *My Zeppelins.*

14. Hugo Eckener, *My Zeppelins.*

15. Hugo Eckener, *My Zeppelins.*

16. Hugo Eckener, *My Zeppelins.*

17. Hugo Eckener, *My Zeppelins.*

18. Hugo Eckener, *My Zeppelins.*

8. The Big Ships

1. Charles Rosendahl, *Up Ship.* New York: Dodd, Mead & Co., 1931.

2. Sir Samuel Hoare, Viscount Templewood, *Empire of the Air.* London: Collins Press, 1957.

3. Nevil Shute, *Slide Rule.* New York: William Morrow & Co., 1954.

4. Nevil Shute, *Slide Rule.*

5. Nevil Shute, *Slide Rule.*

6. Nevil Shute, *Slide Rule.*

7. Nevil Shute, *Slide Rule.*

8. Pierre van Paassen in the *New York World* quoted in *The Literary Digest* (February 18, 1928).

9. Sir Samuel Hoare, Viscount Templewood, *Empire of the Air.*

10. *Philadelphia Inquirer* quoted in *The Literary Digest* (November 16, 1929).

11. Maj. G. H. Scott from the *London Daily Mail* quoted in *The Literary Digest* (November 16, 1929).

12. Lt. Col. Vincent Richmond from the *London Daily Mail* quoted in *The Literary Digest* (November 16, 1929).

13. Lord Thomson of Cardington from the *London Times* quoted in *The Literary Digest* (November 16, 1929).

14. Nevil Shute, *Slide Rule.*

15. Nevil Shute, *Slide Rule.*

16. Navy General Board quoted in *Hearings before a Joint Committee to Investigate Dirigible Disasters.* 73rd Congress (1933).

17. Adm. William Moffett from *General Board, Hearings, Vol. 1* (1926), quoted by Richard K. Smith, *The Airships Akron and Macon.* Annapolis: United States Naval Institute, 1965.

18. Nevil Shute, *Slide Rule.*

19. Air Ministry press release quoted by James Leasor, *The Millionth Chance.* New York: Reynal & Co., 1957.

20. Nevil Shute, *Slide Rule.*

21. Nevil Shute, *Slide Rule.*

22. Lord Thompson quoted by James Leasor, *The Millionth Chance.*

23. *R.101* radio transmission quoted by James Leasor, *The Millionth Chance.*

24. Alfred Rabouille quoted by James Leasor, *The Millionth Chance.*

25. Joe Binks from the *New York World* quoted in *The Literary Digest* (October 18, 1930).

9. The End of the Dream of Rigid Airships

1. Hugo Eckener, *My Zeppelins.*

2. Bud Cowart, *Los Angeles Times* (May 12, 1932).

3. Adm. Arthur Willard, commander of Scouting Force to Scouting Force, 23 May 1932, quoted by Richard K. Smith, *The Airships Akron and Macon.* Annapolis: United States Naval Institute, 1965.

4. Lt. Comm. Herbert Wiley's official report quoted in *The Literary Digest* (April 15, 1933).

5. Adm. Ernest King to Admiral Halligan, 11 January 1934, from the private papers of Capt. Garland Fulton quoted by Richard K. Smith, *The Airships Akron and Macon.*

6. Adm. William Standley, *General Board Hearings* (1934) quoted by Richard K. Smith, *The Airships Akron and Macon.*

7. Hugo Eckener, *My Zeppelins.*

8. Hugo Eckener, *My Zeppelins.*

9. Hugo Eckener, *My Zeppelins.*

10. Margaret G. Mather, "I Was on the Hindenburg," *Harpers Magazine* (November 1937).

11. Margaret G. Mather, "I Was on the Hindenburg."

12. Leonhard Adelt, "The Last Trip of the Hindenburg," *The Reader's Digest* (November 1937).

13. Margaret G. Mather, "I Was on the Hindenburg."

14. Leonhard Adelt, "The Last Trip of the Hindenburg."

15. Charles Rosendahl, *Up Ship.* New York: Dodd, Mead & Co., 1931.

16. Herbert Morrison for WLS as quoted by *Time* (May 17, 1937).

17. Leonhard Adelt, "The Last Trip of the Hindenburg."

18. Margaret G. Mather, "I Was on the Hindenburg."

19. Leonhard Adelt, "The Last Trip of the Hindenburg."

20. Margaret G. Mather, "I Was on the Hindenburg."

21. Ernst Lehmann, *New York Times* (May 8, 1937).

10. World War II

1. Hugo Eckener, *My Zeppelins.*

2. Hugo Eckener, *My Zeppelins.*

3. The Durand Committee Report quoted by Charles Rosendahl, *What About the Airship?* New York: Charles Scribner's Sons, 1938.

4. Adm. Ernest J. King to the General Board, 9 June 1936, Record Group 72, BuAer General Correspondence (1925–1942), Box 5561, The National Archives.

5. Comdr. F. R. McCrary quoted by Archibald Turnbull and Clifford Lord, *History of United States Naval Aviation.* New Haven, Connecticut: Yale University Press, 1949.

6. Official report, commander Airship Squadron Twenty-One to the commander-in-chief, U.S. Fleet, 25 July 1943, Naval History Center, Operational Archives Branch, Washington, D.C.

7. Official report, commander Airship Squadron Twenty-One to the commander-in-chief, U.S. Fleet, 25 July 1943, Naval History Center, Operational Archives Branch, Washington, D.C.

8. Samuel Eliot Morison, *History of United States Naval Operations in World War II.* 15 volumes. Boston: Little, Brown & Co., 1962.

9. Petty Officer Antonio Contreras, *New York Times* (July 8, 1960).

10. Petty Officer Joseph Culligan, *New York Times* (July 7, 1960).

11. Hugo Eckener quoted by J. Gordon Vaeth, *Graf Zeppelin.* New York: Harper & Bros., 1958.

12. Fred Nebiker, *Los Angeles Times* (October 28, 1973).

13. Charles G. Grey quoted by P. W. Litchfield and Hugh Allen, *Why? Why Has America No Rigid Airships?* Cleveland, Ohio: Corday & Gross Co., 1945.

11. Ballooning to the Edge of Space

1. Otto C. Winzen, *Proceedings, IXth International Astronautical Congress, Amsterdam, 1958.*

2. James Glaisher, with Flammarion de Fonvielle, and Gaston Tissandier, *Travels in the Air.* London: Richard Bentley, 1871.

3. Gaston Tissandier, *Histoire de mes Ascensions.* Paris: 1888.

4. Ralph Upson, *Free and Captive Balloons.* New York: The Ronald Press Co., 1926.

5. Ralph Upson, *Free and Captive Balloons.*

6. Capt. Joseph W. Kittinger, Jr., "The Long, Lonely Leap," *National Geographic,* December 1960.

7. Capt. Joseph W. Kittinger, Jr., "The Long, Lonely Leap."

8. John Wise, *Through the Air, a Narrative of Forty Years Experience as an Aeronaut.* Philadelphia: 1873.

9. Ed Yost in an interview with Douglas Balz, *Akron Beacon Journal,* October 16, 1977.

10. Ed Yost in an interview with Douglas Balz, *Akron Beacon Journal,* October 16, 1977.

11. Charles McCarry, with Ben Abruzzo, Maxie Anderson, and Larry Newman, *Double Eagle.* Boston: Little, Brown and Co., 1979.

12. Charles McCarry, with Ben Abruzzo, Maxie Anderson, and Larry Newman, *Double Eagle.*

13. Charles McCarry, with Ben Abruzzo, Maxie Anderson, and Larry Newman, *Double Eagle.*

12. The Airship and the Future

1. Adm. Carl J. Seiberlich quoted in the *Los Angeles Times,* September 3, 1979. Admiral Seiberlich was then the U.S. Navy's highest ranking officer with airship experience.

2. Maj. Reed M. Anderson, quoted in 1977 Air University report.

3. Maj. Jimmy L. Badger and Maj. Ronald M. Lebert, quoted in 1977 Air University report.

4. Vladimir Pavlecka in an interview with the author.

5. Vladimir Pavlecka in an interview with the author.

6. Vladimir Pavlecka in an interview with the author.

7. Vladimir Pavlecka in an interview with the author.

8. Vladimir Pavlecka in an interview with the author.

9. Vladimir Pavlecka in an interview with the author.

10. Vladimir Pavlecka in an interview with the author.

11. Translated from the newspaper, *Città del Popolo,* June 12, 1931.

12. Vladimir Pavlecka in an interview with the author.

13. Vladimir Pavlecka in an interview with the author.

· BIBLIOGRAPHY ·

Abbott, Patrick. *Airship*. New York: Charles Scribners Sons, 1973. An account of the British airship *R.34*.

Adams-Ray, Edward. *Andrée's Story*. 1930. Reprint. New York: The Viking Press, 1960.

Allen, Hugh. *The House of Goodyear*. Akron, Ohio: The Superior Printing & Litho. Co., 1936.

Allen, Hugh. *The Story of the Airship*. Akron, Ohio: The Goodyear Tire & Rubber Company, published annually from 1925 until 1932.

Amundsen, Roald, and Ellsworth, Lincoln. *First Crossing of the Polar Sea*. New York: George H. Doran Co., 1927.

Amundsen, Roald. *My Life as an Explorer*. New York: Doubleday, Doran & Co., 1928.

Buoyant Flight. A. D. Topping, ed. Akron, Ohio: Lighter Than Air Society. A bimonthly publication.

Buttlar-Brandenfels, Freiherr Treusch von. *Zeppelins over England*. New York: Harcourt, Brace & Co., 1932.

Byrd, Richard E. *Skyward*. New York: Blue Ribbon Books, 1928. The famous polar explorer missed the fatal flight of the *R.38* by only a few hours.

Churchill, Winston S. *The World Crisis, 1911–1914*. London: Thornton Butterworth Ltd., 1923.

Clarke, Basil. *The History of the Airship*. London: Herbert Jenkins Ltd., 1961.

Cuneo, John R. *Winged Mars: The German Air Weapon 1870–1914*. Harrisburg, Pennsylvania: The Military Service Publishing Co., 1942.

Cuneo, John R. *The Air Weapon 1914–1916*. Harrisburg, Pennsylvania: The Military Service Publishing Co., 1947.

Crouch, Tom D. *The Eagle Aloft: Two Centuries of the Balloon in America*. Washington, D.C.: Smithsonian Institution Press, 1983.

Davy, M. J. B. *Handbook of the Collections Illustrating Aeronautics-II Lighter-Than-Air Craft*. London: His Majesty's Stationery Office, 1934. Includes a history of lighter-than-air flight.

Dollfus, Charles. *The Orion Book of Balloons*. New York: The Orion Press, 1961.

Dudley, Ernest. *Monsters of the Purple Twilight*. London: George G. Harrap & Co. Ltd., 1960.

Duke, Neville, and Lanchbery, Edward, eds. *The Saga of Flight*. New York: The John Day Co., 1961.

Eckener, Hugo. *Count Zeppelin: The Man and His Work*. Translated by Leigh Farnell. London: Massie Publishing Co., Ltd., 1938. A biography of Count Zeppelin by his longtime coworker and successor.

Eckener, Hugo. *My Zeppelins*. Translated by Douglas Robinson. London: Putnam & Co., Ltd., 1958. Eckener's own story of his life in the air.

The Editors of American Heritage Magazine. *The American Heritage History of Flight*. New York: American Heritage Publishing Co., 1962. Primarily about airplanes, with one chapter on ballooning.

Ege, Lennart. *Balloons and Airships*. New York: MacMillan, 1974.

Eiloart, Arnold. *The Flight of the Small World*. New York: W. W. Norton & Co., 1959.

Ellsworth, Lincoln. *Search*. New York: Brewer, Warren & Putnam, 1932. Ellsworth's autobiography before he flew over Antarctica.

Ellsworth, Lincoln. *Beyond Horizons*. New York: Doubleday, Doran & Co., 1937. Ellsworth's autobiography after he flew over Antarctica.

Fraser, Chelsea. *Heroes of the Air*. New York: Thomas Y. Crowell Co., 1926.

Fritsche, Carl B. "The Metalclad Airship and Its Application to Foreign Trade." Manuscript of a speech presented to the Royal Aeronautical Society, London, May 14, 1931. The James Carruthers Collection, Claremont Colleges.

Gilbert, Martin. *Winston S. Churchill, Vol. 3, The Challenge of War 1914–1916*. Boston: Houghton Mifflin Co., 1971.

Glaisher, James, with de Fonvielle, Flammarion, and Tissandier, Gaston. *Travels in the Air*. Richard Bentley, London, 1871.

Glines, Lt. Col. C. V., ed. *Lighter-Than-Air Flight*. New York: Franklin Watts Inc., 1965. A collection of firsthand accounts of airship and balloon flights.

Goldsmith, Margaret. *Zeppelin: A Biography*. New York: William Morrow & Co., 1931. Written just after the crash of *R.101*, the last chapter includes some contemporary material.

Grantham, Frederick W. *Safety in the Air*. Los Angeles: The Wolfer Printing Co., 1931. Grantham was chief engineer on the metal airship, *City of Glendale*.

Hatfield, D. D. *Los Angeles Aeronautics 1920–1929*. Inglewood, California: Northrop Institute of Technology, 1973.

Hearings before a Joint Committee to Investigate Dirigible Disasters. 73rd Congress of the United States, May 22 to June 6, 1933. Washington, D.C.: United States Government Printing Office, 1933. This is 944 pages of testimony after the loss of the *Akron* by everyone with an interest in lighter-than-air, including Charles Rosendahl, Herbert Wiley, Anton Heinen, Garland Fulton, Jerome Hunsaker, Ernest King, and Billy Mitchell.

Heinmuller, John P. V. *Man's Fight to Fly*. New York: Aero Print Co., 1945. Includes an aviation chronology.

Higham, Robin. *The British Rigid Airship, 1908–1931*. London: G. T. Foulis & Co., Ltd., 1961.

Hildebrandt, A. *Airships Past and Present*. New York: D. Van Nostrand Co., 1908.

Hoare, Sir Samuel, Viscount Templewood. *Empire of the Air*. London: Collins Press, 1957. Hoare was air minister during most of the construction of *R.100* and *R.101* but his book is primarily concerned with airplanes.

Hoehling, A. A. *Who Destroyed the Hindenburg?* Boston: Little, Brown & Co., 1962.

Hogg, Gary. *Airships over the Pole.* New York: Abelard-Schuman, 1969.

Jeffries, Dr. John. *Two Aerial Voyages of Dr. Jeffries with Mons. Blanchard.* London: 1786. Reprinted by the Works Projects Administration in the 1930s. New York: No date.

Johnson, Kenneth M. *Aerial California.* Los Angeles: Dawson's Book Shop, 1961.

King, Ernest J., and Whitehill, Walter Muir. *Fleet Admiral King.* New York: W.W. Norton & Co., 1952. A biography of the admiral who succeeded Moffett, only briefly about airships.

Kirschner, Edwin J. *Aerospace Balloons.* Fallbrook, California: Aero Publishers, 1978.

Kirschner, Edwin J. *The Zeppelin in the Atomic Age.* Urbana: University of Illinois Press, 1957.

Kittinger, Capt. Joseph W., Jr., "The Long, Lonely Leap," *National Geographic,* December 1960.

Kittinger, Capt. Joseph W., Jr. *The Long, Lonely Leap.* New York: E. P. Dutton & Co., 1961.

Leasor, James. *The Millionth Chance.* New York: Reynal & Co., 1957. The story of the *R.101* with a spooky last chapter about the return of the dead airshipmen at a séance.

Lehmann, Ernst, and Adelt, Leonhard. *Zeppelin.* New York: Longmans, Green & Co., 1937. Published soon after Lehmann died of burns from the crash of the *Hindenburg,* includes an account of the crash by Lt. Comdr. Charles Rosendahl.

Litchfield, P. W., and Allen, Hugh. *Why? Why Has America No Rigid Airships?* Cleveland, Ohio: Corday & Gross Co., 1945.

Lundborg, Einar. *The Arctic Rescue.* New York: The Viking Press, 1929. By the pilot who rescued Nobile, then crashed on the ice and joined the castaways.

Mabley, Edward. *The Motor Balloon "America."* Brattleboro, Vermont: The Stephen Greene Press, 1969.

Maitland, E. M. *The Log of H.M.A. R.34.* London: Hodder & Stoughton, 1920.

Marion, Fulgence. *Wonderful Balloon Ascents or the Conquest of the Skies.* New York: Charles Scribner & Sons, 1871.

McCarry, Charles, with Ben Abruzzo, Maxie Anderson, and Larry Newman. *Double Eagle.* Boston: Little, Brown and Co., 1979.

McPhee, John. *The Deltoid Pumpkin Seed.* New York: Farrar, Straus & Giroux, 1973. The story of a recent attempt to build a hybrid, helium-filled airplane.

Millbank, Jeremiah. *The First Century of Flight in America.* Princeton, New Jersey: Princeton University Press, 1943.

Miller, Francis Trevelyan. *The World in the Air.* 2 volumes. New York: G. P. Putnam's Sons, 1930. A massive picture history of aviation.

Mooney, Michael. *The Hindenburg.* New York: Dodd, Mead & Co., 1972.

Morison, Samuel Eliot. *History of United States Naval Operations in World War II.* 15 volumes. Boston: Little, Brown & Co., 1962.

Morpurgo, J. E. *Barnes Wallis.* New York: St. Martin's Press, 1972. A biography of the chief designer of *R.80* and *R.100.*

Naval Airship Training and Experimental Command. *They Were Dependable, Airship Operations in World War II.* Lakehurst, New Jersey: 1946. A pamphlet dealing primarily in statistics.

Nielsen, Thor. *The Zeppelin Story.* London: Allan Wingate Ltd., 1955. A biography of Hugo Eckener.

Nobile, Umberto. *Memoirs.* A manuscript published in several languages but not, as yet, in English.

Nobile, Umberto. *My Polar Flights.* New York: G. P. Putnam's Sons, 1961.

Norman, Aaron. *The Great Air War.* New York: Macmillan, 1968.

Peterson, Houston. *See Them Flying.* New York: Richard W. Baron Co., 1969. An eleven-year-old boy's aviation scrapbook with all the newspaper and magazine clippings on aviation that he could find in Los Angeles in 1909 and 1910.

Piccard, Auguste. *Between Earth and Sky.* London: Falcon Press, 1950.

Piccard, Auguste. *In Balloon and Bathyscaphe.* London: Cassell & Co., 1956.

Poolman, Kenneth. *Zeppelins Against London.* New York: The John Day Co., 1961.

Robinson, Douglas H. *Giants in the Sky: A History of the Rigid Airship.* Seattle: University of Washington Press, 1973.

Robinson, Douglas H. *The LZ 129 Hindenburg.* Famous Aircraft Series. Dallas, Texas: Morgan Aviation Books, 1964. Includes the pilot's flight manual for the *Bodensee.*

Robinson, Douglas H. *The Zeppelin in Combat.* Sun Valley, California: John W. Caler Co., 1966.

Rolt, L. T. C. *The Aeronauts.* New York: Walker & Co., 1966.

Rosendahl, Charles. *Up Ship.* New York: Dodd, Mead & Co., 1931.

Rosendahl, Charles. *What About the Airship?* New York: Charles Scribner's Sons, 1938.

Santos-Dumont, Alberto. *My Air-Ships.* New York: The Century Co., 1904.

Shute, Nevil. *Slide Rule.* New York: William Morrow & Co., 1954. The autobiography of the famous author who also worked on *R.100.*

Simons, Maj. David. *Man High.* New York: Doubleday, 1960.

Smith, Richard K. *The Airships Akron and Macon.* Annapolis: United States Naval Institute, 1965. The definitive work on these two ships.

Snowden Gamble, C. F. *The Story of a North Sea Air Station.* London: Oxford University Press, 1928.

Swanborough, Gordon, and Bowers, Peter M. *United States Navy Aircraft since 1911.* New York: Funk & Wagnalls, 1968.

Toland, John. *Ships in the Sky.* New York: Henry Holt, 1957.

Tuchman, Barbara W. *The Guns of August.* New York: Macmillan, 1962. Only two references to dirigibles in this complete account of the beginning of World War I.

Turnbull, Archibald, and Lord, Clifford. *History of United States Naval Aviation.* New Haven, Connecticut: Yale University Press, 1949.

Turnor, Hatton. *Astra Castra, Experiments and Adventures in the Atmosphere.* London: Chapman & Hall, 1865.

Upson, Ralph. *Free and Captive Balloons.* New York: The Ronald Press Co., 1926.

Vaeth, J. Gordon. *Graf Zeppelin.* New York: Harper & Bros., 1958.

Vittek, Jr., Joseph F., ed. *Proceedings of the Interagency Workshop on Lighter Than Air Vehicles.* Cambridge, Massachusetts: Massachusetts Institute of Technology Flight Transportation Library, 1975. Sixty-three scientific papers representing the most complete examination of current technology.

Wellman, Walter. *The Aerial Age.* New York: A. R. Keller & Co., 1911.

Whale, George. *British Airships Past, Present and Future.* London: John Lane, The Bodley Head, 1919.

Whitehouse, Arch. *The Zeppelin Fighters.* Garden City, New York: Doubleday & Co., 1966.

Williams, Archibald. *Conquering the Air.* New York: Thos. Nelson & Sons, 1926.

Wirth, Dick. *Ballooning: The Complete Guide to Riding the Winds.* New York: Random House, 1980.

Wykeham, Peter. *Santos-Dumont: A Study in Obsession.* New York: Harcourt, Brace & World Inc., 1963.

· I N D E X ·

Page numbers in *italics* refer to captions.